D1205994

THE PRACTICE OF STRATEGY

The Practice of Strategy

From Alexander the Great to the Present

Edited by
JOHN ANDREAS OLSEN
AND COLIN S. GRAY

OXFORD
UNIVERSITY PRESS

*This book has been printed digitally and produced in a standard specification
in order to ensure its continuing availability*

OXFORD
UNIVERSITY PRESS

Great Clarendon Street, Oxford OX2 6DP
United Kingdom

Oxford University Press is a department of the University of Oxford.
It furthers the University's objective of excellence in research, scholarship,
and education by publishing worldwide. Oxford is a registered trade mark of
Oxford University Press in the UK and in certain other countries

© John Andrea Olsen and Colin S. Gray 2011

First published 2011
Reprinted 2012

British Library Cataloguing in Publication Data
Data available

Library of Congress Cataloging in Publication Data
Data available

ISBN 978-0-19-960863-8

Preface

The Practice of Strategy: From Alexander the Great to the Present focuses on the nature and logic of grand strategy and military strategy through the lens of twelve case studies, from ancient times to contemporary conflicts in Afghanistan and Iraq. The book is intended for military professionals; 'officer-scholars'; postgraduate students in history, international relations, and strategic studies in its various forms; and all who have a wide interest in strategy and history. While the book is designed as a cohesive whole, each chapter can be read in isolation.

The book's point of departure is Professor Colin S. Gray's thesis from his study *Modern Strategy*: 'there is a unity to all strategic experience: nothing essential changes in the nature and function (or purpose)—in sharp contrast to the character—of strategy and war'. To shed light on this claim, and to deepen understanding of both the uniqueness and the universality of grand strategy and military strategy, Professor Gray and I decided to select a range of historical case studies drawn from more than two millennia. Next, we identified leading experts to conduct independent research and write the respective chapters.

I am deeply thankful to the authors, all of whom showed both scholarly professionalism and personal dedication as they crafted their contributions to this volume. I am most obliged to Margaret S. MacDonald, who once again committed her unique editorial skills to, and showed great enthusiasm for, yet another project. I am grateful to the Norwegian Defence University College and the Swedish National Defence College for having sponsored this project, Commander Tore J. Rosseid for administrative assistance, Dr. H. P. Willmott for constructive insight, and Laurien Berkeley for editorial support. It is also my pleasure to thank the University of Reading's Liberal Way of War Programme, conducted with the support of the Leverhulme Trust. In addition, I would like to thank Dominic Byatt, Jenny Lunsford, Sarah Parker, Lizzy Suffling, Carla Hodge and Vijaysankar Natesan at Oxford University Press and SPi for their professionalism.

Finally, special thanks to Colin Gray—a profound scholar, always pushing the envelope, and full of ideas and enthusiasm. It has been a great pleasure to co-edit this book with him. I especially enjoyed our honest and refreshing exchanges as we developed and then realized this book project.

John Andreas Olsen
Sarajevo

Contents

Introduction

John Andreas Olsen

This book focuses on grand strategy and military strategy as practised over an extended period of time and under very different circumstances, from the campaigns of Alexander the Great to insurgencies and counter-insurgencies in present-day Afghanistan and Iraq. It presents strategy as it pertained not only to wars, campaigns, and battles but also to times of peace that were overshadowed by the threat of war. The terms 'grand strategy' and 'military strategy' as we understand them today were unknown to rulers and generals in ancient, medieval, and even the early portion of modern times. Yet, although they may never have received formal teaching about military or political theory, and some may not have read much history, nonetheless, when faced with decisions about their national policies and about combat, these leaders practised strategy. This does not mean that all Roman, Byzantine, and Ottoman emperors had overarching grand strategies through which they assessed how to combine political, economic, and military resources, or that all military action was based on deliberate planning, but all of them undoubtedly sought some sort of gain, some sort of victory, and most did so by combining desired objectives, concepts of operations, and available resources: 'Just as the laws of physics governed the universe long before there were physicists to study them, so those who command nations in war are subject to the logic of strategy even if they know nothing of strategy.'[1] Indeed, from the historical record it is not self-evident that the self-consciously strategic politicians and soldiers of modern times have demonstrated superiority in strategic performance over their far-distant predecessors.

This book is intended to deepen the understanding of the phenomena and logic of strategy by reconstructing the considerations that shaped imperial and nation-state policies. Through historical case studies, the book seeks to shed light on a fundamental question: is there is a unity to all strategic experience? The working hypothesis is that nothing essential changes in the nature and function (or purpose)—in sharp contrast to the character—of strategy and war.

For Carl von Clausewitz (1780–1831), 'the greatest student of strategy who ever lived',[2] and for others who tried to develop a theory for strategy in the nineteenth century, the focal point was the relationship between strategy and tactics. They defined strategy as the use of the battle for the purposes of the war. The term 'strategy', derived as it was from the Greek *strategos* (general), was inextricably related to the battlefield and combat, and was considered the art of the commander. Strategy formed the plan of the war, mapped out the proposed course of the different campaigns which composed the war, and regulated the battles that had to be fought in each of the campaigns.[3]

In the twentieth century, Basil H. Liddell Hart (1895–1970) and others expanded the term beyond its military meaning by referring to 'grand strategy' rather than the Clausewitzian 'military strategy' or 'pure strategy'. According to Liddell Hart, Clausewitz's definition was too narrow and battle-centric,[4] implying that battle was the only means to a strategic end. Liddell Hart sought to broaden the definition by suggesting that strategy should rather be defined as 'the art of distributing and applying military means to fulfil the ends of policy' in which 'the role of grand strategy—higher strategy—is to co-ordinate and direct all the resources of a nation, or band of nations, towards the attainment of the political object of the war—the goal defined by fundamental policy'.[5] Stated differently, while the horizon of strategy was bounded by the war, grand strategy had to look beyond the war to the subsequent peace.

It has since become popular to place strategy in a rigid hierarchy that descends from political vision and policy to grand strategy, of which military strategy is but one part, which in its turn is implemented by operations that are expressed tactically. Such a hierarchy makes sense, but it presents challenges. First, it is hard to distinguish *purpose* from *action*, and to recognize that every 'level' in the hierarchy is both the instrument for the 'level' above and the purpose for the 'level' below. As tactics is an application of military strategy on a lower plane, so military strategy is an application of grand strategy on a lower plane.[6] Bereft of political guidance, strategy is meaningless; further, in the absence of assessment of operational and tactical feasibility, it is likely to prove fruitless.

Though technically distinct, the levels of war that typically are presented and treated as discrete steps are in truth wholly interdependent. The implication of these mutual dependencies is that even when one focuses upon strategy, and strives to define it clearly, the subject cannot be examined intelligently in isolation from policy or from operations and tactics. Edward N. Luttwak emphasizes these dilemmas when he refers to 'the paradoxical logic of strategy', where there is no natural harmony between the levels of war. What works today in strategy may not work tomorrow, precisely because it worked today: 'it is only in war that a bad road can be good precisely because it is bad and may therefore be less strongly defended or even left unguarded by the enemy.'[7]

Another challenge to a strict hierarchy of levels of war is that strategy often is confused with policy on one hand and operations on the other. With reference to the 'war on terror', Professor Hew Strachan notes:

> By 2003 [strategy] had lost its identity: part of it had been subsumed by policy and part of it by operational thought. Because neither politicians nor the soldiers had a clear grasp of what strategy was, they could neither put the pieces back together again nor develop a clear grasp of the nature of the wars in which they were engaged. Moreover, without a clear grasp of strategy, they could not see what had really changed in war as opposed to what merely seemed to have changed. By confusing strategy with policy, and by calling what are, in reality, political effects strategic effects, governments have denied themselves the intellectual tool to manage war for political purposes, and so have allowed themselves to project their daily political concerns back into strategy.... Strategy has to deal in the first instance not with policy, but with the nature of war. To be sure, strategy should serve

the ends of policy, but it cannot do that if it is not based on a clear-eyed appreciation of war.[8]

One way of rectifying the situation is to go 'back to basics'. In its most generic sense, strategy is 'the art of winning by purposely matching ends, ways and means'. *Ends* are the objective, such as unconditional surrender, conditional victory, stalemate, or victory denial; *ways* are the forms through which a strategy is pursued, such as a military campaign, diplomacy, or economic sanctions; and *means* are the resources available, such as soldiers, weapons, and money.[9] It follows that military strategy is the bridge between military power and political purpose, wherein ends are the political end-state, ways the operational plan of campaign, and means the military forces at the leader's disposition. According to Alan Stephens:

It is a military axiom that time spent on reconnaissance is never wasted. The maxim could be paraphrased for strategists. The time any decision-maker, from a president to a commanding general to a private soldier, spends on two critical considerations will never be wasted. First, they must clearly understand what, in the prevailing circumstances, they mean by winning. And second, they must ensure that their desired ends are realistic, clearly defined, and consistent with political objectives; that the ways chosen to pursue those ends are feasible; and that the available means are suitable and sustainable. The importance of establishing and maintaining a logical relationship between winning and ends, ways and means cannot be overstated.[10]

With today's wider interpretation of the term strategy, there is a greater case for continuity in what is essentially an exercise in statesmanship in times of peace and war, than with its nineteenth-century usage. In this vital sense, at least, our contemporary understanding of strategy probably is closer to Sun Tzu on the art of war than it is to Clausewitz.

BRIEF SUMMARY

Adopting the working definition of strategy as 'the art of winning by purposely matching ends, ways, and means', this book explores how strategy has been applied throughout history. It consists of three parts, each containing four chapters: case studies from ancient to medieval times, medieval to modern, and modern to contemporary.

Ancient and Mediaeval

The opening chapter, by David J. Lonsdale, focuses on the wars and campaigns of Alexander the Great. By the time of his death in 323 BC, Alexander had added the Persian Empire to Macedon's European territories, thus controlling most of the world as known to the ancient Greeks. Lonsdale examines Alexander's campaigns over a twelve-year period, from the early conflicts in Greece and the Balkans through his great conquests in Persia, his expedition into India, and his eventual return to Babylon. Although Alexander inherited an established and favourable military and political situation from his father, Philip II, much of his success was apparently due to his own supreme strategic abilities, combining military and political leadership. Within this one individual, the military and political components of strategy came together in an extremely powerful manner. Alexander at times applied non-military instruments of what we today would refer to as grand strategy, showing sensitivity to religion as well as cultural and societal factors, and at other times acted with brute force, slaughtering inhabitants, or selling them into slavery. As a military commander, he proved himself successful in set-piece battles as well as irregular warfare, often engaging the enemy indirectly and with inferior numbers. Yet, despite his extraordinary levels of success over a long period of time, Alexander was prone to mistakes, and this opening chapter also deals with the factors that explain Alexander's reduced strategic efficiency as he tried to conquer India. In the end, Alexander succeeded as long as he managed to combine the tactical, operational, strategic, and grand strategic levels of war, but, like great commanders before and after him, he did not recognize the need to consolidate his gains, failed to keep his ambitions in check, and went beyond what Clausewitz defined as the culminating point of victory: to some extent 'he enjoyed campaigning too much and lost sight of the bigger picture'. Genius has to recognize limits to its ambition, but frequently does not.

In the second chapter, Israel Shatzman examines grand strategy and military strategy during the period of the Roman Republic. Rome, a city-state of about 800 square kilometres and a population of some 30,000 people at the end of the sixth-century BC, had established its rule in Italy in a series of wars from the fifth to the third centuries, during which its manpower and territory increased considerably. Rome defeated Carthage in two great wars (264–241 and 218–201), crushed the armies of the Macedonian kingdom (197 and 168) and the Seleucid monarchy (191 and 189), and vanquished various other enemies. Along the way, the Roman authorities had to make a range of strategic decisions concerning, notably, the size and structure of the regular army, the mobilization of additional forces in militarily critical situations, the allocation of resources during wars conducted on several fronts, the treatment of defeated enemies, the establishment of Roman and Latin *coloniae* in Italy, the administration of annexed territories and subject peoples, and the relations with nations and states outside Roman rule. Shatzman discusses how these strategic considerations shaped the Roman strategy for the then-emerging empire, maintaining that the overall strategy evolved gradually. The author argues that the military component of the Roman strategy—characterized by extensive recruitment of manpower and huge tactical formations, lines of communications made possible by networks of roads, military discipline combined with *virtus*, an offensive spirit in pitched battle, and military leaders with both wisdom and determination—was central to sustaining and further expanding the republic. The author concludes that the economic, social, and political aspects were equally important in determining the success of the strategy that the Romans practised.

The Byzantine Empire—the *de facto* continuation of the Roman Empire—lasted more than twice as long as its Western counterpart, which dissolved in the fifth century. Its endurance—approximately 800 years—is all the more remarkable because it was favoured neither by geography nor by military dominance. It survived because its rulers were able to adapt strategically to deteriorating circumstances by devising new ways of coping with successive, sometimes simultaneous, enemies. In Chapter 3, Edward Luttwak asserts that the Byzantine Empire relied less on military strength than on persuasion—to recruit allies, dissuade threatening neighbours, and manipulate potential enemies into attacking one another. Even when the Byzantines fought, they were less inclined to destroy their enemies than to contain them, for they knew that today's enemies could be tomorrow's allies. The Byzantine emperors had no formal statements of 'national strategy' that attempted to define 'interests', the means to protect and enhance them, and the alignment of the two in rational or at least rationalized terms. Yet they had a grand strategy, even though it was never stated explicitly, and applied it so consistently that one might refer to it as the Byzantine 'operational code'. The Byzantine strategy—grand and military—continued to be refined over the centuries, leaving several instructive guidelines defining the relationship between statecraft and war. Luttwak concludes that a key to the Byzantine success was that 'military strategy was subordinated to diplomacy instead of the other way round, and used mostly to contain, or intimidate rather than to attack or defend with full force'.

The next chapter centres on the Hundred Years War, a prolonged conflict lasting from 1337 to 1453 and encompassing the Edwardian War, the Caroline War, the Lancastrian War, and the decline of English fortunes after the appearance of Joan of Arc. The Hundred Years War offers an ideal opportunity to consider strategy in the context of medieval European warfare in general, while also considering the specifics of the Anglo-French conflict of the fourteenth and fifteenth centuries. Between 1337 and 1453, English armies invaded and occupied France with the ostensible aim of making English kings' claim to the French throne a reality. In Chapter 4, Anne Curry argues that the war must be seen in terms of phases. In some, English strategy consisted largely of raids through enemy territory, while in others it consisted of deliberate conquest and occupation. The author explains why certain strategies were chosen at particular points, noting that strategic decisions in medieval warfare often appear to be the result of personal choices by kings and princes at particular moments in time, with little attention to theory or to 'lessons of history'. Curry therefore considers how and why rulers behaved as they did, and also how they attempted to put their preferred strategies into practice both by their own actions and through those of others. She concludes that throughout the period rulers and commanders did not see warfare simply as action against armies, with the ultimate goal of engaging in battle. Instead, they also sought to demoralize the population, reduce economic sustainability, and weaken political authority. In the process, both sides sought alliances with continental rulers. Strategy was therefore also influenced by international relations, not least in choice of theatre, and throughout the period political elements were always more significant than military factors.

Mediaeval and Modern

The second section marks the transition from the ancient and medieval to the modern period, beginning with a chapter on the strategy of the Ottoman Empire, whose military power endured for nearly 700 years. From its rise around 1300, and continuing from the mid-fifteenth century until its demise during World War I, the Ottoman Empire was a crucial player in European and Asian power politics: first as a major Islamic threat to Christian Europe and later as a weakening military power over whose territories and resources the European Great Powers competed. In Chapter 5, Gábor Ágoston examines the grand strategy of the early Ottomans, focusing on how the small Turkic principality that emerged around 1300 in western Asia Minor evolved into an empire with the conquest of Byzantine Constantinople (1453). Ágoston suggests that until the late sixteenth century, the Ottoman rulers equated winning to 'the gradual expansion of earlier Ottoman frontiers into a world empire by defeating Christian and Muslim neighbours and rivals and incorporating their territories'. Changes in the geopolitical setting during the mid-sixteenth century then caused the Ottoman strategy to shift towards defending earlier gains, using fortresses, garrisons, and provisional forces. The Ottomans established one of the first permanent armies of late medieval Europe, and military power was the basis of the rising empire, but, crucially, the Ottomans also sought alliances across religious and ethnic boundaries, including through dynastic marriages. Ágoston emphasizes the coming together of geopolitics, threats, ideologies, political and military objectives, and military structures and techniques of resource mobilization. He uses a handful of pivotal wars and battles to illustrate the execution and effectiveness of strategies and strategists, and therein the relationships between grand strategy and military strategy.

Moving on to one of the most destructive episodes in European history, the sixth chapter centres on the Thirty Years War. Waged between 1618 and 1648, it was a series of conflicts that merged rather than a single war, devastating central Europe in general and Germany in particular. David Parrott argues that the Thirty Years War was about two different, albeit interconnected, sets of aims and security concerns. The first was the struggle over the political form of the Holy Roman Empire, focused upon the relationship of the constituent territories to the Austrian Habsburg monarchy. The other lay outside the Empire itself and reflected two different struggles: one between the Spanish Habsburg monarchy and the breakaway United Provinces, and the other between the French monarchy and the Habsburg Imperial system. Other concerns, especially the religious tensions that had been mounting since the latter part of the sixteenth century, gravitated around these political issues, and this in turn explains the successive involvement of other states, such as Denmark, Poland, Sweden, Savoy-Piedmont, and Portugal. It was also a conflict of almost unparalleled destructive futility: a war which lasted for thirty years because the aims of the belligerents and the military resources at their disposal seemed totally incompatible. Parrott sets out to unravel the strategic implications of this apparent dichotomy. He also focuses on strategy in the narrower, 'eighteenth-century' context of strategic theory, providing a clearer perspective from which to view the wider 'strategic' issues raised in the earlier sections of his chapter that relate to the interactions among war aims, alliances and diplomacy.

Jeremy Black next focuses on British policy and strategy in the so-called 'long' eighteenth century, beginning with the Glorious Revolution of 1688 and the overthrow of King James II of England and ending with the battle of Waterloo in 1815. Chapter 7 provides a contextual debate on the relationship between policy and strategy, discussing the dynamics between strategy and dynasticism, the complexity of strategic culture, the character of British imperialism, and the concept of power, with the associated challenge of reach and overreach. These factors collectively explain what the author refers to as the limitations to strategic planning. Black next discusses the dynamics between strategy and policy in three case studies: the Seven Years War (1756–63), the American War of Independence (1775–83), and the French Revolution (1789–99)—and briefly analyses the Napoleonic Wars. Each of the wars exhibited important geopolitical and strategic continuities as well as important political differences. The Seven Years War was in no small part driven by anti-Catholicism, and thus was characterized by religious passion that made compromise difficult. The American War of Independence had a different political context, which led to a strategy of pacification. The conflict also centred on a revolution in a part of the empire, while the French Revolution posed the threat of similar revolutionary movement in the British Isles. The author maintains that the struggle with France was not a new type of war, but that the strategy itself was new, being concerned with two aspects of domestic politics: 'first, potential supporters of the foreign power, and, secondly, conventional high politics'. Thus, while mastery of the sea and economic warfare were important, so was national reform—political, economic, and military. As a result, domestic policy was pushed to the fore as a component of strategy.

In Chapter 8, Charles Esdaile examines 'Britain and the Napoleonic Wars'. He shows that for Britain, control of the seas lay at the heart of both the conduct and strategy of the Napoleonic Wars. Control of the seas enabled Britain to sustain the war, in the sense that maritime commerce provided her with the resources of money and raw materials needed to continue the fight. At the same time, it rendered her invulnerable to direct attack, while also strengthening her against assaults of a more insidious nature. Sea power ensured that Britain would not be starved into submission and provided a source of social stability in a time of crisis. It was also a force multiplier, enabling extensive expeditions. Britain's mastery of the seas brought the additional advantage of forcing Napoleon, at least in the early years of the conflict, to do battle with Britain on her own terms. Economic warfare as an extension of naval warfare, especially in the forms of raiding commerce and closing many ports, was an integral part of Napoleon's strategy, but the emperor never appreciated that this should have been the centrepiece of his strategy. Esdaile argues that it is very difficult to discern any coherent strategy in the actions of the 'God of War', other than that battle lay at the heart of it, with the consequence that the lack of unity of strategic aim proved to be Napoleon's Achilles heel. Napoleon ultimately lost because he did not match ends, ways, and means, while the Allies ultimately won because they did. Esdaile also contends that 'whatever else they did, the Napoleonic Wars settled the patterns of modern war' and that these patterns were 'in effect, timeless'.

Modern and Contemporary

To begin the third section of the book, Williamson Murray asserts that the key to success in developing and executing grand strategy lies in the ability to focus and act beyond the demands of the present, to take 'a longer view beyond simply reacting to the events of the day', and therein to allow grand strategy to 'envelop military strategy as well as diplomatic strategy and political strategy'. This view forms the basis for his examination of how two aspects of strategy influenced or failed to influence the American Civil War (1861–5). Chapter 9 focuses on the relationship between the evolution of grand strategy and military strategy, assessing generals and battles on both sides, as well as the immense cost in lives and treasure. Murray puts emphasis on the symbiotic relationship between Abraham Lincoln's grand strategy—the preservation of the Union with its form of government—and Ulysses S. Grant's ability to execute the military portion of it—the generalship and combat required to meet such an objective. In the process, both men acknowledged that the appointment of political generals was necessary to maintain political support for the war in the North, despite the reduced military effectiveness, increased casualties, and prolongation of the war that resulted from their incompetence. Murray argues that the real explanation of why it took the North four years to defeat the Southern states resides in the vast size of the theatre of operations and the logistical challenges that posed for one side, and the revolution in military and social affairs occurring in the other: a revolution that saw the blending of the French Revolution and the Industrial Revolution. Lincoln's grand strategy succeeded because the verdict that 'the United States *is* a country', singular rather than plural, was never seriously challenged again. However, it would take another 100 years for Americans to deal with the other consequence of Lincoln's grand strategy: the ending of slavery and the establishment of civil rights for blacks.

Martin van Creveld next focuses on grand strategy and military strategy in the First and Second World Wars. The first part of the chapter examines the similarities between the two wars at the highest level: 'to wit, the one where national policy and politics, strategy, diplomacy, economics, and mobilization meet and interact'. The second part discusses the military strategy of the principal belligerents: Germany, Austria-Hungary, Italy, France, Britain, Russia (the Soviet Union), the United States, and Japan. The author then highlights the differences between the two wars, the role of armored formations on the ground, naval warfare, and the extensive use of air power. He maintains that, in reality, these two total wars should be seen as parts of a single protracted struggle of attrition, with victory ultimately gained by the side with greater resources in terms of bigger military forces (army, navy, and air force), backed by larger populations, a stronger military-industrial base for scientific research and production, and greater economic leverage. The author notes that the two wars, when viewed as a single conflict, present a Janus face to history. One face, looking backward, marked the culmination of centuries of Great Power wars. The other, looking forward through the debris left by the two nuclear explosions, marked the beginning of the period in which we live today. Van Creveld concludes that wars between nuclear-armed states have ceased to make sense because nuclear weapons have cut the long-standing link between victory and survival, and that, with ever more states joining the nuclear club, large-scale inter-state warfare is relegated 'to the dustbin of history'.

In examining the Soviet-American Cold War of 1945–91, Colin Gray posits seven categories of context: political, sociocultural, economic, technological, geographical-geopolitical, historical, and military-strategic. He also divides the Cold War into separate periods, defined by what he considers the three strategically 'decisive moments': the outbreak of, and the American-led reaction to, the war in Korea (June 1950); the Cuban Missile Crisis (October 1962); and the fall of the Soviet Union (December 1989). His analysis leads to the conclusion that 'when all the caveats concerning the wisdom, cunning, and skill, in strategy, grand and military, as well as the ever lurking role of chance, are accorded their due, there is no escaping the overall judgement that the cold war was a struggle that the Soviet Union was never likely to win, at least not by any reasonable definition of victory'. Gray deliberately weights political over military considerations—and grand strategy over military strategy. Grand strategy was practised from the beginning to the end of the contest, military strategy fortunately was not, at least not as it would have been expressed in action. Gray acknowledges the real dilemma posed by the need to devise strategy for a category of weapons (atomic, thermonuclear, and ballistic missiles) that strain the basic logic of strategy to its limits and beyond. Importantly, Gray argues that despite this revolutionary weapon, the nature of strategy itself has not changed. The strategic experience of the Cold War supports his main hypothesis: namely, that strategy has eternal and universal characteristics.

The final chapter explores the nature and character of strategy in two conflicts: Afghanistan (2001–present) and Iraq (2003–present). Treatments of these and other contemporary wars all too often devolve into discussions about the success or failure of policy, the roles played by individual personalities, and the elusive nature of irregular warfare. Moreover, the strategy underlying such conflicts is all too often examined from the perspective of only one of the combatants. James Kiras seeks to place these wars in their proper context by outlining the characteristics that set contemporary asymmetric wars apart from more traditional, conventional armed conflicts, asking if these wars are historically unique or just contextually different. The author provides a brief historical survey and assessment of the two case studies, identifies the unique challenges that contemporary wars pose for both sides, and examines the dynamics of strategy as it applies to these wars. In particular, by assessing the individual strategies of the Taliban, Saddam Hussein, and the US-led coalitions, he explores how adversaries adapt to one another and try to use their strengths against the weaknesses of their opponent. The chapter ends with an assessment of how the gap between policy and operations is about to be bridged in Iraq and can be bridged in Afghanistan. Kiras highlights three attributes of strategy that are identifiable in all wars, but even more apparent in contemporary conflicts. First, strategy is not an academic discipline but rather a practical one—it has to be *done*. Second, strategy is 'executed by, with, and through a number of actors'. Third, strategy is never static, but is influenced dynamically by enemy actions as well as one's own. These attributes of strategy are quintessentially relevant to all of the case studies in this book.

STRATEGY APPLIED

Individually and collectively, then, these chapters deal with the intrinsic nature of war and strategy and the characteristics of a particular strategy in a given conflict. They show that a specific convergence of political objectives, operational schemes of manoeuvre, tactical moves and countermoves, technological innovations and limitations, geographic settings, transient emotions, and more made each conflict studied unique. Yet, despite unique circumstances, enticing continuities emerge, revealing a pattern of universality to all these strategic experiences. Certain elements seem common to war and strategy in all periods, in all geographies, and with all technologies.

What follows from this is that security communities in all historical periods have applied strategy for certain purposes to reach certain objectives. Practised more or less competently, more or less consciously, and with considerable variation in terminology depending on the language of the historical time and place, strategy as a phenomenon has endured throughout history. By surveying the history of warfare, examining the Greek wars of Epaminondas, Philip, and Alexander, the Roman wars of Hannibal, Scipio, and Caesar, and the Byzantine wars of Belisarius and Narses, and comparing them with the wars of the nineteenth and twentieth centuries, we recognize that strategic reasoning has very strong elements of constancy and continuity.

Strategy is a 'how to do it' study—a guide to accomplishing something and doing it effectively. With that comes the option of encapsulating centuries of experience by defining enduring and universal dicta because generalization in its abstract form offers an excellent starting point especially for commanding officers who lack the time or the interest to study the history of warfare in detail. But that stated, the commanding officer cannot rely on these dicta blindly; he needs to adapt these simple axioms to the imminent situation. As Bernard Brodie has observed, we must understand that by its very nature strategy cannot be a true science: 'In short, the catalogue of principles must be recognized for what it is, which is a device intended to circumvent the need for months and years of study of and rumination on a very difficult subject, presented mostly in the form of military and political history and the "lessons" that may be justly derived there from . . .'[11]

With this perspective in mind, Professor Colin Gray offers a conclusion to this volume that focuses on strategic theory and strategic practice—continuity and change. He offers some observations on the enduring function of strategy, the importance of theory and the link between strategic theory and its political purpose. In the conclusion he offers a general theory of strategy in the form of 'twenty-one dicta'—not to be 'rote-learnt and repeated as a credo', but rather 'the author's best current effort to present such a general theory'.

In sum, by examining strategy in all its aspects, from higher statecraft down to military tactics in a wider political and social context, this volume seeks to shed further light on both the uniqueness and the universality of grand strategy and military strategy, and the relationship between those two levels of war. It emphasizes the interplay of adversaries that threatened to use, or used force, to resolve their conflict, and it does so by focusing on the difficulties related to winning wars, campaigns and battles militarily as well as demonstrating the perpetual challenges of imposing political control beyond military victory into an enduring peace settlement.

NOTES

1. Edward N. Luttwak, *Strategy: The Logic of War and Peace*, revised and enlarged edition (London, 2001), 57.
2. Ibid., 267.
3. Basil H. Liddell Hart, *Strategy*, second edition (London, 1967), 319.
4. Ibid., 319.
5. Ibid., 321–2, 335–6.
6. Ibid., 321.
7. Luttwak, *Strategy*, 3.
8. Hew Strachan, 'War and Strategy', in John Andreas Olsen (ed.), *On New Wars* (Oslo, 2007), 15, 23.
9. Alan Stephens and Nicola Baker, *Making Sense of War: Strategy of the 21st Century* (New York, 2006), 8.
10. Ibid., 13.
11. Bernard Brodie, *War and Politics* (New York, 1973), 448.

Part I

Ancient and Mediaeval

1

The Campaigns of Alexander the Great

David J. Lonsdale

INTRODUCTION

There can be no better way to start a volume on the practice of strategy than with Alexander the Great.[1] His performance as a strategist gives us a rare insight into best practice, and sets an extremely high benchmark against which to judge those who followed. The young Macedonian king successfully campaigned for twelve years, revealing adroitness with all of the tools of grand strategy, against a range of foes, and in a host of different geographical environments and forms of warfare. At the end of his short life, his empire reached from the Balkans, down into Egypt, and on into India. In order to achieve this he had to defeat decisively the great Persian empire under Darius III. Remarkable as these exploits appear on the surface, the skill of Alexander's grand strategy is fully revealed by the fact that he entered Persia with a mere 40,000 men. Facing an estimated 15:1 disadvantage in manpower against Darius, Alexander had to masterfully obtain maximum effect from his limited forces and operate a fully integrated grand strategy in order to achieve his objectives.

In order to understand how Alexander achieved such a feat, this chapter will initially detail the main protagonists. This will include an analysis of Alexander's control over the Greek world and the forces at his disposal. It will also include a brief analysis of Macedonian warfare. Since this is a volume primarily concerned with the higher levels of strategy, tactical issues will not be addressed in any real detail. Nonetheless, Alexander's success cannot be understood without a minimal knowledge of the style of warfare that he inherited from his father and evolved further. The initial section of the chapter will also include an examination of the Persian empire at this time. It will be shown that, although somewhat in decline, Persia was still the dominant actor of the period. Other significant actors and locales will be detailed as required throughout the main body of the chapter.

Alexander's campaigns will be broken down into three main sections. The first section will deal with his actions in Greece and the Balkans, which he undertook to secure his home base before heading into the Persian empire. This will provide an early example of his astute grasp of coercion, as well as the significance of his ability to perform rapid operational manoeuvres. The second section details Alexander's destruction of the Persian centres of gravity, leading to the collapse of the empire. This will include an analysis of the three great battles against the forces of Darius, neutralization of the Persian naval threat, capture of the three capital cities, and the pursuit and death of Darius. Of particular significance in this part of his campaigns was Alexander's astute grasp of grand strategy. The final section of the work will focus upon Alexander's campaigns in the East. Particular attention will be paid to counter-insurgency operations in central Asia and his last great battle at the River Hydaspes in India. It will be shown here that Alexander was able to take a military instrument primarily designed for large conventional battles and transform it into an excellent instrument of irregular warfare. The final section will close with an examination of Alexander's increasingly brutal campaign through India. This will give us an insight into the faults of his style of command and leadership, and his inability to identify the culminating point of victory.

Overall, it is hoped that this chapter will provide the reader with an insight into one of the most extraordinary strategic careers in history. Napoleon advised that budding commanders should study the campaigns of the great captains of the past.[2] There can be few worthier of study than Alexander.

ALEXANDER'S INHERITANCE: POLITICAL AND MILITARY CONTEXT

At the age of 20, Alexander became king of Macedonia after the assassination of his father, Philip II, in 336 BC. At the time of his accession, Macedonia was the hegemonic power in Greece. Following the Macedonian victory over the Greek states at the battle of Chaeronea, Alexander's father established a political settlement in Greece that recognized Macedonian hegemony and provided material and political support for the kingdom's foreign policy. The League of Corinth, as this political settlement was known, bound together the states of southern Greece in a collective security organization. However, the League was barely a year old when Philip was killed, and so it was Alexander who had to establish fully the new political settlement. In the immediate aftermath of Philip's death (events described below), Alexander campaigned through Greece, persuading the various states, through a combination of coercion and political compromises, to honour their League commitments.

Alexander's main foreign policy goal was clearly the invasion of Persia. Thus, his principal objective in Greece was the maintenance of stability. To that end, the League guaranteed the autonomy and sovereignty of its member states (under Macedonian hegemony), and forbade any reforms or initiatives that promoted radical political change within these same states. A. B. Bosworth notes that the League acted as a court of arbitration among the states of southern Greece, where disputes could be settled peacefully. The procedural workings of the League were somewhat vague. This seems to have been deliberate in order to give Alexander and his representative in his absence, Antipater, flexibility in maintaining order.[3]

However, although the diplomatic and procedural niceties of the League may have been vague, it is clear that peace and unity within the Greek world rested upon Macedonian military power. To that end, Alexander left Antipater with a substantial military force when he left for Persia. The force comprised 12,000 phalangites and 1,000 Companion cavalry, with supporting light infantry and light cavalry. This typifies Alexander's entire approach to grand strategy. He was an astute practitioner of the non-military instruments of grand strategy. However, these other elements were always underpinned by military power.

On the military front, Alexander was fortunate to inherit a well-developed military instrument from his father. Prior to the rise of Macedonia, Greek warfare had been dominated since the seventh century by part-time hoplite infantry.[4] Although varying in the type and amount of armour worn, the hoplite was essentially a heavy infantryman. The main armament for the hoplite was a spear (between 7 and 9 feet in length) and shield (hoplon). The dominant formation was the phalanx, in which tightly packed hoplites, gaining protection from their neighbours' shields, would slowly advance upon their opponents. As the phalanxes came together, battles would be won or lost by one side pushing their opponents off the main field of battle. Hoplite warfare was quasi-ritualistic in nature, regulated by well-understood rules of engagement (e.g. no pursuit of a routed enemy), and typically resulted in relatively light casualties. Light infantry (including slingers and archers) and cavalry had minimal roles on the hoplite battlefield. Although this pattern of warfare had begun to evolve somewhat during the Peloponnesian War, it remained essentially the same until being swept away by Macedonian innovation under Philip II.

Macedonia retained the phalanx formation, but it was now manned by Macedonian phalangites, who wielded the substantially longer, 16-foot sarissa (a heavy wooden pike) and a small shoulder shield. With such armaments, the Macedonian phalanx was even more restricted in its movements than the hoplite version. However, it no longer represented the unit of decision. Rather, Philip II used the phalanx in the centre of his line to fix the enemy in place, so as to enable his heavy cavalry, the Companions, to break the enemy's line. Light infantry forces, including archers, slingers, and the mobile hypaspists (shield bearers), were given much greater prominence in Macedonian tactics. These tactical changes created the potential for more decisive victories. However, this was only truly realized with accompanying cultural shifts. Macedonia abandoned the quasi-ritualistic nature of Greek warfare and placed emphasis on pursuit and destruction of the enemy, both on and off the battlefield. Macedonia also made significant changes at the operational level. Most importantly, the logistical requirements were significantly reduced. This in turn enabled a smaller baggage train, which ultimately produced a force capable of significantly more rapid manoeuvre over operational distances. Finally, Macedonia developed a highly skilled and much more aggressive team of siege engineers. Rather than starving a city into submission, time and again the Macedonians were able to breach a city's defences in a fairly short time-frame. The whole Macedonian military enterprise was underpinned by a core of professional soldiers with personal loyalty to the king. Indeed, Alexander had grown up and trained with many of his leading officers. The military instrument created by Philip II, and developed by his son, would prove to be disciplined and highly adaptable in the coming Persian campaign.

Clearly, Alexander had inherited a state well placed for military adventure. However, this should not blind us to the fact that in Persia he faced a substantial foe. By the time he crossed the Hellespont on his conquest, the Persian empire had been established for over 200 years. Within that period the empire had created well-structured political, economic, and social systems. The first was centred on the authority of the king, but with delegation of that authority down to the provincial level for administrative purposes. In his study of ancient Persia, Josef Wiesehöfer notes that the sources (both archaeological and written) do not present us with a clear description of the imperial political system in the provinces. Various administrative offices are mentioned. The most important appear to be satraps, governors, and provincial military commanders. However, whatever the minutiae of provincial governance, it is clear that the king acted as the unifying point for this diverse empire. The monarch was not worshipped as a god, but was perceived to be the gods' representative on earth. The centre of the Persian empire was the province of Persis. High office in the royal court was almost exclusively the preserve of the Persian aristocracy. Thus, the king and his closest relatives were vital components of imperial power. Their destruction or removal could prove catastrophic to the empire.

Unlike the Roman empire, there were no opportunities for outsiders to attain Persian citizenship. This did not mean, however, that non-Persian subjects felt alienated within the empire. Indeed, provincial elites often regarded the Persian king as a guarantor of stability, and therefore also of their political and economic position.[5]

The scale of the empire was impressive. Darius's domains reached from the Hellespont, down to Egypt and the Persian Gulf, and as far east as India. Although ethnically diverse, the empire was held together not only by the person of the king but also by an official language (Aramaic), a well-developed fiscal system (including an official currency), and an impressive road and communications network. The 'royal roads', which extended for hundreds of miles and were often paved or laid with bitumen, were lined by forts, posts, and the equivalent of milestones. Imperial control of these routes was well established, to the point that contemporary authors, such as Xenophon, commented positively upon the relative safety of the general traveller. Similar levels of security were also evident within the cities of the empire, which boasted imperial garrisons under the command of men chosen by the monarch. These obvious signs of development were supplemented further by the central administration's upkeep of a substantial irrigation system. Finally, it is worth noting that the Achaemenid monarchy enacted a policy of tolerance towards their subjects' many religions. Indeed, some of these religions were actually supported by the central administration via various measures, including tax exemptions.[6] All told, the picture we have of ancient Persia suggests that Alexander faced a well-organized empire, with well-developed fiscal and agricultural systems, and populated by inhabitants who were not overburdened by high taxes, and who could practise their religion without interference from the central imperial administration.

Despite the impressive development of the Persian empire, there is some historical debate about its condition at the time of Alexander's invasion. One school of thought, based mainly upon Graeco-Roman sources, describes a period of decline from Cyrus the Great onwards. This decline is attributed to, among other things, a growing effeminization of the Persian monarchy and mounting resistance within the empire to increasingly despotic rulers. This perception of decline has been challenged by more recent scholars, such as Wiesehöfer, who questions the validity of the Graeco-Roman sources.[7] While there is some evidence of challenges to the authority of the Persian king, there is also evidence of the monarchy's ability to deal effectively with these challenges. This was certainly the case in Egypt just prior to Alexander's arrival in the empire. In the final analysis, the empire that Alexander invaded appeared to be essentially stable. During the war with Alexander, it was also able to put into the field three substantial armies superior in number to his own.

In military terms, like Alexander, Darius had a core of very competent forces at his disposal. Particularly worthy of mention are the various cavalry units serving in the Persian empire. The Bactrian cavalry are generally regarded as being the equal of the Macedonian Companions. Darius also had the equally well-respected horse archers among his forces. However, despite these advantages, the Persians had one fatal weakness in their military instrument: infantry. Aside from the 10,000 Immortals and trained Royal Bodyguards, the mass of Persian infantry was generally part-time, consisting of conscripted farmers who were poorly armed. The Persians had sought to overcome this problem with the employment of Greek hoplite mercenaries. Although these provided Darius with a solid, reliable force to face Alexander, it has already been noted that the age of the hoplite was passing in the face of Macedonian innovation. Nonetheless, as the third section in this chapter will show, the Persians made essentially sensible tactical decisions when facing the Macedonians. In particular, they would rely upon their strong cavalry forces, hoping to neutralize the Macedonian instrument of decision. However, in the event, against a commander of Alexander's ability, the Persians' well-designed plans were overturned and the weak infantry could not hold the line against the Macedonians.[8]

On the battlefield, the Persians could not match Alexander and his army. However, the fate of the empire did not rest entirely on land. Darius was also in command of a substantial navy. Drawn primarily from Phoenicia, Persian naval forces offered an alternative strategic option: an attack on mainland Greece, thereby bypassing Alexander's army in Persia. The power of the Persian navy was such that Alexander did not attempt to defeat it at sea. Rather, as we shall witness in the third section, the young Macedonian king found a novel way of neutralizing this substantial threat.

GREECE AND THE BALKANS

A number of Greek states (including Athens, Thebes, and Ambracia) saw the death of Philip II as an opportunity for change: a possible end to Macedonian hegemony. In Athens, Demosthenes stirred up political discontent, while the Ambracians declared a democracy and expelled the Macedonian garrison. Alexander realized that he had to assert his authority rapidly, and promptly moved south with his forces. Along the way his advance and authority were challenged by Thessalian tribesmen, who blocked his path on a mountain pass. By cutting steps into the mountainside Alexander's forces outflanked the entrenched Thessalians, who promptly surrendered and reaffirmed Macedonian leadership of the Thessalian League. Not only did this ensure a regular financial contribution from the tribesmen, but more importantly it secured for Alexander the use of the well-respected Thessalian cavalry, who would prove to be invaluable in the coming campaigns. The pace of Alexander's advance south, and the early competence he had shown as a young ruler, quenched any enthusiasm for rebellion in Greece. Alexander also displayed his deft political hand by recognizing the democracy in Ambracia and granting a pardon to Thebes. As a result of these actions, at Corinth the Greek city-states reaffirmed Alexander's position as hegemon of the League of Corinth. In his first strategic test, he had displayed the hallmark of his coming imperial rule: a blend of military brilliance allied to subtle political manoeuvres. All that was missing at this stage was an act of brutal coercion. However, it would not be long before the Greek world would witness that element of Alexander's strategic art.

With Greek support assured, Alexander moved north to complete his father's Balkan ambitions. With discontent and ambition stirring in Thrace, it was vital for him to subdue the region before he left for Persia. He moved north into the Balkans in the spring of 335, leading a combined arms army that included most of his quality units: phalangites, hypaspists, Agrianians, archers, and Companion cavalry. The main threat in the area emanated from the Triballians under the rule of King Syrmus in the Danube region. Prior to reaching the Danube, Alexander had already killed 3,000 Triballians in battle with a brilliant ruse. A Triballian force was entrenched in a thick wooded glen. In order to draw them out, the young Macedonian harassed them with slingers and archers. When forced to counter-attack, the Triballians were met by the disciplined phalangites, who pinned them in place, thus enabling the Companion cavalry to encircle them. This overwhelming victory cost Alexander the deaths of only forty infantry and eleven cavalry. Widely disproportionate kill ratios would become a mainstay of Alexander's battles.

As Alexander approached the heart of the Triballian kingdom, Syrmus and his people retreated to the island of Peuce in the Danube. Alexander sensibly abandoned an initial attempt at a risky amphibious attack on the island. Instead, he opted for a more indirect approach by devastating Triballian crops in an act of coercion. As the campaign of devastation commenced, a 14,000-strong force of Getae arrived on the northern bank of the Danube. Their aim was to deter Alexander from crossing the great river into their territory. Rather than being deterred, Alexander led 5,500 of his men across the river at night, and fell upon the unprepared Getae forces, who fled, leaving their main settlement open to attack. Inadvertently, the Getae had presented Alexander with an ideal opportunity to display both his military competence and coercive technique. King Syrmus had seen enough, and promptly accepted Macedonian rule in the region. In this, he was joined by a number of fellow tribes in the coming days.

Despite this stunning success, Alexander still faced significant opposition in the Balkans. Two Illyrian chiefs, Cleitus and Glaucias, had allied against him and even planned an attack upon the Macedonian homeland. They received some support from the Autariatae, who planned to harry the Macedonian forces as they marched to engage the Illyrians. Alexander negated the latter threat with the help of his ally King Langarus of the Agrianians. With his flank secure, Alexander headed to Pelium, a fortified city where Cleitus was due to meet up with Glaucias's forces in preparation for the invasion of Macedonia. While besieging Pelium,

Alexander's forces became surrounded when Glaucias's army arrived in the area earlier than expected. As Alexander's supplies ran down, he was left in an increasingly desperate situation, faced as he was by an enemy superior in number and occupying the high ground. On this occasion, his actions were in tune with Sun Tzu's comment on knowing when and, just as importantly, when not to engage the enemy.[9] He sensibly opted for the latter, leading the Macedonians on a skilful tactical withdrawal without suffering a single loss. The withdrawal was accomplished by a series of feints, well-disciplined manoeuvres, and courageous attacks, made possible by the quality of his professional troops.

The operations at Pelium had revealed that Alexander was not just a master of aggressive offensive action. However, although his masterful withdrawal had saved the army, the Illyrian threat still loomed large over Macedonia. Fortunately, the Illyrians believed Alexander would continue his retreat all the way into Macedonia. Instead, his effective intelligence machinery brought the king information that the Illyrians seemed to be displaying a false sense of security and had left the safety of their fortifications. Alexander moved quickly, and fell upon his unprepared enemy at night. Once again, the pace and surprise of the Macedonian attack destroyed the cohesion of the enemy. Many Illyrians were killed and captured, leaving Cleitus and Glaucias with little choice but to abandon their planned invasion of Macedonia. Instead, they agreed to provide Alexander with forces for the invasion of Persia. The Balkans were pacified.

However, at the moment of triumph in the north, and possibly with the encouragement of Darius, a rumour began circulating Greece that Alexander had been killed in the Balkan campaign. Athens and Thebes once again jumped at the opportunity to rid themselves of Macedonian control. Alexander responded with typical speed. His army arrived outside Thebes and immediately began attacking the city. In contrast to the leniency he had previously shown to Greek rebels, on this occasion he used Thebes as an example to deter any future thoughts of rebellion. Six thousand Thebans were killed in the attack, the city was razed to the ground, and the remaining 30,000 inhabitants were sold into slavery. However, conscious of the cultural significance of Athens and the value of its navy to his future campaigns, Alexander showed leniency towards the city. This act of mercy helped to retain the unity of the League of Corinth. This unity was further entrenched by declaring the destruction of Thebes an act of the League, and thereby treating Thebes as a rebel against the whole Greek world rather than just Macedonia.

This episode raises some interesting questions concerning Alexander's approach to clemency. For the most part, his treatment of defeated foes can be best understood through the lens of strategic pragmatism. However, there were occasions, such as at Tyre and during the Indian campaign, when resistance to his will did seem to provoke an emotionally charged increase in the levels of violence. Alexander was prudent, but he was still a young monarch who expected to be obeyed.

In his efforts to secure Macedonia's position in Greece and the Balkans, Alexander revealed a surprising degree of maturity and strategic flair. With a mixture of rapid operational advances and skilful manoeuvres in the face of the enemy, he had achieved remarkable results from little military effort and had suffered few casualties. These results can be partly explained by his appreciation of the coercive use of force, and partly by his ability to surprise his enemies by crossing rivers or attacking at night. In Greece, military force was used more sparingly than in the Balkans. Indeed, Alexander relied as much upon political manoeuvres as he did upon his forces. His careful use of the League of Corinth to cement his position and justify his actions enabled him eventually to unify and stabilize the Greek world behind Macedonian ambitions. However, it is important to note that underpinning all of Alexander's political moves was the threat and use of force. The attack on Thebes was a perfect demonstration of this. His professional, loyal army was the deciding factor in Alexander's relations with his neighbours.

DESTROYING PERSIA'S CENTRES OF GRAVITY

Carl von Clausewitz theorized that each strategic actor has centres of gravity, characteristics or capabilities upon which their strategic potential rested: 'One must keep the dominant characteristics of both belligerents in mind. Out of these characteristics a certain centre of gravity develops, the hub of all power and movement, on which everything depends. This is the point against which all our energies should be directed.'[10]

Although it is often the case that we search for one dominant centre of gravity in each actor, in some cases, pressure may have to be exerted upon a number of different capabilities. This was certainly the case in relation to the Persian empire. Alexander appears to have understood that such a powerful foe had at least four main attributes that sustained it: army, navy, capital cities, and Darius III. This section will discuss each of these centres of gravity in turn, and analyse how their destruction or capture eventually resulted in the fall of the empire.

Destruction of the main Persian army was of vital importance for Alexander's campaign. The army was an important symbol of Persian power and rule over the provinces of the empire. During military campaigns, the Persian king would lead the army with a substantial proportion of his royal court in attendance. Thus, Macedonian victory over Darius's forces would signal a shift of power in the region. However, there was another, more tangible reason for defeating the army in battle. As previously noted, Alexander began his campaign with a relatively small force. Thus, in order to retain a sufficient offensive instrument, he was able to leave only small garrisons in the areas he conquered. That being the case, he could not afford to leave substantial Persian forces roaming around the empire, retaking his gains as they went. This was a problem later faced by Hannibal during his invasion of Italy.[11]

Conscious of these two factors, Alexander eagerly engaged the Persian army early in the campaign at the River Granicus. As with all of Alexander's three battles against Darius's forces, the Granicus ended in decisive victory, but had a moment of crisis for the Macedonians. Quite understandably the Persian commander, the Greek mercenary Memnon, deployed his strongest forces (the cavalry) along the steep riverbank facing Alexander's men. Perhaps less understandable is Memnon's decision to hold 20,000 Greek mercenaries well back from the front line in reserve. In the event, the battle unfolded so rapidly that the Greek mercenaries were unable to play any significant part. The rapid turn of events hinged on an act of deception by Alexander, which drew some of the Persian cavalry away in pursuit and thereby opened a gap in the Persian line that Alexander's Companion cavalry was able to exploit. In the midst of his victory, Alexander was almost slain, only to be saved by the intervention of Clietus the Black. Alexander's style of command was suited to the heroic culture of the Greeks, but clearly had attendant dangers.

Alexander's victory at the Granicus gave him a window of opportunity in Asia Minor while Darius began raising another army from his vast manpower reserves. The Macedonian spent this time liberating Greek cities along the coast from Persian control and dealing with the Persian naval threat. Alexander's approach to those whom he conquered reveals an astute grasp of grand strategy. It also suggests that he had studied the Persian empire well and understood its methods of control. Conscious that he did not have the forces available to be engaged constantly in putting down rebellions throughout the empire, he sought to gain the support, or at least the acquiescence, of his new subjects. More often than not, he achieved this through political, economic, and cultural measures. Since his primary goal was stability, in most cases he would leave the current political and economic systems intact. This would involve leaving taxes at established rates and even retaining existing Persian officials in their posts. This was not an abrogation of control, however, because trusted Macedonians were placed alongside the existing officials to monitor events and protect Alexander's interests. Occasionally, as in the case of the liberated Greek cities, Alexander would make some popular changes, often replacing oligarchies with democracies (subject to Alexander's rule).

On the issue of religion, Alexander appears to have understood existing Persian policy, and would normally leave religious practices to the locals. However, he would sometimes go even further and honour local religious traditions. For example, in Egypt he participated in religious ceremonies, including a sacrifice to their god Apis. This approach paid significant dividends, and contributed to the Egyptians' decision to pronounce Alexander Pharaoh. What is evident from these examples is that Alexander's intelligence apparatus provided good information on the particulars of each region he operated within. Once he understood local circumstances, he would adjust his policies to ensure a stable transfer of power from Persia. It is important to note, however, that he was equally prepared to use excessive and brutal force when his rule was challenged. This occurred at the sieges of Gaza and the island city of Tyre. After an unusually long (seven-month) siege at Tyre, Alexander slaughtered the inhabitants or sold them into slavery for their refusal to fully accept his authority.

Tyre was a major Phoenician naval port, and as such was an important part in Alexander's campaign to neutralize the Persian navy. The threat from Darius's naval forces had become real with an invasion of the Greek islands in 333. Without sufficient forces to defeat the Persian navy in battle, Alexander sought to weaken it by capturing and destroying its bases along the Mediterranean coast. As he marched south through Asia Minor, many of the main Phoenician ports surrendered to him, having recognized the shift of power in the region. Thus, not only could Alexander deny the Persian navy safe harbour but his own naval strength also grew as the Phoenician states pledged their allegiance to the Macedonian king.

The victory at the Granicus and the treatment of Tyre were clear indicators of Alexander's military power. However, he was given another opportunity to display his pre-eminence at the battle of Issus in November 333.

Having raised a new army in Persia, Darius, more by luck than judgement, managed to fall upon Alexander's lines of communication along the coast. Alexander, conscious of the Persians' substantial numerical advantage, man-oeuvred rapidly and caught the Persian army in the narrows at Issus. As at the Granicus, the Persian battle plan rested upon their cavalry. Darius, now unable to outflank the Macedonians through sheer length of line, sought to envelop the Macedonian centre by defeating the Macedonian light cavalry on the left wing. In the event, one of Macedonia's most trusted generals, Parmenion, led a successful defence of the left, and once again Alexander broke through the enemy's line with a cavalry-led combined-arms attack in the centre-right of the line. Despite the success, there was a moment of crisis for Alexander when his central phalanx split, exposing its vulnerable flanks. Defeat was averted by the rapid collapse of the Persian line and subsequent tactical readjustment by the Macedonian forces. The Persian defeat secured Alexander's position and reputation in the western pro-vinces of the empire. However, Darius escaped capture and returned to the centre of the empire to raise an even larger army for one final battle with Alexander.

At Issus, Alexander did manage to capture Darius's mother and the very substantial royal tent. The latter was so vast that it has been described as a mobile palace. Although these gains seem of little significance at first glance, it is possible that Alexander was availing himself of the trappings of Achaemenian rule, and thereby developing a sense of legitimacy as ruler in the eyes of the empire's subjects: 'Alexander was not only perfectly familiar with the conditions for the Achaemenid rulers' legitimacy, but he did everything to fulfill them himself.'[12]

With the escape of Darius, allied to his ability to raise yet another army, Alexander had thus far failed to neutralize these two important Persian centres of gravity. Nonetheless, with the Persian navy now impotent, the young Macedo-nian could drive deep into the Persian heartland, secure in the knowledge that his home base was safe from Persian attack. Before pushing on into Persia, he completed his conquest of the western Persian provinces by advancing into Egypt. The Egyptians accepted his rule without a fight, and he thereby gained an important grain-producing region without cost. This was an important politi-cal and economic move for Alexander because Greece was a net importer of grain.[13] Thus, by securing Egyptian supplies, he could reveal to some of his reluctant Greek allies the benefits of supporting his campaigns. He appears to have been acutely aware of keeping the Greeks on board. He wasted few oppor-tunities to present the campaigns in Persia as a Greek enterprise in revenge for previous Persian invasions of the Greek homeland. For example, after the capture of the Persian capitals, he returned captured Greek artefacts home for display. Greek support not only ensured a regular supply of fresh troops, but it also helped to stave off or undermine any rebellions against Macedonian rule in Greece. Rebellion proved to be a genuine threat when a Sparta-led coalition briefly challenged Macedonian hegemony in late 331.

In the period between the battles of Issus and Gaugamela, Darius made a diplomatic attempt to salvage his monarchical rule. In exchange for peace, he offered Alexander all of the territory west of the Euphrates. Even though this represented a substantial gain for Macedonia, Alexander refused these peace overtures. His objectives reached far beyond the Euphrates. Upon setting foot in Asia Minor, it is reported that he threw his spear into the sand and proclaimed that he would be lord of Asia, won by spear.[14] In light of this, Darius's offer suggests that the Persian monarch seriously underestimated the scale of Alexander's ambition. In addition, after the victories at the Granicus and Issus, and his success against the Persian naval bases, Alexander was understandably brimming with confidence. At this stage of the campaign, the culminating point of victory was still some way off.

Alexander's push into Persia eventually brought him to the final showdown with Darius at Gaugamela. The Macedonian's path through the Persian heartland was partly dictated by logistical requirements.[15] However, this necessity does not entirely excuse him from the folly of meeting Darius on a battlefield chosen and prepared by the Persians. By accepting Darius's chosen site, it appears that Alexander had fallen victim to overconfidence. This decision looks especially problematic when one considers that Alexander faced a 5:1 numerical disadvantage on a wide-open battlefield. In addition, Darius had flattened the ground to accommodate his forces, particularly the cavalry and scythed chariots.

Facing these tactical challenges, Alexander deployed his men in a rectangular formation to guard against Persian outflanking manoeuvres. Despite this sensible response, the Macedonian line came under substantial pressure from Persian cavalry, some of which broke through to the Macedonian baggage train. The scythed chariots proved ineffective, however, mainly because Darius threw them at the Macedonian line in isolation. As the chariots reached the enemy's forces, the well-drilled Macedonians opened their lines and cut the chariot drivers to pieces.

The moment of decision in the battle came when Alexander identified a gap appearing in the Persian line as Darius's cavalry poured towards the Macedonian right, seeking what they thought was the moment of victory. As at Issus, Alexander led the Companion cavalry into the gap, and, once exposed to this attack, the inferior Persian infantry was routed. Darius again fled the battlefield, an act that precipitated a further collapse of the Persian line. Despite a lengthy pursuit, the Persian king escaped. However, the Macedonians' slaughter of the routed enemy ensured that the Persian army, an important centre of gravity, was finally taken out of the equation. The route to the Persian capitals was now open.

Although the Persian army ceased to exist after Gaugamela, Alexander still had much to do in order to secure his new empire. In the first instance, Darius was still at large. Until this could be rectified, the Persian king represented a legitimate source of authority in the empire and a potential rallying point against Alexander. Also, Alexander had to secure and stabilize the central satrapies of the empire, which included the three capital cities: Susa, Persepolis, and Ecbatana. Gaining control of these important centres would solidify Alexander's political standing among the people and the ruling classes. Control would also confer significant financial rewards by capturing the main imperial treasuries.

From Gaugamela, Alexander marched into Babylon. The Babylonians treated him as a liberator from Persian occupation. In December 331, he entered the first capital, Susa, without any resistance. There he took control of an abundant treasury. He also discovered Greek artefacts taken during Persian invasions of Greece. As noted above, ever conscious of Greek perceptions of his campaign,

Alexander returned the artefacts to the homeland to emphasize the unified nature of his endeavours.

After Susa the next great prize was the capital Persepolis, in the satrapy of Persis, the centre of the empire. Persepolis housed the residence of the Persian rulers and in many respects was the very heart of the entire empire. After the bloodless capture of Babylon and Susa, Persepolis presented a much more challenging proposition. Geographically, the Macedonians were entering more mountainous terrain. In addition, Alexander's men would receive a more hostile reception as they left Persian-occupied territory and entered Persia proper.

Since Gaugamela signalled the end of set-piece battles for this part of the campaign, Alexander created smaller, more mobile units. These included smaller companies of the Companion cavalry, as well as eight infantry commando units of 1,000 men each. Light cavalry was given greater prominence in operations, and across the army Alexander's forces were given extra training in mountain warfare against irregular foes. Finally, there was further delegation of command authority to the unit commanders to enable more rapid and dispersed operations. These actions indicate that Alexander had moved even further away from the restrictive, one-dimensional warfare of Greece in the pre-Macedonian period. As a commander, Alexander was proving to be adaptable and flexible, as the challenges he faced demanded.

One of the first tests of the revised army was against the mountain-dwelling Uxians. The Persian empire had failed to subdue the Uxians for almost two centuries. Even Darius's men had to pay a toll to traverse Uxian land. Alexander defeated these stubborn mountain dwellers in one night, through guile and brutality. He feigned submission to draw the Uxian forces away from their villages. Once exposed, the villages were devastated. From there, Alexander moved rapidly and ambushed the Uxian men in a mountain pass, inflicting a crushing defeat. Reeling from their defeat, the Uxians submitted to the Macedonian, agreeing to pay an annual tribute.

With the Uxians defeated, Alexander headed quickly towards Persepolis. He needed to reach the second Persian capital before the contents of the treasury could be removed. However, the ruling satrap, Ariobarzanes, controlled the Persian Gates pass in the Zagros Mountains with over 40,000 men. Alexander sent the slower-moving elements of his army via a longer alternative route. This left him with the elite mobile units, such as lighter Companion cavalry, Macedonian infantry, Agrianians, and archers. Utilizing local intelligence from a captured enemy prisoner, Alexander was able to outflank Ariobarzanes via a precarious mountain path 17 kilometres in length. He hid his flanking manoeuvre by distracting Ariobarzanes with what appeared to be a full army camped on the mountainside. Once in position, he was able to crush the Persian force between the two parts of his army. Yet again, he had managed to inflict a crushing defeat on a far superior force via an astute operational manoeuvre. Persepolis was quickly captured, along with its substantial treasure. To strengthen Greek unity further, Alexander burnt parts of the Persian royal palace in an act of revenge for the prior invasions of Greece.

While waiting for the winter snow to clear in the Zagros Mountains, Alexander received intelligence that Darius had reached the third Persian capital, Ecbatana, 827 kilometres to the north-west. As the snow receded, he began an extraordinarily rapid pursuit of the Persian king, the one remaining centre of gravity of significance in the empire (Ecbatana would fall shortly). It is reported that horses and men died of exhaustion, such was the pace that Alexander maintained. As Alexander reached Ecbatana, Darius's position in the empire was waning. Much of the ruling elite had accepted the new political order, and the Persian king was becoming increasingly isolated. The issue came to a head when Bessus, the satrap of Bactria, deposed and killed Darius. Alexander recovered the body, and with a gesture designed to ingratiate himself with his new subjects and further foster the legitimacy of his rule, gave Darius a royal burial. This act once again reveals Alexander's knowledge of the land he was operating in. Before taking the throne, Persian monarchs traditionally had to fulfil certain duties. One of these duties was to provide an appropriate burial for their predecessor.[16]

With the death of the old king, and the capture of the three capitals, the Macedonian-led Greek war of revenge was over. Greek allied forces were either sent home or retained on a mercenary basis. The nature of the campaigns now became directly concerned with the establishment of Alexander's new empire, within which he would be lord of Asia.

Alexander's neutralization of the Persian centres of gravity was all about a shift in the balance of power in the empire. Darius's ability to rule was based upon the army, navy, central organization based around the capital cities, and the symbolic significance of his own royal persona. In pursuing these centres of gravity Alexander played to his strengths and relied primarily upon the army as the chosen means to attain power. In a series of battles and sieges his army destroyed Persian military power on land and at sea, leaving Darius and his capitals vulnerable. The growth in Alexander's power was recognized by many provincial rulers, who often chose to accept the new reality without resistance. This process was aided by Alexander's coercive technique, which received notable boosts from his brutal actions at Tyre and Gaza. As important as military power was in this section of the campaign, the non-violent components of Alexander's grand strategy also deserve mention. His soft touch on political, social, cultural, and economic issues eased the decisions of many to accept his rule.

ESTABLISHING THE EASTERN FRONTIER

Although all of the pre-existing Persian centres of gravity had been dealt with, and Achaemenid rule had collapsed, the security of Alexander's conquests was still in doubt. First, he had to deal with Bessus, both to prevent him from becoming a rallying point for a rebellion, and also to enhance his own claim to the Persian throne by dealing with the man who had killed Darius. Second, Alexander wanted to establish a secure eastern frontier for the empire. Both of these objectives led him and his army into central Asia and India. Bessus failed to engender enough support in Bactria, which initially accepted Alexander's rule. He fled into neighbouring Sogdiana, where he was himself deposed and handed over to the Macedonian by Sogdian noblemen led by Spitamenes. Alexander established the northern border of his empire at the River Jaxartes, occupied the Sogdian capital,

Samarkand, and built a new city, Alexander the Farthermost. However, any sense of stability was short lived when both Bactria and Sogdiana rose in rebellion under the leadership of Spitamenes.

For a commander famed for his set-piece battles, Alexander now faced a protracted eighteen-month insurgency. As witnessed during his operations in the mountainous regions of Persia, he adapted well to the new challenge. As always, he moved quickly. Revealing a surprisingly modern understanding of counter-insurgency, he recognized the need to act quickly to prevent the insurgency from becoming established and cohesive. His first tangible objective was the capture of seven fortified cities in the region. These would act as pacified bases of operations from which he could extend his influence. The cities fell relatively quickly in the face of superior Macedonian siege techniques. In addition to this success, Alexander defeated Scythian forces massing on the northern bank of the Jaxartes.

The Macedonian next had to lead his men to relieve his garrison at Samarkand, which had come under attack from Spitamenes. As is usually the case in irregular warfare, Alexander's primary challenge was bringing the enemy to battle. In the absence of such an opportunity, Alexander further divided his forces into smaller, more mobile units with delegated command authority. These detachments engaged in search and destroy operations against the rebels. He also sought to weaken the support base of Spitamenes by devastating the countryside and dealing harshly with those towns and villages that supported the rebellion. These measures, alongside the establishment of a series of hill forts and fortified settlements, eventually isolated Spitamenes in Sogdiana. Alexander had successfully isolated the battlefield and restricted his enemy's freedom of movement.

As a result of Alexander's actions, Spitamenes was forced to engage in ever more dangerous raids. On one occasion, a large raiding party was intercepted by a Macedonian detachment commanded by Coenus. In the ensuing battle, Spitamenes lost 800 cavalry. As Alexander's counter-insurgency measures took effect, increasing numbers of rebels laid down their weapons and accepted the stability offered by Alexander's control. In the end, as Spitamenes had done to Bessus, so others did to him. A group of his men, fearing the imminent arrival of a force led by Alexander, killed him and presented his head to the Macedonian king.

The death of Spitamenes brought the main insurgency to an end. A few pockets of resistance remained, including a group sheltering atop the seemingly impregnable Sogdian Rock. Alexander took the rock with an audacious attack up the sheer rock face. The defenders were so caught by surprise that they submitted with minimal resistance. A similar feat led to the capture of the Rock of Chorienes. On both occasions, Alexander used innovative and audacious manoeuvres to break the will of the enemy, and thereby achieved great results from minimal effort. He cemented his political position in the region through a series of marriages, including his own to Roxanne, the daughter of a local ruler named Oxyartes. As was always the case with Alexander, in central Asia the political stability of the region was built upon the foundation of military power. To that end, he left a garrison of 10,000 infantry and 3,500 cavalry in the pacified region. In return, his army gained cavalry forces of high quality from Bactria, Sogdiana, Massagetae, and Dahae.

Alexander's campaigns in India, as he searched for an eastern border for his empire, reflected those in central Asia. His army retained its more mobile form with decentralized command and control. Much of the fighting was of an irregular character, with the capture of centres of population that would serve as bases of operations and development.

Such an approach seems entirely sensible. However, many of the potential benefits were undermined by Alexander's increasingly less subtle, and more brutal approach to strategy. As he worked his way through India, wholesale slaughter of populations became more common. Explanations for this change are varied and include issues relating to Alexander's personality. He was becoming more paranoid and isolated among his men. His excessive drinking began to have a significant effect on his personality. Furthermore, a number of plots against him had been unearthed. One included Philotos, the son of the reliable general Parmenion. The execution of Philotos and the assassination of his father further eroded the relationship between Alexander and his Macedonian veterans. This relationship was already under pressure as Alexander increasingly adopted Persian customs in his court. Many of his men saw this as the king going native. In fact, it is more likely that the pragmatic Alexander was merely enhancing the legitimacy of his claim to the imperial throne. He was not a mere conqueror satisfied with raping his new territories of their resources. As his city-building projects reveal, he was trying to establish a durable empire that brought together the Greek and Persian worlds in a new cohesive whole. However, as his empire began to take shape, he felt increasingly isolated and became volatile in the face of any resistance to his rule, either from within or outside his own forces.

These personality traits were magnified by his increasing belief in his own divinity.[17] The seed of this idea had been planted in his mind from an early age by his mother, Olympias. It received confirmation during a famous visit the young Macedonian made to the oracle at Siwah in Egypt, where a priest addressed him as the son of a god. Taken together, all of these elements of Alexander's personality made him resentful of disobedience and resistance.

However, it would be wrong to attribute the decline in Alexander's strategic performance merely to his own emotional failings. We should also consider the fact that he possessed little information on India. As noted above, much of the success of his grand strategy in Persia was enabled by a wealth of information on the workings of the Persian empire. Without the corresponding intelligence on India, Alexander was not able to judge the political or social desires of the population. In an absence of intelligence, he had to rely more on brute force and its coercive effects.

The political landscape of India, characterized as it was by many competing kingdoms, complicated Alexander's task. However, he was at least able to take advantage of this situation to some degree and enact a divide-and-rule approach. Such an approach led him to his last significant battle, against the rajah Porus, who was an enemy of Alexander's ally King Ambi of Taxila. Porus hoped to hold Alexander's forces across the River Hydaspes, and thus took up position on the far bank in great numbers (35,000). This gave Alexander the opportunity to achieve arguably his greatest victory. A complex and lengthy campaign of deception led Porus to believe that he was facing Alexander's entire army on the opposite bank. In fact, Alexander was able to move 15,000 men 25 kilometres upriver and cross unopposed. When this manoeuvre was discovered, Porus initially sent his son with a holding force, which was quickly pushed aside by Alexander's army.

When the two main armies met in the field, Alexander was presented with a new tactical dilemma. His instrument of decision, the Companion cavalry, would not be able to repeat its feats of previous battles. Porus had deployed elephants along the centre of his line. Horses possess an innate fear of elephants and thus will not engage them. Consequently, Alexander used his cavalry on the wings to isolate and then destroy the Indian cavalry, so that they ceased to be a threat to the slow-moving phalanx that would perform the decisive role. In the event, the Indian line was decimated as Alexander's infantry attacked the elephants and their mahouts, forcing them back into their own lines. The Macedonians manoeuvred in such a way as to concentrate the Indian forces into a small area, where the elephants could inflict maximum damage upon their own men. The loss ratio was once again outstanding. Alexander lost approximately 1,000 men compared to the 15,000–20,000 reported Indian losses. As was so often the case, Alexander did not humiliate his defeated enemy. Rather, he increased Porus's territory, and thereby gained an important ally in the region.

Following the victory over Porus, Alexander's eastward journey continued with relative success. Many tribes submitted without conflict. However, others put up serious resistance. In response, Alexander's treatment of them mirrored his actions at Tyre. For example, at Sangala, 17,000 of the inhabitants were slaughtered and the remaining 70,000 enslaved. This pattern of repression continued throughout the remainder of the campaigns when Alexander met resistance.[18]

However, it was not enemy forces that eventually brought a halt to the Macedonian's progress. At the River Beas in Punjab, after ten years of fighting, the core of Alexander's army refused their commander's order to advance further. Seventy days of monsoon rain, rumours of substantial enemy forces waiting in the Ganges valley, and increasing dissatisfaction with Alexander's kingship all contributed to the mutiny. With little indication that a reachable objective was in sight, it appeared that Alexander's court was now simply engaged in campaigning for its own sake. The culminating point of victory was well past. After four days of tense negotiations, Alexander agreed to lead the army back home, and thus began the final stages of his campaigns.

Notable incidents during the three-year journey back to Babylon include Alexander's serious injury during the siege of Multan, and the decimation of his army while crossing the Makran Desert. These two incidents give us an illuminating insight into Alexander's style of command. His courageous lead at the siege of Multan, which left him fighting the enemy inside the city walls almost alone, fits perfectly with the heroic style of the age, and provides an excellent case study of command by example.[19] However, while culturally correct, Alexander's actions at Multan (and elsewhere) raise questions about his judgement. By risking his life so often, he was potentially putting his army and the entire campaign in jeopardy. If he fell in battle, so far from home, his army would be left without its leader, and the court would be left without its king. Clearly, he had to operate within the boundaries of his own cultural reality. However, pragmatism should also be part of the command equation. This is a difficult balance to get right. Perhaps Clausewitz got it right when he wrote:

We can thus only say that the aims a belligerent adopts, and the resources he employs, must be governed by the particular characteristics of his own position; but they will also conform to the spirit of the age and to its general character. Finally, they must always be governed by the general conclusions to be drawn from the nature of war itself.[20]

The losses in the Makran Desert provide an example of a situation where even the most thorough logistical preparations can fall foul of events. So serious were the consequences that Engels describes the desert as 'Alexander's most formidable opponent... which came closer to destroying him and his army than any enemy he encountered'.[21] In order for his troops to survive the arduous journey along the Makran coast, Alexander established a joint land-sea operation. The forces needed to take four months' worth of provisions with them. These were stored on a navy flotilla of over 500 ships. Without the burden of transporting their own supplies, the army marched ahead with nine days' worth of supplies. Their task in this joint endeavour was to dig wells along the route to provide the necessary water for themselves and the fleet. However, the monsoon weather was far more severe than expected, and the departure of the fleet was delayed for three months, unbeknown to Alexander, who had marched ahead with the army.

As the days passed with no sign of the fleet, the Macedonian king had to make a choice. Alexander and his men could either stay where they were, to await a fleet that might not appear, or they could return to Pattala (where the expedition had begun) through a land already raped of its resources by the army. As it was, Alexander chose a third option, and pushed onwards through the desert towards the Jhau tract, which he knew had cultivable land and a small population. Engels claims that this was the only viable option for him to take.[22] Even so, three-quarters of the men with him did not survive the march. Fortunately, the fleet, carrying approximately half of the entire army, completed their journey safely. Having defeated so many foes in battle, Alexander's forces were decimated by friction. Only his decisive leadership enabled some of them to survive the Makran Desert.

Despite the tragedy of the Makran Desert, Alexander continued to plan for the future of his empire and to that end developed the army further. In another move that alienated his Macedonian veterans, he pushed forward with the integration of subjects of the Persian empire (especially Persians, Bactrians, and Medians) into his political and military structures. Upon his return to Susa, Alexander conducted a mass marriage of Macedonian men to Asian women. Perhaps more significant was the integration of Asian forces into the central units of Alexander's army. For example, 30,000 boys of the Persian empire, whom Alexander had trained in military schools and who were now reaching maturity, were brought together in newly formed phalanxes. Most worryingly for the Macedonian phalangites, Alexander named these new units 'Epigonoi', or 'the next generation'.[23]

The tensions between Alexander and his Macedonian veterans finally came to a head in 324 at Opis, when elements of the army once again mutinied. As before, a few days of negotiations brought a degree of reconciliation. Nonetheless, the Opis incident is yet more evidence of how Alexander had lost the confidence of key components of his army.

Upon finally reaching Babylon in 323, Alexander did not settle down to administer his vast empire. Rather, he began planning another campaign in

Arabia. The great strategic pragmatist failed to understand the need to consolidate his gains. Clausewitz noted that one of the characteristics of a military genius was ambition.[24] Although ambition was clearly a vital driving force in pushing Alexander to achieve extraordinary feats, he failed to keep his ambition in check, went far beyond the culminating point of victory, and ultimately put his successes at risk. As it was, the Arabian campaign never got under way. Alexander fell ill while at Babylon and died on 10 June 323. In his absence the empire slowly fell apart.

Alexander's campaigns in the east reveal an increasing dichotomy in his exercise of strategy. On the one hand, he displayed outstanding tactical innovation at the Hydaspes and a mature appreciation of counter-insurgency in central Asia. On the other hand, some of the subtlety of his earlier campaigns was gradually lost. The increasing brutality of the Indian campaign often gave his opponents little choice but to resist. Increasingly, Alexander's grand strategy was becoming unbalanced, with the non-violent means being overwhelmed by direct and destructive force. By operating well beyond the culminating point of victory, Alexander also weakened the resolve of his Macedonian veterans. The schism between Alexander and his men was exacerbated by his increasing integration of Persians and their ways into his court and army. Although these failings can be partially attributed to frailties in Alexander's personality, shortcomings in intelligence and a logical attempt to stabilize relations with his new subjects must also be recognized. Perhaps most importantly, a clear and attainable objective was missing from the later campaigns. Without a good understanding of the ends, it is difficult to order the means effectively.

CONCLUSION

As with any case study, attempting to decipher the reasons behind Alexander's outstanding success in the practice of strategy is difficult. A good place to start is by examining his performance throughout the levels of strategy. When doing so, it quickly becomes apparent that he excelled in all of the levels. Although in some of the battles the Macedonians may have faced moments of crisis (such as when the phalanx split at Issus), Alexander's record of tactical success is outstanding. As a commander he never suffered any serious setbacks. He met all of his military objectives, regardless of the context. His forces destroyed the largest armies the Persian empire could field, but were equally effective at neutralizing small irregular forces. At the operational level, his speed of manoeuvre often proved decisive without the need for battle.

As our analysis moves beyond the tactical and operational, it becomes clear that Alexander achieved a balance and harmony among the levels. The non-violent instruments of grand strategy were just as carefully tailored as his military forces. Although undoubtedly young and ambitious, and with an occasionally impulsive nature, he showed great maturity and forethought. As his army marched through the empire, the need for stability was met by careful consideration of the political and social needs of the population. Nonetheless, as brilliant as Alexander's overall grand strategy was, it must be remembered that the whole enterprise was under-pinned by his military strategy.

With limited forces at his disposal, time and again Alexander revealed an astute grasp of the political and psychological effects of military power. His use of coercion and deterrence often brought substantial gains with minimal effort. Likewise, he understood that military prowess was a vital symbol of power in the Persian empire. Thus, he embraced battle and sieges as a means to announce the changing political environment. In the military sphere, the young Macedonian ruler undoubtedly benefited from having such a fine instrument at his disposal. Much of the credit for this must go to his father, who had created a potent instrument of decision. This was the case in terms of both tactics and a new cultural approach to warfare in the Greek world. The latter should not be under-estimated. Although it is correct to make reference to the achievements of Philip II, it was Alexander who took this instrument and made it so adaptable, and therefore so capable across the spectrum of warfare (the polymorphous character of war).

In military affairs, Alexander also understood that details matter. The Macedo-nian king left little to chance. His army was supported by an excellent logistics operation, which, among other things, facilitated the aforementioned rapid man-oeuvres over large distances. When the army met resistance in the form of fortifications, the Macedonian siege engineers were able to achieve decisive results in a relatively short time-frame. For the enemies of Alexander, it must have seemed that resistance really was futile.

Just as impressive was Alexander's intelligence organization. Although the sources reveal little detail on this subject, the results speak for themselves. As at the Persian Gates, he was often able to surprise his opponents on the basis of superior intelligence. Perhaps more importantly, he relied upon his intelligence organization to provide solid information on the political, social, and economic conditions of the areas he was about to enter. The knowledge he built up from this intelligence enabled him to tailor his grand strategy to fit the circumstances. And, in the case of the Persian empire, seemingly it enabled him to identify correctly the Persian centres of gravity.

This picture of Alexander as a great practitioner of strategy at all the levels may be called into question by the fact that in the aftermath of his death the new empire rapidly collapsed. This may suggest that the means-ends relationship lacked a substantive foundation. In this sense, it could be argued that he had a greater affinity with the means than the long-term objectives. Or, to put it another way, he enjoyed campaigning too much and lost sight of the bigger picture. However, such a conclusion would overlook a number of important factors. Alexander's city-building programme, establishment of long-term garrisons, edu-cational programmes for young Persians, and later changes to the army's military structure all indicate that he sought stability and growth for his new empire. As it was, his early death made it impossible for him to establish a secure succession or a stable future for his new acquisitions.

For much of his career, Alexander created a workable balance of means to achieve his desired policy objectives. When this smooth process was knocked out of kilter, it was the result of a number of factors. Notable amongst these were his growing personality problems, an increasing scarcity of intelligence and an un-clear end-state. Alexander undoubtedly over-extended himself in India. However, even then he managed to bring a substantial portion of his army back to Babylon and quell a number of small rebellions that had arisen in the central provinces. When his grand strategy did succeed, which was most of the time, the process was beautifully balanced and underpinned by an outstanding military instrument led by a genuine military genius. Alexander's performance in grand strategy may have wavered towards the end, but his use of military force could almost always rectify any problems. Clausewitz wrote that a successful battle could change everything. Alexander exemplifies this point.

NOTES

1. For detailed historical accounts of Alexander's campaigns, see Arrian, *The Campaigns of Alexander* (London, 1971); A. B. Bosworth, *Conquest and Empire: The Reign of Alexander the Great* (Cambridge, 1988); R. Lane Fox, *Alexander the Great* (Harmondsworth, 1986); and N. G. L. Hammond, *The Genius of Alexander the Great* (London, 1998).
2. Quoted in D. Chandler, *The Campaigns of Napoleon* (London, 1966), 139.
3. For a detailed analysis of the workings of the League, see Bosworth, *Conquest and Empire*, 187–97.
4. For detailed analysis on the development of Greek warfare, see F. E. Adcock, *The Greek and Macedonian Art of War* (Berkeley, 1957); J. K. Anderson, *Military Theory and Practice in the Age of Xenophon* (Berkeley, 1970); Bosworth, *Conquest and Empire*; J. Cassin-Scott, *The Greek and Persian Wars 500–323 BC* (Oxford, 1977); H. Delbrück, *Warfare in Antiquity* (Lincoln, NE, 1975); A. Ferrill, *The Origins of War: From the Stone Age to Alexander the Great* (London, 1985); J. F. C. Fuller, *The Generalship of Alexander the Great* (Ware, 1998); V. D. Hanson, *The Western Way of War: Infantry Battle in Classical Greece* (Berkeley, 1989); id. (ed.), *Hoplites: The Classical Greek Battle Experience* (London, 1993); id., *The Wars of the Ancient Greeks: And their Invention of Western Military Culture* (London, 1999); W. K. Pritchett, *The Greek State at War*, 4 vols (Berkeley, 1971–85); N. Sekunda, *The Army of Alexander the Great* (Oxford, 1984); W. W. Tarn, *Hellenistic Military and Naval Developments* (Chicago, 1930); J. Warry, *Warfare in the Classical World: War and the Ancient Civilisations of Greece and Rome* (London, 1998); and H. van Wees, *Greek Warfare: Myths and Realities* (London, 2004).
5. For a discussion of the workings of the Persian empire, see J. Wiesehöfer, *Ancient Persia* (London, 2001).
6. Ibid. 57.
7. Ibid. 80.
8. For details on the development of the Persian army, see N. Sekunda, *The Persian Army* (Oxford, 1992); Cassin-Scott, *The Greek and Persian Wars*; and Delbrück, *Warfare in Antiquity*.
9. Sun Tzu, *The Art of War*, trans. S. B. Griffith (London, 1971).
10. C. von Clausewitz, *On War*, ed. and trans. M. Howard and P. Paret (London, 1993), 720.
11. For more details on Hannibal's campaign in Italy, see N. Bagnall, *The Punic Wars: Rome, Carthage and the Struggle for the Mediterranean* (London, 1999); and A. Goldsworthy, *The Punic Wars* (London, 2000).
12. Wiesehofer, *Ancient Persia*, 105.
13. Lane Fox, *Alexander the Great*, 198.

14. Arrian reports this incident from the work of Diodorus, and claims that, if true, it reveals Alexander's intentions for the coming campaign; *The Campaigns of Alexander*, 66.

15. D. W. Engels, *Alexander the Great and the Logistics of the Macedonian Army* (Berkeley, 1980), 10.

16. Wiesehöfer, *Ancient Persia*, 31.

17. For discussion of Alexander's deification, see I. Worthington, *Alexander the Great: A Reader* (London, 2002), esp. ch. 9.

18. A. B. Bosworth, *Alexander and the East: The Tragedy of Triumph* (Oxford, 1998), 27.

19. The significance of leading by example is examined in J. Keegan, *The Mask of Command* (London, 1988).

20. Clausewitz, *On War*, 718.

21. Engels, *Alexander the Great and the Logistics of the Macedonian Army*, 110.

22. Ibid. 115.

23. Hammond, *The Genius of Alexander the Great*, 188.

24. Clausewitz, *On War*, 105.

2

The Roman Republic: From Monarchy to Julius Caesar

Israel Shatzman

INTRODUCTION: THE SOURCES AND THEIR LIMITATIONS

The history of Rome, traditionally founded by Romulus in 753 BCE, is conventionally divided into three periods according to the different forms of government that prevailed: the monarchy, the republic, and the empire. The republic was founded by the patrician aristocracy who expelled the last king in, traditionally, 509. Rule by a single man was re-established by Octavian, who defeated Antony in 31, thus ending a series of violent internal dissensions and civil wars that had started in 133. The empire as a type of regime was devised by Octavian, the first emperor (*imperator*), also known by the title Augustus, which was conferred on him by the senate in 27. Given the limitations of space, this chapter concentrates on the republic.[1]

What was the nature of Roman strategy during the republic? Can we reconstruct it? To understand the difficulties faced in answering these questions, it is necessary to give a brief account of the sources at our disposal, which, for the history of Rome and her army, are varied and uneven. We have narrative history for stretches of many years, for instance from the legendary beginnings of Rome to 293 BCE (Livy and Dionysius of Halicarnassus) and 218–167 (Polybius, Livy, and Appian). We have monographs on specific wars or themes, such as an account of the First Punic War, 264–241 (Polybius); the Roman wars in Spain and against Mithridates VI, king of Pontus (Appian); the Roman civil wars (Appian and Caesar); the war against Jugurtha, king of Numidia, 112–106 (Sallust); and the Gallic wars of Caesar (Caesar). But there are also long gaps: for example, 293–264, 241–218, and 167–133. Several other literary sources supplement to some extent the narrative histories, especially Plutarch's Roman biographies and the copious writings of Cicero, and a great deal of relevant information can be found in other literary works, including legal writings and poetry.

But there are other difficulties beyond the lack of a narrative source for certain stretches of time. The early history of Rome, a formative period for the important themes of Roman bellicosity and imperialism, is beset with problems. Livy and Dionysius of Halicarnassus, our main sources for this period, drew on past historians, the earliest being Fabius Pictor, who was writing at the end of the third century. His work was a major source for Polybius, but it has not survived: nor have any of the works of Fabius's immediate successors. The various sources for those early historians contained facts—bare particulars about people, places, and events. The main concern underlying these early sources was to preserve the memory of the 'deeds performed' (*res gestae*)—the achievements of the people who did them. A distant relation of sources of this kind is the *Res Gestae* of Augustus, his own record of 'the deeds by which he subjected the world to the dominion of the Roman people', which has been preserved. This detailed document enumerates the wars and conquests made under Augustus, and the peoples who submitted to him, but the causes and objectives of the wars and of the expansion of the empire are not explained, except for a few nebulous references to peace. In sum, there did not exist in Rome original, contemporary sources that dealt with Roman strategy in early times.

Although Roman (and Greek) historians made wars the focus of their works, their aim was to tell the story, and they were interested in vivid descriptions of the action. When they mention planning, their reports usually relate to the tactical or operational aspects of battles or campaigns. Strategies designed for specific wars are seldom explained, and accounts of strategic consultation or planning at a national level are barely mentioned. Hence, our reconstruction of Roman strategy depends to a large extent on extrapolation from the factual information contained in the narrative histories.

Some military treatises survive, all written during the period of the empire, notably Onasander's *The General* (*c.*54 CE), Frontinus's *Stratagemata* (late first century), Arrian's *Tactica* (136 CE), and Vegetius's *Epitome of Military Science* (late fourth century). These works provide a wealth of precepts and practical information about army organization and the management of war, the structure and size of units, the use of ruses, and training and discipline. However, the focus of these writings is on the tactical, operational, and technological level rather than the strategic, although the general rules prescribed by Vegetius and Onasander are also instructive for the period of the republic. The epigraphic, papyrological, and archaeological sources abound with documentary and material evidence on the military institutions of Rome and the workings of the army. Much of the information they provide has a bearing on the study of Roman strategy, but, unfortunately, the vast majority of these sources date from the period of the empire.

One major drawback with the available sources is that, as already mentioned, with few exceptions they do not give access to the deliberations that probably took place in consultations involving strategic decision-making. The evidence of the narrative sources concerning Roman military, political, and diplomatic modes of operation can only partly compensate for the absence of original reports on the plans and purposes of the decision-makers. Still, ends may be inferred from the ways in which wars were conducted, the structuring of the army and its size, the deployment of units, and so forth, and sometimes the narrative sources do provide direct testimony on aims. If, then, strategy is conceived as the art of matching means and ends, there is some basis for the reconstruction of Roman strategy, but bearing in mind the gaps in, and limitations of, the available sources, it is not surprising that different scholars have arrived at different interpretations.

THE POLITICAL AND MILITARY INSTITUTIONS
OF THE REPUBLIC

Polybius ascribes the phenomenal political and military achievement of Rome, namely the subjection of almost all the inhabited world within fifty-three years (220–167 BCE), to the superiority of her constitution (1. 1. 5). In book 6, he presents in detail the powers of the three components that made up the constitution (the consuls, the senate, and the people) and the way in which they worked together, as well as the organization of the army. That is to say, the success of Roman foreign policy, and by implication of Roman strategy, depended on the particular properties of the political and military institutions that obtained in Rome under the republic. There is much to say for Polybius's view on this, and it is essential for an understanding of Roman strategy to give an account of the senate, the assemblies of the people, the magistrates,[2] and the military system.

Originally an advisory council to the kings, the senate accumulated powers under the republic as an outcome of Roman expansion, the increasing complexity of the state's affairs, and the unsuitability of the magistrates and the assemblies of the people to control and coordinate how those affairs were managed. The traditional number of senators was 300, and it rose to 600 after the year 80, a figure which Augustus sanctioned in 18. The senators were at first chosen by the consuls, and from 312 by the censors; former holders of magistracies were entitled to membership of the senate and, in addition to them, people of high social and economic standing were chosen. Its members being the only people with knowledge and experience of the affairs of state, the senate was the only permanent body with the expertise to oversee the government of the state. Although its powers rested mainly on custom and tradition, and not on statutes, it gained control of taxation and public expenditure, the allocation of funds to the army commanders, the levy and disposition of troops, the assignment of tasks to magistrates and extension of their command (*prorogatio imperii*), foreign affairs, legislation, maintenance of law and order, and religious life.

Male Roman citizens had the franchise, but only those who attended the meetings of the assemblies of the people, which took place in Rome, could vote. There were two main assemblies under the republic, the Comitia Centuriata and the Comitia Tributa. The first was based on the division of the citizens into 193 voting units called *centuriae* ('centuries'), which were organized in five graded property classes, and the latter on their division into *tribus* ('tribes'), in fact districts (there were thirty-five from the year 241). The Comitia Centuriata elected the consuls, praetors, and censors; enacted laws; and held trials for capital and political offences. Declarations of war and treaties needed its ratification, after their endorsement by the senate, but it rarely rejected them. The Comitia Tributa, called the Concilium Plebis if confined to plebeian citizens only, elected lower magistrates, enacted laws, and held trials for non-capital offences; in some cases its legislation treated foreign affairs and the conduct of war in the late republic.

All magistrates, save for the dictator (a temporary magistracy in emergency) and censors, served one year in office, and all magistracies, with the exception of the dictator, consisted of two or more colleagues with equal power. Every magistrate had *potestas*, that is, legal power based on statute or custom. The pair of censors conducted the *census*, that is, prepared a national register of the Roman citizens, including their domicile and amount of property, which served them in registering the citizens in the *tribus* and the *centuriae*; taxation and recruitment of the citizens were based on that register. The censors also revised the lists of the senators and of the members of the eighteen equestrian *centuriae* of the Comitia Centuriata, leased out public property, and drew up contracts for the collection of taxes in the provinces.

The power held by the consuls, praetors, and the dictator was called *imperium*; it included military command, jurisdiction, use of coercive means to maintain law and order, the right to consult the gods, and many other rights. When it was deemed necessary for military purposes, the *imperium* of consuls and praetors was extended, usually by the senate, beyond the annual term of their magistracies, and they then became proconsuls and propraetors. The two consuls elected annually spent their year of office partly in Rome and partly in their *provinciae* (see below), with conduct of war as their main business. The number of the praetors increased gradually from one in 367 to eight in 81 and twelve under Augustus. Although their *imperium* was inferior to that of the consuls, the praetors were legally capable of carrying out the same duties; jurisdiction in Rome, however, became their main occupation after 81. The number of quaestors, lower magistrates responsible for financial administration and other duties and usually working with holders of *imperium*, increased over the years from one in the fifth century to twenty in 81; many of them continued to function as proquaestors after their year of office ended.

The multiplication of magistrates and promagistrates reflected Roman expansion in Italy and abroad and an increase in the number of *provinciae*. The term *provincia* originally referred to a duty or sphere of command assigned by the senate to a Roman holder of *imperium*; it was only during the second and first centuries that there came to be *provinciae* in the sense of defined territories outside Italy that were regularly administered by Roman governors who were holders of *imperium*. The senate's yearly discussion and allotment of the *provinciae* to magistrates and promagistrates, to the extent that these are reported in the extant sources, provide an opportunity to gain insight into Roman foreign policy and strategy.

The Roman military system under the republic is characterized by, *inter alia*, the duty of the citizens to serve in the army, the enduring functioning of the legion, and the maintenance of military discipline and strict procedures.[3] Roman citizens who were physically fit and of military age (17–45) were liable to military service for sixteen campaigns; from the third century onwards, this was, in effect, sixteen years. Wealthy citizens with the equestrian property *census* (400,000 sesterces in the late republic) were eligible for service in the cavalry for ten years. Citizens with no property (*proletarii*) were normally exempt from service except in emergency or as rowers in the navy.

The following is a reasonable conjecture regarding the evolving structure of the Roman legion. The legion (literally 'levy') of the monarchic period consisted of sixty *centuriae* with 100 heavily armed men each and 2,400 lightly armed troops. Following the foundation of the republic, when command of the army began to be shared by the two consuls, it was divided into two units with the same name and structure but half the men. This outline is compatible, among other things, with the fact that this sixty-*centuria* structure, with a *centuria* of a reduced number of soldiers as the smallest tactical unit, remained constant through the imperial period. The annual levy had increased from two to four legions by 311, and probably by 340, and this remained standard, as described by Polybius. Originally, the legions raised served to the end of the campaigning season and were then disbanded, but when wars became protracted over long periods, the legions remained in being for several years. With the expansion of Rome's military commitments, the number of legions in service began to exceed the regular annual levy; the first cases of this seem to date from the late fourth century, and some time later it became the norm. In addition, the Roman army included contingents supplied by Rome's Latin and Italian allies (*socii*; see below), which were grouped to form units similar in size, and probably structure, to the legions. The two-legion consular army was normally accompanied by two such units, and the total number of allies serving in the Roman army surpassed that of Roman citizens from the mid-third century onwards.

The Greek hoplite equipment and the massed phalanx formation were adopted in Rome early on. The phalanx formation was replaced by the flexible manipular legion, of which Polybius provides the best available description (6. 20–4); the crucial stage in the development of the new formation had probably taken place by 340,[4] although some changes were introduced later. Every legion had six military tribunes, senior officers in charge of various duties, with two of them probably serving as the legion's commanders in rotation but subject to the holder of *imperium* in command of the particular army.

The standard complement of this legion consisted of 3,000 heavily armed and 1,200 lightly armed troops, and 300 cavalry divided into ten squadrons (*turmae*). Equipped with several javelins, a sword, and a small circular shield, the lightly armed men (*velites*), the youngest and poorest troops, served as skirmishers. Three groups made up the heavily armed infantry: the youngest 1,200 *hastati*, the senior 1,200 *principes*, and the oldest 600 *triarii*; each group was divided into ten *manipuli* ('handfuls') with two *centuriae* each, and each maniple had two centurions, the senior one in command. For protection, they were all equipped with a helmet, a breastplate, greaves, and an oblong, curved shield (*scutum*), which could also be used to stun the enemy. For offensive fighting, the *hastati* and the *principes* had the *gladius*, a double-edged sword, good for slashing and particularly for thrusting, and two heavy javelins (*pila*); the *triarii* had a sword and a spear.

Arrayed for battle in three lines, with the skirmishers in front of them, the *hastati* occupied the first, the *principes* the second, and the older *triarii* the third line. The maniples of each group were so deployed as to leave an interval as wide as the maniple between each, with the maniples of the second line covering the intervals in the first line and those of the third line covering the intervals in the second line. The structure and battle order of the manipular legion enabled the tactical units, the maniples, or even, possibly, the *centuriae*, to charge or withdraw through the intervals; left the individual soldier, mainly in the first two lines, sufficient space to manoeuvre and operate the *scutum* and *gladius* efficiently; and maintained the *triarii* as a reserve force. The ability to hurl the *pila* at a short distance from the enemy, followed by the use of the sword and the *scutum* in face-to-face combat, made the fighting of the manipular legion more aggressive than that of the phalanx.

The cohort had replaced the maniple as the principal tactical sub-unit of the legion by the 50s. It is mentioned as a formation consisting of three maniples as early as 210, and it appears that it was subsequently utilized on several occasions, notably in Spain, but it was only during the first half of the first century that it supplanted the maniple.

Several other changes occurred simultaneously. First, the *velites* and the Roman citizen horsemen disappeared with the growing employment of foreign auxiliary troops as the lightly armed and cavalry forces, respectively, of the army. Second, Roman citizenship was extended to the Latin and Italian allies in 90–88, who from then on served in the legions and not in separate divisional units (*alae sociorum*). Third, recruitment of volunteers, including the poorest citizens (*proletarii*), who normally had not been enlisted in the legions, became the more common way for raising and maintaining armies, although the obligation to serve in the army remained in force and conscription of eligible citizens was occasionally applied. Fourth and finally, the spear (*hasta*) was discarded and all the legionaries used the sword and the throwing *pilum* as their offensive weapons. Supplied with arms and equipment, the cohortal legion comprised ten cohorts, each one made up of six eighty-man *centuriae*, each commanded by a centurion.

Caesar's writings provide our best evidence for the capabilities of the cohortal legion. The army need not be arrayed for battle in three lines but might also be ranged in a single line, two lines, or even four lines. Cohorts or groups of cohorts could be manoeuvred to outflank the enemy, to give support to other cohorts, to launch surprise attacks, or to counter-attack an outflanking enemy movement, and so on. They could also be used to carry out actions independently of pitched battle.[5] In other words, the army cohortal structure put at the disposal of the commander ample options in planning for battle and coping with the vicissitudes of battle. The manoeuvrability and flexibility of the cohortal legion so much impressed Hans Delbrück that he declared that 'The cohort tactics marked the apogee of the development which the fighting skill of ancient infantry could reach.'[6]

WARS, IMPERIALISM, AND FOREIGN POLICY

The seeds of the Roman empire-building process were planted by the early kings, who sought to establish Roman rule over the neighbouring city-states of Latium. After the expulsion of the kings, the Roman republic, at that time a city-state of about 800 square kilometres with a population of perhaps 30,000 people, had to fight—together with her allies the Latins and the Hernici—the Etruscan city of Veii and the Volsci and Aequi, mountainous tribes who invaded the plain of Latium in the fifth century. Having won this deadly struggle, Rome suffered a terrible defeat by a marauding Gallic tribe in the early fourth century, but she managed to recover from that catastrophe and, in a series of wars that culminated in the so-called Great Latin War (340–338), established her rule over Latium, Campania, and southern Etruria.

Over the next eighty years or so, Rome fought the Gauls, the Umbrians and the Etruscans of northern Italy, and the Samnites and various other tribes of central and south Italy, as well as King Pyrrhus of Epirus, who came to save the Greek city of Tarentum. Successively defeating all these enemies, Rome had completed her conquest of Italy south of the Po by the 260s.

No sooner had Rome consolidated her dominion in peninsular Italy than she embarked on a series of overseas wars. She defeated Carthage in two great wars (264–241, 218–201), winning Sicily in the first and laying the foundations for the conquest of the Iberian peninsula in the second—a long process that was to continue to the late first century. She also expanded her rule as far as the Alps (Cisalpine Gaul) in wars against Gallic and Ligurian tribes (230s–150s); vanquished the armies of the Macedonian kingdom (197 and 168) and the Seleucid king Antiochus III (191 and 189), and thereby established her hegemony in the Hellenistic world; destroyed Carthage in the Third Punic War (149–146); annexed the kingdom of Pergamum (133–126); gained control of Transalpine Gaul (later the province of Gallia Narbonensis) in the late second century; defeated the Numidian king Jugurtha (109–106); and then crushed the Cimbri and Teutones in two decisive battles (102 and 101).

The great wars of expansion in the first-century BCE were conducted by ambitious and powerful leaders, notably Pompey, who extended Roman rule in Asia Minor after permanently vanquishing Mithridates VI, king of Pontus, and annexed Syria (66–63); and Julius Caesar, who conquered the whole of Gaul as far as the Rhine (58–51). The invasion of Parthia by another ambitious leader, Marcus Crassus, ended in a crushing defeat of the invading army at the battle of Carrhae (53). Caesar was about to leave Rome for a grand expedition against Parthia when he was stopped by the daggers of the conspirators on the Ides of March 44. A few years later, in 36, Antony, too, failed in his attempt to overcome the eastern kingdom, and the confrontation with Parthia and Sassanian Persia was to last until late antiquity. All in all, warfare and expansion dominated Roman foreign relations throughout the period of the republic.

The historian Livy expresses the blunt view that Rome's wars, like all wars, were fought for dominion and the subjugation of the vanquished (1. 23. 7, 25. 3). As far as the archaic period of Rome is concerned, Livy's is no more than an educated view, but it may well hold good for the wars conducted from the fourth century onwards. The outcome of the Samnite wars (343–341, 326–304, 298–290), clearly fought for mastery of central and southern Italy, left Rome with no rival for the dominion of Italy.[7]

It was during that period, probably as early as the late fifth century, that the Romans became accustomed to annual military service, and the regularity of Roman warfare from 440 to the late republic, with some fluctuations, is amply evidenced in the available sources.[8] In addition to hunger for fighting and dominion, there were other incentives to go to war. Successful wars brought in indemnities and plenty of booty, including precious metals and slaves, and increased the extent of public land, confiscated from the vanquished enemies, from which the soldiers, citizens (particularly the rich), and the state benefited from the early fourth century onwards.[9]

The awareness that war opened up opportunities to win triumphs and glory, prestigious and politically valuable for the upper-class commanders, became deeply rooted in the mind of the Romans during the wars by which they built up their empire in peninsular Italy. It is noteworthy that only those citizens who had completed ten annual military campaigns were allowed to run for political office, starting with the lowest,[10] and thus would-be senators and senior magistrates were schooled in war from youth, competing with one another to win military glory. In sum, there were many benefits to be gained by going to war—for the state, the senatorial aristocracy, and the common people. Roman society was extremely militaristic, bellicose, and aggressive.

This is one way to account for the expansion of Roman dominion in Italy and of Roman imperialism in general, which is basically the theory of offensive imperialism, fully argued by William V. Harris.[11] In contrast, the theory of defensive imperialism holds that Rome went to war because of fear of dangerous threats, real or imagined, to her and her allies' vital interests from other states. Roman dominion and empire were the incidental, unintentional outcome of defensive wars (see Cicero, *De Republica* 3. 35: 'our people has now taken control of the whole world by defending its allies').[12] However, even if fear and defensive considerations played a major role in the Roman decision-making process, the available means and the preferred policy were, generally speaking, aggressive and offensive, which is reflected in Cicero's assertion that 'if we want to benefit from peace, war should be conducted',[13] and, as Tacitus frankly recognizes, the Romans, ever seeking dominion, riches, and glory, achieved peace by destruction and subjugation.[14] Moreover, Rome was constantly taking care to maintain or improve her superiority over her adversaries, real and present or potential; that is, to have and to develop the capabilities to promote her interests or attain her goals. No matter whether it was offensive or defensive, there is no denying the fact that Roman imperialism was efficient and successful in the long run.

The last point is highlighted in a recent study by Arthur Eckstein, who endorses the view that Rome 'was a highly militarized, militaristic, and assertive state, led by an aristocracy imbued with a strong warrior ethos, which in turn was backed by a populace that accepted war as a fact of life'. But in this respect Rome was not exceptional; given the anarchy and multipolarity that prevailed in the Graeco-Roman world, all or most states had to fight for survival and were characterized by those traits. The only alternatives were to achieve superiority or to succumb to foreign dominion. In other words, the grim conditions of the ancient anarchic inter-state system drove Rome to acquire more and more power. She was exceptional in her success in winning universal power, and the key to this success was her ability to assimilate and integrate non-Romans into the Roman polity.[15]

Eckstein's study is novel in its application of the theory of 'realism' developed by one school of political scientists to inter-state relations obtaining in the Graeco-Roman world.[16] This theory maintains, in a nutshell, that in an environment of inter-state anarchy, with no international law and no accepted law-enforcing institutions, all states compete for power and have to employ it to achieve security. In essence, they are all imperialists seeking to augment their dominion and, when one achieves superiority over the rest, the anarchic multipolar system is replaced by a unipolar system.[17]

Another innovation of Eckstein's study lies in its characterization of the Graeco-Roman world, based on comprehensive discussion and analysis of the evidence, as an anarchic inter-state system, and its demonstration that Roman diplomacy and warfare were the norm. On the whole, Eckstein's is a refreshing and well-argued study, but his insistence that the Roman ability to assimilate others is the sole factor in Rome's success neglects to take into account several other important factors, as a discussion of Roman strategy can show.

One important aspect of Roman foreign affairs and wars needs to be clarified at this point. An ideology of world rule developed in Rome in the second and first-century BCE, culminating under Augustus. This was an ideology of Roman empire without limits in either space or time;[18] all peoples were or should be under the dominion of the Roman people (*sub imperio populi Romani*). That is to say, the notion of the Roman empire (*imperium Romanum*), as the Romans perceived it, did not correspond to the administered provinces under direct Roman rule and the polities in alliance with Rome alone, but was broadened to comprise the whole world. This perception of the Roman empire, inevitably incompatible with peace, underlay and legitimized much of the tendency to expand indefinitely.[19] Any situation, even 'the mere existence of an independent power',[20] that might be regarded by the Romans as a threat to the *imperium Romanum* could serve as a cause for going to war in order to eliminate the danger, whether the initiative lay with the senate or with a holder of *imperium*, with the latter's actions usually endorsed later by the senate.[21] If one follows Polybius, the beginnings of the notion of world rule in Rome go back to the early second century, and there is no compelling reason not to accept his view on this theme.[22]

Ideology, of course, is not strategy, and from all we know about the allocation of tasks (*provinciae*) and troops to holders of *imperium* in the second and first centuries, it appears that the senate did not have any concrete plan to realize the claim to world rule. Yet the Roman ideology of world rule arose against a background of proven, unprecedented military and political success, won thanks to real, rational factors and not simply by the grace of the gods, that is, won by observing the rituals intended to maintain *pax deorum* ('peace with the gods'), particularly those related to the conduct of 'just war' (*bellum iustum*), which indeed the Romans performed scrupulously.[23] These factors are treated in the next section.

ROMAN STRATEGY DURING THE REPUBLIC

For all their defects, the available sources provide enough significant information to make it possible to discern the means, methods, principles, and modes of operation Rome developed, adopted, or used in her efforts to win the almost incessant wars she conducted, as well as to overcome any adversaries that stood in the way of her increased power and wider dominion. It is essential for an understanding of Roman strategy during the republic that we enumerate and discuss all these factors, including the personal qualities and moral values of both leaders and common people.

Integration of Non-Romans into the Roman Polity

The settlement the senate devised and imposed on the communities Rome conquered in the Great Latin War of 340–338 illustrates two strategic-political methods she used in her treatment of defeated enemies, except for those who suffered complete destruction such as the Etruscan city of Veii (396) or polities that sought alliance with her of their own accord.[24]

The first method established a category of communities who retained their autonomy but were obliged to supply troops for the Roman army in times of war. They served in separate contingents, with their own officers, but subject to the Roman general who commanded the particular army in which they served. According to the other method, communities, Latin and non-Latin, were incorporated into the Roman state and their citizens became, to all intents and purposes, full Roman citizens. Whether or not the senate found precedent in 338 in the tradition of forcible incorporation of several Latin communities into Rome in the regal period and the granting of Roman citizenship to immigrant leaders and their retainers in the early republic,[25] this decision broke new ground in that the method was applied, then and later, to non-Latin communities far away from Rome. That is to say, ethnicity and locality were not to hinder the extension of Roman citizenship.

Halfway between these two methods were the self-governing *municipia*, with partial Roman citizenship (*civitas sine suffragio*). Although their citizens could not vote in the Roman political assemblies nor hold Roman offices, they shared all the other rights and obligations of Roman citizens, and hence were liable to military service in the Roman legions.[26] By the mid-third-century BCE, there were more than 150 nominally independent Latin and Italian allied communities (*socii nominis Latini et Italici*) who contributed troops to the Roman army, each one allied to Rome by a separate treaty or according to its status as decided by Rome, and all of them bound not to go to war with one another and practically debarred from pursuing individual foreign policy.

Four factors mitigated the loss, in practice, of independence by Rome's allies in Italy: Rome refrained from garrisoning or taxing her allies; the Roman system of bilateral treaties put an end to all wars between the states of Italy; the ruling classes of the allied states knew they could get Roman support if threatened by internal dissensions; and Rome's allies obtained a share of the booty gained in successful wars. These factors, as well as the heterogeneous character of the allies in respect of ethnicity, language, culture, and sentiment, were to preclude joint action to cast off Roman rule.

Build-up of Military Manpower

From Rome's point of view, the incorporation of whole communities of former enemies or allies into the Roman citizen body and the system of allies she established in Italy, often regarded as the implementation of the strategic-political principle of *divide et impera*,[27] not only ensured her dominion in Italy but also put at her disposal enormous military manpower that could be mobilized in future wars. To help his readers appreciate the formidable enterprise Hannibal undertook in attacking Rome, Polybius details the numbers of men on active service and the numbers of men eligible for it in 225, when Rome was alarmed by an invasion of north Italy by some 70,000 Celts.[28] In this case, he took the information from Fabius Pictor and the detailed figures were derived from original documents.[29] The total number of men capable of bearing arms—Romans, Campanians (i.e. those with partial Roman citizenship), and Italian allies—was more than 700,000 foot and 70,000 horse, of whom 210,300 were serving in 225: 52,300 Romans and Campanians and 158,000 Italians. Of the total number of men capable of bearing arms, there were 273,000 Romans and Campanians (250,000 infantry and 23,000 cavalry). Although there is disagreement among scholars over the interpretation of some of these figures,[30] Rome's overwhelming superiority in manpower over any of the big contemporary powers, whether Carthage, Macedon, or the Seleucid or Ptolemaic kingdoms, stands out clearly. This superiority did not come about fortuitously; rather, the build-up of military manpower was pursued as a primary objective in Rome, a major factor in her strategic arsenal.

Alliances and Allies

The building and exploitation of alliances, both formal (*foedera*) and informal (*amicitiae*, i.e. relations of friendship), were practised by Rome for strategic purposes from early on, beginning with the formal alliances with the Latins and Hernici in the wars for survival against the Volsci and Aequi in the fifth century. Successive alliances with various Italian communities helped Rome to win mastery of Italy in the fourth and first half of the third centuries. The alliance with Messana gave Rome a foothold in Sicily, and that with Saguntum, in Spain. In her wars with Philip V of Macedon (214–206, 200–197) and the Seleucid ruler Antiochus III (192–189), Rome benefited from alliances she made with various Hellenistic polities, notably the Aetolian League, Athens, Rhodes, and Eumenes II, king of Pergamum. Alliances, formal and informal, were made with small polities as well.[31]

In many cases, Rome received significant military aid from her allies; for instance, Eumenes II and his cavalry played a decisive role in defeating Antiochus III at the battle of Magnesia. Allies were also helpful in supplying the Roman armies with food, ships, weapons, and other commodities.[32] Alliances served another important function: they marked the zones of Roman interests, that is, where Rome had a claim to dominion, to be realized immediately or in the future. In these cases, an attack on Roman allies could be exploited to go to war against the aggressors, a 'just war' from the Roman point of view, which is what Rome did, for example, in the First and Second Punic wars (justified by the alliances with Messana and Saguntum, respectively).

Conversely, by the mere application for treaties of alliance (*foedera*), many minor Greek city-states acknowledged Roman supremacy. Although the senate was reluctant to send troops to support allies in these cases, preferring diplomatic means, 'as symbols of loyalty to Rome and of Roman favour,' the treaties 'served to advertise and affirm Rome's *imperium*'.[33] In one case at least, the alliance with Judaea, there was a concrete goal: to weaken the Seleucid kingdom.[34] In sum, Rome made alliances, formal and informal, as strategic-political means for a variety of purposes, both in Italy and overseas.

Colonization

Colonization was another strategic means Rome utilized to overcome her enemies and to consolidate her dominion in Italy.[35] One way was to settle Roman citizens on land confiscated from vanquished enemies, which led to the gradual extension of Roman territory (*ager Romanus*) settled by Roman citizens from the Tyrrhenian Sea to the Adriatic; by mid-third century the total area amounted to 24,000 square kilometres, concentrated in central Italy. This was a process of consolidation, since the settlement followed the crushing of the enemies. Most important, strategically, were the so-called *coloniae Latinae*. Rome and her allies the Latin League had founded in the fifth and the early fourth centuries new political communities on land conquered from their common enemies. The land was allotted to colonists, both Romans and Latins. The new community constituted an independent and sovereign state, with its own political institutions and territory, and its citizens, the colonists, forwent their former citizenship. Each such community became a member of the Latin League and sent a contingent to the allied army. Its citizens possessed Latin communal rights, hence the term *colonia Latina*.

Although Rome dissolved the Latin League in the settlement of 338, she subsequently employed the institution of the Latin colony for herself. From 334 to 264, at least nineteen Latin colonies were founded, with the number of colonists, each with his family, ranging from 2,500 to 6,000. In each case, the foundation was authorized by a law (specifying the type and site of the colony, the number of colonists, the size of plots, etc.) that was discussed in the senate and ratified by the people's assembly. All the settlers, whether formerly Romans, Latins, or members of any Italian community, became citizens of the new community and possessed Latin status, which gave them certain rights relative to Rome. The new colonies, independent communities like the old *coloniae Latinae*, had each to send contingents to the Roman army. More importantly, founded as they were on strategic sites conducive to safeguarding troublesome areas and protecting or blocking lines of communication, and planted progressively closer to or among enemy polities during the conduct of wars, they were to serve as strongholds of Roman dominion throughout peninsular Italy. Given the Roman origin of a substantial part of their population and their special rights relative to Rome, and with Latin as the spoken language, the Latin colonies were the most loyal of Rome's allies, a major factor in the consolidation of Rome's conquest of Italy.

A third form of colonization is represented by the colonies of Roman citizens that were founded on the sea coast, ten from the years 338 to 218 and eight more by 190, each comprising 300 settlers with their families. Planted along both the Tyrrhenian and the Adriatic coasts of Italy (e.g. at Ostia, Antium, and Sipontum), they were to guard the coastline and prevent enemy raiders from landing. The colonists were normally exempt from legionary service, but had to stay in place in order to perform their guard duties.

Finally, whatever the form of the colonization, most of the settlers were poor Roman citizens who now became landlords. That is to say, colonization served as a means of solving socio-economic problems, thereby contributing significantly to the cohesion of Roman society and the political stability and strength of the state, which is another aspect of the strategic importance of the colonization policy.

Supplying the Army and Road-Building

Logistics is aptly defined as 'the practical art of moving armies and keeping them supplied',[36] and a well-planned and well-organized system of logistics is surely a major factor in general strategy. As long as the Roman army was operating in

Latium and its close vicinity, logistics did not pose a grave problem, but this situation began to change with the extension of the Roman wars to all parts of peninsular Italy from the late fourth century and progressively to almost all the Mediterranean countries, and even beyond them, from the First Punic War through to the wars of Pompey and Julius Caesar in the first century. During these 300 years or so, the Romans developed a logistics system that was not planned in advance but piecemeal, not perfect but quite workable, and certainly superior to what other ancient empires had evolved.[37]

It was characteristic of this system that the state took care of supply: living off enemy land was practised relatively little, to complement the state supply in certain war conditions, mainly by foraging. In practice, this meant that the senate regularly allocated funds to each holder of *imperium* whose *provincia* was to conduct war. Several mechanisms were employed to have food, particularly wheat and barley, personal military equipment, and various war materials prepared or acquired in advance of or during wars, including competitive tendering by private contractors, provincial taxation in kind, purchase in the market, requisitioning of supplies from subject communities, and gifts from allies.

These materials were first transported to magazines established outside and sometimes within the war zone, often on the seashore and navigable rivers, to be later forwarded by a kind of shuttle system to the army. Transportation of supplies—and of troops as well—was by sea and river, and over land; the task was performed by private contractors, by requisition of ships, pack animals, and wagons, and possibly by state-owned vessels, and was paid for by voluntary contributions from allies. To facilitate the movement of legions and the transportation of goods to war zones, the state gradually constructed a network of roads in Italy from 312 onwards, and in the provinces from about 130.[38] Despite occasional delays and failures, due to difficult weather or terrain conditions, enemy attacks, or human frailty, broadly speaking the system enabled the armies and their commanders to accomplish their goals, an impressive achievement given the tens of thousands of men and animals involved and the enormous quantities of food, ships, equipment, and other war materials required.

The main structural deficiency of the system was its lack of permanency; that is, the state did not establish a permanent administrative apparatus responsible for supplying the army. Although the ways and means of achieving their logistical aims, and even the conceptual approach to the problems, were known and available, every general had to start afresh to set up the logistical machinery he deemed appropriate to supply the needs of his army.

Discipline

Military discipline (*disciplina militaris*) was considered by the Romans to be a major factor in their success in winning wars and world dominion. Originating in the early days of Rome, it had developed into a systematic art based on a comprehensive set of precepts,[39] the mainstay of the *imperium Romanum*.[40] Military discipline went hand in hand with training, protocols of behaviour, and rules concerning marching, pitching camp, keeping guard, deployment and advance in battle, fighting, and so on. It meant a system of punishment for any infringement of the rules or reward for excellence in display of courage in battle.[41] Whether committed by the rank and file or by officers, offences such as falling asleep on guard duty at night, abandoning one's weapons in battle, or deserting one's post were punished by death, usually by being beaten or stoned to death by fellow soldiers. If a whole unit deserted its position in battle, one-tenth of its men were selected by lot and put to death. Fines and flogging were applied for less serious offences, such as slowness in the execution of orders. Rewards included oral commendations by the general, military decorations, and cash donations. This system of harsh punishments and honourable and material rewards, all performed or bestowed in public, served to maintain military discipline, although it did not completely preclude incidents of panic in battle, desertions, and even occasional mutinies.[42] Polybius and Josephus,[43] both outside observers, praised the effectiveness of Roman training, discipline, and orderliness, and considered them major strategic factors in Rome's overall military success.

Integrating Valour with Discipline and Tactical Formations

Authors[44] sometimes put *disciplina Romana*, as a cardinal cause of Roman military superiority, on a par with *virtus*, that is, originally and primarily, military prowess, manly courage.[45] According to Sallust, Julius Caesar 'desired a great command, an army, and a new war where his *virtus* could shine out'.[46] In a play staged in the early second century, the Roman playwright Plautus has a wife express the view that by victory in war a man wins glory and proves his *virtus*; *virtus* comes before all other things, that is, it safeguards liberty, security, life, property and parents, homeland, and children.[47] Gaining reputation for valour was essential for political career and public esteem, and the best way to prove one's *virtus* was to engage and overcome an enemy in single combat.[48]

The trouble was that *virtus*, a competitive quality, might clash with military discipline (*disciplina militaris*), as is brought out clearly by Livy in the story of the young nobleman Titus Manlius Torquatus, who slew an enemy in single combat, thereby proving his *virtus* but violating the express order of his father, the consul, not to engage in battle. By leaving his position to fight the enemy, the young Roman warrior had subverted military discipline, by which 'the Roman state has stood firm until then', and to restore it the consul had his son executed. Indeed, the terrible punishment was effective, since thereafter the soldiers performed their duties with attention and did well in the ensuing battle.[49]

Thus, *virtus* proved by individual fighting, ideally in a duel, posed a potential threat to a system of corporate fighting. If monomachy had obtained in Rome from early times, as it may well have done, the dichotomy became real with the Roman adoption of the Greek hoplite phalanx, which could not work efficiently without the implementation of military discipline.[50] The imposition of strict military discipline became imperative with the introduction of the manipular formation, a more advanced and complex system of corporate fighting.

Given the inherent conflict between the political-cultural ethos of individual fighting and the requirements of the new system, the Romans worked out means, probably gradually, by trial and error, to contain or resolve this conflict. As described by Polybius, even in a pitched battle the age-based division of the manipular legion into echelons and the slightly loose array of the maniples enabled the young *velites* as well as *hastati* and *principes* to seize opportunities for individual distinction in combat. Foraging and various independent missions offered such opportunities for the well-to-do and noble cavalrymen and for poor *velites* as well. In addition, in certain circumstances single combat was occasionally allowed and indeed practised until the end of the republic. More importantly, not only were the various rewards for feats of valour bestowed in front of the army but they were also publicized later in Rome.[51] In sum, in practice there evolved a strategy that fostered the introduction of successive new tactical formations, imposed a two-faceted military discipline, and allowed the realization of *virtus* in battle—three major factors that combined to make the Roman war machine so successful over a long period.

Terror and Clemency

The Greek historian Diodorus Siculus (32. 2), probably following Polybius, argues that those whose object is to gain dominion use valour (*andreia = virtus*) and sagacity to obtain it, clemency (*epieikeia = clementia*) to extend it, and terror to secure it, an argument that is valid, as he adds, for the creation of the Roman empire. In fact, all three factors played a role in the acquisition, extension, and protection of the Roman empire. About the first factor, enough has already been said, and the other two can be presented here in broad terms only.

That the senate and generals alike used both terror and clemency as calculated means to subdue an enemy or win his cooperation is amply evidenced throughout the republic. For instance, after the successful conclusion of the Great Latin War in 338, the senate could exercise, as Livy has one of the consuls explain, extreme cruelty and severe punishment, or forgiveness and generous treatment, to solve permanently the relations with the Latin League; the senate decided to apply these means to each of the Latin city-states according to its individual deserts.[52]

The sacking and destruction of captured cities, and even sometimes of those surrendered by agreement, is an application par excellence of the system of terror, and in this case it was also lucrative for both the soldiers and the state.[53] For example, Polybius reports that, at the conquest of New Carthage in 209, Scipio Africanus sent his soldiers, 'as is the Roman custom', to massacre all the inhabitants they encountered, an expedient, he claims, that the Romans employed with fearful brutality when they took cities in order to inspire terror; the looting stage followed later, on the general's signal.[54] On the other hand, shortly after the conquest of New Carthage, Scipio restored hostages of the Carthaginians to their relatives, an act of clemency which he used, among other means, to win the 'friendship', that is, the military and political support, of various Iberian tribes.[55]

As Diodorus notes, earlier empires also used terror and clemency to establish dominion; what perhaps made the Romans exceptional was their systematic implementation of one or the other of these means, depending on the circumstances. Whether exceptional or not, numerous particular instances testify to regular use by the Romans of the strategy of terror and clemency, often efficiently and successfully, thus confirming Diodorus's observation, even though in certain circumstances some peoples preferred death in battle or suicide to falling into Roman hands.[56]

Ways of Conducting War

Seeking out the enemy offensively in order to engage him at once in pitched battle was one way to conduct war, and that strategy could work well when the opponent was willing to accept the challenge. A perfect and celebrated example is the battle of Zela, in which Caesar routed the army of Pharnaces, king of Pontus, in 47 (*veni, vidi, vici*).

The extreme opposite is the war of delay or attrition, best illustrated by the way in which Fabius Maximus sought to reverse the effect of Hannibal's first stunning victories upon Rome's Italian allies, to revive the spirit of the Roman troops, and to wear down the enemy. That strategy worked well for a while, but then the Roman inclination to maintain honour and reach a conclusion through all-out battle prevailed, and the senate instructed the consuls in 216 to fight a decisive battle, resulting in the catastrophic defeat at Cannae. Thereafter the 'Fabian strategy' was usually followed in Italy, and to good effect, thwarting Hannibal's plan to win the support of Italian polities and to overthrow the system of alliances that Rome had established in Italy.

The overall victory in the Second Punic War, decisive for the rise of Rome to Mediterranean dominion, was achieved by launching offensive campaigns in Spain, Sicily, and eventually Africa, characterized by Liddell Hart as a strategy of indirect approach.[57] Victory was due to Rome's superiority in manpower, stubbornness, and relatively efficient logistics system, as well as the loyalty of her allies, itself a triumphant proof of Rome's shrewd system of alliances.

Broadly speaking, Roman generals aimed at overcoming the enemy in pitched battle, but they were careful to fight on advantageous or at least equal terms. Sometimes this worked perfectly. For example, a single full-scale battle put an end to the dreaded invasion of the Gauls in 225, who were trapped between two Roman armies at Telamon. Marius destroyed the Teutones at Aquae Sextiae in 102, launching his attack from a defensive, superior position, helped by an ambush carefully planted in advance.

However, the enemy was not always willing to give battle, and certainly not at a disadvantage, and so the war would drag on. Ravaging the country and other manoeuvres might be tried to induce the enemy to engage in battle, which sometimes occurred by accident, as at Pydna in 168, when the Macedonian phalanx succumbed to the Roman legion.

Another strategy was applied by Metellus Numidicus and Marius in the war against the Numidian king Jugurtha, who, having lost two battles, turned to daring guerrilla tactics. Both Roman generals tried to subdue the elusive enemy by destroying or garrisoning the places that might provide the king with a base. This they did with much success, but the war ended only when Jugurtha was betrayed to the Romans through a ruse.

Occasionally, wars were concluded by the capture of the enemy's central city, which is how Numantia was brought down by Scipio Aemilianus in 134–3. However, it was rare that wars were won swiftly. Indeed, Rome suffered at least ninety major defeats during the period of the republic,[58] but she never gave in, always continuing her wars to a successful end. All in all, Roman wars were conducted in a variety of ways and means, depending on the nature of the enemy and on geopolitical and other conditions, with the generals inclined to prosecute offensive, aggressive campaigns, though using restraint and maintaining military discipline, and by adapting the available methods of conducting war to the circumstances.

Military Sapientia, Invention, Determination

Finally, three matters that pertain to Roman general strategy need to be mentioned. Contrary to what many a Roman writer later averred, military *sapientia* ('wisdom'), characterized by foresight and expediency, and use of stratagems, including ambushes, surprise attacks by night, and pretended flights, constituted hallmarks of good generalship and were highly esteemed in Rome until the second century. Even later, when such actions were attributed to Punic perfidy for propagandistic purposes, cunning and stratagems continued to be practised.[59] Secondly, a positive approach to innovation in military affairs, including organization, tactics, and technology, prevailed throughout the period of the republic, underlying the adoption or adaptation of foreign offensive and defensive weaponry (e.g. Celtic helmets and ring-mail, the Spanish sword, and Greek arms for cavalry),[60] war machinery (notably Greek artillery),[61] and the formation of the Greek hoplite phalanx, as well as original inventions such as boarding devices to permit fighting on enemy ships in naval warfare[62] and the manipular and cohortal formations. This approach served to maintain steady improvement of the military capabilities of the Roman army vis-à-vis its enemies. Thirdly, it was typical of Rome to conduct wars with inexorable determination and perseverance, whatever the suffering and costs in human and material resources, until victory was achieved. Except for the agreement made with the Samnites after a Roman army was trapped and surrendered in 321 BCE, Rome never made peace except after utterly defeating the enemy.

The use of stratagems, improvement of military means, and perseverance in carrying on wars despite severe losses were not unique to Rome, nor were the several other factors enumerated above, and yet there was a difference: a difference in degree and, in a few respects, also in kind. More importantly, the combination of all these factors made Rome exceptional and gave her strategic superiority over each and every polity that stood in the way of the expansion of her dominion.[63]

CONCLUSION

The questions posed at the beginning of this chapter were: What was the nature of Roman strategy during the republic, and can we reconstruct it? There is no trace or indication in the extant sources of the existence of strategic theory in Rome. As one scholar has aptly pointed out, Rome had no institutes of strategic studies;[64] indeed, it did not even have a general staff.[65] What the sources do show us is strategy in practice, which may or may not have features in common with modern strategic conceptions and ways of thinking. On certain occasions during the republic, Rome had to reach decisions on issues we may call strategic, such as the declaration of wars and the making of peace; the conclusion of treaties, especially including the rights and the military and other obligations of allies;

the treatment of defeated enemies; the annexation and administration of conquered territories and the management of subject peoples; relations with nations
and states outside direct Roman rule; the size and structure of the regular army;
the mobilization of troops in militarily critical situations; the allocation of forces
during wars conducted on several fronts; methods of raising financial resources;
supply of the army; the creation of material infrastructure conducive to the
functioning of the army; etc. These decisions may be construed as reflecting a
general strategy that embraced certain fundamental principles and forms of action
and behaviour that were followed in the conduct of foreign affairs and wars, as
well as the practical methods that were fostered.

This general strategy evolved gradually over time, hand in hand with
continuing violent confrontation with other polities and the growth of the
Roman empire, and was not an outcome of theoretical scientific thinking. In a
sense, it was a collective enterprise, a cumulative result of the senate's debates and
resolutions on specific issues, as well as of proposals concerning concrete matters
that were submitted for ratification to the people's assemblies. Sometimes these
issues were also discussed in public speeches. The strategy expressed and responded to foreign policy purposes, concerns of internal politics, economic
interests, social considerations, moral values and habits, religious beliefs and
scruples, and ideological notions.

Needless to say, the Roman general strategy should be distinguished from a
specific strategy that was applied in a particular war, although it naturally bore
upon the plans, means, and actions that made up the latter, and itself was influenced
by the ways in which generals conducted campaigns. Conflicting views, incoherent
behaviour, blunders, and cases of mismanagement of foreign affairs are on record,
but they do not undermine the strategic factors delineated in the previous section.
Conversely, Roman general strategy suffered from lack of strategic intelligence on a
national level, indicating the absence of long-term planning.[66]

Seen from one angle, Roman general strategy provided the senate and the
generals with the means to win all the wars that Rome conducted during the
period of the republic, which is the essence of every strategy. Seen from another
angle, this strategy served the political ambitions, ethical-cultural aspirations, and
economic interests of the Roman ruling classes, in particular the narrow group of
the nobility, as well as the material needs of the soldiers and citizens at large.
Given the values and ideas that came to dominate Roman society and political life,
Roman general strategy realized the tendency towards the relentless expansion of
Roman dominion and the establishment of the Roman empire.

NOTES

1. For brevity, ancient sources are sparsely mentioned and references to modern works are
   minimal; controversial topics cannot be dealt with. Basic information on people
   (authors, statesmen, generals, kings, etc.), technical terms, historical events, and so
   forth can easily be found in S. Hornblower and A. Spawforth (eds), *The Oxford Classical
   Dictionary*, 3rd edn (Oxford, 1996). Unless mentioned otherwise, all dates are BCE.
2. A. Lintott, *The Constitution of the Roman Republic* (Oxford, 1999).

3. L. Keppie, *The Making of the Roman Army* (Oxford, 1984), 1–131; P. Erdkamp (ed.), *A Companion to the Roman Army* (Oxford, 2006), 1–179 (the republican period); and P. Sabine, H. V. Wees, and M. Whitby (eds), *The Cambridge History of Greek and Roman Warfare* (*CHGRW*), i (Cambridge, 2007), 303–516 (the Hellenistic world and the Roman republic).

4. Livy 8. 8.

5. J. E. Lendon, *Soldiers and Ghosts* (New Haven, 2005), 222–8.

6. H. Delbrück, *History of the Art of War within the Framework of Political History*, 2 vols (trans. of the 3rd German edn, 1920; Westport, CT, 1975), i. 416.

7. See Polybius 1. 6. 3–6.

8. W. V. Harris, *War and Imperialism in Republican Rome 327–70 BC* (Oxford, 1979), 9–10; S. Oakley, 'The Roman Conquest of Italy', esp. 14–16; and J. Rich, 'Fear, Greed and Glory', esp. 44–9 (trends and fluctuations), both in J. Rich and G. Shipley (eds), *War and Society in the Roman World* (London, 1993).

9. Appian, *Civil Wars* 1. 7.

10. Polybius 6. 19. 4.

11. See Harris, *War and Imperialism in Republican Rome*, ch. 1.

12. The leading exponents of this view are T. Mommsen, T. Frank, and M. Holleaux, on whom, see J. Linderski, '*Si vis pacem, para bellum*: Concepts of Defensive Imperialism', in W. V. Harris (ed.), *The Imperialism of Mid-Republican Rome* (Rome, 1984), 133–64.

13. Cicero, *Philippics* 7. 19; cf. Livy 6. 18. 7.

14. Tacitus, *Agricola* 30. 4–5.

15. A. M. Eckstein, *Mediterranean Anarchy, Interstate War, and the Rise of Rome* (Berkeley and Los Angeles, 2006), esp. 33–5, 182–3, 241–3, 245–57. For the view that there existed in Classical Greece a normative framework that shaped inter-state relations, see P. Low, *Interstate Relations in Classical Greece* (Cambridge, 2007). Understandably, Low does not address the arguments of Eckstein.

16. See, however, P. J. Burton, '*Clientela* or *Amicitia*? Modeling International Behavior in the Middle Republic (264–146 BC)', *Klio*, 35 (2003), esp. 349–51, curiously ignored by Eckstein.

17. See Eckstein, *Mediterranean Anarchy, Interstate War, and the Rise of Rome*, 1–2; also K. N. Waltz, *Theory of International Politics* (New York, 1979).

18. E.g. Virgil, *Aeneid* 1. 278–9; 6. 851–4.

19. See P. A. Brunt, *Roman Imperial Themes* (Oxford, 1990), 297–302.

20. Ibid. 439.

21. See A. M. Eckstein, *Senate and General* (Berkeley and Los Angeles, 1987), 319–24.

22. Polybius 23. 14. 10; cf. Livy 38. 48. 3–4, 60. 5; and Plutarch, *Tiberius Gracchus* 9. 5. See I. Shatzman, 'The Integration of Judaea into the Roman Empire', *Scripta Classica Israelica*, 18 (1999), esp. 54–8 (with the literature therein).

23. See Brunt, *Roman Imperial Themes*, 294–7, 305–8; and N. Rosenstein, *Imperatores Victi* (Berkeley and Los Angeles, 1990), 53–94.

24. Livy 8. 13–14.

25. Livy 1. 28–30, 33; 2. 16.

26. On the settlement of 338 BCE, see T. J. Cornell, *The Beginnings of Rome* (London, 1995), 347–52.

27. See e.g. E. T. Salmon, *The Making of Roman Italy* (London, 1982), 71.

28. Polybius 2. 23.

29. Polybius 2. 24; cf. Diodorus Siculus 25. 13; Eutropius 3. 5; and Orosius 4. 13. 6.

30. See D. W. Baronowski, 'Roman Military Forces in 225 BC (Polybius 2. 23–4)', *Historia*, 42 (1993), 181–202 (with ample bibliography). See also E. Lo Cascio, 'Recruitment and the Size of the Roman Population from the Third to the First Century BCE', in

W. Scheidel (ed.), *Debating Roman Demography* (Leiden, 2001) (a higher estimate of the size of the Roman population), 111–37.

31. See e.g. R. K. Sherk, *Rome and the Greek East* (Cambridge, 1984), 24–5, 32–3, 56–7.
32. See J. P. Roth, *The Logistics of the Roman Army at War (264 B.C.–A.D. 235)* (Leiden, 1999), 158–9, 225; and A. M. Eckstein, '*Unicum Subsidium Populi Romani*: Hiero II and Rome, 263–215 BC', *Chiron*, 10 (1980), 183–203..
33. On these treaties, see R. M. Kallet-Marx, *Hegemony to Empire* (Berkeley and Los Angeles, 1995), 184–97, cited at 197.
34. Shatzman, 'The Integration of Judaea into the Roman Empire', 59–71.
35. See E. T. Salmon, *Roman Colonization under the Republic* (London, 1969).
36. M. van Creveld, *Supplying War* (Cambridge, 1978), 1.
37. See, in particular, P. Erdkamp, *Hunger and the Sword: Warfare and Food Supply in Roman Republican Wars (264–30 B.C.)* (Amsterdam, 1998); and Roth, *The Logistics of the Roman Army at War*.
38. See, in general, R. Chevalier, *Roman Roads* (London, 1976); cf. T. P. Wiseman, 'Roman Republican Road-Building', *Papers of the British School at Rome*, 38 (1970), 122–53; and R. Laurence, *The Roads of Roman Italy* (London, 1999).
39. Livy 9. 17. 10.
40. Valerius Maximus, *Memorable Deeds and Sayings* 2. 7, preface.
41. See A. D. Lee, 'Morale and the Roman Experience in Battle', in A. B. Lloyd (ed.), *Battle in Antiquity* (London, 1996), esp. 23–6; and S. A. Phang, *Roman Military Service* (Cambridge, 2008), esp. chs 2, 4, 6, and 7.
42. Five incidents of mutiny are recorded in the period 280–90; for a good discussion of the mutiny under Scipio Africanus in 206 CE, see S. G. Chrissanthos, 'Scipio and the Mutiny at Sucro, 206 BC', *Historia*, 46 (1997), 172–84.
43. Polybius 6. 26. 10–39. 11, 40. 1–42. 6; Josephus, *Jewish War* 2. 577–82; 3. 14–15, 70–107. On Polybius, see A. M. Eckstein, '*Physis* and *Nomos*: Polybius, the Romans, and Cato the Elder', in P. Cartledge, P. Garnsey, and E. Gruen (eds), *Hellenistic Constructs* (Berkeley and Los Angeles, 1997), esp. 183–6.
44. E.g. Cicero, *Tusculan Disputations* 1. 2.
45. See M. McDonnell, *Roman Manliness: Virtus and the Roman Republic* (Cambridge, 2006), esp. 1–71. As McDonnell shows, the ethical aspects of *virtus* developed in the wake of Hellenic ideas.
46. Sallust, *Catiline's Conspiracy* 54. 4.
47. Plautus, *Amphytruo*, 641–53.
48. On single combat, see S. P. Oakley, 'Single Combat in the Roman Republic', *Historia*, 35 (1985), 392–410.
49. Livy 8. 6. 16–8. 1.
50. On this topic, see Lendon, *Soldiers and Ghosts*, 181–91; and id., 'War and Society', in *CHGRW*, i. 509–15.
51. See Polybius 6. 39.
52. Livy 8. 13. 10–14. 1.
53. On the sacking of cities, see A. Ziolkowski, '*Urbs Direpta*, or, How the Romans Sacked Cities', in Rich and Shipley (eds), *War and Society in the Roman World*, 69–91.
54. Polybius 10. 15. 1–6.
55. Polybius 10. 34–5; 37. 6–38. 6. On Scipio's severity and clemency, see also Dio 16. 42–3, 48.
56. E.g. Astapa in Spain (Livy 28. 22. 1–23. 5; Appian, *Iberike* 33). On the strategies of terror and clemency, see C. M. Gilliver, 'The Roman Army and Morality in War', in Lloyd (ed.), *Battle in Antiquity*, 219–38.
57. B. H. Liddell Hart, *Strategy* (New York, 1954), 50.
58. For a list, see Rosenstein, *Imperatores Victi*, 179–203.

59. On this topic, see E. L. Wheeler, '*Sapiens* and Stratagems: The Neglected Meaning of a *Cognomen*', *Historia*, 37 (1988), 167–95; and id., 'The Modern Legality of Frontinus', *Militärgeschichtliche Mitteilungen*, 43 (1988), 7–29.

60. See B. C. Bishop and J. C. N. Coulston, *Roman Military Equipment*, 2nd edn (Oxford, 2006), 54–6, 63, 65; Polybius 6. 25. 8–11; and Sallust, *Catiline's Conspiracy* 51. 38.

61. See E. W. Marsden, *Greek and Roman Artillery: Historical Development* (Oxford, 1969), 83–5, 170–9.

62. See P. de Souza, 'Naval Battles and Sieges', in *CHGRW*, i, esp. 437–9.

63. Eckstein, *Mediterranean Anarchy, Interstate War, and the Rise of Rome*, 182–216.

64. J. C. Mann, 'Power, Force and the Frontiers of the Empire', review of E. N. Luttwak, *The Grand Strategy of the Roman Empire, Journal of Roman Studies*, 69 (1979), 180.

65. Cf. F. E. Adcock, *The Roman Art of War under the Republic* (Cambridge, MA, 1940), 94.

66. On Roman intelligence and its limitations, see N. J. E. Austin and N. B. Rankov, *Exploratio* (London, 1995), 12–38, 107–8; and A. C. Bertrand, 'Stumbling through Gaul: Maps, Intelligence, and Caesar's *Bellum Gallicum*', *Ancient Historical Bulletin*, 11 (1997), 107–22.

3

The Byzantine Empire: From Attila to the 4th Crusade

Edward N. Luttwak

INTRODUCTION

The Roman empire of the East, which we now call Byzantine, warrants the attention of all who are interested in strategy for two distinct reasons. The first is the empire's unique longevity: estimates of its duration could be stretched to 1,123 years, starting with Constantine's consecration of his capital on 11 May 330 and ending on 29 May 1453, when what remained of Constantinople within its majestic walls fell to the Ottomans. For most historians, except perhaps those who focus exclusively on the history of religion, this conflates too much history—successive political, administrative, demographic, and geographic transformations leave no other continuity. But even by my own much shorter reckoning, from the advent of Attila's Huns in the fifth century to its downfall in the twelfth century, which culminated in the Latin conquest and sack of Constantinople in 1204, the Byzantine empire outlasted all other empires in history, including the longest-lived Chinese dynasties, and also its only worthy competitor, the earlier Roman empire in the West.

The second reason why strategists should study Byzantium is that its survival and indeed prosperity were very much strategic artefacts. The administrative division of the Roman empire in 395, which bisected the Mediterranean basin and left Constantinople the capital of the eastern half, endowed the western half with a much better geography. It had the safe hinterlands of what are now France, Italy, and Spain, as well as North Africa, while the eastern half was lacking in geographic depth, yet had to guard the always threatened Danube frontier exposed to the Eurasian steppes, and also face the powerful and chronically aggressive Sassanid empire of Persia. This severe imbalance between threats and resources was not supposed to matter, because after 395, as before it, all mobile Roman army forces of East and West were meant to be equally available to face threats anywhere. But with the western half of the empire declining and finally extinguished in the later fifth century, the east Romans, or Byzantines, had to face alone undiminished threats once confronted by the resources of both halves of the empire. They overcame this fundamental material weakness with two immaterial strengths: their strategy, which applied intellect to the task of making the best use of such strength as they still had; and their morale-enhancing triple identity: they were Christian in religion, Hellenic in culture, and Roman politically and institutionally. It helped that the Eastern Church fully accepted the entirety of classical culture, erotic poetry included, with none of the ambivalence periodically manifested within the Roman Church.

This chapter argues that the Byzantine empire greatly outlasted its western counterpart because its rulers were able to adapt strategically to diminished circumstances by devising new ways of coping with successive enemies instead of seeking to destroy them in the classic Roman manner. Overall, the Byzantine empire relied less on military strength and more on persuasion: to recruit allies, to dissuade threatening neighbours, and to manipulate potential enemies into attacking one another. Even when the Byzantines fought—which they often did, usually with much skill—they were less inclined to destroy their enemies than to contain them, for they knew that today's enemies could be tomorrow's allies. This chapter focuses especially on the fifth and sixth centuries, for it was then that the new strategy emerged.[1]

THE EMERGENCE OF THE NEW STRATEGY

In facing Attila, the mild and scholarly Theodosios II (408–450) and his experienced civil officials were doubly constrained.[2] They had no military forces that were tactically effective against the Huns, and they had more urgent priorities on two other fronts.

As always, the strongest foreign power was Sassanian Persia. It had been exceptionally peaceful until 420, in the time of the shah Yazdgird, but there was a sharp deterioration under his successor, Bahram V (420–438).[3] The ancient quarrel over the Armenian lands was rekindled and there was a new quarrel over religion. Modern historians have described the Armenian statelets as 'buffer states', but the evidence suggests that their existence between the two empires was more often conflict-inducing than conflict-avoiding, as each tried to assert its authority over the fractious petty rulers of narrow valleys who made up political Armenia.[4]

The religious quarrel was quite new. Whether coincidentally or reciprocally, there was a sharp rise in the Christian militancy of the Byzantine empire and the Zoroastrian militancy of the Sassanians. In the former, the official persecution of remaining pagans and Jews notably intensified, non-Greek churchmen suspected of Christological deviations were ferociously investigated, and there were more violent attacks on non-Christians and their places of worship. In the latter, the arrival of a new Sassanian ruler was in any case habitually marked by new military initiatives—no doubt they were useful to affirm his authority—and Yazdgird II, who succeeded Bahram in 438, duly launched an attack on the frontier city of Nisibis, until the *magister militum per Orientem* (the highest military commander east of Constantinople) Anatolios arrived to negotiate a peace treaty. There was no more fighting while Theodosios lived, in part because Yazdgird himself lived until 457, but troops had to remain available to defend the Persian front anyway, because no peace could long outlast their absence. Unlike Attila's incursions, a

Sassanian invasion could easily lead to the permanent loss of imperial territory; hence that frontier retained its priority.

The second front was in Africa—that is, North African territory corresponding to modern Tunisia and coastal Algeria. It belonged to the western empire, whose boundary started in the middle of Libya, but it remained a joint responsibility. In October 439, Vandals and Alans who arrived from Spain under their formidable warlord Gaiseric seized Carthage, the capital of Africa, then the major source of grain for Rome and central Italy.[5] The immediate damage was to the western empire, but Carthage was a major port with shipyards, a fleet was under construction, and thus the eastern empire was also threatened. Constantinople was further away and well defended, but with a fleet favoured by the prevailing westerly winds, Gaiseric could cut off its grain supply from Egypt by attacking the great port city of Alexandria.

The grand fleet of some 1,100 vessels assembled by the eastern empire to pre-empt a Vandal offensive never reached Carthage, instead returning quickly to Constantinople, but the expedition was not wasted. It seems that Gaiseric was thoroughly intimidated. At any rate, he never attacked Alexandria or any other eastern possession, and did not attack anywhere until 455, when his expedition sacked Rome, by then undefended, apparently inflicting more damage than Alaric had in 410.

Intimidation had worked with Gaiseric as far as the eastern empire was concerned; even his seizure and sacking of Rome was precipitated by a court intrigue. But intimidation failed with Attila; he had nothing to fear even from an all-out attack, the land equivalent of the naval expedition against Gaiseric.

In later times, the Byzantines would have an excellent diplomatic remedy against enemies from the steppe: again and again, they persuaded different steppe powers to fight one another instead of attacking the empire. But Attila's empire was too large for that: the Byzantines could not reach behind it to find new allies. The most profound historian of the Huns opined that it was a 'thankless task' to determine the geographic extent of Attila's domain because to do so would 'clash with long-cherished myths'.[6] He then rejected more expansive estimates to settle for a rather modest territory stretching from central Europe to the shores of the Black Sea. But there is negative evidence that disproves the eminent historian: there is no sign that any independent steppe power existed west of the Volga, that is, behind the Huns but within reach of Byzantium.

In between, the advent of major steppe powers, lesser nations, tribes, and war bands also alternated between fighting against the empire and fighting for it. All were subject to the dynamics of pastoralism in the steppe: the natural increase of unmolested herds provoked struggles over pasture that made it easy for Byzantium to find allies; while nomads who had plenty of meat, milk, leather, and horn but nothing else had a perpetual need of gold to purchase grain and everything else.[7]

The entire steppe corridor west of the Volga that runs below the forests and over the Black Sea all the way to the Danube became the permanent arena of Byzantine diplomacy, which was routinely successful in converting the very multiplicity of potential enemies into its own remedy. But in the time of Attila that did not happen, either because of an improbable absence of other peoples on the steppe, or because his power really did extend much further east than the

Danube, indeed all the way to the Volga. Either way, from a diplomatic point of view, Attila's empire might as well have spanned the entire distance to Vladivostok, because when Byzantium urgently needed allies in the eastern steppe who might be persuaded to move westward to attack the Huns from the rear, there were none to be found, neither large ones nor small ones.

That left only an inferior though still useful form of diplomacy: instead of using gold to persuade others to attack the Huns, it had to be used to buy their restraint. Keeping both infantry and cavalry at home, Theodosios II instead sent envoys to negotiate with Attila to induce him to stop raiding imperial territory. It was more effective than sending more forces that would be defeated, and cheaper than the tax revenues lost when provinces were ravaged. There had been earlier annual payments to Attila of several hundred pounds of gold, and the tribute was increased to 2,000 pounds of gold a year, but not paid until 447, when a comprehensive agreement was reached that required the lump sum payment of 6,000 pounds of gold and future annual payments of 2,100 pounds of gold.[8]

In the event, the remedy was successful: Attila did not attack the eastern empire, instead attacking westward. By 451 he was in Gaul. The year before, Theodosios had been succeeded by the talented Marcian (450–457), who refused to pay the annual tribute, but by then Attila was committed in the West and could not retaliate.

Had Theodosios II pleased the traditionalists by making peace with Persia, leaving Gaiseric's Vandals alone, accommodating Isaurians, Tzanni, and other tribesmen making trouble at home to send all his troops to fight Attila instead with maximum strength, it is almost certain that the imperial army would have been destroyed and the empire with it, for there would have been nothing left to stop Persians, Vandals, and assorted tribesmen as well as the Huns and their allies from seizing imperial territory.

That is the conclusion one would reach theoretically, considering the tactical, operational, and theatre-strategic advantages of Attila's Huns, who fought with the added mass of subjected Germanic and Iranic warriors. And that is also the conclusion one would reach empirically, on the basis of the only relevant evidence there is—which is more than enough: when Attila moved west to invade what is now France, in the great battle of Campus Mauriacus, the combined strength of the Salic Franks, Alans, Bretons, Liticians, Burgundians, Saxons, Riparian Franks, former Roman auxiliaries, numerous Vesi Goths, and a few Roman soldiers was only sufficient to repel Attila's army, not to destroy it or even damage it enough to prevent the subsequent invasion of Italy. It is therefore reasonably certain that the eastern army would have been defeated.

Instead of gambling with the survival of the empire, the Byzantine rulers contained the extraordinary threat of Attila's Huns without large-scale warfare, until it passed away with no lasting injury. A new strategy was thereby affirmed, which marked another transition from Rome to Byzantium: diplomacy first, force second, for the costs of the former were only temporary, while the risks of war could be fatal.[9]

In their constant search for potential allies, the Byzantines sent out diplomatic missions to distant lands—even very remote allies could be useful if they had the fast strategic mobility typical of nomadic steppe powers. The Byzantines maintained an impressive linguistic capability, with a professional bureau of interpreters. We read of Maniakh, the Sogdian potentate who in the year 568 first brought word to Constantinople of the sudden rise of the first Türk Qaganate, which was also the greatest of all subsequent Turkic states. When he was admitted to the court, Maniakh was able to communicate his important information through a translator, who was evidently proficient in Sogdian—even though we hear of no prior Sogdian visitors to the court.

The Byzantines also exploited the assorted attractions of the imperial court, with its banquets and entertainments, and all the other amenities of Constantinople to win over visitors and recruit them as allies or agents. Detailed instructions on how to entertain and impress visiting foreign potentates survive in the tenth-century *Book of Ceremonies* of the emperor Constantine Porphyrogennetos. They reveal considerable psychological sophistication; for example, to dazzle visitors with the golden robes of court officials without evoking resentment, equally magnificent robes were provided for the visitors, on loan. This too was an expression of the emperor's benevolence; indeed, even when on the offensive, the emperor was not to be viewed as a predator, but always as a protective and generous patron. Gold coins were given as tips to dinner guests at the palace, including foreign visitors, while the wording of the prescribed greetings for foreign envoys and their masters in *The Book of Ceremonies* is redolent with concern for their well-being and good health. From the same text we learn that great numbers of lesser rulers, some little more than local chieftains, also received the recognition of their own personalized imperial greeting—very flattering, no doubt.

For visitors used only to yurts, tents, and huts, the vast Hagia Sophia church must have been a veritable vision of heaven. We have contemporary accounts by foreign visitors awed by the multi-media spectacle of its gilded mosaics and soaring dome, the choral chanting, billowing incense, and golden-robed priests. Even when it did not induce religious conversion, as the *Russian Primary Chronicle* would have it, the great church was a powerful instrument of Byzantine diplomacy.

The essential aim of Byzantine strategy was to minimize reliance on costly force: instead of trying to destroy successive enemies systematically in the Roman manner, enemy threats were to be contained or deflected by every form of diplomacy from religious conversion and dynastic marriages to plain bribery, as well as the mutual accommodation of interests.

Under this strategy, varied means of persuasion were employed, but gold was consistently the most important. Combined with effective military forces to set firm limits to extortion, gold was successfully employed to cope with many dangerous enemies. The cost of tribute was evidently less than the double cost of resisting attacks: both the military expenditure and the damage inflicted on civilian lives and property.

Nor was the payment of tribute deflationary. The circulation of gold, from taxpayers to the imperial treasury and from the treasury back to the taxpaying economy by way of imperial salaries and purchases, was only briefly diverted when tribute was paid. The Huns and all their successors inevitably tended to use their tribute gold to buy both necessities and baubles from the empire (special arrangements were negotiated for border markets); hence the gold given to the Huns and later claimants quickly returned to circulate within the empire, except for the small fraction retained for jewellery. To be sure, tribute converted products that could have been consumed locally into unrequited exports, reducing the standard of living within the empire. But the payment of tribute did not depress production—in fact, it probably stimulated economic activity by increasing the velocity of the circulation of gold.

From a strategic point of view, the payment of tribute was an effective way of exploiting the empire's greatest comparative advantage: its financial liquidity. Egypt was more fertile and parts of Mesopotamia also; Persia was better placed for long-range trade, having better access to both the central Asian routes to China and the Persian Gulf sea route to India and the Spice Islands. But the wealth of nations is one thing, the wealth of states quite another. It depends on their extractive capacity—their ability to collect revenue—for which the Byzantine empire had the superior system. Even after the catastrophe of 1204, the diminished state restored in Constantinople by Michael VIII Palaiologos (1259–82), a Greek kingdom that was imperial only in name, still had more gold in its treasury than any kingdom of Europe, simply because it routinely collected taxes as they could not.

THE TACTICAL REVOLUTION

A further response to Attila's greater-than-expected threat was entirely different, but it too marked a transition from Rome to Byzantium. In a huge simplification, it has often been asserted that the cavalry displaced the infantry as the primary arm of the Roman army after the devastating defeat it suffered at Adrianople in 378. Actually, it was the solid and stolid heavy infantry of the classic legions that was displaced, not cheaper foot-soldiers in general—and that process was well under way more than a century before Adrianople. In the time of Gallienus (260–268), the emperor's massed cavalry force became the most effective form of military strength at a time of acute crisis. It was equally useful to repel foreign incursions swiftly or to suppress internal revolts before they could spread; his *dux equitum*, commander of the cavalry, Aurelianus, unsurprisingly became emperor in 270. It was also before Adrianople, under Constantine, who died in 337, that standing mobile forces for the empire as a whole, *comitatenses*, were added to the provincial frontier forces.[10]

As compared to these large and complicated changes, whose authorship and timing are still the subject of debate, the tactical revolution was perfectly straightforward: having found no effective way of defeating the Huns with their existing forces of infantry and cavalry, the Byzantines at some point decided to copy the Hun mounted archers, adding some armour to make them more versatile. That was no easy accomplishment. In the absence of a steppe culture of hunting and warfare, in which instruction in riding and archery begins in early childhood, only very intensive, very prolonged training programmes could convert recruits into skilled horsemen, skilled archers, and, finally, skilled mounted archers. There is no clear evidence on how and when the transformation occurred, but by the time Justinian came to power in 527, the most effective forces of the Byzantine army were certainly its units of mounted archers. Even if they lacked the fullest riding skills and endurance of the steppe riders, they had compensating advantages of their own: body armour that made them more resilient, a lance strapped to their back, which they could pull out to mount a charge, and very thorough combat training.

These troopers could fight in close combat as well, and not only with their missiles from afar, as Homeric bowmen did with their simple wooden self bows, acquiring a cowardly reputation thereby. That was true of the Huns also: they too could fight with sword and spear, and their archery could be dismounted as well, contrary to their caricature as centaurs who could barely walk, let alone fight on foot.

There was more than tactics to the tactical revolution: it had clear strategic implications. The old heavy infantry of the legions, trained and equipped to hold its ground firmly, to dislodge others from their ground, and to kill enemy soldiers relentlessly in close combat face to face, was most suitable for 'attrition', whose aim is to destroy the enemy, paying the proportionate cost in casualties. The tacit assumption was that once the enemy was destroyed, there would be peace.

The Byzantines knew better. They knew that peace was merely a temporary interruption of war, that as soon as one enemy was defeated, another would take his place in attacking the empire. Hence, the loss of scarce and valuable soldiers to inflict attrition was final and irrevocable, while the strategic gain could be very short-lived. Not even the utter destruction of an enemy was an unqualified gain because, in the unending struggle, yesterday's enemy can become today's best ally. Because they fully recognized this, the Byzantines rejected the old Roman striving to maximize attrition that was embodied in the measured pace, elaborate armour, heavy throwing spears, and short stabbing swords of the classic legions—veritable meat grinders. Whenever possible, the Byzantines tried to avoid the frontal attacks and rigid stands that inflict and cost high casualties, to rely instead on manoeuvre— that is, to fight by raiding on the offensive and by ambushing on the defensive, by skirmishing, by outflanking, and by enveloping, in order to defeat by disruption rather than destruction. The Byzantines therefore favoured the more mobile and more flexible cavalry over the infantry, because it was better suited for all forms of manoeuvre at least in open country, and could usually retreat safely under pressure instead of being trapped into last stands.

The tactical revolution was therefore a major military innovation that trans-cended the tactical level: it amounted to a new style of war that left only siege warfare unchanged, and also such rare combat as took place in rugged mountains and forests, which remained the domain of the light infantry, as is still the case today for the most part.

Offensively, the new style of war was employed most successfully in Justinian's wars of conquest in North Africa against the Vandals from 533, and in Italy against the Ostrogothic kingdom, and also in renewed warfare started by Sassani-an Persia in 540—though Byzantine mounted archers had certainly taken part in the previous Persian War under the fortunate and talented Anastasius I (491–518).

Defensively, on the other hand, the great test came with the Avars, the first major steppe power to arrive since Attila's Huns. Formed in the usual way of ethnogenesis around an inner core of Mongols or Turks from Inner Asia, possibly the Jou-jan (or Juan-juan, or Ruan-ruan) of the Chinese sources, they accumulated Turkic and other subjects as they moved westwards.[11] They were mounted archers just like Attila's Huns had been, but much better equipped, with armour and thrusting lances as well as bows, and more accomplished in other forms of warfare, including siege-craft. We have detailed information about Avar equipment in the most important of Byzantine military manuals, the *Strategikon* of Emperor Maurikios. It contains the first reference to stirrups—a major innovation—and prescribes that various items of Byzantine equipment are to be of the 'Avar type'. Perhaps it was from their Chinese antecedents that the Avars acquired the designs that the Byzantines eagerly copied. But mounted archery they already had from the Huns, neutralizing its Avar equivalent or near enough, and that made all the difference: the Avars could be confronted in open-field combat, which had not been the case with the Huns unless they were badly outnumbered or the battle took place in very wet weather.

By 557 the Avars had reached the Volga boundary between the steppe north of the Caspian, in what is now Kazakhstan, and the Pontic steppe north of the Black Sea. In 558 or possibly as late as 560, they sent an embassy to Constantinople with the assistance of the Caucasian Alans, who referred them to the Byzantine commander in nearby Lazica, today's southern Georgia.

At that point, in the steppe corridor west of the Avars there were Turkic Utrigurs and Kutrigurs,[12] who periodically threatened Byzantine possessions in Crimea and along the Black Sea coast. There were also dangerous Antae ahead of them, and a greater mass of other Slavs (Sklavenoi) pressing against the Danube frontier and infiltrating as far as central Greece. The Avars did become a great threat a generation later, but in 558 or 560 it would have been against all the rules of Byzantine statecraft to risk a great army and accept the certainty of many casualties to 'utterly destroy' a potential enemy that was more immediately a potential ally. The Avars did in fact proceed to attack, rout, and subject Utrigurs, Kutrigurs, Antae, and many Slavs. When the Avars did finally attack the empire from *c.*580, the new style of war proved itself. Under Emperor Maurikios (582–602) there were reverses at first—for reasons of operational command rather than tactical ones—but Byzantine forces strong in mounted archers successfully attacked the Avars *c.*590.

The Avars were indeed formidable. They overcame their defeats of the 590s, and by 626 they had reached and besieged Constantinople with great numbers of Slav subjects, in coincidental or planned conjunction with the deepest of all Sassanian offensives, which reached the shore directly opposite Constantinople. After they failed in 626, the Avars lost control of many of their Slav subjects, who were efficiently subverted by Byzantine agents, including the tribes that evolved separately into the Croats and the Serbs, with consequences that endure to this day. Nevertheless, the Avars remained a threat until they moved north into what is now Hungary, where they were decisively defeated by Charlemagne in 791, and later finally dispersed by Bulghar attacks. Long before then, the Avars were no more than a manageable if severe threat for the Byzantines, who were not outclassed as they had been by the Huns because they too had mastered the difficult art of mounted archery. That revolution may have been tactical, but it had strategic implications.

INTELLIGENCE AND COVERT ACTION

In Byzantine field manuals, commanders were invariably urged to do their best to gather intelligence by all means available, given the special need for information of the Byzantine style of war. No single method could suffice. Light cavalry and foot patrols were to probe with hit-and-run attacks, to test the enemy's morale and skill, and to provoke the enemy to send out more of its forces, exposing them to observation and assessment: this was the *reconnaissance* function performed by smaller, faster combat units operating ahead of the main forces. Next, there was the stealthy exploration of terrain and enemy forces further out, deeper in enemy-controlled territory, by small teams of soldiers on foot or on horseback, who were to avoid any combat that would interfere with their primary duty of seeing and reporting back: this was the *scouting* function, in modern terms—clandestine but not covert missions performed by undisguised soldiers with light weapons and no armour, who were to keep out of sight as much as possible by hiding in the terrain. Finally, to go still deeper and obtain less visible information, it was necessary to penetrate enemy encampments, fortresses, and even seats of government, a function performed by covert agents, not hidden in the terrain but protected by false identities as merchants, innocent local civilians, or even enemy soldiers or officials—in other words, *espionage*, in modern terms. In addition to infiltrated agents, there were 'secret friends', enemy citizens, officials, and military chiefs recruited to provide inside information, 'agents-in-place', in modern parlance.[13]

The field manuals established clear distinctions between the three functions. Reconnaissance by light cavalry units—*prokoursatores*, 'those who run ahead'—could not be combined with scouting to observe the enemy as it was, because the presence of even those light units was apt to induce either reinforcements or prudent withdrawals. Likewise, scouts who started fighting the enemy were unlikely to fare well with their light armament and lack of numbers, while failing in their duty of observing and reporting back. Nor could clandestine scouts become useful spies by just walking out of the woods or down the mountain to enter the nearest town: they were trained as soldiers, not as covert agents, whose selection, training, and management are also included in the field manuals.

Intelligence gathering in a broader sense, to strive to understand the mentality of foreign nations and their leaders and not just their immediate intentions, to assess their military strength in the round and not just what forces were in the field and where, was very much a Byzantine concern. Our knowledge of Attila and his Huns largely derives from the detailed account of Priskos of Panium, who was sent with a Byzantine delegation, evidently for the purpose of reporting back on the Huns—a practice already ancient when Tacitus wrote his *Germania*. But aside from such explorations of peoples and land rendered as literature, whatever their purpose might have been, there was also systematic espionage.

Covert operations are a natural extension of espionage, and they had a very natural place in the Byzantine style of war, as a particularly economical way of reducing or even avoiding combat and attrition. Normally, their aim was to weaken the enemy by subversion, that is, an induced transfer of loyalties. Field commanders were urged to get in touch with, and send gifts and promises to, chiefs in the enemy camp, including the garrison commanders of frontier fortresses. Beyond the battlefield, there were persistent efforts to recruit and reward lesser dynasts, officials, and subordinate tribal chiefs to serve the empire in preference to their sovereigns, for whatever reason, from personal resentment, jealousy, or greed to enthusiasm for the Christianity of the true Orthodox Church.

The tasks given to subverted enemy chiefs might be to dissuade counsels of war against the empire, or to promote the merits of fighting for the empire, or simply to argue the virtues of friendship with the empire, all of which might be viewed as wise statecraft anyway. Subversion was more difficult when the conflict of loyalties could not be masked, when it was unambiguously disloyal.

In one most dramatic case, Shahrbaraz, the very successful commander of the Sassanian army that had penetrated all the way to the shore opposite Constanti-nople in 626, was officially and openly contacted at the time for a failed battlefield negotiation. Evidently, contact continued thereafter by covert means, and later—in military circumstances that had become very adverse for the Persians—Shahr-baraz overthrew the shah to make peace with the empire.

This was subversion on a strategic scale, achieved by a combination of official and private negotiations conducted with skill and tact, for which there is some evidence, and above all by victories on the battlefield that had changed the military balance; it was still very useful, however, in diminishing further fighting. It is extremely unlikely that Shahrbaraz could have been subverted by pure bribery: a successful army commander who had recently conquered the richest trading cities of the empire was unlikely to be wanting for gold, which the Byzantine emperor of the time, Herakleios (610–641), sorely lacked in any case: he had to seize and melt down church plate and vessels to pay his soldiers. Even in dealing with much less exalted personages, it was the Byzantine method to wrap bribery in flattery, and to present it as a spontaneous gift motivated by imperial benevolence, all of which made it much easier for the subverted to accept payment.

FORTRESS CONSTANTINOPLE

Overall, the strategic geography of the eastern empire was less favourable than that of the western empire. But there was a huge exception: the geographic setting of its capital city of Constantinople. A promontory jutting out into the Bosporus with the sea on three sides, it was outstandingly defensible. True, no natural barrier protected its landward side, whose defence therefore required fortified walls, which were duly provided on the grandest scale. Nor was there a river or an abundance of nearby springs to supply water as in Rome, so that aqueducts had to reach very far over difficult terrain, and their capacity was often inadequate nonetheless.[14] During sieges, once the aqueducts were cut, there was only the finite supply provided by cisterns; in the worst of times, as in 717, when an extremely prolonged siege by the Jihadi army of Maslama bin Abdul-Malik was correctly anticipated, this forced the partial evacuation of the city. But obviously this defect was less than fatal because Constantinople prospered and grew, even though it never had the abundant water that Rome's magnificent aqueducts supplied (Christian suspicions of public bathing helped to reduce demand). As for cisterns, they could hold a great deal of water—just three in place by the sixth century held 1 million cubic metres.[15] Almost a hundred public and private open and covered cisterns are known, including the spectacular underground cistern built under Justinian, which has become a major tourist attraction as the Yerebatan Sarayi. No cisterns could suffice for unusually prolonged sieges—but such sieges required very effective logistics to feed the besiegers, and indeed Maslama's men eventually starved.

For everything else, the logistic position was excellent. In 430, when the city's population was around 250,000, the authorities did not find it difficult to supply the 80,000 daily free food rations originally offered by Constantine to populate his city.[16] With its ports at the entrance to the Bosporus, Constantinople had ready access to seaborne supplies from the Aegean Sea and the entire Mediterranean on one side, and from the Black Sea on the other. At the meeting point of Europe and Asia, Constantinople had the hinterland of Thrace on one side, and, on the other, the fertile shores of the Propontis (the Sea of Marmara) at the western edge of Anatolia. The Bosporus is only 700 metres across at its narrowest point, between Kandilli and Asiyan some 8 miles up the Thracian shore, but the steep cliffs on the Anatolian side made it much easier to transit through the low-lying shore at the western entrance to the Bosporus, where the adjacent cities of Chrysopolis (Üsküdar) and Chalcedon (Kadiköy) faced Constantinople directly across the water only a mile away.

To starve out the city in a siege, an enemy therefore had to control Thrace to cut off the usual supplies of livestock and produce that reached Constantinople overland, and this did happen several times at the hands of the Avars and later the Bulghars long before the final Ottoman occupation. But to cut off the city from its European hinterland was not enough; unless the Anatolian shore was also controlled, foodstuffs and livestock could arrive from there by vessels as small as one-man rowing boats. The Asian shore of the Sea of Marmara did briefly fall under Persian control in 626, when the Avars and their Slav subjects held the Thracian side, and many parts of it were held by successive Arab expeditions in 674–678 and during the greatest Arab offensive of 717. But until the final Ottoman conquest, it was only threatened by occasional incursions. Even when both Thrace and the Asian shore were in enemy hands, as in 626, Constantinople could still be supplied by ship, at least from the Aegean side, if the Bosporus traffic was cut off. All this meant that Constantinople could not be starved into surrender, but it was only towards the end that it was reduced to a city-state, for which it was enough to survive siege.

An imperial capital with possessions scattered across the Mediterranean and with important outposts on the Black Sea needed much more: naval power. It was therefore the maritime dimension of Constantinople that was most important strategically, and in that respect its natural endowment was uniquely advantageous for reasons both obvious and not so obvious.

In the obvious category there is the Golden Horn (Haliç), a narrow inlet some 4 miles long, sheltered from the wind by the jutting hills of the northern shore. This was the finest natural harbour known to antiquity because it was calm in all weathers, while its entrance has no shallows and could be navigated without a pilot.

Along the shore of the Golden Horn there were the landing stages, quays, slipways, and shipyards of the Byzantine navy, merchant vessels, and local ferries. But the Propontis shore was also sheltered from winds from the north. Several harbours were built along that shore that gave more direct access to the heart of the city, including the landing stage of the palace of Bucoleon, on the edge of the acropolis at the end of the promontory that housed both the imperial palace and the great Church of the Holy Wisdom, Hagia Sophia.

The less obvious maritime attribute of the city was the 'Devil's current'. The Black Sea receives proportionately much more water from its great rivers than from the Mediterranean. There is therefore a surface current through the Bosporus that varies greatly in strength, with maximum speeds of up to 4 metres per second, or 8 knots, with half that speed quite common. That alone made it difficult or impossible for any ancient fleet to effect a landing directly onto the shore of the city jutting out into the Bosporus current. In addition, its large inflows of river water make the Black Sea less saline than the Mediterranean, and because of osmotic pressure there is a subsurface current into the Bosporus.

The interplay of the two currents, and the winds often channelled from the north by the Bosporus, result in a great deal of turbulence, which in turn gives a great advantage to sailors with local expertise. This was an important factor in the defeat of foreign fleets that came to attack Constantinople. With such an excellent base, the Byzantine navy could defend Constantinople, even if outnumbered, by keeping away enemy fleets and preventing landings, and also by bringing reinforcements from anywhere in the empire, both in its own transports and in enlisted merchant vessels. Constantinople was also the greatest base complex of the Byzantine army, with its standing forces of horse guards and foot guards, workshops for the manufacture of armour, weapons, uniforms, and footwear, and the imperial breeding stables. Accordingly, the Byzantine navy was more often employed to convey imperial forces from Constantinople to active fronts around the empire than to bring troops to reinforce the city garrison.

The sources for the history of the Byzantine navy are scant,[17] but even our fragmentary knowledge of individual naval actions and expeditions is sufficient to determine all that needs to be resolved here—that when Constantinople was in good working order as a political capital and naval base, as it mostly was, it was secure from naval attack even on the largest scale. In 717 the greatest Arab offensive mobilized vessels in all the seaports of the eastern Mediterranean to fill the Propontis with warships and transports, yet it too failed.

The triangular promontory of Constantinople has no natural barriers that defend its broad base. Accordingly, when Constantine established his new Rome, work started on a wall reinforced with towers from the Plateia Gate on the Golden Horn to what became the gate of St Aemilianus on the Propontis side. When an earthquake damaged parts of the Constantinian Wall in 408, construction began on what would eventually become the Theodosian Wall 1.5 kilometres further out, and extending some 5.5 kilometres from the Propontis coast to the suburb of Blachernae near the Golden Horn. From the start, it was not just a wall; it was a complete defensive system consisting of three walls (two of them reinforced with ninety-six towers each), a roadway, and a moat—a formidable combination of synergistic barriers. Taken as a whole, the moats, walls, and towers of the Theodosian land wall amounted to a very effective 'force multiplier', in modern parlance, because they could greatly magnify the defensive capacity of any reasonably adequate garrison. Any properly built fortification can be a force multiplier, but the Theodosian Wall system was by far the most effective fortification in the world for centuries thereafter, and of strategic significance in itself.

It was noted at the start of this chapter that the eastern empire was disadvantaged as compared to its western counterpart because of its lack of strategic depth. That is why Constantinople had to function concurrently as the magnificent capital of a great empire and as a fortress that had to look to its own protection. During the fifth century, the Byzantines added another fortified perimeter between Constantinople and the northern threat: the Long Wall, or Wall of Anastasios, which extended for 45 kilometres from the Sea of Marmara 6 kilometres above Selymbria (Silivri) to the Black Sea coast at what is now Evcik İskelesi. It was the great virtue of the Long Wall that it formed a defensive perimeter 65 kilometres beyond the Theodosian Wall, giving much more depth to the defence of Constantinople. If properly manned by sentries and patrols, the Long Wall could stop bandits, small groups of marauders, and localized attacks. On a larger scale, it offered a secure base for field armies sent to intercept enemies at a dignified distance from the capital, instead of allowing them to come right up to its walls.

The great defect of the Long Wall was that the geography was unfavourable: to provide 65 kilometres of depth beyond the Theodosian Wall, it had to extend 45 kilometres in length, and required a commensurate garrison of at least 10,000 to provide an adequate number of sentries, patrols, and reaction units. In the preface to one of Justinian's laws, it is noted that two quite senior officials were in charge of the wall, which implies a substantial establishment.[18] This is certainly the reason why the Long Wall was abandoned in the early seventh century if not before. So it was with very little strategic depth that Constantinople was successfully defended by the garrisons of the Theodosian Wall for almost 800 years.

JUSTINIAN'S REVERSAL REVERSED: VICTORY AND PLAGUE

Sabbatius Iustinianus, our Justinian I or Justinian the Great, St Justinian the Emperor of the Orthodox Church, was born a peasant's child in what is now Macedonia, yet came easily to the throne, having long served as assistant, understudy, co-emperor, and increasingly the effective ruler for his uncle Justin I (518–527). When he was formally enthroned in 527, seventy-seven years had passed since the end of the reign of Theodosios II, and its strategic innovations had been absorbed, consolidated, and institutionalized to good effect.

The empire was much stronger than it had been in 450, but still needed the Long Wall and the Theodosian Wall to protect Constantinople, not against large-scale invasions but rather against plunder raids from across the Danube.

The Sassanian empire of Persia remained the permanent strategic threat, undiminished by mutual respect, frequent negotiations, and formal treaties, including the 'endless peace' of 532. Persistent vigilance and a readiness to deploy reinforcements quickly were always necessary, if often insufficient, to contain Sassanian power in the Caucasus, across contested Armenia and the entire eastern front down to southern Syria. On the other hand, there was no longer any rival power north of Constantinople or beyond the Danube, while across the Adriatic the Ostrogothic kingdom of Italy desired good relations with the empire; at least some of its elite even wanted reunion under the empire. The Vandals and Alans who had conquered Africa in the last century were still there, but no longer threatened naval expeditions against Egypt. As for the dangers of the great Eurasian steppe, the nearest warlike nomads were the Turkic Kutrigurs[19] in what is now Ukraine, at worst a nuisance rather than an irresistible force as Attila's Huns had been.

More powerful steppe enemies were on their way, so it was more important that by the time of Justinian the warriors of the steppe had irreversibly lost their tactical superiority. The imperial army had undergone its tactical revolution, mastering the difficult technique of mounted archery with powerful composite reflex bows while retaining close-combat skills with sword and thrusting lance. Even if their archery could not quite match the best that the Hun mercenaries with them could exhibit, Byzantine troopers could no longer be outclassed tactically. The steppe warriors had also lost much of their operational superiority, because the imperial army had adopted agile cavalry tactics, and what individual riders may have lacked in virtuoso horsemanship could be compensated by the greater resilience of their disciplined and cohesive units.

This also meant, of course, that the imperial army now had tactical and operational superiority over the Vandals and Alans of Africa and the Ostrogoths of Italy. The Alans were primarily horsemen; Vandals and Goths were formidable fighters at close quarters, fully capable of organizing major expeditions and not unskilled in sieges, but all now found themselves lacking in missile capability and battlefield mobility. Prokopios of Caesarea, who was there, reports how Belisarios, Justinian's celebrated commander, explained the difference that made:

> practically all the Romans and their allies, the Huns [Onogur mercenaries], are good mounted bowmen, but not a man among the Goths has had practice in this branch, for their horsemen are accustomed to use only spears and swords, while their archers enter battle on foot and under cover of the heavy-armed men [to ward off cavalry charges]. So the horsemen, unless the engagement is at close quarters, have no means of defending themselves against opponents who use the bow, and therefore can easily be reached by the arrows and destroyed; and as for the foot-soldiers, they can never be strong enough to make sallies against men on horseback.[20]

This was only tactics, not strategy, but without this advantage it may be doubted whether Justinian would have embarked on his plan of reconquest, first of North Africa in 533–534 and then of Italy from 535.

Modern historians almost unanimously assert that he was excessively ambitious and that his conquests overextended the empire—true enough in retrospect, though only because of unforeseeable catastrophe. Not even his harshest critics consider Justinian a fool, or irrational, or incapable of sober calculation, but he was severely constrained by logistics.[21] The inescapable fact was the impossibility of sending large armies by sea. In the biggest expedition, Belisarios set out from Constantinople to what is now Tunisia in the summer of 533 with some 10,000 infantry and 8,000 cavalry carried in 500 transport ships manned by 30,000 crewmen and escorted by ninety-two war galleys.[22] It was certainly a most impressive armada, but 18,000 soldiers were not enough to take on the Vandals and Alans in North Africa, let alone the Ostrogoths, whose fighting manpower was sustained by the resources of the whole of Italy.

It could only be done, and then only just, with the tactical and operational advantages of manoeuvre with forces of mounted bowmen: it also required a successful theatre strategy, and good generalship overall. Justinian was famously well served by talented field commanders, especially the eunuch Narses, who was perhaps the better tactician, and the more celebrated Belisarios of the many stratagems and ingenuities. Belisarios is still remembered today by unlettered Romans for his improvised floating mills powered by the current of the Tiber that ground corn into flour during the siege of 537–538. Successful stratagems are the classic force multipliers, and it was with Belisarios that they first became a Byzantine speciality, along with his systematic avoidance of attrition and maximum exploitation of manoeuvre.

In the record of both the Vandal and the Gothic wars left by his secretary Prokopios, an admirer but not uncritical, we read how Belisarios would undertake long marches on more perilous routes to avoid the expected direction, and reach instead the enemy's flank or, better, his rear, and we read how he was willing to hazard the most risky stratagems to avoid direct assaults. To win with few against many, he replaced the mass he lacked with high-pay-off, high-risk manoeuvres and bold surprise actions, *coups de main* that all would praise in the successful aftermath, but which were gambles indeed.

Stratagems aside, it was mostly its archery as well as good tactics that enabled the Byzantine army to defeat enemies with larger numbers quite regularly. In an authoritative reconstruction of two major battles of the Italian campaign, at Tadinae, or Busta Gallorum, on the Via Flaminia in what is now Umbria in 552, and at the River Casilinus, now Volturno, near Naples in 554, the Byzantine forces commanded by Narses included assorted foreign contingents of Lombards, Heruls, and even Persians. In both cases, it was the bowmen of the imperial army who made the critical difference in the crucial phase of the fight with their volleys of powerfully lethal arrows.[23]

In sum, the army's tactical and operational superiority was the *sufficient condition* for the two campaigns of North Africa and Italy; the *necessary condition* was the negotiated peace with the Sassanian Persians.[24] Italy was hardly restored to a better condition (*in melius convertere*) by being liberated from the Ostrogoths in fighting that lasted until 552 through many destructive vicissitudes. From 568 the Lombard invasion started a new round of destructive fighting, which began only after Justinian's death in 565, and long after the unforeseeable catastrophe that invalidated all his strategic plans.

Whatever the future held, Justinian achieved his ambitions almost in full. His forces conquered North Africa from Tunis through coastal Algeria to what is now the northern tip of Morocco, thus reaching the Atlantic; and, across the straits, a coastal slice of the Iberian peninsula in what is now south-east Spain; all the islands of the western Mediterranean—the Balearics, Corsica, Sardinia, and Sicily; and all of Italy. Except for a tract of the Iberian coast and the southern coast of Gaul, where no rival naval power existed in any case, the entire Mediterranean was once again a Mare Nostrum, with none to contest the Byzantine navy.

Nor was this the achievement of a military adventurer, but merely the military dimension of even broader ambitions. Justinian was notoriously indefatigable, demonstrably very intelligent, unchallenged by rivals, and quite unfettered by conventions—he married a woman with the social status of an ex-prostitute. He also had two more attributes that empowered him greatly: a full treasury at his accession, and a particular talent in finding the especially talented to serve him. Thus, Justinian could have been an even more successful version of Anastasios, who ruled for twenty-seven years, built a great deal including the Long Wall and the fortress city of Dara, lost no wars, reduced taxes, yet supposedly left 320,000 pounds of gold in the treasury for his successor, Justin.[25]

But Justinian had much larger aims. In the legal sphere, he set out to codify all the extant *costitutiones*, imperial pronouncements with the force of law. Theodosios II had also issued a codification, but it was incomplete, while Justinian's code, already published in 529, which implies that it was started as soon as he gained the throne, collated all the *costitutiones* in the Theodosian code with those in two unofficial collections, adding more recent laws including his own to produce the *Codex Iustinianus*, in twelve books. The lawyer Tribonian was in charge, another of Justinian's highly talented appointments. Tribonian was also the chief author of the *Pandectae, Pandektes*, or *Digesta*, the jurisprudential treatise that followed the Codex, which contains in fifty books the legal opinions on all manner of cases of thirty-nine legal experts, notably Ulpian and Paulus. Once issued with official authority, the Digest became in effect an additional code of jurist-made law, not dissimilar from the body of English common law—except that Romans were involved, hence the code is organized. Tribonian and his colleagues next produced a much shorter work, the *Institutiones*, in four books, a manual of legal training. By 534 the *Codex Iustinianus* was issued in a new edition with corrections and additions, including Justinian's laws issued in the interim, and 168 new laws, *novellae*, mostly in Greek, were added by the time Justinian died in 565.

The sum total has been known since the sixteenth century as the *Corpus Iuris Civilis*. Long before then, by the end of the eleventh century, it was rediscovered in Italy and came to form the foundation of canon law, of secular legal studies at Bologna and of the first real university along with them, and of the Western jurisprudence that now extends worldwide. The continued use of untranslated Latin in English and even more in American courts—*sine die, nolle prosequi, ad litem, res iudicata*, etc.—symbolizes a much deeper persistence; these phrases all come from the *Digesta* of the *Corpus Iuris Civilis*.

Equally vast and equally successful was Justinian's ambition in the realm of public works. Prokopios wrote an entire book, *Peri Ktismaton* ('On Buildings'), to describe the churches, fortresses, and all else that Justinian built or enhanced—sometimes attributing to him the edifices of other emperors. But we know that under Justinian dozens of fortresses and other fortifications were built, or substantially rebuilt, in many parts of the empire, and that thirty-nine churches were built or rebuilt in Constantinople alone, including the great church of Hagia Sophia, whose immense floating dome still amazes visitors, and whose design is reproduced with varying degrees of fidelity and felicity in thousands of churches all over the world. From the detailed description in Prokopios of how Hagia Sophia was built, we learn that the men chosen by Justinian in person to build a radically innovative building, Anthemios of Tralles and Isidore of Miletus, used mathematical engineering to calculate the statics of the delicately counter-weighted dome.[26] Once again the talented Justinian had found exceptional talents to realize his inordinate ambitions, and the evidence remains intact in Istanbul to prove that he was highly successful, just as it does in his ambitious jurisprudential project, whose influence is even wider now than it was at his death in 565.

So why were Justinian's military ambitions different? That they were not grossly unrealistic we know from the simple fact that the maritime expedition sent in 533 to conquer Africa was neither shipwrecked nor defeated on arrival, so that what is now Tunisia and coastal Algeria were duly conquered. The conquest of Italy from the Ostrogoths, which started in 535, was a much more demanding undertaking, but it too was successfully completed in May 540, when Belisarios entered the Ostrogothic capital and last refuge of Ravenna to accept the surrender of King Witiges, or Vitigis, and his wife, Mathesuentha.

As noted, most modern historians hold that Justinian's military ambitions were unrealistic, because they exceeded the capacity of the empire to sustain them. One year after Belisarios ceremoniously concluded his Italian war in May 540, because no powerful garrison remained in Italy to control them, the Goths were able to start fighting again, and with increasing success once Totila became their king. One established explanation is that Justinian did not reinforce Belisarios and his army because he was 'afraid of the threat that a mighty general could pose'.[27] Even Rome was lost in 546 to the Gothic counter-offensive that persisted until 552. And because Sassanian Persia had repudiated the 'endless peace' treaty to resume fighting in 540, continuing with interruptions until 562, the empire had to sustain simultaneously two large-scale wars on widely separated fronts, so that in 559 hardly any troops were left in Constantinople to fight off an incursion of Kutrigurs and Slavs. That was certainly evidence of overextension, and presaged an inability to defend the Danubian frontier and the Balkan peninsula with it, and therefore Greece also, from Avar invasions and Slav occupations.

The charge of overextension therefore implies a charge of strategic incompetence, or more simply a lack of ordinary common sense: having himself inherited a war with the perpetually aggressive Sassanians when he came to the throne, Justinian had to know that the Persian front had to be well guarded at all times, in peace as in war. What military strength was left would be needed for the 'northern front' of the empire, from Dalmatia to the Danube, which was not under attack in 533 but which was bound to be attacked sooner or later, as the turbulence of peoples continued beyond the imperial frontiers. That northern front was indeed the primary defence perimeter of the empire; it protected the valuable sub-Danubian lands all the way to the Adriatic, and shielded Greece as well as Thrace and therefore Constantinople itself. The northern front also contained prime recruiting grounds for the imperial army, including the village near the fort of Bederiana where Justinian himself was born and lived his first years when he was still called Sabbatius.

To launch expeditions far away, even to conquer the rich grain fields of Africa and the hallowed first Rome, while neglecting the defence of the very hinterland of the imperial capital, was therefore a strategic error so gross that it betokens a foolish mind—not the mind of the Justinian we know. It is true, of course, that history is the record of the crimes and follies of mankind, and many a foolish war of conquest has been launched since 553.

But there is an altogether different explanation, based on evidence in part very old and in part very new—so new that it is not yet incorporated in the broader research on Justinian and his wars, let alone more general histories.[28] Entirely new historical evidence of large significance is very rare, and almost always the product of fortunate digging. That is true in this case also, even if the evidence itself is neither epigraphic nor numismatic, or conventionally archaeological, for it consists of skeletal DNA and ice cores.

First the old evidence. In book 2, chapter 22, of the *History of the Wars* of Prokopios, we read:

> During these times [from 541] there was a pestilence, by which the whole human race came near to being annihilated. Now in the case of all other scourges sent from Heaven some explanation of a cause might be given by daring men . . . But for this calamity it is quite impossible either to express in words or to conceive in thought any explanation . . . For it did not come in a part of the world nor upon certain men, nor did it confine itself to any season of the year, so that from such circumstances it might be possible to find subtle explanations of a cause, but it embraced the entire world . . . It started from the Aegyptians who dwell in Pelusium. Then it divided and moved . . . And in the second year it reached Byzantium in the middle of the spring, where it happened that I was staying at the time. . . . With the majority it came about that they were seized by the disease without becoming aware of what was coming. . . . They had a sudden fever . . . And the body showed no change from its previous color, nor was it hot as might be expected when attacked by a fever, nor did any inflammation set in . . . It was natural, therefore, that not one of those who had contracted the disease expected to die from it. But on the same day in some cases, in others on the following day, and in the rest not many days later, a bubonic swelling developed . . . not only in [the groin] . . . but also inside the armpit, and in some cases also beside the ears . . . . there ensued for some a deep coma, with others a violent delirium . . . Death came in some cases immediately, in others after many days, and with some the body broke out with black pustules about as large as a lentil and these did not survive even one day but all succumbed immediately. With many also a vomiting of blood ensued . . . and straightaway brought death . . . [29]

In the next chapter, 23, we come to the demographic consequences:

> Now the disease in Byzantium ran a course of four months, and its greatest virulence lasted about three. And at first the deaths were a little more than the normal, then the mortality rose still higher, and afterwards [the number of] dead reached five thousand each day, and again it even came to ten thousand and still more than that . . . [30]

Three months, or ninety days, of the greatest virulence at 5,000 a day comes to 450,000; if we take the 10,000 estimate, we reach 900,000, and Prokopios mentions a still-higher daily mortality, yielding seemingly impossible numbers. When writing as a historian and not as a polemicist, Prokopios is generally deemed a trustworthy source by his modern colleagues, but on the subject of the pandemic he was wrongly suspected, for two different reasons. First, in an age without statistics there were no mortality figures to peruse and incorporate in a text, while impressionistic assessments of the effects of epidemics are notoriously misleading—anyone who read prose accounts of the early years of AIDS in the United States would never guess that it had insignificant demographic effects. The second reason acquired greater resonance with the advent of structuralist approaches to the study of texts. Like any sane person, Prokopios immensely admired Thucydides, and tried to write in his prose, by then a millennium removed from the common Greek of his day. Thucydides famously wrote of the plague of his own days most poignantly (in book 2, as now edited) and Prokopios clearly strove to echo his prose.[31] Hence his testimony is wrongly discounted.[32]

Of course, it is universally accepted that there was a pandemic, and a very severe one, not only because Prokopios was trusted that far, but also because other extant contemporary texts concur.[33] One such is by Evagrius Scholasticus of Antioch;[34] he too refers to Thucydides. But uncontaminated sources also depict an unprecedented catastrophe, notably the *Chronicle of Pseudo-Dionysius of Tel-Mahre*, which was written in Syriac (late eastern Aramaic), in eighth-century Mesopotamia, but which preserves a lost contemporary text on the pandemic specifically written by the prelate and historian John of Ephesus. Under the Seleucid year 855 (= 543/4) the text reads, 'there was a great and mighty plague in the whole world in the days of the emperor Justinian'.[35] The chronicler then lists the affected provinces of the empire: all the Egyptian provinces and Palestine as far as the Red Sea, Cilicia, Mysia, Syria, Iconium (Konya, central Anatolia), Bithynia, Asia (western Anatolia), Galatia, and Cappadocia.[36]

This is no mere literary emulation but rather the recollection of a demographic catastrophe. And it would also have been an institutional catastrophe: when half the soldiers of cohesive army units become casualties, those units do not lose half their combat capability but all of it, or almost. All components of the imperial military system—tax collection offices, central administrative commands, weapons workshops, supply depots, fortress construction teams, warships and fleets, and army units everywhere—would have been in the same predicament, with their surviving personnel much more likely to have scattered to flee the pandemic or to tend to sick survivors, or simply shocked into immobility, or weakened by the disease, or just demoralized, so that 50 per cent mortality would have caused more than 50 per cent incapacitation.

The old narrative evidence would thus immediately explain why Justinian's military capabilities declined so drastically from 541, irremediably ruining his ambitious plans. But that evidence could not be conclusive because it was devoid of credible, comprehensive figures. Hence it has been said that Prokopios exaggerated. In the account of Justinian in the latest edition of the most authoritative survey of late antiquity, the principal evidence is presented—including fiscal legislation necessitated by the death of many taxpayers—but the implication is that it was just another disaster ('there were other disasters, notably earthquakes, one of which destroyed the famous law school at Berytus') whose consequences were incremental: 'Justinian's difficulties were increased by a severe outbreak of bubonic plague . . . '.[37]

The new evidence, which comes in two parts, definitely proves that Prokopios was accurate: it was not just another outbreak of disease, not just another disaster soon assuaged, it was a historically unprecedented pandemic that may well have killed even more than one-third of the population, radically altering the strategic situation.

First, a study published in 2005 contains the first definitive DNA evidence that the disease of Justinian's pandemic was caused by an exceptionally virulent *and* exceptionally lethal biovar of *Yersinia pestis*, the bubonic plague.[38] That is an entirely different disease from the plague narrated by Thucydides or any other malady known until then. When *Yersinia pestis* reappeared as the agent of the Black Death from *c.*1334 in China and from 1347 in Europe, some residual acquired immunity would have persisted, but for the populations of the empire in 541 it was an entirely new pathogen against which none had acquired any immunity, as opposed to much less prevalent natural resistance.

Hence the pathogen was exceptionally virulent; that is, its ability to cause the disease was very high—a single bite from a flea carrying *Yersinia pestis* in 541 was enough to infect, which is certainly not the case with established pathogens, because many people have acquired immunities against them. Infection rates of 90 per cent or more were therefore possible for people in contact with fleas, which meant practically everyone in antiquity. Justinian contracted the disease, as did our witness Evagrius among other survivors. To be sure, virulence is one thing, lethality another. Actually, for obvious reasons, highly virulent diseases are not usually highly lethal: common influenza biovars kill minimal numbers of their many victims. But that was not true of the biovar of *Yersinia pestis* in 541 because it was entirely new for the affected population—a lethality of 30 per cent or even as much as 50 per cent was thus very likely, at least in well-connected parts of the empire, though not in remote backwaters of course.

A second stream of new evidence indicates that what could have happened, did in fact happen. Climatology is now infected by partisan polemics, but ice-core studies that show rising carbon dioxide levels in the atmosphere over the last 10,000 years are undisputed. According to an 'anthropogenic' explanation offered by an eminent climatologist with much persuasive evidence, agricultural deforestation, which replaces natural greenery with bare planted fields and increasing livestock herds, especially methane-producing cattle, has measurably contributed to rising levels of carbon dioxide over the last several thousand years. In any case, carbon dioxide levels in the ice show two abrupt and drastic declines, one of which correlates with *c.*541, providing independent evidence of an unprecedented demographic collapse, which would have caused the widespread reversion of cleared fields to natural greenery, and the predation of abandoned cattle—imperial territories still had populations of wolves, bears, lions, and cheetahs, and also Caspian tigers in eastern Anatolia.[39] The climatological evidence is more decisive than the archaeological evidence, but the latter is perfectly consistent. A recent overview concludes: 'the expansion of settlement that had characterized much of rural and urban Syria in the fifth and early sixth centuries came to an abrupt end after the middle of the sixth century. There is evidence that housing starts almost ceased.'[40]

Taken together, the new biological evidence and the climatological theory compel a reassessment of the realism of Justinian's ambitions. He could have been as successful in his military ambitions as he was in his jurisprudential and architectural ambitions. It was not overextension but *Yersinia pestis* that wrecked the empire, drastically diminishing its military strength as compared to that of enemies less affected. The invaders were less infected because they were less urbanized, or simply less organized to begin with, hence less vulnerable to institutional breakdown.

Quite suddenly, with frontiers denuded of their defenders (the post-541 disappearance of coinage from Byzantine military sites on the frontiers of Syria and Arabia has long been attested, if misunderstood[41]), with strongholds abandoned, once prosperous provinces desolate, and its own administrative machinery greatly enfeebled, the empire found itself in a drastically altered world, in which the nomads of the steppe and the desert were greatly favoured as compared to empires, and in which the less urbanized Persian empire was relatively favoured also.

Still, what Justinian did would not have been done by his successors. It was his policy to destroy totally the power of the Vandal conquerors of Africa, and he succeeded. Therefore, when the native tribes started raiding from the desert and the hills of the Aurès, there was no pliant Vandal militia to resist them, let alone a functioning Vandal client state, so the overburdened imperial army had to fight them instead. Likewise, there were promising opportunities for a negotiated acquisition of Italy instead of an invasion followed by all-out war to destroy the Ostrogothic power. The landing of Byzantine troops from reconquered Sicily to the mainland of Italy in 535 was preceded by secret negotiations with King Theodahad. One proposal would have retained him as client ruler of a dependent state, another would have seen him off with the award of landed estates yielding 86,400 *solidi* a year, the income of 43,200 poor men. Justinian's successors would have found such a compromise solution, but he rejected all compromise—before the pandemic. After it, Justinian too had no other choice but to revert to the embryonic Theodosian strategy of avoiding war by paying off enemies if necessary.

When the Turkic Kutrigurs of the Pontic steppe under their leader Zabergan mounted raids in 558 that penetrated Greece and approached Constantinople, indulging in the usual outrages that allowed Agathias Scholasticus to indulge himself and his readers ('well-born women of chaste life were most cruelly carried off to undergo the worst of all misfortunes, and minister to the unbridled lust of the barbarians', etc. etc.),[42] Justinian called out Belisarios from retirement (he was 53) to repel them with ceremonial palace guards, 300 veterans, and a mob of volunteers, but then took more decisive action by enlisting the aid of the leader of the Utrigurs.[43] The alternative of waging war could be very successful tactically and operationally, but even in total victory the only definite result would be the cost of it, while the benefit would only be temporary, as the demise of one enemy merely made room for another.[44] It is hard to imagine that the empire could have overcome the ensuing century of acute internal crises and devastating invasions without its new strategy. It generated disproportionate power by magnifying the strength obtainable from greatly diminished forces, and by combining that military strength with varied means and techniques of persuasion.

CONCLUSION: BYZANTINE STRATEGY

All states have a grand strategy, whether they know it or not. That is inevitable because grand strategy is simply the *level* at which knowledge and persuasion, or in modern terms intelligence and diplomacy, interact with military strength to determine the outcomes in a world of other states, with their own 'grand strategies'. The Byzantines had no central planning staffs to produce documents in the modern manner, including the recent innovation of formal statements of 'national strategy' that attempts to define 'interests', the means to protect and enhance them, and the alignment of the two in rational or at least rationalized terms. But they assuredly had a grand strategy, even if it was never stated explicitly, and it was applied so repeatedly that one may even extract a Byzantine 'operational code'. The key elements are nowhere stated in any Byzantine source as compressively as in what follows, but can be inferred legitimately on the basis of observed behaviour, as well as the recommendations of Byzantine guide-books and field manuals. A normative summary that minimizes duplication is one way of defining an operational code.

Avoid war by every possible means in all possible circumstances, but always be ready to fight at any time. Train both individual recruits and complete formations intensively, exercise units against each other, prepare weapons and supplies to be ready for battle, but do not be eager to fight. The highest purpose of maximum combat-readiness is to reduce the probability of having to fight at all.

Gather intelligence on the enemy, his means, and his mentality, and monitor his movements continuously. Patrols and reconnaissance probes by light cavalry units are always necessary, but not sufficient. Spies are needed inside the enemy territory to provide early warning of war threats, or at least to report preparations for war, and help divine enemy intentions. In between reconnaissance by combat units and espionage in civilian garb, the middle layer of intelligence gathering is often the most productive: clandestine scouting, that is, passive observation and reporting. Efforts to scout and prevent enemy scouting are seldom wasted.

Campaign vigorously, both offensively and defensively, but attack mostly with small units; emphasize patrolling, raiding, and skirmishing rather than all-out attacks. Avoid battle, and especially large-scale battle, except in very favourable circumstances—and even then avoid battle if possible—unless the enemy has somehow fallen into a condition of complete inferiority, as in the case of a fleet badly damaged by storms.

Replace battles of attrition with 'non-battles' of manoeuvre. On the defensive, do not confront superior forces head-on; instead, fall back or sidestep invading armies, remaining just beyond their reach to pounce quickly on outnumbered detachments and baggage trains, and to intercept looting parties. Prepare ambushes large and small in the path of enemy forces, and lure them in by feigned retreats. On the offensive, mount raids, but without persisting if they encounter stiff resistance. Rely on constant activity to demoralize and materially weaken the enemy over time.

Strive to end wars successfully by recruiting allies to change the overall balance of power. Diplomacy is therefore even more important in war than at peace—not for the Byzantines the foolish aphorism that when the guns speak, diplomats fall silent. In recruiting allies to attack the enemy, *his* allies are the most useful recruits, because they are likely to know how best to fight his forces. Enemy commanders successfully subverted to serve the imperial interest are even better allies, and the best of all might be found at the enemy's court, or within his family. But even peripheral allies that can only help a little are worth recruiting in most cases.

Subversion is the best path to victory. It is so cheap as compared to the costs and risks of battle that it must always be attempted, even with the most unpromising targets infused with hostility or religious ardour. When facing an imminent jihadi offensive, the strategos is advised to befriend the emirs of the frontier castles, sending them 'gift baskets'. No exception was to be made for known fanatics: the Byzantines had discovered that religious fanatics could also be bribed, being especially creative in inventing religious justifications for taking bribes (with Islam's victory inevitable in any case why not . . .).

When diplomacy and subversion are not enough and there must be fighting, it should be done with 'relational' operational methods and tactics that circumvent enemy strengths and exploit enemy weaknesses. To avoid consuming the major combat forces, it may be necessary to patiently whittle down the enemy's moral and material strength. That may require much time. But there is no urgency because, as soon as one enemy is no more, another will surely take his place, for all is constantly changing as rulers and nations rise and fall.

The operational code here outlined allows for no historical evolution. Having claimed that the construct here called 'Byzantine strategy' was invented during the fifth century in response to the specific circumstances of the time, I recognize that the very different circumstances of subsequent centuries left their mark on Byzantine strategy. It is a lesser claim that is here advanced—that there was enough continuity to define an 'operational code'. Strategic practice is not the mere application of techniques that could be applied anywhere and by anyone: it is always the expression of an entire culture. But the strategic culture of Byzantium is in part applicable even today, or perhaps especially today.

The genius of Byzantine grand strategy was to turn the very multiplicity of enemies to advantage by employing diplomacy, deception, pay-offs, and religious conversion to induce them to fight one another instead of fighting the empire. Only the Byzantine rulers' firm self-image as the only defenders of the only true faith preserved their moral equilibrium. In the Byzantine scheme of things, military strategy was subordinated to diplomacy instead of the other way round, and was used mostly to contain, punish, or intimidate rather than to attack or defend with full force.

NOTES

1. For more detailed studies of the subject, see my *The Grand Strategy of the Byzantine Empire* (London, 2009) and its predecessor, *The Grand Strategy of the Roman Empire: From the First Century A.D. to the Third* (Baltimore, 1976).

2. For an overview, see A. D. Lee, 'The Eastern Empire: Theodosius to Anastasius', in *The Cambridge Ancient History* (*CAH*), xiv, ed. A. Cameron, B. Ward-Perkins, and M. Whitby (Cambridge, 2000), 34.

3. R. C. Blockley, *East Roman Foreign Policy: Formation and Conduct from Diocletian to Anastasius* (Leeds, 1992), 56.

4. C. Toumanoff, 'Armenia and Georgia', in *The Cambridge Medieval History*, iv/1, ed. J. M. Hussey (Cambridge, 1966), 593.

5. See A. Cameron, 'Vandal and Byzantine Africa', in *CAH* xiv. 553.

6. O. J. Maenchen-Helfen, *The World of the Huns* (Berkeley, 1973), 125.

7. In an immense literature, see A. M. Khazanov, *Nomads and the Outside World*, 2nd edition (Madison, WI, 1994), 69, on the 'non-autarky of the pastoral economy'.

8. *Excerpta de Legationibus Gentium ad Romanos* 3, in R. C. Blockley, *The Fragmentary Classicising Historians of the Later Roman Empire* (Liverpool, 1983), ii. 237–9.

9. See J. Haldon, 'Blood and Ink: Some Observations on Byzantine Attitudes towards Warfare and Diplomacy', in J. Shepard and S. Franklin (eds), *Byzantine Diplomacy* (Aldershot, 1992), 281.

10. In a vast literature the standard work remains A. H. M. Jones, *The Later Roman Empire* (Oxford, 1964), i. 608.

11. The 'pseudo-Avar' question (in Theophylact Simocatta 7. 7. 10—which reads as a romanticized version of Menander's fragment 19. 1, Müller–Dindorf 43) is of scant interest; P. B. Golden, *Introduction to the History of the Turkic Peoples* (Wiesbaden, 1992), 109. Professor Golden was more definitive on the Avar–Jou jan connection in a personal communication, 23 Oct. 2003. See W. Pohl, *Die Awaren: Ein Steppenvolk in Mitteleuropa 567–822 n. Chr.* (Munich, 2002), 158.

12. Greek 'Outrigouroi' from 'Utur' or 'Otur Oghur' = the thirty Oghurs—clans or tribes; and 'Koutrigouroi' from 'Quturghur', from 'Toqur Oghur' = the nine Oghurs; Professor Golden, personal communication, 15 Apr. 2008.

13. See N. Koutrakou, 'Diplomacy and Espionage: Their Role in Byzantine Foreign Relations, 8th–10th Centuries', in J. Haldon (ed.), *Byzantine Warfare* (Princeton, 2007), 137; first pub. in *Graeco-Arabica*, 6 (1995), 125–44.

14. C. Mango, 'The Water Supply of Constantinople', in C. Mango and G. Dragon (eds), *Constantinople and its Hinterland* (Aldershot, 1995), 13.

15. Ibid. 16.

16. J. Durliat, 'L'Approvisionnement de Constantinople', in Mango and Dragon (eds), *Constantinople and its Hinterland*, 20.

17. Most recently collated in J. H. Pryor and E. M. Jeffreys, *The Age of the Dromon: The Byzantine Navy ca 500–1204* (Leiden, 2006); cf. the earlier H. Ahrweiler, *Byzance et la mer: La marine de guerre, la politique et les institutions maritimes de Byzance aux VIIe–XVe siècles* (Paris, 1966).

18. Novel 26: *De Praetore Thraciae, Praefatio*: 'In Longo enim Muro duos quosdam sedere vicarios . . .' (vicars, in effect deputy praetorian prefects); conveniently from <http:// web. upmf-grenoble.fr/Haiti/Cours/Ak/Corpus/Novellae.htm>.

19. Golden, *Introduction to the History of the Turkic Peoples*, 98–100; private communication from Professor Golden, 23 Mar. 2008.

20. Prokopios, *History of the Wars* 5. 27. 27–9, in *Procopius*, trans. H. B. Dewing (London, 1961–78), iii. 261.

21. Cf. the appraisal in A. Cameron, 'Justin I and Justinian', in *CAH* xiv. 67. (I wrote the above before reading Cameron.)

22. Prokopios, *History of the Wars* 3. 11. 2, in *Procopius*, trans. Dewing, ii. 101.

23. J. Haldon, *The Byzantine Wars: Battles and Campaigns of the Byzantine Era* (Stroud, 2001), 37–44.

24. As Justinian himself explained by way of incidental comment in the text of a new law on the administration of Cappadocia, 'We have undertaken such great labours, incurred so much expense, and fought such great wars, in consequence of which God has not only granted Us the enjoyment of peace with the Persians and the subjugation of the Vandals, the Alani, and the Moors, as well as enabled Us to recover all Africa and Sicily, but has also inspired Us with the hope of again uniting to Our dominions the other countries which the Romans lost by their negligence, after they had extended the boundaries of their Empire to the shores of both oceans, which countries We shall now, with Divine aid, hasten to restore to a better condition' (Novel 30: *De Proconsule Cappadociae*, ch. 11. 2).

25. See below for Long Wall and Dara. For the 320,000 pounds of gold, see *Anecdota* 19. 7, in *Procopius*, trans. Dewing, vi. 229.

26. *Buildings* 1. 1. 24, in *Procopius*, trans. Dewing, vii. 11.

27. J. Moorhead, 'The Byzantines in the West in the Sixth Century', in *The New Cambridge Medieval History*, i, ed. P. Fouracre (Cambridge, 2005), 127.

28. Not even the very recent book by Guy Halsall, *Barbarian Migrations and the Roman West, 376–568* (Cambridge, 2007), where the plague merely 'erodes morale' (504).

But now see L. K. Little (ed.), *Plague and the End of Antiquity: The Pandemic of 541–750* (Cambridge, 2006).

29. *Procopius*, trans. Dewing, 1. 451–65.
30. Ibid. 465.
31. Thucydides, *History of the Peloponnesian War*, trans. C. F. Smith (Cambridge, MA, 1951), chs 48 and 49, 343, 345.
32. Notably by J. Durliat, 'La Peste du VIme siècle, pour un nouvel examen des sources byzantins', in V. Kravan, J. M. Lefort, and C. Morrisson (eds), *Hommes et richesses dans l'Empire byzantin*, i (Paris, 1989), 107–19. For the historiographical context, see L. K. Little, 'Life and Afterlife of the First Plague Pandemic', in Little (ed.), *Plague and the End of Antiquity*, 3–32; and on Durliat, ibid. 17.
33. See, e.g. P. Allen, 'The 'Justinianic' Plague', *Byzantion*, 49 (1979), 5–20.
34. Evagrius Scholasticus of Antioch was a well-educated lawyer who had started his elementary education in 540, a year before the pandemic began, and who lost his wife, daughter, grandson, and other relatives in a later recurrence that he himself survived. Written *c.* 593, his *Ecclesiastical History* offers a description of the pandemic 'in its 52nd year'. He starts with the origins: 'It was said, and still is now, to have began from Ethiopia . . .'. Then he describes the symptoms: 'in some it began with the head, making eyes bloodshot and face swollen' (*The Ecclesiastical History of Evagrius Scholasticus*, trans. M. Whitby (Liverpool, 2000), 229–31).
35. The text then proceeds with a plangent jeremiad of laments: 'over corpses which split open and rotted in the streets with nobody to bury [them]; over houses large and small, beautiful and desirable which suddenly became tombs . . . over ships in the midst of the sea whose sailors were suddenly attacked . . . and became tombs . . . and they continued adrift in the waves . . . over bridal chambers where the brides were adorned, but all of a sudden there were just lifeless and fearsome corpses . . . Over highways which became deserted' (*Pseudo-Dionysius of Tel-Mahre, Chronicle: known also as The Chronicle of Zuqnin, Part III*, trans. W. Witakowski (Liverpool, 1996), 74–5).
36. The text records what 'we saw' on a journey from Syria all the way to Thrace beyond Constantinople: villages 'void of their inhabitants; staging-posts on the roads [checkpoints, and so relay posts of the imperial courier service] full of darkness and solitude filling with fright everyone who happened to enter and leave them; cattle abandoned and roaming scattered over the mountains with nobody to gather them; flocks of sheep, goats, oxen and pigs which had become like wild animals . . . fields in all the countries through which we passed from Syria to Thrace, abundant in grain which was becoming white and stood erect, but there was none to reap them' (*Pseudo-Dionysius of Tel-Mahre, Chronicle, Part III*, 80–1).
37. Cameron, 'Justin I and Justinian', 76, 77, order reversed.
38. A biovar similar to Orientalis; I. Wiechmann and G. Grupe, 'Detection of *Yersinia pestis* DNA in Two Early Medieval Skeletal Finds from Aschheim (Upper Bavaria, 6th Century AD)', *American Journal of Physical Anthropology*, 126 (2005), 48–55. It was earlier presumed that the biovar was Antiqua (so named because of the 541 pandemic), which persists and is less lethal.
39. See W. F. Ruddiman, 'The Anthropogenic Greenhouse Era Began Thousands of Years Ago', <http://courses.eas.ualberta.ca/eas457/Ruddiman2003.pdf>; see also 'Debate over the Early Anthropogenic Hypothesis', *Real Climate*, 5 Dec. 2005, <http://www.realclimate.org/index.php/archives/2005/12/early-anthropocene-hyppothesis>. In regard to predation, the last lion in Anatolia was killed in 1870; the last Caspian tiger was killed in 1959; a few cheetahs survive.
40. H. N. Kennedy, 'Justinianic Plague in Syria and the Archaeological Evidence', in Little (ed.), *Plague and the End of Antiquity*, 95.

41. R. Alston ('Managing the Frontiers: Supplying the Frontier Troops in the Sixth and Seventh Centuries', in P. Erdkamp (ed.), *The Roman Army and the Economy* (Amsterdam, 2002), 417) writes that in *Anecdota* 24. 12 Prokopios is malevolent (true) and exaggerating (not true).

42. Agathias Scholasticus, *Histories* 5. 2. J. B. Bury (born 1861), on whom we happily depend, must be allowed his titillation—it is the volume's longest citation; *History of the Later Roman Empire: From the Death of Theodosius I to the Death of Justinian* (New York, 1958), ii. 305.

43. ' . . . applying pressure to Sandilkh, the leader of the Utrigurs [other Ogur tribes]. He made continual attempts to rouse him somehow to war against Zabergan, sending a stream of embassies and trying various means to provoke him. . . . Justinian added in his own messages to Sandilkh that if he destroyed the Kutrigurs the Emperor would transfer to him all the yearly tribute—monies were paid by the Roman Empire to Zabergan. Therefore, Sandilkh, who wished to be on friendly terms with the Romans, replied that utterly to destroy one's fellow tribesmen was unholy and altogether improper, 'For they not only speak our language, dwell in tents like us, dress like us and live like us, but they are our kin, [Ogur Turks] even if they follow other leaders. Nevertheless we will deprive the Kutrigurs of their horses and take possession of them ourselves, so that without their mounts they will be unable to pillage the Romans.' This Justinian asked him to do; *Excerpta de Legationibus Romanorum ad Gentes* 1. 13–30, in *The History of Menander the Guardsman*, trans. R. C. Blockley (Liverpool, 1985), 43–5. On the Kutrigurs and Utrigurs, see Golden, *Introduction to the History of the Turkic Peoples*, 98–100.

44. *Excerpta de Legationibus Romanorum ad Gentes*, 4. 13. 7–13 in M. and M. Whitby, *The History of Theophylact Simocatta* (Oxford, 1986), 121–2. See W. E. Kaegi, *Byzantium and the Early Islamic Conquests* (Cambridge, 1992), 32.

4

The Hundred Years War, 1337–1453

Anne Curry

INTRODUCTION

The Hundred Years War is an artificial construction, but so standard has usage of the term become that readers might expect discussion of the strategy of the war as a single conflict. There was superficial unity throughout, in that English royal armies invaded and occupied France in the name of the English king's claim to the French throne; the French tried to stop them and to reconquer the territory they had taken.[1] Yet, given that the war is an invention, we could consider every campaign as having a separate and individual strategic aim. Both interpretations would be misleading. Wars have phases and this one was no exception.

The first phase (1337–60) displayed continuities with Anglo-French conflicts of the previous century over the landholdings of the English king in France. Not least, it began with the confiscation of these lands by the French king in May 1337, just as previous wars had been triggered. But, in contrast with earlier conflicts, Edward III was able to respond with a claim to the French crown itself, even though it was through the female line. The main question is whether and how this new element affected the strategies both sides pursued. The first phase ended with the Treaty of Brétigny in 1360, which extended English landholdings and made them independent of French feudal control. In return, Edward dropped his claim to the French throne. Within nine years, however, loopholes in the treaty enabled Charles V to confiscate Edward's lands once more. Not surprisingly, the latter responded by resuming the title 'king of France', a title his successors preserved.

The second phase lasted until a long truce was agreed in 1396, neither side having been able to gain the military upper hand, although the English had lost most of the territories won in 1360.

The third phase opened in 1415, when Henry V invaded Normandy. It saw major successes, which included the conquest of Normandy and the acceptance of Henry as heir to the French throne in the Treaty of Troyes of 1420. His son Henry VI was recognized as king in much of northern France, but the Valois claimant, Charles VII, was able to recover his position from 1429 onwards, thanks initially to the inspiration of Joan of Arc. The third phase ended between 1449 and 1453 when the English were driven out of all of their lands except for Calais, a town captured by Edward III in 1346.

Although English kings launched invasions of France after 1453 and only lost Calais in 1558, and although they called themselves kings of France until 1801, historians have not counted post-medieval wars as part of the Hundred Years War on the grounds that the English no longer had major territorial interests within France.

THE NATURE OF STRATEGY

Unlike later periods, there are relatively few explicit statements in contemporary sources about military strategies. At the level of grand strategy, rulers tended to make general pronouncements on the recovery of rights, the need to act against the evil intentions of the enemy, and so on. As for campaign planning and execution, assumptions have often to be made about intentions and plans, and strategy is mainly revealed by what happened. Therefore, the consideration of strategy in this chapter will be largely through the principal events of each phase.

We can also use the evidence of military organization. There were no standing armies. (That said, the intensity of invasions and occupations of France by the English did much to create a pool of professional soldiers, and the desire to drive out the English was the catalyst for the formation of a more regular French army from the mid-1440s onwards.) For every campaign a new army had to be raised. Therefore, the nature of the army is indicative of proposed strategy as well as anticipation of enemy response. The maintenance of garrisons and the building of fortifications is also a useful measure of defensive strategies.

In all phases, most of the action took place within France. It must not be forgotten, however, that from time to time the French tried to bring the war to the English by means of hit-and-run raids on the south coast and by actions at sea against transports and merchant shipping of the English and their allies. In addition, throughout the war the French maintained an offensive and defensive alliance with the Scots. This prompted Scottish raids of the north of England. Sometimes this was part of coordinated Franco-Scottish military action, most notably in 1346 (when the Scots invaded England as revenge for the French defeat at Crécy but were themselves defeated and their king captured at Neville's Cross) and in 1385 (when a French army was sent to Scotland to launch an invasion of England alongside Scottish forces). This created an important second front for the English (not least as they had been at war with the Scots since the late thirteenth century), but it was not the only international dimension. Throughout the war, English and French kings sought alliances with continental rulers in order to implement their strategies. In turn, allies sought to pursue their own aims vicariously by giving assistance to one or the other side in the principal Anglo-French conflict.

Military strategy was therefore strongly influenced by international relations, not least in the choice of theatre, although this also led to competition for resources between different theatres. The Hundred Years War was a truly international conflict, arguably the first pan-European war.[2] In the second phase of the war, and even in the ostensible years of peace between 1360 and 1369, the French and English fought each other outside France, most notably in the Iberian peninsula and in Flanders (technically part of France but an area whose counts and towns were powerful enough to pursue their own interests).

The war also assumed a religious dimension when the protagonists supported rival popes during the papal schism (1378–1417). The war of words, an integral part of medieval strategy as much as in other periods, escalated into full crusading ideology and justified English invasions of Flanders and of Castile in the name of a war against schismatics.

Political divisions within France, in particular the civil war between Armagnacs and Burgundians in the early fifteenth century, also heavily influenced English strategies. Between 1419 and 1435, the English and Burgundians pursued a joint military strategy, best symbolized, perhaps, by the joint force detailed to the capture of Joan of Arc at Compiègne in May 1430.

The war is characterized therefore by a number of 'sideshows' enmeshed to a greater or lesser degree in the main Anglo-French debacle. Protagonists used informal means of waging war, such as encouraging privateering at sea, and entering into short-term deals with routiers on land to act on their behalf.[3]

The strategies of both the English and the French were heavily influenced by the legacy of the past.[4] They were already traditional enemies before the Hundred Years War because of the difficulties of the English king holding lands as the vassal of his French counterpart. By 1337, English-held territories were Guyenne (the coastal strip between Bordeaux and Bayonne, with an inland extension into the Dordogne) and Ponthieu (around the mouth of the Somme). This was but a shadow of the great Angevin empire of the twelfth century, which had also included Normandy, Anjou, Maine, and Poitou.[5] The English had given up their rights to these areas in 1259 but disputes persisted on the extent and status of their remaining lands.

English kings had a consistent grand strategy to remove French feudal over-lordship. Victory for the English consisted of gaining full sovereignty over their French lands but they were also keen to extend their territories. For instance, they retained a lingering desire to recover the lost lands of the Angevin empire: both Edward III and Henry V resurrected the title of duke of Normandy at particular stages of their wars to exploit Norman provincial separatism. They also exploited their claim to the throne of France to gain influence within France and on the European stage.

The grand strategy of French kings was to remove the English from France altogether. Philip IV and Charles IV had already triggered wars in 1294 and 1324, pursuing the same strategy as Philip II had done in 1202, and as Philip VI was to do in 1337 and Charles V in 1369. They assembled an army on the frontier, and as soon as the legal confiscation was proclaimed, they dispatched it swiftly and suddenly to seize English territory. This was medieval blitzkrieg, effective because the English could not afford to maintain garrisons in their lands and could only respond by sending an expeditionary army from England after the event. This remained a constraint during the Hundred Years War. The English established a stronger defensive provision in the fifteenth-century phase, but blitzkrieg tactics in 1449–53 enabled the French to achieve their long-standing ambition to remove the English from French soil.

Guyenne had almost been lost to the French in the war of 1294–7 when a French army took Bordeaux, but external pressures (not least the Flemish victory over the French at Courtrai in 1302) restored the status quo. In the war of 1324–7, the French fared less well militarily but in the peace treaty of 1327 secured the surrender of the key frontier area of the Agenais. For the ten years leading up to the outbreak of the Hundred Years War, there was a 'cold war' exacerbated by French diplomatic support for the exiled Bruce king of Scots at the very time Edward III was pursuing campaigns in Scotland in support of his puppet, the Balliol claimant. In this context, it is hardly surprising that Edward should seek to put pressure on the French by exploiting an advantage which none of his predecessors as kings of England had enjoyed—a claim to the throne of France itself.

THE FIRST PHASE, 1337–60

Given the recent deposition of Edward II (1327), the English had not been in a position to take advantage of Edward III's claim to the French throne at the death of Charles IV in 1328, but the new French king, Philip VI (1328–50), was certainly afraid that it might be exploited in the future. His strategy was to keep the English in check while he built up his own position. In this he was assisted by the political disarray in England, which had contributed to disadvantageous peace settlements with France in 1327 and Scotland in 1328. Philip forced Edward III to pay homage for his French lands by threatening to sequestrate their revenues. By paying homage in 1329, and confirming it in 1331, Edward publicly acknowledged Philip's kingship. Philip subsequently refused to negotiate further unless the Scots were included in any settlement, thereby interfering in matters that Edward considered to be his domestic concern.

Fissures deepened when Philip's erstwhile friend but now bitter enemy Robert of Artois went to England as an exile, and encouraged Edward to make more of his claim to the French throne. Both sides began to seek allies. The French aimed to pre-empt any military action on the part of Edward while preparing for invasion of Edward's French lands. In 1336, Philip ordered his fleet to be brought from the Mediterranean to the north coast, thereby stimulating an invasion scare in England. He continued to emphasize his feudal rights over English lands in France and used the presence of Robert of Artois in England as a *casus belli* by summoning Edward as duke of Guyenne to surrender Robert. When Edward refused, Philip confiscated his lands: he had already prepared troops to take Ponthieu and to harry the frontiers of Guyenne. Essentially, this was the same French strategy as in 1294 and 1324. Edward's claim to the French throne enabled English strategy to move away from the defensive approach of earlier wars, which had focused largely on the sending of expeditionary armies to Guyenne to reinforce the inhabitants' own resistance. (The Gascons always preferred distant English rule to French interference.)

Strategy in this period was heavily influenced by concepts of the just war. Before 1328, English kings had no justification for actions outside their own lands of Guyenne and Ponthieu. The claim to the throne liberated them. If Edward claimed to be king of France, he did not need to restrict his strategy to the defence of his lands. He could attack Philip anywhere within the kingdom of France. Indeed, he would need to do so to make the claim meaningful. Therefore, the claim had the potential to change English strategy fundamentally, and it most certainly did so.[6]

Significantly, Edward sent no army to Guyenne after its confiscation. As a result, Philip needed to invest little effort in that area until the mid-1340s in response to a new English initiative.[7] Encouraged by Robert of Artois, whose own interests lay in the north, and in response to Philip's acts of aggression (which included major raids on south coast ports of England between 1337 and 1339), Edward decided that any meaningful attack needed to be made in northern France, where the French king's heartlands lay. However, executing this strategy was not simple. In comparison with the defensive campaigns in Guyenne in 1294–7 and 1324–7, it would necessitate a much larger army in the field for longer, operating wholly in hostile territory. The English did not have enough military resources on their own. In numerical terms, large armies had been raised for use in Scotland but only by virtue of the easy availability of archers and of general infantry. For his planned French campaign, Edward had only 1,800 English men-at-arms at his disposal, and around 4,600 troops overall. Given the number and strength of men-at-arms in French royal armies, Edward needed to find skilled mounted men-at-arms elsewhere. This explains alliances with the rulers of the Low Countries and Germany, whereby Edward bought military support to the tune of 6,200 men-at-arms.[8] It also explains why he established his base at Antwerp in the duchy of Brabant in 1338, and also why there was a delay in military action until he had enough troops as well as enough money to pay them.

The reliance on allies also explains the strategies of the two opening campaigns. The first was launched by Edward and his allies in 1339 into the Cambrésis. The second, in 1340, was aimed at the capture of Tournai. While both offered Edward the opportunity to attack France directly, both were fought for the interests of others as much as for himself. Edward invaded the Cambrésis not as king of France—he had not formally adopted the title at this point—but as vicar-general of the emperor Ludwig IV in the only part of France that lay within the empire. Strained Franco-imperial relations made the emperor responsive to Edward's approaches: this in turn was instrumental in gaining the aid of imperial vassals, although some rulers, such as the count of Hainault and the count of Flanders, chose to support Philip VI.

The strategy of this first campaign was one of scorched-earth activity against local inhabitants, carried out by detachments from the army operating separately and swiftly. The level of damage was greater than at any other phase of the Hundred Years War, as is shown by the evidence surviving for a subsequent mission of relief conducted by papal envoys. Edward's strategy was to challenge Philip's kingship by showing that the latter could not defend his people. Not surprisingly, this goaded Philip into raising an army and marching to meet Edward in battle at Buironfosse in July 1339. Given the determination with which the English had gathered the army of allies, at great expense, it had surely been Edward's intention all along to bring Philip to battle. This suggests the English king hoped for a short sharp shock and, hopefully, a victory that would give him the upper hand in subsequent negotiations. In the event, Philip decided not to engage. Without any focus, the campaign collapsed but left Edward bankrupt because of the price he had had to pay for his allies' support.

Nonetheless, his strategy of using others continued. By the end of 1339, he was able to secure the support of the major industrialized towns of Flanders—Ghent, Bruges, and Ypres—then in revolt against their count, who was himself a vassal of the French crown. The towns, also swayed by economic factors of access to English wool, were pleased to recognize Edward as king of France in order to justify their rebellion against their count, who had fled to the court of Philip VI. This explains why it was now necessary for Edward formally to declare himself king of France, and why this took place in Ghent on 26 January 1340.

The second campaign of the summer of 1340 was, as a result, focused on the recovery of Tournai for the Flemish, a town that had been lost to the French in 1328. This was the first siege of the war, and Edward may again have hoped to draw Philip into battle through an attempt to relieve the siege. But this did not happen, partly because Edward could not feed his army in hostile territory, a problem that prevented almost all efforts during the Hundred Years War to take major fortified centres by siege and that has beset commanders in many periods. It was therefore possible for papal mediators to persuade Edward to accept a temporary truce. He had achieved success, however, when the French navy was defeated off Sluys on 24 June 1340. This was a severe blow to Philip's strategy of trying to prevent English and Flemish military coordination, and also curtailed his and his successors' ability to continue the raids on English coasts.

Edward's strategy in the early years of the war was original in that it attacked royal France directly, but in other respects it emulated the policy of Edward I. The latter had sought to distract the French by joining with allies in Flanders, and had spent much money in doing so.[9] Edward I had also established an important precedent by not campaigning in person in Guyenne but instead crossing to Flanders in 1297. At no point in the Hundred Years War did an English king campaign in person in Guyenne. Even when a king was not present, the largest armies of the war were sent to northern France in order to undermine French royal authority.

Edward continued in the early 1340s to pursue a strategy that exploited allies. A succession dispute in the duchy of Brittany led to the English and the French supporting rival claimants. The strategy for both sides was identical: the military occupation of territory in the name of their candidate, with such sieges, skirmishing, and small-scale engagements as necessary. This war affected civilians by its inconclusiveness: never did either side control the whole of Brittany.

The strategies that Edward developed in 1345 and 1346 indicate a move away from reliance on allies, although not a total shift, in that coordination with his Flemish supporters was initially intended. Plans were developed for a three-pronged attack through Guyenne, Normandy, and Flanders. In practice, only the Guyenne campaign materialized in 1345, when the earl of Derby was sent to the area, conducting a series of small-scale invasions into French territory with the emphasis on capture of fortresses and plunder.[10] In response, Philip sent a large army led by his son John to besiege Aiguillon, a key location on the frontier of Guyenne. This encouraged the implementation in the summer of 1346 of Edward's invasion through Normandy. In strategic terms this was a major initiative. The king raised a large army in England, at least 12,000 strong: this had necessitated the extension of military obligations to the crown in order to generate a larger number of men-at-arms (nearly 3,000) and mounted archers, giving a ratio of 1:5 overall between men-at-arms and archers.[11]

The resulting Crécy campaign, which began with Edward's landing at St Vaast la Hougue, on the east coast of the Cotentin peninsula, was a *chevauchée* akin to that conducted in the Cambrésis in 1339, conducted at around 10–12 miles per day, with attacks on towns as well as villages. Edward was not aiming at conquest even though he had gained the assistance of some Norman renegades. Caen was taken, but it was reoccupied by the French as Edward took his army northwards. The point was to bring Philip to the battlefield. Edward goaded him by moving within a short distance of Paris before turning northwards into his own territory of Ponthieu. This destination had surely been chosen at the outset since Edward had already ordered victuals and materials to be taken to Le Crotoy to await his arrival. He had visited Crécy twice in the early years of his reign, and it is tempting to believe that his strategy had always been to ensure that the battle was in a location beneficial to the English.

Edward also had in mind from the start of his campaign the need to establish a more permanent point of entry in France, bearing in mind that there was increasing uncertainty over the Flemish alliance. This manifested itself by his moving immediately after his battle victory at Crécy to besiege Calais. This was by no means an easy task and success was achieved only after eleven months. If Edward had hoped to gain another victory over Philip, he was disappointed: the French king raised a relieving army but decided against engagement, no doubt in light of the defeat of the previous year.

In fact—and this is an interesting point—English successes had made the French reluctant to pursue any offensive strategies at all. In the early years of John II (1350–64), their emphasis was on a negotiated settlement. It was only successes by the count of Armagnac in Guyenne that prompted them to withdraw from peace talks. This forced Edward to focus his offensive strategies on the south. His eldest son, Edward (the Black Prince), was sent with a small Anglo-Gascon army (*c*.5,000) to harry Armagnac's own lands by means of a *chevauchée* (at around 10 miles per day) from the Atlantic almost to the Mediterranean. The ease and success of this led to the prince wintering at Bordeaux and conducting a similar movement northwards the next year, with the intention of joining up with the duke of Lancaster. The latter was conducting a campaign in Normandy to secure the possessions of a new ally, Charles of Navarre. This continued the strategy of support for those in rebellion against the French crown. To advance this particular situation, Edward had assumed the title duke of Normandy and had initially intended to campaign in person in the duchy.

Problems in Scotland turned his attention elsewhere. The armies of the prince and Lancaster were too small and did not manage to join forces. The French decided that relative English weakness made an offensive strategy, aimed at avenging Crécy, feasible, and raised a large army. John II successfully intercepted the prince but lost the ensuing battle at Poitiers, where he was captured, being taken to England the following year. Edward III was at first keen to use this to reach a negotiated settlement, but finally decided in 1359, presumably on the assumption that the French would not be in a position to resist, to invade with a large English army (at least 10,000) to besiege Reims and have himself crowned king. Although the French could not raise an army to oppose him, the campaign had to be aborted because of a shortage of victuals. Edward accepted terms at Brétigny near Chartres on 8 May. This was an English victory in that it gave full sovereignty over extended lands in south-west France, but Edward's experiences had demonstrated some perennial strategic limitations, not least the difficulty of coordinating troop movements and ensuring supply within enemy territory. That said, the claim to the throne had given him freedom to operate across all theatres and had provided him with allies within and outside France, reminding us that specific political factors have a role to play in dictating strategy.

THE SECOND PHASE, 1360–96

Edward's experience shows that short-term military success did not necessarily generate lasting achievement. That the English realized this is suggested by moves to keep the French in check vicariously after the Treaty of Brétigny. First, the marriage of the king's fourth son to the heiress of Flanders was negotiated, thereby envisaging a great English enclave, including Calais and Ponthieu, on the northern frontier of France. Secondly, support was given to the recently deposed Pedro II in Castile against his French-sponsored half-brother Henry of Trastamara. Both plans misfired. The Pope was persuaded by the French not to allow the English marriage but to let the heiress marry John II's younger son, Philip (duke of Burgundy), ensuring French control of Flanders. Although Pedro was restored thanks to Prince Edward's victory at Najera in 1367, he was deposed two years later: Castile fell into the French nexus. By 1369, Charles V saw himself as legally, politically, and militarily strong enough to challenge the Brétigny settlement and confiscated the English lands as his predecessors had done, a reminder of the consistency in French grand strategy. Following past precedent too, Charles had troops ready to occupy the English lands. By 1372, the English were reduced to what they had held in 1337 plus Calais. Edward had invested in its defence but had not done the same for his newly gained lands in the south-west. This may appear as folly to the modern eye, but it reminds us of two things: first, that Edward considered the Brétigny settlement as binding on its signatories, and, second, that it was hard to maintain an effective defensive strategy in peacetime as taxation could not be levied to pay for it.

The English found it difficult to decide upon a strategy to recover their position because they had lost so much initiative. They simply returned to strategies that had brought success in the past. For instance, they encouraged the defection of the duke of Brittany to give them a foothold in France but found the duke unreliable as an ally.[12] They also conducted long-distance *chevauchées*, with deliberate burning and plundering. While these caused concern, they did not bring the French to battle, nor did they lead to major sieges being laid or territory being gained. The armies the English sent to France between 1369 and 1388 were small (on average 4,000) and had an equal balance of men-at-arms and archers.[13] Given the importance of archers in battle successes at Crécy and Poitiers, it is unlikely that the English were any more minded to engage in battle than were Charles V and his leading general, Bertrand du Guesclin. There is no doubt that French strategy was not to raise large armies in response but simply to harry English armies in a quasi-guerrilla fashion.

The lack of engagements and of attempts to reconquer territory led to stalemate in France but vicarious wars elsewhere: English assistance to the opponents of the Trastamara dynasty in Castile, to the Portuguese, and to the men of Ghent against the count of Flanders, as well as exploitation of the papal schism to justify 'crusades' in Castile and Flanders.[14] That said, these were often competing strategies. Edward III's third son, John of Gaunt, who was married to Pedro II's daughter, was determined to pursue his own interests in Castile, while other lords were keen to support Brittany, and the Commons favoured support for Ghent. As a result, no strategy was adequately resourced or timely.

From the very reopening of the war in 1369, the French aimed to take the war to England through raids, a reason why Charles had been keen to ally himself with the Castilian pretender to gain access to his fleet.[15] This policy continued, with major raids in 1376–7 and 1385, the latter timed to coincide with a Franco-Scottish invasion of the north. The English responded by formulating a new strategy combining offence with defence. This is best described as a 'barbican policy'— the idea of capturing key ports on the French mainland as English bases. That it was announced in parliament in 1377 suggests that it was a strategy devised to please the Commons, who were always concerned with the defence of the realm and Channel. None of the direct attacks (on St Malo and Harfleur) succeeded, but Brest and Cherbourg were acquired on lease from the duke of Brittany and the heirs of Charles of Navarre.[16] These saw English garrisons installed, which lived off the surrounding area. They are in many ways the medieval equivalent of Hong Kong or Gibraltar. Both were returned to their owners after a twenty-eight-year truce was agreed between the French and English in 1396.

This phase of the war saw many strategies, often competing but none wholly successful. Behind this lies a lack of leadership. Edward III did not campaign in person again after 1360, Richard II was only ten at his accession in 1377, and Charles V died in 1380 leaving a minor on the throne. Most importantly, a lack of royal involvement dissuaded battle-seeking by either side. Whilst both sides remained committed to their grand strategies—the English to restore their Brétigny gains and the French to boot them out of France—without definitive outcomes there could only be stalemate. This is surely a perennial in military strategy across all ages.

THE THIRD PHASE, 1415–53

There were no formal hostilities in the reign of Henry IV (who deposed Richard II in 1399), but both sides maintained a 'cold war' strategy, in which a war of words was accompanied by sporadic raids on each other's coasts and shipping. There was an overt, but unsuccessful, attempt by Louis, duke of Orléans, over the winter of 1406–7, to secure control of the Gironde by besieging English-held Bourg, and there were periodic fears of an attack on Calais by John the Fearless, duke of Burgundy. These actions, however, were competing strategies in France, reflecting the personal interests of the respective dukes. Any unified approach to the English was impossible because of intense political rivalries within the French royal family, fanned by the recurrent madness of Charles VI. The situation worsened after the assassination of Orléans at the behest of Burgundy (November 1407). By 1410, there was a complete rift between the Burgundian and Orléanist (now known as Armagnac) camps. In the civil war that followed, both sides sought military assistance from the English.

There was a division of opinion in England over the best way of exploiting French approaches in order to regain the territorial position of the Brétigny settlement. When the future Henry V was in control of the government during his father's illness in 1410–11, he chose to send 2,000 troops to the duke of Burgundy. On recovery, Henry IV chose to dispatch an army of 4,000 men under his second son, Thomas, newly created duke of Clarence, to the Armagnacs. Before this army, which landed at St Vaast as Edward III had done in 1346, was able to join the Armagnacs at Blois, peace had been brokered. As Edward III had found, there was no guarantee of success in a strategy of fighting other people's wars.

These experiences are important, however, in establishing English strategy under Henry V, encouraging the great invasion of France in 1415 with an army of close to 12,000 men, the largest since 1346 (although Richard II and Henry IV raised over 13,000 for very brief shows of force in Scotland in 1385 and 1400). The French civil war had erupted again in 1414, with the Armagnacs carrying out a campaign of sieges in Burgundian-held Artois. Although there was a superficial reconciliation by the time Henry invaded, he might have anticipated French difficulties in making a unified response.

But what precisely was Henry's strategy? Although we know a good deal about the campaign, there is debate over his intentions, and, in particular, whether he had planned from the outset to bring the French to battle.[17] The indentures for his army show that he proposed to campaign for twelve months. That suggests a strategy of conquest, as does the provision of miners, guns and gunners, and other craftsmen—support staff relevant to a siege-based advance. A large army was needed so that conquered places could be garrisoned.

Henry landed on the north bank of the Seine and proceeded immediately to besiege Harfleur. There is enough evidence to suggest that this had been his intention all along. The fact that some early indentures were for service at Guyenne and that Southampton was chosen as the point of embarkation was classic subterfuge on Henry's part, akin to that of Edward III in 1346, when the actual destination in the Cotentin was kept secret while making it seem as though preparations were for a campaign in Guyenne.

There has been a suggestion that, after taking Harfleur, Henry intended to move southwards in a great *chevauchée* to Bordeaux. This is counter-intuitive, since Harfleur lay to the north of the Seine and any southward march would need to cross the river, never an easy move with a large army, especially when the lowest bridging point was at Rouen, one of the largest and best-fortified cities in northern France. The source that is cited in support of a march to Bordeaux is a private letter written on 3 September by the archdeacon of Médoc from the siege of Harfleur to the mayor and *jurats* of Bordeaux, and reflects local patriotism:

> my lords, do make every effort to please him [Henry had sent a simultaneous request to Bordeaux that the city should send him 500 to 700 tuns of wine] for he will look kindly on you in his heart and has great confidence in you, and in the city [of Bordeaux], and it is his intention to come thither before he returns to England.[18]

In fact, later in the same letter, the writer gives a different account of Henry's plans.

> And when he has taken Harfleur, I have heard that it is not his intention to enter the town but to stay in the field. In a short while after the capture of the town, he intends to go to Montivilliers, and thence to Dieppe, afterwards to Rouen and then to Paris.

Henry's strategy of conquest was unprecedented and indicates a new phase in the Hundred Years War. Normandy had already been a theatre of choice, as in 1346 and 1356, but never had there been an effort at taking the duchy or even part of it systematically. Henry's choice of Normandy is significant. He had no right there save as putative king of France. The treaty of Brétigny explicitly confirmed the duchy to the French. A campaign there was a direct strike at the heartlands and resources of the French monarchy. Henry had not ignored other areas of English interest, however. Immediately after his father's death, he had kept in Guyenne under the earl of Dorset most of the army that had crossed in 1412, ordering a blitzkrieg into Saintonge.[19] The French sent an army under the duke of Bourbon to retaliate, which prompted Dorset to come to truce since he was short of money to maintain his troops. Dorset was heavily involved in planning Henry's invasion in 1415 and was appointed captain of Harfleur at its fall. It seems likely, therefore, that Henry's decision to shift the war to Normandy was influenced by the experiences of Clarence and Dorset in the south-west, which had shown how difficult it was to make meaningful progress there.

Yet, if Henry's intention in 1415 was to conquer territory in Normandy, thereby putting pressure on the French to negotiate, he failed. After the surrender of Harfleur, he decided not to proceed to further conquests. His army had been reduced in size by illness and by the need to install a large garrison of 1,200 men in Harfleur. Ironically, bombardment had rendered the town less easily defensible. Early French recovery efforts were deemed likely, since the six-week siege (longer than Henry had anticipated) had allowed the French to start to raise taxation to gather their army at Rouen. By early October, Henry decided to withdraw from France by moving the remainder of his army as quickly as possible, using the route that Edward III had taken in 1346, to Calais, whence it could easily and cheaply effect a short crossing home. All of the narrative sources agree that this was Henry's strategy but that rumours of a large French army awaiting him on the north bank of the Somme near Blanchetaque forced him to turn west along the river, and to march inland in search of a safe crossing point. None suggests that he intended to engage the French. All have it that it was the French strategy to seek battle—they formally summoned him to battle after he crossed the Somme—and that they chose the battlefield at Agincourt, reckoning no doubt that English defeat in that vicinity would facilitate the subsequent recapture of Calais.

Throughout his march, Henry feared an attack on his army: before the crossing of the Somme, he ordered all archers to provide themselves with a stake in order to create a defensive palisade to protect them if attacked. He was not a strategic risk-taker: this is shown by his efforts to cover all scenarios as he prepared to launch his campaign, and also by his ordering the killing of the prisoners at Agincourt when he feared the French might return to the fight. He could not count on any support within France: there is no evidence of an Anglo-Burgundian pact in 1415. Even though the duke was not at the battle, two of his brothers died there fighting on the French side. The response to Henry's invasion was reasonably unified, but the speed of his march (at an average of 15 miles per day) had made it difficult for the French to assemble a very large army quickly enough. At the battle, he most certainly out-generalled his opponents.

After Agincourt, Henry abandoned his campaign of conquest with a view to resuming it in the spring of the following year. This left Harfleur vulnerable in the face of an obvious French strategy to retake it, involving blockades by land and sea. As a result, the 7,000-strong army which Henry raised in the summer of 1416 could not be used to continue the conquest by land but was sent to sea under his second brother, John, duke of Bedford, where it defeated a French fleet on 16 August. This reveals Henry's ability to change tack in order to maintain his bigger goals. The conquest of Normandy, which he had intended all along, was finally resumed with great success from 1 August 1417.

Henry also learned from the lessons of 1415. In 1417, he chose a landing in Lower Normandy at the mouth of the River Touques, well away from major fortifications or settlements.[20] He thereby secured a long coastal bridgehead for resupply before moving off to the first siege, that of Caen. The town agreed to surrender after two weeks, cut off from assistance by neighbouring garrisons thanks to Henry's sending his lieutenants to secure the fortifications in the vicinity. He then moved swiftly southwards from Caen, taking places into his control as he went, bisecting Lower Normandy. Once he had secured the corridor to Alençon, separate armies of conquest were sent simultaneously eastwards and westwards under his brothers. By July 1418, with most of Lower Normandy in English hands, the king was able to regroup his army with reinforcements from England to lay siege to Rouen. Significantly, in the light of the problems caused by bombardment at Harfleur, Henry chose to starve the city into submission even though this required him to keep his army surrounding it for six months. This had the deliberate effect of undermining support for the French monarchy, which did not have the confidence or unity to relieve the city by engaging Henry in battle.

The king garrisoned the largest places in his conquest with royal troops but gave the smaller places to his captains in land grants, thereby passing on the cost and responsibility of defence to them. Adopting the title duke of Normandy from the outset of the campaign, he pursued a strategy towards the civilians of the duchy, offering them opportunities and incentives to enter his allegiance, and also ensured, by deploying an army of administrators, that the government of the duchy passed with little disruption into his hands. It did not take long, therefore, for Henry to be able to raise money from the duchy or to use its inhabitants in its defence.[21]

Henry's conquest was secured not only by his effective military and political strategies but also by French disunity. In May 1418, John the Fearless took control of Paris and the king, forcing the Dauphin, Charles, by then the leader of the Armagnacs, to flee to the Loire. An effort at reconciliation ended disastrously on 10 September 1419 on the bridge at Montereau when John was assassinated by the henchmen of the Dauphin. With the English now almost at the gates of Paris, serious negotiations had to be entered into with Henry. Not surprisingly, his terms were high (the inheritance of the throne of France after the death of Charles VI), but they were acceptable to Burgundians determined to revenge themselves against the Dauphin. They were ratified in the Treaty of Troyes of 21 May 1420.

Although Henry had to await the death of Charles VI, he was regent in the interim. This raises an important point. Effectively, the treaty meant an end to the 'English' strategy of conquest which Henry had hitherto pursued. He was now committed to a French strategy, or, more accurately, a Burgundian strategy. This commitment was enshrined in the treaty itself, where clause 12 reads as follows:[22]

Item, that our said son shall labour with all his might, and as soon as profitably can be done, to put in our obedience all the cities, towns, countries, castles, places, areas and persons within our realm which are disobedient to us, and rebels holding to or being of the party commonly called that of the Dauphin and of Armagnac.

Fulfilment of this obligation is manifested in the military actions that Henry undertook over the rest of his life to secure the major places close to Paris that were still in the control of the Armagnacs. Significantly, an early objective was the taking of Montereau as part of the revenge for the murder of the duke.

Henry's strategy before the treaty had been highly successful. On the face of it, his post-treaty strategy was equally successful. He took all the places he besieged but some proved exceptionally difficult. Armagnac resolve and support had been boosted rather than diminished by the disinheriting of the Dauphin. This was revealed by the defeat in battle at Baugé on 21 March 1421 of an army led by Clarence, in which the duke and many Englishmen were killed, and others taken prisoner. Worse still, Henry died from siege-induced dysentery on 31 August 1422, leaving as heir to the double monarchy a nine-month-old son, who came to his grandfather's French throne on 14 October.

Although the war continued for another thirty years, strategies changed little. The English focused on the maintenance of Henry's successes and on the implementation of the Treaty of Troyes. John, duke of Bedford (d. 1435), as regent, and the succession of lieutenants-general who followed, continued to defend Normandy as the heartland of English rule following the deathbed advice of Henry to do so. Never before had the English maintained such a large defensive establishment in a concentrated area (up to 6,000 men in 1436). This allowed not only the preservation of local order (even in Normandy there was guerrilla activity against the English) but also the use of garrison detachments for field campaigns alongside expeditionary armies sent from England almost every year.[23] In addition, following precedents set by Henry V, there was a revival of feudal obligation to provide troops from the local nobility and also from the English who had been given lands in Normandy. This was a highly militarized position.

Strategies were uncompromising. The English, until 1435 assisted by the Burgundians, were committed to extending the area that accepted the Treaty of Troyes. The Dauphin and his supporters strove to stop them and to retake territory. Even though his resources were limited and he was largely dependent on troops provided by his Scottish ally, the Dauphin sought to take the war to the English and their allies, but defeats in battle at Cravant (1423) and Verneuil (1424) forced him into a defensive position. After Verneuil, the English pursued a strategy of expansion into Maine and Anjou between 1424 and 1427. This was intended to continue in 1428–9 under the prompting of Bedford, who had a personal interest through his creation as duke of Anjou. But a rival strategy was developed in England, led by Humphrey, duke of Gloucester, in liaison with the veteran commander the earl of Salisbury, to advance instead towards Orléans, the gateway to the Dauphin's main power base south of the Loire. As in the second phase of the war, divisions in strategic thinking were likely to emerge when there was not a king in charge. Furthermore, it did not prove any easier to coordinate English and Burgundian efforts than it had been for Edward III to control his allies. In the mid-1420s, Duke Philip of Burgundy developed his own strategy of expansion in the

Low Countries, which led to armed conflicts with Duke Humphrey, who was keen to secure the territorial interests of his wife, Jacqueline of Hainault.

The plan to take the war to the Dauphin prevailed but failed. Orléans held out until relieved by the Dauphin's army, inspired by Joan of Arc. Charles went on to defeat the English in battle at Patay and to take all of the important places as far as Reims, where Charles was crowned king on 17 July 1429. Initially, English strategy focused on the recovery of Reims so that Henry VI could be crowned there as king of France. To that end, the largest army of his reign—almost 5,000 men—was dispatched with the young king in the spring of 1430, and major efforts were made to coordinate with the Burgundians.[24] But it proved impossible to recover the lost places, and Henry had to make do with a coronation in Paris in December 1431.

The English had little choice thenceforward but to follow a largely defensive strategy since Charles's supporters had penetrated into Normandy and were holding clusters of garrisons, which constantly harassed the English occupiers. In 1435, the French took Harfleur, Dieppe, and much of the Pays de Caux. With the defection of the Burgundians around the same time, and the loss of Paris without any possibility of resistance in 1436, English strategy concentrated on the recovery of the lost places of Normandy. Harfleur was recovered in 1440, but Dieppe remained in French hands. Mont-Saint-Michel had eluded English capture throughout, despite several major sieges by land and sea.

The early 1440s provide an example of the difficulty the English experienced in identifying the best strategy when the tide was turning against them. This was exacerbated by differences of opinion between the members of the royal family to whom the task of ruling English France fell, since the king was not interested in campaigning in person. While the duke of York wished to concentrate on consolidation in Normandy, John Beaufort, duke of Somerset, saw advantage in conducting an old-style *chevauchée* southwards to impress the Bretons and the French that the English were still a force to be reckoned with.

This debate between defence and offence had begun in the mid-1430s in the face of the increasing vulnerability of the English position in Normandy, as is demonstrated by the advice that Sir John Fastolf wrote in September 1435.[25] Fastolf's proposal was for a fourteenth-century approach to a fifteenth-century problem, urging scorched-earth policies to force the local population to submit, and ran counter to the strategies that Henry V and Bedford had consistently maintained. Henry had emphasized throughout his conquests an intention to protect the civilian population, never pursuing a scorched-earth campaign. In this, his military strategy supported political strategy: Henry sought to legitimize his claim to the French throne and to the duchy of Normandy by his good lordship, and to distinguish his stance from the violence of Armagnacs and Burgundians. Bedford's platform was very much the continuation of his brother's policies. Disciplinary control of soldiers was strict—so much so that the local population praised their occupiers for it in the 1420s. Although this approach continued after 1435, the decline in English fortunes, and the isolation caused by the defection of the Burgundians, undermined civil-military relations. Increasingly, the Normans resented paying taxes for their own occupation. The inhabitants of Lower Normandy complained at paying for the recovery and defence of the more vulnerable Upper Normandy north of the Seine. The English parliament was equally reluctant to pay for the support of what was left of Henry VI's French monarchy.

The strategy of temporary truce that was arrived at in 1444 needs to be seen against this resource context. Almost overnight it allowed garrisons to be reduced to 2,000 men, although the problem of demobilized soldiers threatened to undermine civil-military relations further. Henry VI and his advisers failed to develop a clear forward strategy. There were only feeble efforts to come to a negotiated settlement or to prepare the remaining English-held territories for the recommencement of open war. Even worse, the king's naivety led him to surrender Maine to Charles VII secretly, much to the amazement of those continuing to defend it. By contrast, Charles implemented a clear strategy to remove the English from France once and for all. From the truce onwards, he reformed military organization to provide the troops he would need, and he negotiated the support of the duke of Brittany away from a traditionally pro-English position. By contrast, the English tried to put pressure on the Bretons by ordering an Aragonese soldier in their service, Sir François de Surienne, to capture the fortress of Fougères on the Breton-Norman border, prematurely breaching the truce and providing justification for Charles's invasion.

Charles's reconquest of Normandy was swift and decisive. The way was paved by those in the French-held garrisons in Normandy capturing by surprise neighbouring key points, such as Pont-de-l'Arche. The main royal invasion shows striking parallels with the strategy of Henry V's conquest. Invasion from the south cut Lower Normandy in two, and facilitated armies being sent simultaneously to the west (with Breton assistance) and east. Once it was clear that Charles would be successful and that the English could not send troops to relieve, most places offered no resistance. The surrender of Rouen, as of other places, was at the behest of its citizens, who wished to avoid war damage, and triggered the automatic surrender of Harfleur and other key locations. The English fell back on Caen, and subsequently Cherbourg, a piecemeal strategy of resistance having foundered in battle at Formigny on 15 April 1450. The following year, Charles turned his attention to Guyenne, employing a similar strategy of blitzkrieg so that places fell to him without resistance. A rebellion in Bordeaux briefly returned control of the city to the English, but an expeditionary army sent to protect what was left of the English position was defeated at the battle of Castillon on 17 July 1453.

In this third phase of the war, political divisions in France prompted the English to move away from the grand strategy which they had pursued since the opening of the Hundred Years War. The coincidence of Henry V's military success with the assassination of the duke of Burgundy gave the English the crown of France. Once won, there was no room for negotiation. The English position thereafter could only be sustained by support within France. In this context, military strategy became overdependent on political factors. We also see the tensions between good treatment of conquered peoples and military effectiveness which have dogged many subsequent occupations.

CONCLUSIONS

What can we deduce in terms of strategic ideas and assumptions in this period? No one was a trained strategist. In all of the countries involved in the Hundred

Years War, princes and nobles received a didactic, rather than scholarly, education that was based on classical exemplars. Governors of young princes were often
veterans who passed on not only their experience of actual events but also their
knowledge what the heroes of the past did, or did not do, under certain circumstances. The same military treatises were in use across Europe.[26] Many dated from
the late Roman period. The most renowned was Vegetius's *De Re Militari*, which
was increasingly consulted in vernacular translations,[27] but also available was
Frontinus's *Strategemata*, as well as Valerius Maximus's *Factorum et Dictorum
Memorabilium*. New works such as Honoré de Bouvet's *L'Arbre des batailles*
(1387), Christine de Pisan's *Livre des fais d'armes et de chevalerie* (1405),
Nicholas Upton's *De Studio Militari* (1430s–1440s), and Jean de Bueil's *Le
Jouvencel* (1461–6) were heavily influenced by earlier works but were amended
to suit present circumstances, as, for instance, in de Pisan's mention of gunpowder
artillery. De Bueil added advice from the recent past, such as the adage of La Hire,
one of Charles VII's captains (as well as a hardened routier): 'if you want to stop
yourself being frightened, make sure you always strike the first blow'.[28] All of the
works contained more on tactics than strategy, although areas such as spying and
discipline crossed the boundary between the two. All made clear the need for
preparation for campaign, especially in terms of ensuring food supplies for armies.

In terms of mindset, there were no real differences among the protagonists of
the war. Nor is it obvious that there were changes in strategic thinking over the
course of the period. By the end of it, gunpowder artillery was in greater use. This
was certainly a contributory factor to Charles VII's swift reconquest of Normandy,
not least as places preferred to surrender than to be bombarded, although political
factors also played a role in such decisions. In 1415–19 the Normans were
resisting an alien invader, in 1449–50 they were being liberated by the king of
France—who by then was accepted by the remainder of the French population—
from an occupier in whom they had lost confidence.

As we have seen in the chronological discussion, military strategies were
moulded and remoulded according to political and diplomatic circumstances, as
well as financial and manpower resources. Generally, it was the French who were
forced to respond to English initiatives, but there were occasions, such as in 1369,
when the French acted as aggressors and forced the English into a defensive
strategy. However, we must remember that the main protagonists were very
similar to each other culturally, and shared the same strategic assumptions and
ideas as well as the means to implement them. Both were hereditary monarchies
with well-established bureaucracies and means of raising armies. On the face of it,
with a larger land-mass and population, the French had potentially greater
military and financial resources at their disposal, and the king could levy taxation
without the need for public consent. However, forward planning was restricted
because in practice taxation could only be raised in response to emergency and for
defensive purposes: this explains why there were delays in the French response to
the invasions of 1346 and 1415. Furthermore, royal power was restricted in the
great apanages such as Flanders, Brittany, Burgundy, and of course, English-held
Guyenne.

On the English side, from the 1290s onwards, English kings needed the consent
of the Commons in parliament to raise direct taxation. In the middle of the
fourteenth century, this was also needed for indirect taxes such as customs duties.

This system of funding allowed English kings to plan offensive campaigns ahead, even though these were often presented to parliament as protective moves for England on the grounds that attack was the best form of defence.

When the English held lands in France, they were able to raise taxation and troops from them. Resources could become overstretched, however, and strategies were often undermined or curtailed by shortages of wages for troops and by a lack of victuals. This was a particular problem for the English, who were operating at a distance from their homeland in hostile territory. The predominance of *chevauchées* in the first and second phases of the war is explained by the need to keep armies moving in order to keep them fed. Such swift raids brought quick gains and little loss of life to the army, but they had short-lived strategic value. It is also notable that cessation of war had an undermining effect on the preparedness of the defending side. This is seen in the opening stages of the second phase, when the French were able to retake English gains easily. The English were to experience the same difficulty after the Truce of Tours of 1444, when, to save money, troops were stood down, and fortifications, victualling, and artillery not maintained. On both occasions, peace reduced military effectiveness and made it difficult for commanders to re-adopt an offensive strategy quickly enough. The advantage always lay with the attacker. Despite the use of spies, which is well evidenced across the whole period, it was extremely difficult to arrange relieving armies quickly enough, especially when they had to cross the Channel.

It is clear that throughout the period, rulers and commanders did not see warfare simply as action against armies, with the ultimate goal being to engage the enemy in a pitched battle. They also intended armies to act against the enemy population as a whole in order to demoralize them and to weaken the economic infrastructure.[29] The two strategies were complementary facets of the overall aim to damage the opponent by whatever means possible. Civilians were potential victims in the many sieges, as well as in raids, where the principal purpose was to cause damage and upheaval, and to reduce the economic resources and political authority of the enemy. Whether by land or sea, raids were difficult to counter since the attackers were constantly on the move and operated over a front of around 13 miles at a time. That said, they did not bring an immediate advantage, nor were they conclusive unless followed up by another action such as a siege or battle, or by repeated attrition in the same area (as practised by the routiers in particular).

All phases of the war saw all strategies, but the relative balance between them varied. The use of allies was significant at some times but not others. In the fifteenth-century phase, the English did not need international allies, as they had the support between 1419 and 1435 of a major peer within France. Both sides adopted a battle- and siege-avoiding stance in the second phase because of relative weaknesses on both sides. Raids on England were only part of French strategy when the French were in a strong position at home and could afford to turn to the offensive. In the third phase of the war, the English gave much greater attention to the protection of the civilian population. In other words, they sought, in the wake of military activity, to win hearts and minds so that they could facilitate their subsequent defensive position.

Despite Edward III's capture of Calais, there remains a basic difference between the fourteenth- and fifteenth-century phases. At no time in the fourteenth century was there an effort by the English to conquer and occupy extensive territory. The fifteenth-century strategy focused on this almost exclusively. Henry V emerges as a more consummate strategist than Edward III. His campaign of 1417–19 is surely the most successful English endeavour of the whole Hundred Years War. His planning and execution were superb, especially the geographical dimension. The king focused his own efforts on taking the major fortified places while sending out his lieutenants to take the surrender of smaller places in the vicinity. He often granted these places to their captors, which gave a collective incentive to preserve the conquest. Military actions were complemented by efforts to win over the local population rather than to damage it as Edward III had done in 1346, and to take over local administration, thereby making it possible to access taxation and food supplies legitimately. The securing of Harfleur and of the coast of Lower Normandy made it possible to bring in foodstuffs from England. Henry was therefore not short of victuals in the way Edward III had been in 1340 and 1359. Only with an adequate supply of food could a large army be sustained for a long siege. Rouen was the largest place ever successfully besieged by the English over the whole course of the Hundred Years War.

Henry was lucky that France was divided and its king incapable. Edward was able to draw on the support of a handful of defectors such as Robert of Artois and Godfrey de Harcourt. It is interesting to note from newsletters home that the king's military decisions were taken in consultation with 'the men of the country'. But Edward never enjoyed widespread support within France except perhaps in that part of Brittany that acknowledged the ducal claimant the English supported. Whether Henry could have achieved what he did without the support of the Burgundians is questionable. The English could not have held onto their conquests without the support of the local population. In explaining success in the strategic domain in the Hundred Years War, political elements were always more significant than military ones. The nature of warfare was such that it could not prove decisive in itself, even with the most talented strategist as commander and even with victory in pitched battle.

NOTES

1. The best single-volume narrative remains É. Perroy, *The Hundred Years War*, trans. W. B. Wells (New York, 1965). Also useful are C. T. Allmand, *The Hundred Years War* (Cambridge, 1988); and A. Curry, *The Hundred Years War* (Basingstoke, 1993; 2nd edn, 2003). A multi-volume study by Jonathan Sumption, *The Hundred Years War*, has reached 1399: *Trial by Battle* (London, 1990), *Trial by Fire* (London, 1999), and *Divided Houses* (London, 2009). For an excellent overview of military matters, see M. Prestwich, *Armies and Warfare in the Middle Ages: The English Experience* (New Haven, 1996); and P. Contamine, *War in the Middle Ages*, trans. M. C. E. Jones (Oxford, 1984).
2. More detail is given in Curry, *The Hundred Years War*, ch. 4.
3. I am grateful for the discussion with Dr Guilhem Pépin on this point.
4. M. G. A. Vale, *The Origins of the Hundred Years War: The Angevin Legacy 1250–1340* (Oxford, 1996).
5. J. Gillingham, *The Angevin Empire*, 2nd edn (London, 2001).

6. For an excellent discussion, see C. J. Rogers, *War Cruel and Sharp: English Strategy under Edward III 1327–1360* (Woodbridge, 2000). His views on Edward's battle-seeking strategy are summarized in 'Edward III and the Dialectics of Strategy, 1327–1360', *Transactions of the Royal Historical Society*, 6th ser., 4 (1994), 83–102; repr. in id. (ed.), *The Wars of Edward III* (Woodbridge, 1999).

7. For a complete study, see M. G. A. Vale, 'The War in Aquitaine', in A. Curry and M. Hughes (eds), *Arms, Armies and Fortifications in the Hundred Years War* (Woodbridge, 1994).

8. Rogers, *The Wars of Edward III*, 62. For background, see H. S. Lucas, *The Low Countries and the Hundred Years War 1326–1347* (Ann Arbor, 1929; repr. Philadelphia, 1976).

9. M. Prestwich, *Edward I* (London, 1988), 386–95.

10. C. J. Rogers, 'The Bergerac Campaign (1345) and the Generalship of Henry of Lancaster', *Journal of Medieval Military History*, 2 (2004), 89–110.

11. A. C. Ayton and P. Preston, *The Battle of Crécy* (Woodbridge, 2005), provides a full account of all aspects of the army and campaign.

12. M. C. E. Jones, *Ducal Brittany 1364–1399* (Oxford, 1970).

13. J. W. Sherborne, 'Indentured Retinues and English Expeditions to France, 1369–89', *English Historical Review*, 79 (1964), 718–46.

14. P. E. Russell, *English Intervention in Spain and Portugal in the Time of Edward III and Richard II* (Oxford, 1955); and J. J. N. Palmer, *England, France and Christendom 1377–99* (London, 1972).

15. J. W. Sherborne, 'The Battle of La Rochelle and the War at Sea 1372–75', *Bulletin of the Institute of Historical Research*, 42 (1969), 17–29.

16. Jones, *Ducal Brittany*, ch. 6.

17. For contrasting views, see A. Curry, *Agincourt: A New History* (Stroud, 2005); and C. J. Rogers, 'Henry V's Strategy in 1415', in D. J. Kagay and I. J. A. Villalon (eds), *The Hundred Years War: A Wider Focus* (Leiden, 2005).

18. A. Curry, *The Battle of Agincourt: Sources and Interpretations* (Woodbridge, 2000), 445.

19. Curry, *Agincourt*, 13–14.

20. R. A. Newhall, *The English Conquest of Normandy 1416–24* (New Haven, 1924); and J. Barker, *Conquest: The English Kingdom of France* (London, 2009).

21. C. T. Allmand, *Lancastrian Normandy: The History of a Medieval Occupation 1415–1450* (Oxford, 1983).

22. Translated from the text of the treaty in French, repr. in E. Cosneau, *Les Grands Traités de la guerre de Cent Ans* (Paris, 1889), which derives from the official versions in Archives nationales, Paris, Xia 8603 (ordonnances royales) and JJ171 (trésor des chartes).

23. For details on the expeditionary armies and garrisons, see A. Curry, 'English Armies in the Fifteenth Century', in Curry and Hughes (eds), *Arms, Armies and Fortifications*; and A. Curry, 'Field Armies in Lancastrian Normandy', in M. Strickland (ed.), *Armies, Chivalry and Warfare in Medieval Britain and France* (Stamford, 1998).

24. A. Curry, 'The 'Coronation Expedition' and Henry VI's Court in France, 1430–32', in J. Stratford (ed.), *The Lancastrian Court* (Stamford, 2003).

25. *Letters and Papers Illustrative of the Wars of the English in France*, ed. J. Stevenson, Rolls Series, 22, 2 vols (London, 1861–4), ii/2. 575. There has been debate on this document. See R. Brill, 'The English Preparations before the Treaty of Arras: A New Interpretation of Sir John Fastolf's 'Report', September 1435', *Studies in Medieval and Renaissance History*, 7 (1970), 211–47; and M. G. A. Vale, 'Sir John Fastolf's Report of 1435: A New Interpretation Reconsidered', *Nottingham Medieval Studies*, 17 (1973), 78–84.

26. Contamine, *War in the Middle Ages*, 210–12.

27. Professor Allmand's full study of Vegetius in the Middle Ages is eagerly awaited. In the meantime, see C. T. Allmand, 'Fifteenth-Century Versions of Vegetius' *De Re Militari*', in Strickland (ed.), *Armies, Chivalry and Warfare*.

28. *Le Jouvencel par Jean de Bueil suivi du commentaire de Guillaume Trignant*, 2 vols (Paris, 1887–9), ii. 62–3.

29. For an important discussion, see C. J. Rogers, 'By Fire and Sword: *Bellum hostile* and Civilians in the Hundred Years War', in M. Grimsley and C. J. Rogers (eds), *Civilians in the Path of War* (Lincoln, NE, 2002).

Part II

Mediaeval and Modern

5

The Ottomans: From Frontier Principality to Empire

Gábor Ágoston

INTRODUCTION

The Ottomans, named after the founder of the Ottoman (*Osmanlı*) imperial dynasty, Osman (d. 1324?), emerged in western Asia Minor in the last decades of the thirteenth century as one of many Turcoman emirates or principalities formed in the wake of the Mongols' destruction of the empire of the Seljuk Turks in 1243. Osman's successors built one of the greatest- and longest-lived multi-ethnic and multi-religious empires in history that can only be compared to the better-known Mediterranean empires of the Romans and Byzantines, the similarly multi-ethnic continental empires of the Habsburgs and Romanovs, and the other great Islamic empires of Asia: the Abbasid caliphate, Safavid Persia, and Mughal India.

In 1352 the Ottomans established their first bridgehead in the Balkans, on the European shore of the Dardanelles. Within fifty years, through military conquest, diplomacy, dynastic marriages, and the opportunistic exploitation of the Byzantine civil wars, the third Ottoman ruler, Murad I (1362–89), more than tripled the territories under his direct rule—territories that were evenly distributed between the Balkans and Anatolia. The conquest of Adrianople (Edirne), most probably in 1369, and the fact that Murad I made the city his new capital indicate that the Ottomans considered themselves both an Asian and a European power. Bayezid I (1389–1402) continued the Ottoman expansion on both continents, extending his rule up to the banks of the Danube and the Euphrates.

While the victory of the Mongol conqueror Timur Lenk (Tamerlane) over Bayezid I (1402) checked Ottoman expansion for a decade, European attempts to halt the Ottoman advance failed repeatedly (in 1396, 1443–4, 1448). In 1453, Sultan Mehmed II (1444–6, 1451–81) conquered Constantinople, the capital of the thousand-year-old Eastern Roman, or Byzantine, empire. Declaring himself Caesar, the heir to the Byzantine emperors, and lord of 'two lands' (the Balkans and Anatolia) and 'two seas' (the Black Sea and the Aegean), Mehmed II announced to the world that a new empire had been born, firmly rooted in both Europe and Asia.

In 1516–17, Sultan Selim I (1512–20) defeated the Mamluk sultanate of Egypt and Syria, incorporating their realms into his empire. Süleyman I (1520–66) added Iraq and central Hungary to his empire, and in 1529 unsuccessfully besieged Vienna, the capital of the Austrian Habsburg empire. Following further conquests in the mid-seventeenth century in Hungary (1660–4), Crete (1669), and the Polish province of Podolia in modern-day Ukraine (1672), the Ottoman empire reached its largest territorial extent. The Ottomans ruled over a vast territory from Hungary in the north to Yemen in the south, and from Algeria in the west to Iraq in the east, approximately 3.8 million square kilometres (40 per cent of the mainland United States) if one includes loosely held lands and unproductive deserts.

The second Ottoman siege of Vienna in 1683 under Grand Vizier Kara Mustafa Pasha provoked a major rescue operation on the part of European Christian states, and by 1699 an international coalition of the Habsburg empire, Poland–Lithuania, Venice, the papacy, and Muscovite Russia managed to re-conquer most of historic Hungary (including Croatia, Slavonia, and the principality of Transylvania), Podolia, as well as parts of Dalmatia and the Morea (Peloponnese). However, the Ottomans continued to rule over most of the Balkans until 1878 and in their Middle Eastern lands until the First World War, a formidable accomplishment even when one recognizes that Istanbul's control over provinces far from the capital was often nominal in the eighteenth and nineteenth centuries.

In the sixteenth and seventeenth centuries, Ottoman-Habsburg rivalry played an important role in shaping the future of both Europe and Asia, and can only be compared to the sixteenth-century Valois-Habsburg struggle over Europe or to the competition between the United States and the Soviet Union and their respective allies during the cold war. In the eighteenth century, Romanov Russia replaced Habsburg Spain and Austria as the Ottomans' main European rival, and southward Russian expansion against a weakening Ottoman empire became the major concern of Ottoman strategy. That expansion also dominated and shaped Ottoman and great power politics in the late eighteenth and nineteenth centuries, and has become a major subject of history and international relations textbooks under the now-antiquated heading of 'the Eastern question'.

For centuries the Ottomans managed to keep law and order among ethnically and religiously diverse peoples in the Balkans and the Middle East—territories that have seen so much violence since the demise of the empire in the First World War. The longevity of the Ottoman empire, its territorial expansion into three continents, and the important role that the Ottomans played in shaping European and Middle Eastern policy for centuries warrant special attention in a book that deals with imperial strategy—defined as 'the art of winning by purposely matching ends, ways and means'. Up to the late sixteenth century, 'winning' meant the gradual expansion of the early Ottoman frontier principality of Osman into a world empire by defeating Christian and Muslim neighbors and rivals and incorporating their territories into the growing Ottoman realms, as well as the consolidation of Ottoman rule in the conquered territories. In this process, the conquest of Constantinople, the Byzantine imperial capital, was a symbolic turning point. In strategic terms, it marked the unification of the Ottoman realms in the Balkans and Asia Minor, and also the birth of the patrimonial Ottoman empire that replaced the frontier principality.

Conquests and consolidation of Ottoman rule continued for some three generations. From the end of the sixteenth century on, however, the main strategic concern of Ottoman policymakers was the defence of earlier conquests rather than territorial expansion, although the 1660s and 1670s brought some new conquests. The late sixteenth century also witnessed yet another turning point in the history of the empire: the transformation from the medieval patrimonial empire into an early modern one, in which the central government's access to resources and means of organized violence were more limited than in the previous era.[1] Thus, this chapter is divided into two time periods. The first major section is devoted to the ascendancy of the Ottomans from the formation of the Ottoman emirate *c.*1300 through their conquest of Constantinople in 1453. It seeks to clarify how the small Turkic principality of Osman poised itself to evolve into an extremely powerful empire. The second major section examines the mid-fifteenth to the late seventeenth centuries, a span of time that witnessed both the heyday of the empire and important readjustments of Ottoman strategy and military capabilities.

STRATEGY AND STRATEGIC CULTURE

Historians have applied the concept of grand strategy—a global vision of the geopolitics and the military, economic, and cultural capabilities of states—to explain the formation, strengths, and weaknesses of empires. Although the term 'grand strategy' was unknown to policymakers of past empires, recent scholarship has argued that it is possible to discern and reconstruct the global strategic visions that informed imperial policy and mobilized economic and human resources to achieve particular policy goals.[2] However, it would be misleading to assume that the Ottomans (or any of their rivals) had a single, unified grand strategy that guided their policies throughout the centuries. While such theories might seem attractive to political scientists and sociologists for their theoretical coherence and elegance, they usually simplify and distort historical realities that are more complex.[3] Ottoman history especially lends itself to interpretations that overemphasize strategy and state intentionality because of the state-centred nature of Ottomanist historiography, which has told the story of the Ottomans from the perspective of the state, using sources generated by the state's bureaucracy.

At times, especially in the era of early conquests, it is not clear whose strategy was behind Ottoman expansion, who the decision-makers were, what motivated them, and what role, if any, political, ideological, social, and economic motives played in their acts. Our knowledge of early Ottoman history is especially shaky, full of black holes and speculations. Some of the most important events of early Ottoman history are recorded under different dates in the scholarly literature, such as Osman's first important victory over a Byzantine army (*c.*1300, 1301, 1302), his death (*c.*1324, 1324, 1326), or the year of the conquest of Adrianople (Turkish Edirne) (the 1360s, 1361, 1367, 1369).[4] This is largely due to the nature of our sources. They include Ottoman chronicles, poems, legends, and dynastic myths, the majority of which were recorded in the fifteenth and sixteenth centuries, in an era when the successors of Osman ruled over a rather different polity: a patrimonial Sunni Muslim empire with complex institutions, ideology, and legitimacy. We also have a few Ottoman dedicatory inscriptions and endowment deed documents; a handful of contemporary or near-contemporary narratives written by the Ottomans' rivals and enemies, mainly Byzantines; and contemporary and later narratives and literary-religious works that historians use to reconstruct the religio-cultural and social landscape of Asia Minor in the thirteenth and fourteenth centuries.[5]

To assume that Ottoman conquests were led by an overarching grand strategy is to discard human agency. Similarly, to posit that military actions were always planned by the ruler and his advisers negates the role of local forces, endows the ruler and the Ottoman centre with overwhelming power that it did not exercise even in the heyday of the empire, and turns Ottoman sultans into the caricature of 'oriental despot'. March, or frontier, lords along the expanding emirate's fringes often initiated raids in the 1300s, just as border governors did in later centuries, leading to major military confrontations, often against Istanbul's intentions. The long war against the Habsburgs in Hungary (1593–1606) is not the only example of an exhausting confrontation that evolved from border skirmishes independent of the imperial centre, which had been fighting a devastating war on its opposite, eastern frontier with Safavid Persia since 1578 and had no wish to engage in a similar struggle in the west.

While I do not believe that there was a single overarching Ottoman grand strategy that guided Ottoman conquest and rule throughout the centuries, it is possible to detect strategies used by individual rulers to conquer, subjugate, and rule over the conquered peoples. In other words, the Ottomans did not lack strategic thinking and some of their strategies spanned longer time periods. Indeed, the strength of Ottoman methods of conquest and rule lay in the ability of the Ottoman decision-makers to promptly adjust their strategies according to new geopolitical conditions. Halil İnalcık examined certain methods of Ottoman conquest more than fifty years ago. Research since then has brought more evidence to light, partly strengthening, partly questioning his findings. İnalcık detected a gradual incorporation of conquered lands in two distinct stages: first, the Ottomans 'sought to establish some sort of suzerainty over the neighbouring states', and then in the second stage they 'sought direct control over these countries by the elimination of the native dynasties'.[6] With regard to the Ottoman conquest of Hungary, the idea of 'step-by-step' conquest and 'gradual incorporation' had been suggested as early as 1897, and was further elaborated on in the 1970s.[7] A recent work suggested that the Ottomans—geographically an Asian and North African empire but geostrategically a European land power—were unable to recalibrate their geostrategy to the changed geopolitical reality following the discovery of the Cape of Good Hope.[8]

While the above theses concerned Ottoman strategy in the long term, other historians restricted themselves to the examination of strategies of individual rulers. Süleyman I, in particular, attracted much attention, though the conclusions are rather contradictory. One historian could not detect any coherent strategy under this ruler and called his era a 'crisis of orientation', blaming the sultan for not adjusting Ottoman foreign policy to the new age of international relations 'after the crossing of the Atlantic'.[9] Others, to the contrary, endowed Süleyman with especially rational strategic thinking. The Hungarian military historian Géza Perjés suggested that Süleyman realized that Hungary lay beyond his army's 'action radius', or the outermost limit of operation of his army, and concluded that Hungary's conquest was undesirable or too expensive. The defence of such a distant province would have resulted in an immense deficit. After recognizing these limits, Süleyman decided not to conquer Hungary; instead, he aimed at turning it into a pro-Ottoman vassal state, a buffer zone between his own empire and that of the Habsburgs.[10] The specific motives behind Süleyman's policies towards his rivals remain the subject of debate. It is possible, however, to discern under his rule a more general vision of empire, which amounted to what may be called his 'grand strategy'.[11]

With regard to military culture, it is unhelpful to describe the Ottomans as 'a near-perfect military society'[12] because it unduly implies an especially violent or militaristic culture. Looking at the records of the Ottomans, it is clear that they were no more belligerent than any of their rivals, and that Ottoman society was no more militarized than that of the Habsburgs or the Romanovs.

While religious beliefs and superstitions were important in shaping culture and ethos, to suggest that religion was the main and unchanging driving force behind Ottoman expansion throughout the centuries is untenable. Research has long questioned Paul Wittek's thesis that the early Ottomans were bound together by the ideology and ethos of *ghaza*—a 'holy war' fought against the infidel—and that the Ottomans' rise and decline can best be explained by this ideology. It is now clear that Wittek privileged only one of the many forms and interpretations of *ghaza* current in Anatolia in the fourteenth and fifteenth centuries. This stands in contrast to those chroniclers who used the Arabic term *ghaza* and the Turkish word *akın* (raid, without any religious connotation) interchangeably to describe all kinds of early Ottoman military operations directed against both their Christian and Muslim neighbours and rivals. Research in recent decades has also constructed a more complex picture of the late thirteenth- and early fourteenth-century Byzantine-Ottoman frontier, and of Asia Minor in general, where alliances were formed across religious boundaries and where Muslims and Christians often joined forces against their rivals.[13]

This is not to say that religion played no role in strategy or in motivating the common soldier, but its influence has been unduly exaggerated in both contexts. The use of religion is most obvious in the Ottoman imperial ideology, propaganda, and legitimization techniques, and will be treated in the relevant sections of this chapter.

FROM FRONTIER PRINCIPALITY TO EMPIRE, C.1300–1453

Geopolitics

There were three cataclysmic events that reshaped power relations in Asia Minor in the twelfth and thirteenth centuries and created a power vacuum in which numerous independent Turkic principalities emerged, including that of the Ottomans: the battles of Manzikert (1071) and Kösedağ (1243), and the fourth crusade (1202–4). Manzikert led to the establishment of the Seljuk sultanate of Rum and opened a floodgate for Turcoman nomads. Their migration changed the ethnic and religious landscape of Anatolia so that by the early 1300s it had become predominantly Turkic and Muslim.[14]

The Byzantine empire, already pushed back to western Asia Minor by the Seljuks of Rum, never recovered from the destruction and carnage caused by Venetian, French, and other Latin crusaders during the sack of Constantinople in 1204. Though Michael VII Palaiologos (1261–82) managed to evict the Latins from Constantinople (1261) and resurrect the Byzantine empire, he and his successors were largely preoccupied with policies aimed at regaining control of the Balkans rather than fighting against the Turks along the Anatolian frontier.[15] The Mongols' defeat of the Rum Seljuks at the battle of Kösedağ (1243) led to the Seljuks' decline and the emergence of numerous Turcoman emirates in Asia Minor. Osman was but one of the Turcoman leaders in the region. The location of the small Ottoman emirate, next to the Byzantine frontier province of Bithynia, offered Osman's warriors both booty and glory for fighting against the 'infidels'. Osman's victory over a Byzantine army in 1302, and the lucrative raids into Byzantine realms, brought more and more Turcoman warriors under his banner.

The Ottomans' first major success was the capture of the Byzantine town of Prousa (Turkish Bursa) in 1326 by Orhan, Osman's son and successor. Orhan promptly made Prousa the capital of his principality. In 1352, during the Byzantine civil war (1341–7), Orhan acquired the Ottomans' first bridgehead in Thrace through marriage and political alliance. Two years later, his son Süleyman Pasha captured the important Byzantine fort of Gallipoli, whose defences had just been destroyed by a devastating earthquake. By conquering Adrianople (Edirne), which is located at the confluence of the Maritsa and Tunca rivers, in 1361 and making it the new capital of his empire, Murad I gained access to Thrace and Bulgaria. This action also signalled that the Ottomans were in Europe to stay and that they considered themselves a power with strategic interests in both Europe and Asia.

Although Murad I was killed at Kosovo (1389), the battle strengthened Ottoman positions in the Balkans. Stephen Lazarević, who succeeded his father, Lazar (also killed in the battle), became the vassal of the new Ottoman ruler, Bayezid I. The Ottoman victory at Kosovo put Hungary, which now shared a border with the Ottomans, on its guard. However, Hungary was unable to halt the Ottomans, and the crusading army led by King Sigismund of Hungary suffered a crushing defeat at Nikopol (1396) on the Danube. Byzantine support for the anti-Ottoman crusade provoked a long Ottoman blockade of Constantinople (1394–1402).

Europe's response to this threat remained lukewarm, and Constantinople was saved not by European crusaders but by Timur's invasion of Anatolia. Timur's victory at Ankara fundamentally changed geopolitics in Asia Minor and the Balkans. He restored the lands in eastern and central Anatolia, recently seized by Bayezid, to their Turcoman lords. A decade of interregnum and civil war among Bayezid's sons almost led to the downfall of the Ottoman sultanate. Fortunately, for the Ottomans, however, basic institutions of state—such as the military, the Ottoman land tenure system, and the structures of central and provincial administration—had already taken root, and large segments of Ottoman society had vested interests in restoring the power of the house of Osman.

Europe's last major effort to halt the Ottoman advance came from the Hungarians, following Murad II's subjugation of Serbia, Hungary's vassal and ally (1439), and the five-month siege of Belgrade (1440), which had since 1427 been the key fortress of the Hungarian defence line. The Hungarians' 'winter campaign' of 1443–4, led by King Wladislas (1440–4) and his governor, János Hunyadi, and a renewed offensive by the Ottomans' most stubborn Anatolian rival, the emir of Karaman, again threatened the very existence of the Ottoman state and forced Murad II to seek peace. The Hungarian-Ottoman peace treaty of 1444 re-established the pre-1439 status quo by returning Serbia to its ruler, George Branković. After restoring peace at both ends of his empire, Murad II abdicated in favour of his 12-year-old son Mehmed II. When, however, the Hungarians broke the treaty, he returned, defeated the crusaders at Varna (10 November 1444), and consolidated Ottoman rule in the Balkans.

Military Power

The early Ottomans' most important asset was the continuous influx of Turkic warriors under Osman's and his successors' banner. As a result of this, by the late fourteenth century, Ottoman forces enjoyed numerical superiority against most of their Anatolian and European rivals. They were strong enough to defeat a coalition of Serbian lords in 1371 and in 1389 another Serbian army strengthened by Bosnian troops at the battle of Kosovo Polje. It seems that the Ottomans also outnumbered the crusaders at Nikopol in 1396 by some 10,000 men (40,000–45,000 Ottomans to 30,000–35,000 crusaders). However, Bayezid's forces were no match for Timur, whose army enjoyed a decisive numerical superiority over the Ottomans at Ankara in 1402, even relying on the most conservative estimates (140,000 Timurids to 85,000 Ottomans).

Ottoman forces under Osman consisted principally of mounted archers and excelled in raids and ambushes rather than formal battles and sieges. However, by the reign of Orhan and Murad I, the Ottoman military had been transformed from the ruler's raiding forces into a disciplined army, and was capable of conducting regular campaigns and sieges.

In the fourteenth century, young volunteer peasants were recruited for the infantry *yaya* (footman) and cavalry *müsellem* (exemptee) corps. Paid by the ruler during campaigns, they returned to their villages after campaigns, and were exempted from certain taxes in return for their military service. Under Murad I, the *müsellems* were gradually replaced by the salaried palace horsemen, and the *yayas'* place was taken by *azab* infantrymen—a kind of peasant militia originally composed of unmarried (*azab*) young men levied from and equipped by the peasants—and by the janissaries. The *yayas* and *müsellems* became auxiliary forces, transported weapons and ammunition, and built and repaired roads and bridges during campaigns.

Organized similarly to the janissaries, and armed with bows and swords, infantry *azabs* were expendable conscripts who fought in the first rows of the Ottoman battle formation, in front of the cannons and janissaries. Although the number of *azabs* was significant in the fifteenth century (20,000 at the conquest of Constantinople in 1453, and 40,000 in the 1473 campaign against Uzun Hasan, mentioned below), the janissaries gradually took over their role, relegating them to garrison and naval duties.

The janissaries (from the Turkish *yeni çeri*, meaning 'new troops') were established in the 1370s as the sultan's elite guard and comprised only few hundred men. At first the sultan used prisoners of war to create his own independent military guard. Later, in the 1380s, the *devşirme* ('collection'), or child levy system, was introduced to recruit soldiers for the janissaries. Under this system, Christian youths between 8 and 20 years of age (principally from the Balkans, though with some exceptions) were conscripted periodically and at varying rates. After conversion to Islam and seven to eight years of service in Anatolian peasant farms, the boys joined the ranks of janissary novices, began their military training, and worked in the imperial dockyards or the imperial cannon foundry. After several years of such service, they became janissaries or joined the corps of gunners, gun-carriage drivers, bombardiers, and armourers. With the broadening of the pool of recruitment, the initial guard was soon transformed into the ruler's elite household infantry, numbering approximately 2,000 men at the battle of Kosovo (1389) and about 3,000 men before Mehmed II's second reign.

Changes in the structure of the Ottoman armed forces, as well as the related fiscal and economic policies under Mehmed II, aimed at strengthening imperial sovereignty. Following the rebellion of janissaries upon his accession in 1451, Mehmed II purged the corps, replacing the dismissed units with new ones formed from the keepers of the sultan's hounds (*sekban*), and raising the total number of the corps from 3,000 to 5,000 men. By the end of his rule in 1481, the number of janissaries had doubled, reaching 10,000 men. The janissaries remained about 10,000–12,000 strong until the end of the sixteenth century. These elite forces, along with the more specialized units of the standing army (such as gunners and armourers) and the palace horsemen, afforded the sultan a strong professional army, which the march lords could not match with their raiders. Mehmed II also deployed janissaries in strategically important frontier garrisons, further strengthening central control over the march lords, whom he turned into ordinary district governors. To pay his standing army, however, Mehmed II needed more revenue, which led him to introduce unpopular fiscal measures: repeated devaluations, confiscations of endowment lands, tax-farming, and so on. These measures caused social discontent that forced his successors to reverse some of these policies. However, the centralized bureaucracy and army survived up to the late sixteenth century.

The bulk of the Ottoman army, however, remained cavalry. Until the beginning of the sixteenth century, the freelance light cavalry *akıncı* raiders remained militarily significant. In 1475, Mehmed II mobilized 6,000 such raiders, whereas Süleyman I (1520–66) brought 20,000 of them to his 1521 campaign against Hungary. Although the six cavalry units of the household army remained modest, numbering about 5,000 men in the early sixteenth century, their number had doubled by 1567, reaching more than 11,000 men. More importantly, a large cavalry force was maintained through the Ottoman *timar*, or prebendal, system of remuneration. In return for the right to collect revenues from his assigned fiefs, the Ottoman provincial cavalryman (timariot, or sipahi) had to provide his arms (short sword and bows), armour (helmet and mail), and horse, and to report for military service along with his armed retainers when called upon by the sultan. In order to keep track of the number of fief-holding cavalrymen and their obligations, the Ottomans introduced survey registers, perhaps as early as the reign of Bayezid I. During campaigns, muster rolls were checked against these registers in order to determine if all the cavalrymen had reported for military duty and had brought the required share of retainers and equipment. If the cavalryman did not report for service or failed to bring with him the required number of retainers, he lost his military fief, which was then assigned to someone else.

The strength of the timariot army deployed in campaigns in the 1430s and 1440s is estimated at about 10,000–15,000 men. The imperial budget of 1528 listed 28,000 provincial timariot fief-holders who could supply an additional force of 23,000 retainers, which would put the number of the provincial cavalry troops at over 50,000 men. As mentioned above, until the beginning of the sixteenth century, the freelance light cavalry, the *akıncı* raiders, descendants of the old nomadic Turcoman warriors, played a major role in Ottoman conquests. Numbering up to 20,000 men in major campaigns, they were under the control of the march lords. Out of this force potential, Mehmed and his successors were able to mobilize professional field armies in the range of 70,000–80,000 men, an achievement that few of their enemies could match until the late sixteenth century. These estimates do not include the garrison forces, the raiders, and the various auxiliary troops who repaired roads and bridges in front of the marching army, helped to transport cannons, or performed various engineering works. From the late fifteenth century on, the Ottomans also could count on their Crimean Tatar auxiliaries, whose light cavalry troops performed important services as raiders and scouts for the Ottomans, especially in their campaigns against Muscovy, Poland-Lithuania, and Hungary in the sixteenth and seventeenth centuries.[16]

Owing to Ottoman flexibility and conquest strategy, Ottoman forces habitually included Christian troops of the sultans' vassals. At Kosovo, Murad I's vassals from south-eastern Europe fought against the Serbian prince Lazar. The 5,000-strong Serbian heavy cavalry played a crucial role in Bayezid I's victory at Nikopol, and at Ankara the Serbian vassal contingents proved to be the most loyal to the Ottomans, fighting to the end on the sultan's side along with the elite janissaries. However, employing troops from recently subdued vassalages had its hazards too. At Ankara, the Kara (Black) Tatars on the Ottoman left wing, in treacherous agreement with Timur, attacked the Ottomans' back. This caused the cavalrymen from the Anatolian Turcoman emirates, whose emirs fought in Timur's army, to desert Bayezid I.

Under Mehmed II and Bayezid II (1481–1512), the Ottomans acquired the common naval technology of the Mediterranean, adopting the oared galley as their principal vessel. From the 1560s, following their Mediterranean rivals, the Ottomans too adopted the 'al scaloccio' system, by which all oarsmen on the same bench pulled a single oar. This arrangement helped to increase the number of oarsmen. Ottoman galleys usually carried a centre-line cannon and two smaller flanking culverins. Impressed by the Venetian galeasses, which played an important role in the Christians' victory at the battle of Lepanto, the Ottomans were quick to imitate these large and heavily armed galleys that could fire broadsides. During the rebuilding of the fleet, destroyed at Lepanto, the Ottoman shipyards in Sinop and Istanbul constructed some four or five galeasses. The size of the Ottoman navy was already impressive under Mehmed II, who employed 380 galleys in his naval expeditions against the Genoese-administered Crimean port town of Caffa in 1475. During the 1499–1503 Ottoman-Venetian war, Bayezid II considerably strengthened the navy, ordering the construction of no less than 250 galleys in late 1500 alone. The reorganization of the Ottoman navy under Bayezid II transformed the originally land-based empire into a formidable naval power. The navy was instrumental in halting Portuguese expansion in the Red Sea and the Persian Gulf and in the Ottoman conquest of Mamluk Egypt in 1516–17.[17]

The bulk of the Ottoman army (infantry *azabs*, cavalry timariots, and *akıncıs*) used swords and bows. The Ottomans adopted firearms in the latter part of the fourteenth century, and established a separate artillery corps as part of the sultans' standing army in the early fifteenth century, well before their European opponents. Direct military conflicts, contraband trade in weaponry, and the employment of European military experts ensured the dissemination of up-to-date technologies and military know-how into the Ottoman realms. Initially, the janissaries were equipped with bows, crossbows, and javelins. Under Murad II, they began to use matchlock arquebuses, and by the mid-sixteenth century most of them carried firearms. Murad III (1574–95) equipped his janissaries with the more advanced matchlock musket, although flintlock muskets with the Spanish *miquelet*-lock were also manufactured in the empire from the late 16th century. However, the janissaries' traditional weapon, the recurved bow, remained a formidable weapon well into the seventeenth century.

The Ottomans also established cannon foundries and gunpowder works throughout their empire. Major foundries operated along the Adriatic (Avlonya and Prevesa), in Hungary (Buda and Temesvár), the Balkans (Rudnik, Semendire, İskenderiye, Novaberda, Pravişte, and Belgrade), Anatolia (Diyarbekir, Erzurum, Birecik, Mardin, and Van), Iraq (Baghdad and Basra), and Egypt (Cairo). The centre of cannon casting, however, was the Imperial Cannon Foundry in Constantinople, which was established by Mehmed II after the capture of the city. It was one of the first arsenals in late medieval Europe that was built, operated, and financed by a central government, in a time when most of Europe's monarchs acquired their cannons from smaller artisan workshops. The foundry could easily multiply its capacity before and during major wars, casting several hundreds of cannons before the campaign season. The Ottomans also operated gunpowder works in Constantinople and almost all of their provincial centres and thus remained self-sufficient in the production of weapons and ammunition until the late eighteenth century.

Despite allegations to the contrary in the literature, the Ottomans managed to keep pace with Europe regarding weapons technology. More importantly, their military-industrial complex in the capital, supplemented by smaller provincial cannon foundries and gunpowder workshops, enabled the Ottomans to establish a long-lasting firepower superiority in eastern and central Europe, the Mediterranean, and the Middle East. While factors such as numerical superiority, cavalry charge, and better logistics and tactics were important in the Ottoman victories at Çaldıran (1514), Marj Dabiq (1516), Raydaniyya (1517), and Mohács (1526) against the Safavids, Mamluks, and Hungarians, respectively, Ottoman firepower superiority also played a crucial role in all these field battles. In siege warfare, that superiority remained the Ottomans' strength until the mid-eighteenth century.[18]

Strategies of Expansion and Leadership

The main objectives of Ottoman strategy in the fourteenth and fifteenth centuries were the gradual expansion of territory and wealth through varied means and through the avoidance of simultaneous military conflicts on more than one front. Under this strategy, Ottoman methods of conquest and rule included dynastic marriages and marriage alliances; the incorporation of the pre-Ottoman Christian nobility and military men into the Ottoman military and bureaucratic elite (*askeri*) through the assignment of prebends; Ottoman pragmatism and flexibility in provincial administration and taxation in accordance with the Islamic principles *istimalet* (accommodation); and the Ottoman policy of forced resettlement (*sürgün*).

Until about the 1450s, inter-dynastic marriages remained an important means of Ottoman strategy to subjugate (and eventually annex) both Christian and Muslim neighbouring polities, and in this regard Ottoman marriage strategy differed from that of the Byzantines and Habsburgs. Through marriage alliances concluded with the Byzantine, Serbian, and Bulgarian royal houses, as well as with the Anatolian Muslim principalities of Germiyan, Isfendiyaroğlu, Aydın, Saruhan, Çandar, Karaman, and Dulkadır, the Ottomans acquired additional territories; furthermore, the fathers and brothers of the brides became vassals who paid tribute and provided troops to the Ottomans. For example, in 1346 Orhan contracted a second marriage, this time to the Byzantine princess Theodora, and subsequently used his troops to help her father, John Kantakouzenos, acquire the Byzantine throne. In return, Orhan got Tzympe, the Ottomans' first bridgehead on the Gallipoli peninsula.

By the reign of Murad I, marriage had become a way of subjugation. After 1371, Murad I married the sister of the Bulgarian tsar Shisman of Turnovo, who in the process became an Ottoman vassal. In the late 1370s, Murad married his son Bayezid to the daughter of Yakub, the lord of the neighbouring Turkish emirate of Germiyan, and through this marriage the Ottomans acquired part of that emirate, including its capital, Kütahya. In 1392, Bayezid I married the sister of Stephen Lazarević of Serbia, thereby reducing Stephen to vassalage. Two years later, Bayezid also married the daughter of a Frankish countess who ruled a small principality to the east of Athens, and half of that principality came with the bride. In 1423, İsfendiyaroğlu, the defeated lord of Kastamonu in eastern Anatolia, gave Murad II his daughter and became an Ottoman vassal. In 1435, Murad II married Tsaritsa Mara, the daughter of the Serbian despot George Branković.[19]

Dynastic marriages were not just used for subduing rival Christian and Muslim lords, and for gaining territories, allies, and vassal troops. They also could and did prove crucial tools in concluding treaties and thus avoiding double-front engagements. In the crisis years of 1443–4, when the Ottomans were attacked by the Hungarians in the Balkans and by the Karamans in Asia Minor, Murad II used his family ties to initiate peace negotiations with the Hungarians through his Serbian wife and her father. Most likely, the sultan communicated his peace initiative in January 1444 via an Orthodox monk, whom Murad's Serbian wife ostensibly sent to his father-in-law. This then led to the Ottoman-Hungarian-Serbian peace treaty (June 1444), which enabled the Ottomans to quell the rebellious Karamans and free their Asian troops. When the Hungarians later broke the peace and a crusader army crossed the Ottoman border in the autumn of 1444, Murad II was ready, and he defeated them at Varna that November.[20]

Whereas dynastic marriages were part of Ottoman strategy of conquest and rule, the sultans were careful not to produce children by these marriages so as to avoid any possible claims on Ottoman sovereignty and territories on the part of the wives' families. Except for Murad I and Selim I, whose mothers (Nilüfer and Ayşe, the daughter of the emir of Dulkadır) came from ruling families, all the Ottoman sultans were the offspring of slave concubines.

Ottoman pragmatism and flexibility and the inclusive nature of early Ottoman governance also proved instrumental in winning over the minds of the defeated peoples and in attracting followers, allies, soldiers, and taxpayers. Adjusting Ottoman taxation regimes to match that of the pre-Ottoman system in a given locality, lowering taxes after conquest, or protecting the taxpaying subjects (*reaya*) from unjust levies through an efficient provincial administration that was to keep law and order were all methods in accordance with the Islamic principle of *istimalet* (accommodation)—but also indications of Ottoman pragmatism. By granting Ottoman *timar* prebends to members of the conquered Christian nobility in the Balkans and the former Byzantine empire of Trebizond (Turkish Trabzon), the Ottomans gained supporters and collaborators who willingly performed military and bureaucratic services for them in territories and circumstances to which they were newcomers. The Balkan Christian lords also profited from Ottoman conquest, for they managed to preserve their religion, privileged status, and at least parts of their pre-Ottoman military fiefs (*pronoias*) and hereditary possessions (*bashtinas*). Many of these Christian timariots and their sons were called *voynuks* (Slavonic for 'fighting man', or 'soldier'). A social class established in the 1370s or 1380s, *voynuks* were to be found in significant numbers in Bulgaria, Serbia, Macedonia, Thessaly, and Albania. Large numbers of Christian Balkan nomads, called Vlachs, were also incorporated into their ranks. In addition to augmenting the Ottomans' military forces, these troops brought with them valuable tactical diversity and knowledge of the enemy's lands. In order to maintain law and order and thus secure the steady flow of revenues to the imperial centre, the Ottomans allowed pre-Ottoman local communal organizations and their leaders (*knezes* and *primikürs*) to continue to function in conquered Serbia, Bulgaria, and Greece.[21]

Starting as early as the 1350s, another strategy of Ottoman incorporation was state-organized resettlement or forced population transfer (*sürgün*). The strategy was used to achieve a number of goals.

First, by transferring Turcoman and Tatar nomads from Asia Minor to the Balkans, Murad I and his successors increased the number of their Turkic-speaking Muslim subjects in a hostile, Slavic-speaking Christian environment. The transfer of the Christian population, occasionally whole communities, from the Balkans to Anatolia served similar purposes. When this policy was coupled with voluntary Turcoman migration from Anatolia to the Balkans, encouraged by the Ottoman state, it resulted in massive Turkification of the population of Thrace and the eastern Balkans, and expanded Ottoman colonization far beyond garrisons and urban centres.

Second, the Ottomans used deportation to increase Ottoman military presence in the newly conquered lands. The Turcomans transferred from Asia Minor to Europe often belonged to the early Ottoman military formations, such as the *yaya* infantrymen. By granting them farm plots (*çiftlik*) in their new lands, the state financed them locally, using the resources of the conquered territories.

Third, forced migration was also instrumental in establishing or restoring Ottoman control over Anatolia by transferring the unruly and rebellious

Anatolian Turcomans to the Balkans and thus uprooting them from their traditional base. The transfer of Turcomans from the recently subdued Saruhan
emirate to the vicinity of Skopje and Filibe in the 1380s and the relocation of
rebellious Çepni Turcomans from Canik on the Black Sea to Albania and of the
Tatars of the Amasya-Tokat region to the Maritsa valley are just a few examples in
this context.

Fourth, under Murad II and Mehmed II, forced resettlement played a crucial
role in the urban reconstruction projects of the former Byzantine cities of Salo-
nika, Constantinople, and Trabzon. In order to repopulate, rebuild, and Ottoma-
nize them, the Ottoman government transferred Muslim, Christian, and Jewish
peasants, craftsmen, and merchants into these cities from other urban centres
(Bursa, Edirne, Filibe, Gelibolu), and from regions as diverse as Anatolia, Serbia,
Albania, the Morea, the Aegean islands (Euboea, Imbros, Lesbos), the Crimea, and
so on.[22]

Apart from good strategy, fortunate circumstances also played an important
role in the earliest Ottoman military success. In March 1302, floods temporarily
diverted the course of the River Sakarya (Sangarius) into its ancient riverbed. The
forts on the left (Byzantine) bank of the river's new course had recently been
refurbished by Michael Palaiologos in 1281–2, and in places where the forts were
too far apart to guard against enemy crossing the river thick barriers of felled trees
had been set up. However, after the flood all of these became ineffective, which
made it easier for Osman and his small band to cross the river. Osman achieved
his first crucial victory against the Byzantines just a few weeks later, on 27 July
1302, on the plain of Bapheus near Nikomedia (İzmit), on the Byzantine side of
the river.[23] His victory ultimately opened the way to further conquests on the
Byzantine side of the river as far as Constantinople.

Another natural disaster opened Thrace to Ottoman conquests. On the night of
2 March 1354, an earthquake destroyed the Byzantine coastline of Thrace, including the defences of Gallipoli, the largest city on the peninsula, which controlled the
passage from Europe to Asia. Osman's son Süleyman, who learned about the
devastation in Pegai (Biga) on the Asiatic shore, crossed the straits and took
possession of several settlements abandoned by their Byzantine inhabitants,
settling Muslim Turks there. The defences of Gallipoli were repaired and manned
with Ottoman guards, and the fort soon evolved into a naval base and an
important Ottoman bridgehead in Europe.[24]

The early Ottoman rulers were especially successful in forging alliances, building new networks, and thus gaining supporters across the diverse ethnic, religious,
and cultural human landscape of early fourteenth-century Anatolia. A recent
sociological study has shown how Osman and Orhan, the first two rulers of the
Ottomans, used brokerage to build their personal networks, which included
groups of Muslims, Orthodox Christians, and converts. We find several Greeks
and converts among the leaders of the Ottoman *akıncı* forces and garrison
commanders.[25] It is generally accepted that the first ten rulers of the House of
Osman were able strategists and military leaders. They also were successful in
hiring exceptionally talented statesmen, administrators, generals, and military
engineers from a diverse pool of Turks, Byzantine Greeks, Balkan Slavs, and
Europeans.

Supplementing Murad I's qualities as a military commander, Turkish march lords, especially Evrenos in Macedonia and the Mihaloğlus in Bulgaria, played crucial roles in pushing the borders of the expanding Ottoman state further and further. Murad's generals Lala Şahin and Çandarlı Halil Hayreddin Pasha were instrumental in Murad's military conquests. Their service in shaping the military and administrative institutions of the growing Ottoman state, whose administrative structure had become more complex and centralized by the end of Murad's reign, was also of great significance. Similarly, in the 1440s, Murad II's grand vizier, Çandarlı Halil Pasha, the grandson of Halil Hayreddin Pasha, was instrumental in crafting a cautious and balanced Ottoman foreign policy. This policy aimed at avoiding warfare on two or three different fronts at a time when the Ottomans had just recovered from the civil wars and the interregnum of 1402–13 and were threatened by plans of crusades and anti-Ottoman alliances involving all the Ottomans' traditional enemies and rivals: Hungary, Venice, the Byzantine empire, and Karaman.

EMPIRE: MID-FIFTEENTH TO LATE SEVENTEENTH CENTURIES

Geopolitics: Challenges of Empire and Changing Strategies

Modern sociologists do not consider the Ottoman empire a world power, for it did not possess the 'minimal threshold criteria for global and world power'; most importantly, it was not a seaborne empire because its navy did not 'demonstrate ocean-going activity'.[26] Yet, for contemporary Europeans it seemed 'the most powerful' empire.[27] It held this image by virtue of its geopolitical situation, its enormous territory and population, its wealth of economic resources, and a central and provincial administration that was capable of mobilizing these resources according to the strategic interests of the Ottoman sultans and governing elite. The efficient use of resources formed the basis of the Ottoman army, which was considered to be the best and most efficient military known to contemporaneous Europeans. For the Ottomans' contemporaries and main rivals, the sultan's empire was a world power. It is generally accepted that this empire was founded by Mehmed II.

Mehmed II's conquest of Constantinople (1453) was of utmost historical significance. From an Ottoman perspective, the conquest eliminated the Byzantine hostile wedge that had separated the sultans' European and Asian provinces. Whereas neither the Balkans nor Anatolia has a natural geographical or strategic centre, Constantinople's strategic location made the city an ideal capital of both lands. Mehmed II and his successors rapidly rebuilt and repopulated Constantinople, whose pre-conquest population (circa 40,000) doubled by 1477, and reached perhaps as many as 250,000–300,000 inhabitants by the mid-sixteenth century. Owing to the Ottomans' tolerant policy towards the city's former Byzantine inhabitants and European (mainly Genoese and Venetian) resident merchants, as well as to Bayezid II's decision to offer new homes for the Sephardic

Jews expelled from Spain, the population of Ottoman Constantinople was 60 per cent Muslim and 40 per cent Christian and Jewish by the late fifteenth century. This multi-ethnic and multi-religious character (with similar population distribution) remained the hallmark of the Ottoman imperial capital in the sixteenth century, an era when monarchs throughout Europe imposed or at least tried to impose their religions onto their subjects. Mehmed also abandoned the old capital city Edirne and moved into his newly built Topkapı Palace, whose location between the Golden Horn and the Sea of Marmara on the Seraglio Point offered unmatched defensibility and spectacular views.

In strategic terms, the city afforded the Ottomans a commanding position over the trade routes between Europe and Asia, the Mediterranean and the Black Sea, and a perfect logistical centre for mobilizing human and economic resources for campaigns in Asia and Europe. Constantinople was again the seat of a mighty empire's government, the main garrison of its standing forces, a naval base with a formidable armada, a natural harbour (the Golden Horn) with an imperial shipyard to build and repair galleys, a military-industrial complex complete with an imperial cannon foundry, gunpowder works, and workshops to manufacture hand firearms and cold weapons. With its Turkish and Persian artisans and blacksmiths; Armenian and Greek miners and sappers; Bosnian, Serbian, Turkish, Italian, German, and later French, English, and Dutch gun founders and military engineers; as well as Venetian, Dalmatian, and Greek shipwrights and sailors, the Ottoman capital proved to be an ideal place for 'technological dialogue', and helped the Ottomans to keep pace with the latest innovations in military and naval technology. The Ottoman capital was also a centre of international diplomacy, with resident ambassadors from all the major European states and empires, as well as of espionage and intrigues. It was the city of boundless opportunities for political, military, economic, and cultural advancement, which invited talent from all corners of the empire and from Europe, thus affording the empire a large pool of talented people whom the government could and did employ in its army, administration, and economy.

The strategic location of the capital city enabled Mehmed II to consolidate Ottoman rule in the Balkans by annexing Serbia (1459), Bosnia and Herzegovina (1463), Albania (1478–9), the Morea (1458–60), and Euboea (1470). Ottoman performance in the 1463–79 Venetian-Ottoman War signalled that the Ottomans had become an Aegean power. Mehmed II also eradicated the Genoese trading colonies in the Crimea (1475), and made the Muslim Crimean Tatar khanate his vassal (1478), thus establishing Ottoman control over the Black Sea littoral and the steppes to the north of the Crimea, a rich source of grain and slaves. All these would have been unthinkable without the Ottoman navy, which was considerably strengthened under Mehmed and Bayezid II (1481–1512).

However, Ottoman rule in eastern Anatolia remained disputed, and it was not until the 1470s that Mehmed annexed the Karaman emirate (1468–74) and defeated his eastern Muslim rival Uzun Hasan (1453–78) of the Akkoyunlu ('White Sheep') Turcoman confederation (1473). Uzun Hasan ruled over a vast territory from eastern Anatolia to western Iran, and tried to forge anti-Ottoman alliances with the Karamans as well as Christian Hungary and Venice. While such anti-Ottoman leagues never brought tangible results owing to communication difficulties across the religious divide and large distances, they convinced the

Ottoman leadership of the necessity to subjugate the Akkoyunlus, a task that was achieved only under Mehmed II's grandson Selim I (1512–20).[28] By this time, however, the emergence of the rival Safavid dynasty in Persia constituted a new and grave threat to Ottoman sovereignty in eastern Anatolia.

In 1501, Ismail, the head of the militant Shia Safaviyya religious order, defeated the Akkoyunlus, declared himself shah of Persia, and made the Imami or 'Twelver' rite of Shia Islam the official religion of his new empire. Shah Ismail (1501–24) portrayed himself as Mahdi, the prophesied saviour of Islam, and many saw in him the long-awaited hidden imam. For the Turcomans and Kurds of eastern Anatolia, the Safavid style of government, which resembled that of a nomadic tribal confederation, seemed a desirable alternative to the more centralized Ottoman rule that jeopardized the nomads' way of life and social structure.

Sultan Selim I's main strategic concern was the fight against the Safavids. He devoted most of his energies and his empire's resources to confronting the Safavid challenge. Combining sheer military force (his victory at Çaldıran, 1514), propaganda, persuasion, and the policy of appeasement vis-à-vis the shah's followers in his realms, Selim managed to extend Ottoman rule over most of eastern Anatolia, although Ottoman control in these regions remained unsteady until the end of empire. One major consequence of Selim's conquests and claim on the lands of the Dulkadır emirate in south-eastern Anatolia was the Ottomans' confrontation with the Mamluks, the Dulkadır emir's nominal sovereign. The war ended with the destruction of the Mamluk empire and the Ottoman conquest of Bilad al-Sham—territories extending between the Taurus Mountains and Sinai—and Egypt in 1516–17.

The introduction of Ottoman rule in these Arab lands had major political, ideological, and economic consequences. Selim became the master of Mecca and Medina, 'the cradle of Islam', as well as of Damascus and Cairo, former seats of the caliphs. He and his successors assumed the title of 'Servant of the Two Noble Sanctuaries' (Mecca and Medina), and with this the task of protecting and organizing the annual pilgrimage (haj) to Mecca, which gave the Ottomans unparalleled prestige and legitimacy in the Muslim world. His conquests increased the area of the empire to 1.5 million square kilometres, and revenues from Syria and Egypt accounted for approximately a third of the Ottoman treasury's annual income. The protection of the maritime lanes of communications between Istanbul and Cairo thus became vital, and necessitated the further strengthening of the Ottoman navy.

The conquest of Rhodes (1522), the base of the belligerent Knights of St John, and later of Cyprus (1570), then under Venetian rule, was therefore strategically necessary. This led to confrontation with the dominant Christian maritime powers of the Mediterranean: the Knights of St John, who after the capture of Rhodes relocated to Malta, Venice, and Spain. Under Selim's successors, protecting Mecca and Medina against Portuguese encroachment into the Red Sea brought the Ottomans into conflict with the Portuguese. More important for Ottoman maritime interests, in 1519, threatened by Spanish advance in the western Mediterranean, 'the pirate of Algiers', Hayreddin Barbarossa, offered his services to the sultan. Although Selim made him governor (*beylerbeyi*) of Algiers, it was not until his appointment as grand admiral of the Ottoman navy in

1533 that his services brought tangible results for the Ottoman war effort in the Mediterranean.

On the other hand, Selim's wars against Muslims, and the lack of any major campaign against the Christian 'infidels', presented a 'legitimacy deficit'. Constant wars from the early 1510s devastated the eastern provinces, and the imperial army was stretched too thin. Distance and inhospitable climate (early winters and snow), combined with Shah Ismail's tactic of avoiding battle and his use of a scorched-earth policy, which destroyed crops and poisoned wells, caused serious problems for the otherwise well-organized Ottoman logistics, rendering seasonal campaigning ineffective. The sultan's Asian troops also fought reluctantly against the shah's Anatolian followers, and they often deserted. Thus, it was for a combination of ideological, socio-economic, and military reasons that the new sultan, Süleyman I, fundamentally changed the strategic priorities of his empire by embarking on an aggressive campaign against the Ottomans' Christian rivals.

Süleyman's conquest of Belgrade (1521), the key to Hungary and Habsburg central Europe, and Rhodes (1522), especially in light of previous Ottoman failures (Belgrade 1456, Rhodes 1480) under Mehmed II, established Süleyman's image in Europe as a formidable adversary. More importantly, the conquest of Belgrade shows that he either ascended to the throne with his new strategy to attack his European rivals, or made such a decision immediately after he assumed power (30 September 1520). Owing to logistical constraints of the time, preparations for campaigns habitually started during autumn of the previous year, and thus mobilization orders for the 1521 campaign should have been issued in October or November 1520.

Süleyman led his armies on thirteen campaigns, spending perhaps a quarter of his reign on campaign. These brought Iraq (1534–5, 1546) and Hungary (1541) under Ottoman rule. The latter became the theatre of Ottoman-Habsburg rivalry over central Europe for the next 150 years. The other theatre of this rivalry was the Mediterranean, which the Ottomans came to control as far as Tunis and Algiers by 1541. Charles V's conquest of Tunis (1535) proved short-lived. Süleyman's navy, commanded since 1533 by Hayreddin Barbarossa, won a splendid victory at Preveza (1538) off north-western Greece against the joint naval forces of the Holy League of Spain, Venice, Genoa, the papacy, Portugal, and the Knights of St John. The destruction of Charles V's navy on the coast of Algiers (1541), the Ottoman capture of Tripoli (1551), and their victory at Djerba (1560) over yet another Holy League that aimed at retaking Tripoli, cemented Ottoman control in the Mediterranean.[29] They were, however, less successful against the Portuguese. Though the Ottomans managed to defend the Hejaz and the Red Sea, attempts at dislodging the Portuguese from the Indian Ocean had failed repeatedly under Süleyman (1538, 1552, 1554). The idea to deploy part of their Mediterranean fleet in the Indian Ocean via a canal near Suez, which clearly showed Sokollu Mehmed's global strategy, proved technically and economically unfeasible as well.[30]

If Ottoman-Habsburg rivalry in Hungary and in the Mediterranean was one of the epic confrontations that shaped the history of Europe, Süleyman's wars against Safavid Persia (1534–5, 1548–9, 1553) had decisive consequences in the Middle East. Ottoman conquests in Iraq (including that of Baghdad) were acknowledged in the Safavid-Ottoman treaty of Amasya (1555), and the eastern border of the empire, established in 1555, was to remain essentially unchanged until the First

World War. The Ottomans and Safavids fought two more exhausting wars (1578–90, 1603–39), but Safavid gains (recapture of Baghdad) under Shah Abbas (1587–1629) proved short-lived, and the 1555 border was restored in 1639, with some modifications. However, the war caused much destruction and in the long run weakened Ottoman military capabilities, as did the war against the Habsburgs in Hungary (1593–1606). This confrontation brought only modest territorial gains for the Ottomans, and exposed the weaknesses of the Ottoman military machine. These exhausting land wars also showed that by the late sixteenth century the Ottomans had reversed their Mediterranean strategy, thus ending almost a century of maritime rivalry with the Spanish Habsburgs and their allies.

In the Mediterranean, the battle of Lepanto (1571) was the last major confrontation between Muslim and Christian oar-powered navies. Provoked by the Ottoman conquest of Cyprus (1570), the joint fleet of another Holy League (Spain, Venice, Genoa, and their smaller allies), under the command of Philip II's half-brother Don Juan, achieved a resounding victory, destroying almost the entire Ottoman navy with its crew and ordnance.[31] However, to the surprise of the Christians, by next spring the Ottomans were said to have rebuilt their navy, with 150 new vessels, complete with artillery. The Ottomans continued to hold Cyprus, and the Holy League collapsed as Venice concluded a treaty with Istanbul in 1573 and as Spanish resources were redirected to meet new challenges in the Netherlands. In 1574, in a bold strategic move and naval gamble that stretched the logistical and temporal limits—March to late October, known in Ottoman sources as 'sea season' (*deniz* or *derya mevsimi*)—of Mediterranean galley warfare, the Ottomans retook Tunis from Habsburg Spain, with a naval force larger than either party had at Lepanto.

The victory, off the coast of Spanish Habsburg Sicily at such a great distance from Istanbul, the logistical centre of Ottoman operations, demonstrated Ottoman naval resurgence and restored Ottoman military prestige on both sides of the religious divide. Capitalizing on their recent victory, in 1576 Ottoman janissaries and cannoneers helped to unseat the Moroccan sultan Muhammad al-Mutawakkil, who had challenged Ottoman sovereignty and replaced him with Istanbul's client Abd al-Malik of the same Saadi dynasty. Threatened by the recent Ottoman advance in North Africa, the Portuguese launched an attack on Morocco in 1578 under the command of their devout crusading king, Don Sebastian. The expedition resulted in the dramatic battle of Alcazar (1578), which left both Moroccan sultans and the Portuguese king dead. Alcazar was the last major confrontation between Christian and Muslim forces in the Mediterranean. After 1578, the two main adversaries in the conflict, the Spanish Habsburgs and the Ottomans, disengaged and signed a truce in 1580. Both had more pressing concerns: the Ottomans had been fighting the Safavids since 1578, while Spain was busy with the Dutch Revolt and acquiring its weakened Catholic neighbour Portugal (1581).[32]

Sovereignty and Ideology

Mehmed II's second reign (1451–81) marked a major change with regard to Ottoman sovereignty and strategy. Using the prestige that the conquest of Constantinople had afforded him, Mehmed II dismissed and later executed his grand vizier, Çandarlı Halil Pasha, who had been responsible for deposing the young sultan in 1446 and had opposed the siege of Constantinople. According to many contemporaries, Halil Pasha had exerted disproportionate authority under Murad II. His long tenure as grand vizier (1436–53) symbolized both the power of the old Turkish aristocracy and a different style of governing, in an age when the sultan shared power with his viziers and advisers. Mehmed II, however, considered himself an absolute sovereign, and did not want his sovereignty to be restricted by his viziers. Except for Karamani Mehmed Pasha, Mehmed II chose all of his grand viziers from among his *kuls*, or slaves, who had no family ties or regional power base and were thus dependent upon him. Halil Pasha's successor was Zaganos Pasha, of *devşirme* origin and member of the 'war party', whose more aggressive policy, advocated from 1444 on, was more in line with that of the young sultan. Mehmed II's sobriquet, 'Conqueror' (in Turkish *Fatih*) and his insistence of using the Roman-Byzantine title *Caesar (Qayser)*, in addition to the old Turkish *kaghan* and the Islamic sultan, signalled the Ottoman ruler's claim to universal sovereignty and the fact that he considered himself heir to the Roman emperors. His decision not to chair personally the meetings of the imperial council, or *divan*, the empire's highest governing body, which in war also functioned as its high command, was also in line with his policy of royal seclusion, and meant a departure from his father's ruling style. He also ended the old policy of dynastic marriages, for it would have been below the sultan's dignity to marry his sons and daughters to petty princes and princesses of the Balkans and Anatolia. Most of these lands were conquered by the mighty armies of his empire anyhow.

The evolution of Ottoman imperial ideology and propaganda was but one element of a larger imperial vision, which might be referred to as Süleyman's 'grand strategy'. The main elements of this strategy were an imperial ideology and a universalist vision of empire, intelligence-gathering both within and beyond the borders of the empire, a foreign policy and propaganda machine that furthered the Ottoman vision of empire, efficient means of mobilizing human and economic resources, and an effective military power in the service of imperial policy.

Ottoman propaganda portrayed Süleyman in the first three decades of his long reign as 'defender of (Sunni) Islam' and *sahib-kıran*, 'Master of the Conjunction', or 'world conqueror'.[33] The title *sahib-kıran* had also been used by Süleyman's father, Selim I, who probably could have claimed status as a universal conqueror had his premature death not stopped his advance.[34] Süleyman's claim to universal sovereignty developed in the context of Ottoman-Habsburg rivalry and became an important building block of his strategy against his Habsburg antagonist, the Holy Roman Emperor Charles V.

In a recent study that compared and contrasted Ottoman and Habsburg imperial ideologies and political propaganda—advanced most effectively by Grand Vizier Ibrahim Pasha (1523–36) and Mercurino Arborio de Gattinara, Charles V's grand chancellor (1518–30), respectively—I have tried to demonstrate how religion, millenarianism, and competing Habsburg and Ottoman universalist visions of empire were used to strengthen the legitimacy of the two rulers in their own empires and also within the larger Muslim and Christian communities.[35] Süleyman's strategists continued to use religion to legitimize the sultan's rule. As previously noted, he was 'the Servant of the Two Noble Sanctuaries', who protected the pilgrimage routes and restored mosques and other buildings in Mecca and Medina. From the 1540s on, he also started to use the title of caliph in order to counterbalance Charles V's claims to universal sovereignty and that of the Safavid shah's over Ottoman subjects living in eastern Anatolia.[36]

Millenarian prophecies and apocalyptic expectations were also current in both empires in the early sixteenth century. They influenced public opinion and were used by the sultan's propagandists to design and publicize Süleyman's image as *sahib-kiran*, the ruler of a new universal empire. Ibrahim Pasha saw in Süleyman the successor to Alexander the Great, his and his master's favourite historical hero. It seems that Ibrahim Pasha succeeded where Gattinara failed: he managed to strengthen his master's imperial aspirations, whereas Charles V took apocalyptic expectations and his grand chancellor's memoranda, in which Gattinara sought to prepare his master for the task of universal sovereign, with prudent scepticism.

Habsburg military successes against Ottoman Islam (and German Protestantism) as well as Ottoman victories against Habsburg Catholicism (and Safavid Shi'ism) formed an integral part of Habsburg and Ottoman propaganda. Habsburg propagandists seized upon every success against the Ottomans, however ephemeral it may have been, in order to publicize Charles V's image of 'defender of the Catholic faith'. In 1532, both Charles V and his propagandists claimed that his troops stopped Süleyman attacking Vienna,[37] although it seems that neither emperor wanted to risk his prestige and troops in open battle. The stakes were too high and both emperors were aware of their own and their opponents' strengths. It has also been suggested that the 1532 campaign was a skilfully choreographed imperial procession, organized by Ibrahim Pasha to respond to Charles V's coronation celebrations in Bologna (1530), using the language and symbols of imperial propaganda familiar to Europeans. Of these, Süleyman's four-tier parade helmet, mistakenly identified by contemporary Europeans as the sultan's crown, imitated that of the papal tiara and the crown that Charles V had worn during his Bologna coronation. The message was clear: Süleyman was challenging the authority of both the pope and the emperor.[38]

While ideology played a greater role in formulating Ottoman strategy and policy decisions than is usually appreciated, it is clear that it was not ideology but rather a pragmatic approach, often in response to the many challenges the early sixteenth-century Ottoman empire faced, that mattered in the day-to-day conduct of foreign and military affairs. These challenges, as well as opportunities arising from the difficulties and weaknesses of the Ottomans' rivals, were assessed on the basis of incoming information, which, contrary to the general view, was surprisingly correct and up to date. Such intelligence concerned the enemies' military and economic strengths and weaknesses, and was collected through a multi-layered Ottoman information-gathering system. In the sixteenth century, at least four levels of Ottoman information collection can be discerned: central intelligence in Constantinople; information gathering by provincial governors and other local authorities, especially along the empire's frontiers; intelligence provided by Istanbul's client or vassal states; and espionage and counter-espionage carried out by the Sublime Porte's spies and saboteurs in foreign countries. The Ottomans also paid special attention to military intelligence before and during campaigns. They employed local road guides (*kılavuz*), as well as auxiliary forces, such as the raiders, *martolos*, *voynuks*, and Crimean Tatars, who were used for reconnaissance and scouting. Frontier governors habitually kept spies in the major cities of their neighboring enemies and interrogated captured foreign soldiers.[39]

News reached Istanbul through an elaborate courier and communications network, the so-called *ulak* and *menzilhane* system. The Ottoman *ulak* (state courier) and *menzilhane* (post, or relay, station) system, like its Roman and Byzantine antecedents, was built on a sophisticated Ottoman road network, itself inherited from Roman and Byzantine times. The Ottoman road network had three main routes both in Europe and in Asia Minor, which were known as left, centre, and right routes, since the Ottomans viewed their Balkan and Anatolian provinces from Istanbul. These six main routes, each with several smaller branches, radiated from the capital towards Salonika-Athens, Edirne-Sofia-Belgrade-Buda, or the Crimea in Europe, and towards Erzurum-the Caucasus, Diyarbekir-Mosul-Baghdad-Basra, or Aleppo-Damascus-Cairo/Mecca in Asia Minor and the Arab provinces, respectively. Posts established along the road network at intervals of six to twelve hours' ride provided the couriers with post horses and made sure that reports and orders were transported swiftly and efficiently. While abuses of the system occurred as early as the reign of Süleyman, the Ottoman communications network played a crucial role in transmitting intelligence, news, and reports of all kinds, as well as imperial orders, and is rightly regarded as one of the main instruments that held the empire together.[40]

LIMITS TO OTTOMAN STRATEGY AND MILITARY POWER

Contemporaries agreed that, in addition to the power of their army, the strength of the Ottomans lay in their abundant human and economic resources and their army logistics. The road network and *menzilhane* system proved crucial in imperial logistics too, for these way stations also served as major gathering points for troops and depots for food, forage, and ammunition.

In addition, the Ottomans masterfully utilized the empire's river networks. Contrary to general belief, Ottoman viziers and provincial commanders had a good understanding of geography and used this knowledge to their advantage. They recognized the importance of the empire's major rivers and systematically occupied all strategically vital fortresses and towns along them. Many of these towns became provincial centres and/or major military bases, such as Belgrade and Buda on the Danube, and Baghdad and Basra on the Tigris and Shatt al-Arab, respectively. The Ottomans established naval arsenals at their major rivers, building and repairing smaller ships and galleys in the hundreds before military expeditions. Where possible, heavy cannons, cannonballs, and gunpowder were transported on special ships, called 'gun ships' (*top gemisi*) and 'stone [cannonball] ships' (*taş gemisi*) or 'covered' (*örtülü*) boats, for the transport of powder.[41]

The plans and efforts to connect the rivers Don and Volga by a canal, along with the Suez Canal project, clearly demonstrate the strategic thinking of Süleyman I, Selim II (1566–74), and their grand vizier, Sokullu Mehmed Pasha (in office 1565–79). With the Don-Volga canal, Sokullu Mehmed Pasha hoped to dislodge the Muscovites from Astrakhan (captured by them in 1555) and the lower Volga. By transporting the Ottoman Black Sea fleet on to the Caspian Sea, he planned to attack Safavid Persia from the north, conquering the province of Shirwan.[42] Moreover, Ottoman control of the steppes and forests of the lower Volga 'would have strengthened the empire's ecological portfolio, providing grain, horses and timber in abundance',[43] and thus further enhanced the Ottoman strategic position. A sultanic decree written in January 1568 to the governor-general of Egypt ordered the addressee to investigate the feasibility of a canal between the Mediterranean and the Red Seas. With the Suez Canal, Istanbul wanted to transport its main Mediterranean navy on to the Red Sea and the Indian Ocean to check Portuguese expansion there. While both plans failed owing to technological limitations and changing strategic interests, as did similar projects elsewhere in contemporary Europe, they reveal bold and ambitious strategic thinking on the part of Ottoman policymakers.[44]

However, by the mid-sixteenth century, the empire was operating at the limits of its logistical capabilities. In addition, as we saw earlier, seasonal campaigning was already inefficient at the beginning of the sixteenth century against the Safavids, owing to bare terrain, climate, and the shah's rush-and-burn tactics. By the late sixteenth century, power relations on all fronts were more balanced, which made wars longer and increasingly exhausting. Of these, the Long Hungarian War (1593–1606), the war in Hungary (1658–64), the war against the Holy League (1683–99) on the Hungarian frontier, the Iranian wars (1570–92, 1603–11, and 1623–39) on the eastern frontier, and the Cretan War (1645–69) against the Venetians in the Mediterranean required commitments in fighting men, weaponry, supplies, and money on a scale previously unheard of. The maintenance of distant frontier provinces also created financial and logistical problems, since these provinces were not capable of defending themselves by using merely local revenues.[45] From 1592 on, the imperial treasury ended almost every fiscal year with a deficit, which is hardly surprising in light of the fact that the Ottomans waged wars continuously from 1579 to 1611: against the Habsburgs in Hungary, Safavid Iran, and the Anatolian rebels of the Jelali revolts. The seventeenth century also saw the eclipse of the timariot spahi cavalry and the deterioration of the military skills of the once-formidable janissaries. The child levy, once the main method of janissary recruitment, also lapsed.[46]

By the end of the seventeenth century, owing to extensive military and related administrative and financial reforms in Europe, the Ottomans' European opponents established their own standing armies, which were comparable in size to that of the Ottomans. While in the mid-seventeenth century the size of the effective Habsburg forces fluctuated between 14,000 and 53,000 men, in the 1680s and 1690s Vienna was able to mobilize troops numbering between 64,000 and 86,000. In 1705 the effective forces numbered over 110,000 men.[47] Equally important, during and after the Long War of 1684–99, the Viennese central government gradually assumed greater control over recruitment, financing, and supply. Compared to the Ottomans, the control of the relevant Viennese central governmental bodies (the Court War Council, Court Chamber, and War Commissariat) gave substantially more oversight to the emperor, his generals, and administrators than the sultans (or their grand viziers) of the late seventeenth and early eighteenth century could ever dream of.

At the end of the seventeenth century, the Ottomans were still able to mobilize large numbers of forces, and on paper they matched their opponents. According to the account books of the imperial treasury, the Porte paid some 60,000–80,000 men in the late 1680s and early 1690s during its war against the Holy League. The strength of the standing army, at least on paper, climbed to 114,000 men in 1694–5, and stayed just below 100,000 troops in the remaining years of the war. However, the paper figures cited in the literature are misleading, for only a portion of these troops went on campaign. For instance, in 1660–1 only 33 per cent (18,013 men), in 1697 about 30 per cent (21,000 men), in 1701–2 some 25 per cent (9,975 men), and in 1710 approximately 17 per cent (7,255 men) of the total number of janissaries listed in the accounting registers actually participated in military campaigns.[48] Equally important, the soldiers were often poorly trained, and lacked discipline and leadership. Gone were the bold strategists and astute tacticians who were the grand viziers of the fifteenth and sixteenth centuries. In the Ottoman army and military administration, there were no military commanders and strategists comparable to Raimundo Montecuccoli or Eugene of Savoy, who from the 1660s to 1739 directed the military affairs of the Austrian Habsburgs both as heads of the Court War Council and as generals of the field armies.

The Ottomans also seemed less capable of adjusting their military personnel and tactics to the changed nature of warfare, which was now dominated by open battles rather than sieges. This failure to adapt was due partly to Ottoman military culture and the pressure on traditional military units to maintain the status quo, but also partly to Ottoman successes in siege warfare—the dominant type of warfare throughout the 150-year period of Ottoman confrontation with the Habsburgs in Hungary—and the resulting complacency. In siege warfare, the Ottomans still matched the Europeans, as their success in the Morean War against the Venetians proved. However, the weaknesses of the Ottoman military—the uneven quality of the troops, lack of discipline, and so on—were also visible in the Morean War, and these deficiencies proved fatal against the Habsburgs on the battlefield.

CONCLUSION

The Ottoman sultans appear as pragmatic rulers who were capable of adjusting their strategies to the changing geopolitical challenges they faced by using a variety of methods of conquest and rule that spanned across generations. Up to the sixteenth century, their aim was to expand the Ottoman realms and consolidate Ottoman rule in the conquered lands through varied means. From the mid-sixteenth century, the pace of conquest slowed and the main concern of the Ottoman leadership turned to the defence of their gains, using fortresses, garrisons, and provincial forces.

The early Ottoman rulers proved able tacticians who managed to build alliances across religious and ethnic boundaries. They also realized very early that they needed a loyal military force, independent of their allies and the march lords, and thus established one of the first permanent armies of late medieval Europe (elite infantry janissaries, six cavalry divisions, artillery, gun-carriage drivers, and armourers). While other major Islamic empires before them also used soldiers of slave origin, the Ottomans modified this system by collecting and training youths for their elite janissary infantry from among the Christian subject population of their own realms.

Dynastic marriages were an efficient means of forming alliances and augmenting vassal auxiliaries. The policy of appeasement or accommodation (*istimalet*) and that of forced migration (*sürgün*) proved instrumental to consolidate Ottoman rule in the conquered territories. Granting military fiefs (*timar*) to cooperating members of the political and military elites of defeated polities helped the Ottomans to integrate the latter into their provincial cavalry forces and ruling elite. This method helped not only to smooth the transition from the pre-Ottoman regimes to Ottoman rule, but also to establish and maintain law and order following the conquest, and provided the Ottomans with precious knowledge regarding local administration and taxation. The creation of various auxiliary troop formations provided a means to integrate nomadic Turcomans (Yürüks) as well as semi-nomadic and settled Slavs and others (vlachs, *voynuks, martolos*, etc.) into their military system. Some of their troops (such as the *akıncı* raiders and later the Crimean Tatars) were used for reconnaissance as well as for terrorizing populations beyond the Ottoman frontiers.

The integration of pre-Ottoman military men into the Ottoman army and administration also was instrumental with regard to military acculturation, for it acquainted the Ottomans with new skills and tactics and helped them to keep pace with developments in European military technology. Villagers along the military routes and mountain passes were used as auxiliaries who contributed to the maintenance of the Ottoman road network, while others were responsible for providing food and other necessities for the marching army and were, in return for their services, exempted from certain taxes.

We have seen that under certain rulers such as Süleyman, it is also possible to discern what might be called an Ottoman grand strategy. In the sixteenth century, the Ottomans masterfully exploited the growing political (Habsburg-Valois) and religious (Catholic-Protestant) rivalries in Christian Europe, allying themselves with France and England against their common enemies, the Catholic Habsburgs. Throughout our period, Ottoman leaders seem also to have been aware of their limitations, and tried to avoid, as much as possible, waging wars on more than one front at a time.

NOTES

1. For a new interpretation of the post-1580s Ottoman history, see B. Tezcan, *The Second Ottoman Empire: Political and Social Transformation in the Early Modern World* (Cambridge, 2010).
2. E. Luttwak, *The Grand Strategy of the Roman Empire from the First Century* AD *to the Third* (Baltimore, 1976); G. Parker, *The Grand Strategy of Philip II* (New Haven, 1998); and J. P. LeDonne, *The Grand Strategy of the Russian Empire, 1650–1831* (Oxford, 2004).
3. For a similar criticism regarding Russian history, see W. C. Fuller, *Strategy and Power in Russia, 1600–1914* (New York, 1992).

4. Reliable narratives of events can be found in C. Finkel, *Osman's Dream: The Story of the Ottoman Empire, 1300-1923* (New York, 2005); and C. Imber, *The Ottoman Empire, 1300-1650: The Structure of Power*. Second edition (New York, 2009). On the conquest of Adrianople, see E. A. Zachariadou, 'The Conquest of Adrianople by the Turks', *Studi Veneziani*, 12 (1970), 246–71.

5. On the sources and history of the early Ottomans, see C. Kafadar, *Between Two Worlds: The Construction of the Ottoman State* (Berkeley, 1995); H. W. Lowry, *The Nature of the Early Ottoman State* (Albany, NY, 2003); and R. P. Lindner, *Explorations in Ottoman Prehistory* (Ann Arbor, 2007).

6. H. İnalcık, 'Ottoman Methods of Conquest', *Studia Islamica*, 2 (1954), 104–29.

7. See P. Fodor, 'Ottoman Policy towards Hungary, 1520-1541', *Acta Orientalia Academiae Scientiarum Hungaricae (henceforth AOH)*, 45/2-3 (1991), 271–345.

8. J. J. Grygiel, *Great Powers and Geopolitical Change* (Baltimore, 2006).

9. S. Labib, 'The Era of Suleyman the Magnificent: Crisis of Orientation', *International Journal of Middle East Studies*, 10/4 (1979), 435–51.

10. G. Perjés, *The Fall of the Medieval Kingdom of Hungary: Mohács 1526–Buda 1541* (Boulder, CO, 1989).

11. G. Ágoston, 'Information, Ideology, and Limits of Imperial Policy: Ottoman Grand Strategy in the Context of Ottoman–Habsburg Rivalry', in V. H. Aksan and D. Goffman (eds), *The Early Modern Ottomans: Remapping the Empire* (New York, 2007).

12. P. Sugar, 'A Near-Perfect Military Society: The Ottoman Empire', in L. L. Farrar (ed.), *War: A Historical, Political and Social Study* (Santa Barbara, CA, 1978).

13. P. Wittek, *The Rise of the Ottoman Empire* (London, 1938). In addition to the works of Kafadar, Lowry, and Lindner cited above, see Colin Imber's relevant studies in his *Studies in Ottoman History and Law* (Istanbul, 1996); and L. Darling, 'Contested Territory: Ottoman Holy War in Comparative Context', *Studia Islamica*, 91 (2000), 133–63.

14. S. Vryonis, Jr, *The Decline of Medieval Hellenism in Asia Minor and the Process of Islamization from the Eleventh through the Fifteenth Century* (Berkeley and Los Angeles, 1971); and C. Cahen, *The Formation of Turkey: The Seljukid Sultanate of Rum: Eleventh to Fourteenth Century*, ed. and trans. P. M. Holt (London, 2001).

15. G. Ostrogorsky, *History of the Byzantine State*, trans. Joan Hussey (Oxford, 1968), 414–92.

16. On the Ottoman military, see G. Káldy-Nagy, 'The First Centuries of the Ottoman Military Organization', *AOH*, 31/2 (1977), 147–62; H. İnalcık and D. Quataert, *An Economic and Social History of the Ottoman Empire, 1300-1914* (Cambridge, 1994), 88–93; Imber, *The Ottoman Empire*, 193–206; R. Murphey, *Ottoman Warfare, 1500–1700* (New Brunswick, NJ, 1999); and P. Fodor, 'Ottoman Warfare 1300–1453', in K. Fleet (ed.), *Byzantium to Turkey, 1071-1453* (Cambridge, 2009), 192–226.

17. Imber, *The Ottoman Empire*, 295–323; İ. Bostan, *Kürekli ve Yelkenli Osmanlı Gemileri* (İstanbul, 2005); and P. J. Brummett, *Ottoman Seapower and Levantine Diplomacy in the Age of Discovery* (Albany, NY, 1994).

18. G. Ágoston, *Guns for the Sultan: Military Power and the Weapons Industry in the Ottoman Empire* (Cambridge, 2005).

19. For the Ottomans' marriage and reproductive policy, see L. P. Peirce, *The Imperial Harem: Women and Sovereignty in the Ottoman Empire* (New York, 1993), 28–56. For these and other examples, see Imber, *The Ottoman Empire*, 76–83, who, however, thinks that the story regarding Nilüfer, 'like most stories of the early Ottomans', is 'probably a fiction' (77).

20. H. İnalcık, '1444 Buhranı', in id., *Fatih Devri Üzerinde Tetkikler ve Vesikalar* (Istanbul, 1954); P. Engel, 'János *Hunyadi* and the 'Peace of Szeged' (1444)', *AOH*, 47 (1994), 241–57; and C. Imber, *The Crusade of Varna, 1443–45* (Aldershot, 2006).

21. İnalcık, 'Ottoman Methods of Conquest', and id., 'Stefan Duşan'dan Osmanlı İmparatorluğuna: XV. Asırda Rumeli'de Hıristiyan Sipahiler ve Menşeleri', in id., *Osmanlı İmparatorluğu: Toplum ve Ekonomi Üzerinde Arşiv Çalışmaları, İncemelemeler* (Istanbul, 1993), 67–108.

22. Ö. Lûtfi Barkan, 'Osmanlı İmparatorluğunda bir İskan ve Kolonizasyon Metodu Olarak Sürgünler', *İstanbul Üniversitesi İktisat Fakültesi Mecmuası*, 11 (1949–50), 524–70; 13 (1951–2), 56–78; 15 (1953–4), 209–37; repr. in id., *Osmanlı Devleti'nin Sosyal ve Ekonomik Tarihi: Osmanlı Devlet Arşivleri Üzerinde Tetkikler-Makaleler*, ed. H. Özdeğer, 2 vols (Istanbul, 2000), vol. 1, 509–606; İnalcık, 'Ottoman Methods of Conquest', 122–9; id., 'The Yörüks: Their Origins, Expansion, and Economic Role', in id., *The Middle East and the Balkans under the Ottoman Empire: Essays on Economy and Society* (Bloomington, IN, 1993), 97–136; and H. İnalcık and D. Quataert, *An Economic and Social History of the Ottoman Empire*, 31–41.

23. Lindner, *Explorations in Ottoman Prehistory*, 102–16. See also E. A. Zachariadou, 'Natural Disasters: Moments of Opportunity', in ead. (ed.), *Natural Disasters in the Ottoman Empire* (Rethymnon, 1999), 7.

24. Zachariadou, 'Natural Disasters', 7–11.

25. K. Barkey, *Empire of Difference: The Ottomans in Comparative Perspective* (Cambridge, 2008), 45–58, which is largely based on the works of Kafadar and Lowry, cited above.

26. G. Modelski and W. R. Thompson, *Seapower in Global Politics, 1494–1993* (Seattle, 1988), 44, see also P. Brummett, 'The Ottomans as a World Power: What We Don't Know about Ottoman Sea-power', *Oriente Moderno* XX (LXXXI) n. s. 1 (2001) [K. Fleet ed., *The Ottomans and the Sea*], 1–21.

27. L. Valensi, *The Birth of the Despot: Venice and the Sublime Porte* (Ithaca, NY, 1993), 24–5.

28. J. E. Woods, *The Aqquyunlu: Clan, Confederation, Empire* (Salt Lake City, 1999); and L. Tardy, *Beyond the Ottoman Empire: 14th–16th Century Hungarian Diplomacy in the East* (Szeged, 1978).

29. J. F. Guilmartin, *Gunpowder and Galleys: Changing Technology and Mediterranean Warfare at Sea in the Sixteenth Century* (London, 1974).

30. S. Özbaran, 'Expansion in the Southern Seas', in id., *The Ottoman Response to European Expansion: Studies on Ottoman–Portuguese Relations in the Indian Ocean and Ottoman Administration in the Arab Lands during the Sixteenth Century* (Istanbul, 1994), 77–87.

31. N. Capponi, *Victory of the West: The Story of the Battle of Lepanto* (London, 2006).

32. A. C. Hess, *The Forgotten Frontier: A History of the Sixteenth-Century Ibero-African Frontier* (Chicago, 1978); and G. Parker, *The Grand Strategy of Philip II*, 115–46.

33. See C. Imber, 'Ideals and Legitimation in Early Ottoman History', and C. Woodhead, 'Perspectives on Süleyman', in M. Kunt and C. Woodhead (eds), *Süleyman the Magnificent and his Age: The Ottoman Empire in the Early Modern World* (London, 1995), 138–53, 164–90; C. Fleischer, 'The Lawgiver as Messiah: The Making of the Imperial Image in the Reign of Süleyman', in G. Veinstein (ed.), *Soliman le Magnifique et son temps* (Paris, 1992), 159–77; and B. Flemming, 'Sahib-kıran und Mahdi: Türkische Endzeiterwartungen im ersten Jahrzehn der Regierug Süleymans', in G. Kara (ed.), *Between the Danube and the Caucasus* (Budapest, 1987), 43–62.

34. Fleischer, 'The Lawgiver as Messiah', 162.

35. G. Ágoston, 'Ideologie, Propaganda und politischer Pragmatismus: Die Auseinandersetzung der osmanischen und habsburgischen Grosmächte und die mitteleuropäische Konfrontation', in M. Fuchs, T. Oborni, and G. Újvári (eds), *Kaiser Ferdinand I: Ein mitteleuropäischer Herrscher* (Münster, 2005), 207–33.

36. C. Imber, 'Süleyman as Caliph of the Muslims: Ebu's-Su'ud's Formulation of Ottoman Dynastic Ideology', in Veinstein (ed.), *Soliman le Magnifique et son temps*, 179–84.

37. See J. D. Tracy, *Emperor Charles V, Impresario of War: Campaign Strategy, International Finance, and Domestic Politics* (Cambridge, 2002), 145–6.

38. G. Necipoğlu, 'Süleyman the Magnificent and the Representation of Power in the Context of Ottoman–Habsburg–Papal Rivalry', in H. İnalcık and C. Kafadar, *Süleymân the Second and his Time* (Istanbul, 1993), 163–91.

39. Ágoston, 'Information, Ideology, and Limits of Imperial Policy', 78–92.

40. See Colin Heywood's relevant studies in his *Writing Ottoman History: Documents and Interpretations* (Aldershot, 2002); and Y. Halaçoğlu, *Osmanlılarda Ulaşım ve Haberleşme (Menziller)* (Ankara, 2002).

41. See G. Ágoston, 'Where Environmental and Frontier Studies Meet: Rivers, Forests and Fortifications along the Ottoman–Habsburg Frontier in Hungary', in A. C. S. Peacock (ed.), *The Frontiers of the Ottoman World* (Oxford, 2009), 57–79.

42. A. N. Kurat, 'The Turkish Expedition to Astrakhan in 1569 and the Problem of the Don–Volga Canal', *Slavonic and East European Review*, 40 (1961), 7–23.

43. J. McNeill, 'Ecology and Strategy in the Mediterranean: Points of Intersection', in J. B. Hattendorf (ed.), *Naval Strategy and Policy in the Mediterranean: Past, Present, and Future* (London, 2000), 378.

44. G. Ágoston, 'Where Environmental and Frontier Studies Meet', 60–1, where the sources and the relevant literature is cited. See also G. Casale, *The Ottoman Age of Exploration* (Oxford, 2010).

45. G. Ágoston, 'The Costs of the Ottoman Fortress-System in Hungary in the Sixteenth and Seventeenth Centuries', in P. Fodor and G. Dávid (eds.), *Ottomans, Hungarians, and Habsburgs in Central Europe: The Military Confines in the Era of Ottoman Conquest* (Leiden, 2000), 195–228.

46. İnalcık, 'Military and Fiscal Transformation in the Ottoman Empire, 1600–1700', *Archivum Ottomanicum*, 6 (1980), 283–337.

47. M. Hochedlinger, *Austria's Wars of Emergence: War, State and Society in the Habsburg Monarchy, 1683–1797* (Harlow, 2003), 236.

48. M. Genç and E. Özvar (eds), *Osmanlı Maliyesi Kurumları ve Bütçeler*, 2 vols (Istanbul, 2006), ii. 249, 287; and G. Ágoston, 'Empires and Warfare in East-Central Europe, 1550–1750: The Ottoman–Habsburg Rivalry and Military Transformation', in D. Trim and F. Tallett (eds), *European Warfare, 1350–1750* (Cambridge, 2010), 110–34.

6

The Thirty Years War, 1618–48

David Parrott

INTRODUCTION

The conflict which broke out in 1618 with the revolt of the Bohemian Estates against the Habsburg Archduke Ferdinand was unprecedented. Thirty years of campaigns, unbroken by any general truce or ceasefire, ravaged swathes of central and western Europe, spreading devastation from Portugal to Poland. Yet, the war offers a paradox in relation to strategic theory and to the pursuit of strategy in military practice. For, despite its length and scale, many historians and commentators have seen it as a war waged almost entirely without a larger strategic purpose.

A long tradition of German historians has seen the war as a national catastrophe, not one brought about by some titanic clash of political or religious principles, but rather one unleashed and sustained by a series of narrowly opportunistic military initiatives launched by non-German powers. The protracted negotiations for a general peace at Westphalia, which began in earnest in late 1645, reflected the opportunism of these belligerents, as successive moves towards settlement were scuttled by small changes in military fortunes that encouraged powers to increase their demands and change their objectives with scant regard to any original set of war aims. While laying less stress on the predatory nature of foreign involvement, non-German historians have been scarcely more positive about the strategic significance of the war: they agree with Veronica Wedgwood's memorable formulation: 'there was no compulsion towards a conflict which . . . took so long to engage and needed so much assiduous blowing to fan the flame. . . . The war solved no problem. . . . It was the outstanding example in European history of meaningless conflict.'[1]

The political interests of the various belligerents and the means and intensity with which they pursued them appear so diffuse and apparently incompatible that some historians have even argued that the 'Thirty Years War' was a fiction, a simple flag of convenience under which a whole series of distinct and separate conflicts involving different belligerents have been gathered.[2] What gives this argument superficial plausibility is the sequential way in which the belligerents became involved in the conflict. In contrast to most wars of the sixteenth and seventeenth centuries, which were either fought between two particular parties or by alliances of powers who had shared war aims from the outset, the course of the Thirty Years War was shaped by a series of European states whose successive interventions were extended out over two decades. Their involvement reflected a series of apparently separate and individual motives, and any cooperation between them appears essentially contingent.

If the political aims of the belligerents seem so opportunistic and malleable, and unrelated to a wider strategic assessment of means, resources, and ends, then it might be assumed that the strategic imperatives that drove the war must have been those of the military commanders. Though 'leaving war to the generals' is widely regarded as an inherently unsound strategic approach, such an approach follows as a consequence of the military theory that has dominated thinking about the Thirty Years War since it was first put forward by Michael Roberts in the 1950s. For the implication of Roberts's original thesis of the 'military revolution' is that tactical and organizational innovations deployed on the battlefield broke a pattern of indecisive, unpredictable encounters, and allowed commanders to think in terms of far-reaching, war-winning strategies that hitherto would have been beyond their grasp.

The pivotal event for this interpretation is the 1631 battle of Breitenfeld, where the armies of Gustavus Adolphus of Sweden, drawn up in their smaller, more linear formations to maximize firepower and tactical flexibility, overwhelmed the battle-hardened veterans of the Imperial and Bavarian armies.[3] As a result of his confidence in his new tactics, formal drill, and discipline, Gustavus was able to formulate broad strategies to overwhelm his Habsburg enemies, reshape the constitution of the Holy Roman Empire, and destroy the threat of Catholic hegemony in Europe. His death a year later at the battle of Lützen called time on these grandiose designs, and his immediate military successors proved pale imitators of his methods. But the lasting legacy of Gustavus's reforms was a transformation of the art of war and its potential to forge strategy through tactical supremacy on the battlefield.

Alongside a widespread historians' scepticism about the supposed effects of a 'military revolution', there is reason to doubt whether commanders in the Thirty Years War did seek out battles in the belief that they would prove strategically decisive. The contemporary evidence of innumerable manuals and commentaries suggests a widespread perception that the practice of warfare was very largely about sieges, not battles. Yet, thanks to the development of a fortification technology intended to negate the impact of artillery, undertaking a siege was a lengthy and resource-intensive business.[4] Far from pushing wars towards a decisive and rapid outcome, they led to military stagnation: the capture of a major fortified town or city would often represent the sole objective of a campaign.

Even if a commander wished to achieve more, his army might well prove incapable of reconstituting itself, mustering new resources, and continuing the campaign. For the second huge brake on the achievement of military decisiveness was logistical. States could put troops in the field, but they had no effective mechanism to ensure that they could be supplied. Whether supply was supposed to be via the mobilization and stockpiling of food and munitions on home territory, and their transport to the troops via supply convoys, or whether the army was to be supplied by 'living off the land', the consequences were equally dire for military effectiveness and operational capacity. Armies and their commanders were in the grip of a logistical vice, created both by the underdeveloped nature of the early modern economy and by multiple layers of organizational failure, which made it virtually impossible to sustain an ambitious and strategically meaningful campaign plan.[5]

To add to these doubts that commanders in the Thirty Years War had the potential for effective action in pursuit of strategic goals, some accounts also stress the *condottiere* character of many of the armies and their constituent units as created through military enterprise, essentially the product of the financial investment and organizational initiative of their commanders. As with Machiavelli's notorious criticisms of the fifteenth-century Italian *condottiere*, it is assumed that such commanders would seek primarily to preserve their investment, and would be reluctant to engage in warfare that threatened heavy casualties or might demand an exceptional and expensive effort to provide supplies and support. Long-term occupation of territory and systematic extortion from the entire population was the optimal approach to getting a return on an investment in military force, and commanders would prove naturally risk-averse and anxious to avoid military operations that might win wars but would harm their own military or financial interests. Especially in the latter half of the war, military operations are depicted as little more than the battening of military parasites on long-suffering civilian populations; troops who had lost any direct connection with the states whose political interests they notionally served simply acted to preserve themselves and ensure a financial return to their enterpriser commanders.[6] Left to the generals, coherent strategic thinking was apparently in no safer hands than those of narrowly focused, opportunist rulers and their advisors.

THE POLITICS OF THE HOLY ROMAN EMPIRE

The response to the fragmented and sequential involvement of the various belligerents is understandable: a war so apparently lacking in clearly perceived general motives is better treated as an amalgam of smaller conflicts. Yet such a conclusion ignores contemporaries' precisely opposite understanding of the conflict. What began in Bohemia in 1618–19 was seen at the time as inextricably linked to subsequent events: a war lasting ten, fifteen, and ultimately thirty years, as it drew in successive groups of European powers, was directly connected with the issues that had provoked its outbreak.[7] This did not mean that the war *had* to last for thirty years; indeed, the desire to postulate appropriately important causes for a war that was somehow predetermined to be the greatest war to date in European history leads to many of the errors in interpretation of the motives and strategic thinking of the combatants. But the identification of the conflict as a single set of events, beginning in 1618–19 and ending in 1648 with the two Westphalian peace settlements of Münster and Osnabrück, emphasizes what was undisputed at the time: this was a conflict fought about authority within the Holy Roman Empire. Fighting spread well beyond the borders of the Empire and indeed even outside of Europe itself, as Castile and Portugal sought to defend their transatlantic colonies against Dutch, French, and English incursions. It is nonetheless significant that the negotiations that were to settle these latter conflicts occurred outside of the framework of Westphalia, whether the Spanish-Dutch settlement of January 1648, the Franco-Spanish settlement of 1659, or the final concession of Portuguese independence by the Spanish monarchy in 1668. Though military and political events in the Holy Roman Empire interconnected with the struggles fought out elsewhere, there is a direct sense in which the issues that led to conflict in 1618–19 were the same issues that determined each stage of the subsequent struggle in the Empire, and were ultimately negotiated via the settlements at Westphalia.

Nineteenth- and twentieth-century historians had little positive to say about the Holy Roman Empire. It was typically presented as a political system of massive and debilitating complexity, anachronistic and marginal to what was taken as the key political development of the early modern period: the emergence of nation states and the competitive struggle fought out between them. Recent analysis of the Empire attempts to understand it more in its own institutional and political terms.[8] Above all, historians have taken more seriously its capacity to arbitrate and defuse political conflicts and tensions. Imperial arbitration was the strongest defence for the multitude of third- and fourth-rank territories against the ambitions of their larger neighbours. In turn, most of the larger German states valued the collective security offered by the Imperial system, and were prepared to sacrifice opportunistic local advantages for the longer-term benefits of association within the Empire. The management of disputes within territories of the Empire in the later sixteenth century presents a generally positive picture of engagement, negotiation, and compromise.

This capacity to resolve and arbitrate conflicts before they led to war was put under considerable pressure in the decades before the Thirty Years War. The emergence of militant Calvinism in the German states put strain on the 1555 Augsburg Pacification, which had granted equal legal status to rulers who remained Catholic or converted to Lutheranism but which had not envisaged a third force of Protestants outside the framework of the original agreement. Moreover, pragmatic Catholic acquiescence in the Pacification was being eroded by Counter-Reformation militancy.

There were also more diffuse political tensions at work in the Empire. Rulers struggled to meet the demands of upholding princely status, as their revenues and tax grants failed to cope with the impact of steady inflation on the costs of court, government, and their armed forces. Numbers of German rulers found themselves heavily indebted by the end of the century and this aggravated tensions with representative institutions of their subjects. For some of these princes, territorial expansion at the expense of weaker neighbours seemed to offer one route to resolving a financial impasse, while a heightening of tensions within and outside the Empire might create the conditions in which it was possible to strike harder fiscal bargains with their own subjects.[9]

Yet, setting aside knowledge of the post-1618 catastrophe and the evidence of mounting tensions and potential flashpoints within the Empire, there was still an inherent strength to the mechanisms of compromise and arbitration, above all in the underlying attitudes and assumptions of rulers within the Empire. For the great majority of German states, the key to their strategic thinking remained the collective security provided by the Imperial constitution, however anachronistic and backward-looking this might appear in relation to strategic assumptions founded on state-building and competitive advantage. As late as 1609–10, the dispute over the inheritance to the duchies of Jülich-Kleve provoked large-scale military mobilization both by states within the Empire and external powers, but in the event demonstrated the continued reluctance to allow political conflict in the Empire to escalate into warfare.[10] The distinctiveness of the crisis of 1618 was that it brought to a head a conflict of interests both within the Empire—where they might still have been resolved by negotiation—and simultaneously within an overlapping but much broader political structure, the composite monarchy of the Habsburg dynasty.

THE HABSBURGS AND EUROPE

International relations in early modern Europe were dominated by the political fallout from the greatest dynastic coup of all time. A combination of inheritance and conquest established the Habsburg Charles V as ruler of Austria, Bohemia, and Hungary, of Milan and Naples, the Netherlands, the Spanish kingdoms, and the Castilian overseas empire, and in 1519 he was elected Holy Roman Emperor. On his abdication in 1556, Charles divided the Habsburg territories between his son, Philip II of Spain, and his brother Ferdinand, who was granted the territories in central Europe and was advanced as the Habsburg candidate for Imperial election.[11] For several decades, the two branches of the family went their separate political ways. Until the 1580s, the Austrian Habsburg rulers were committed to political and religious compromise in their own lands and in the Holy Roman Empire. In contrast, Philip II pursued an aggressive defence of the Spanish monarchy's Mediterranean and Atlantic commitments, underpinned by an uncompromising assertion of Catholicism.[12] Although it might seem that the two branches of the family had quite separate strategic interests and priorities, in practice various factors ensured that they remained residually interdependent. Above all, from the 1570s Philip II became mired in the long-running political and religious revolt by his subjects in the Netherlands. Imperial authority was also at stake: the Netherlands constituted part of the Burgundian Circle of the Empire, and the Spanish monarchs considered that the Emperor should play a direct, and if necessary a military, role in supporting the struggle to suppress the revolt. Though it was a demand which the Austrian Habsburgs sidelined, it ensured that the possibility of closer relations between the two branches remained on the table.

Within the Holy Roman Empire, the institutions for brokering and handling disputes continued to attract support, so long as the Habsburg Emperors were prepared to maintain an impartial position as the ultimate sovereign authority in the Empire. But during the reign of the third Emperor elected from the Austrian branch, Rudolf II (1576–1612), one of the fundamental tenets of Imperial arbitration, religious neutrality, started to be eroded. Suspicions grew in the 1580s and 1590s that the Emperor would use the mechanisms of conflict resolution to give a priori support to Catholic parties.[13] The suspicions seemed confirmed in 1607 when religious rioting in the South German city of Donauwörth was adjudicated, and Rudolf authorized the ultra-Catholic Duke Maximilian of Bavaria to occupy the city, although it was not within the jurisdiction of the Bavarian Circle of the Empire.[14]

In his assertive support for Catholicism, Rudolf was waging his own struggle against a family revolt led by his brother Matthias, who had pounced on the perceived weaknesses and vacillation of the Emperor's government to challenge his authority and bid for the support of those who favoured a more aggressive pursuit of Habsburg political interests. When Matthias finally succeeded Rudolf as ruler of the Habsburg lands and was duly elected Holy Roman Emperor in 1612, his concern was not just to reassert the grip of the Austrian Habsburgs over their own subjects and the institutions of the Empire, but to recreate the direct links between the Austrian and Spanish branches of the family.

Moreover, by the second decade of the seventeenth century, powerful factions in both the Spanish and Austrian political elites had come to see the strategic benefits of a closer alliance.[15] Though the Spanish had concluded a truce of twelve years with the Dutch rebels in 1609, a strong body of opinion at Madrid opposed the truce, and considered that its conversion into a permanent peace would be a disaster. If war were to be renewed, the support of the other branch of the family could tip the balance, threatening the Dutch with hostile encirclement and economic blockade. As Matthias's declining health raised the question of inheritance to the Austrian lands and a suitable Habsburg candidate for the Imperial election, support from the Spanish branch of the family became a crucial factor in ensuring the succession of Archduke Ferdinand of Styria. In return, the Spanish were able to negotiate the treaty of 1617, a family pact whose secret clauses included the transfer of Austrian Habsburg lands in Alsace to Spain as a means of strengthening the military corridor from Spanish Italy up to the Netherlands. Both Spanish and Austrian parties anticipated that the 1617 treaty would inaugurate an era of far closer diplomatic and military links than hitherto.

It was this Habsburg family treaty that gave strategic logic to the progressive unfolding of events in the Empire over the ensuing months and years. Although it was not fully predictable that political and military cooperation between the two branches would be forthcoming, the clear appreciation in Madrid and Vienna of the common strategic issues gave a coherence to both political and military responses that stands in sharp contrast to the actions and reactions of other powers.[16]

THE CRISIS OF 1618–19

It was always likely that the 1617 election of the Habsburg Archduke Ferdinand as King of Bohemia would generate intense concern amongst large parts of the native elites, who feared that their extensive religious and political privileges would be threatened by an authoritarian ruler with a reputation for uncompromising Catholicism.[17] The 1618 defenestration of Ferdinand's ministers in Prague by a rebellious group of Protestant nobles was thus seen as a challenge from which neither side would back down willingly. Despite his determination not to compromise with his rebellious subjects, Ferdinand was aware that the financial and military resources to crush the revolt did not exist within the Austrian lands. But underpinning his intransigence was his awareness that he now had the powerful backing of the Spanish branch of the family.

Madrid had not anticipated that there would be a call for military support almost before the ink had dried on the 1617 treaty, and initially there was reluctance to commit military force to the cause of their Austrian cousins. But the revolt in Bohemia held particular threats for an emerging Habsburg European strategy. For the king of Bohemia was one of the seven Electors to the Imperial title. A series of Habsburg rulers of Bohemia had previously played their role in ensuring that the Imperial title was kept within the Habsburg family, but a successful revolt would bring an outsider, whether a native noble or foreign interloper, to the Bohemian throne with its electoral vote. The situation was especially threatening since Emperor Matthias's health was collapsing, so that a new Imperial election might be only a few months away. It was concern at the blow to Habsburg prestige and power that the loss of the Imperial title would threaten, and not least to Spain's plans for a resumption of war against the Dutch—this time with Imperial backing—that activated Spanish military support and the beginning of a new strategic commitment to central Europe that was to last until 1648.[18]

The Bohemian rising had activated a Habsburg European strategy, and it was no less clear to the Bohemian rebels that they also needed to look for military allies. Apart from appeals to religious solidarity, they held the potential trump cards of the status of the Bohemian crown, and of the electoral rights that it conveyed. But a plausible alternative to Ferdinand still had to be found—one prepared to bring military support to the rebels and to run the risk of defying Habsburg military power in a territory which the Habsburgs, despite Bohemia's elective monarchy, regarded as their own sphere of influence. Unfortunately, for the peace of Europe, the rebels had just such a candidate in their sights. The militantly Calvinist Palatine Elector, Frederick V, was tempted into the most reckless gamble of his short political career. Already an Elector, and with one of his territories, the Upper Palatinate, abutting Bohemian territory, he saw that the crown offered prestige, access to the vastly greater economic and fiscal resources of Bohemia, and the control of two Electoral votes. With the support of the Calvinist Elector of Brandenburg, not merely would Frederick be in a position to block the election of a Habsburg Emperor, but he would also displace the pro-Habsburg and traditionalist Lutheran Elector of Saxony as the leader of German Protestants.[19]

But for Frederick's gamble to stand any chance of success against the Habsburg military alliance, he would need powerful supporters. And it is here that the gulf between the European strategy of the Habsburgs and the traditional assumptions made about negotiation and compromise within the framework of politics in the Empire becomes apparent. Frederick's position might have suggested that it would be easy to draw allies into the Bohemian conflict: he was son-in-law to James I and VI of England and Scotland; linked by alliance to the Dutch and through the Bohemians to the Calvinist ruler of Transylvania, and thus believed he had the support of the Danes and the French; and aware that the German Calvinists and reformist Lutherans saw him as the leader of opposition to the advance of Catholicism in the Empire. Nevertheless, no financial or military support was forthcoming. The complexities of this political situation became apparent. The Protestant and non-Habsburg powers were certainly concerned over what they saw as a potential shift in the European balance of power, and the larger threat posed by close Habsburg military cooperation. But they also retained the belief that political disputes in the Holy Roman Empire should be resolved by negotiation and peaceful settlement. And indeed, had the dispute occurred before the rapprochement between the Austrian and Spanish Habsburgs, or had the Spanish not felt obliged to underpin the family pact with money and troops, the outcome would probably have justified this reluctance to raise the military stakes. It is certainly clear that the majority of powers within and outside the Empire were not yet prepared to abandon outright the prevailing assumptions that had characterized Imperial politics in the preceding decades.[20]

Frederick's acceptance of the Bohemian throne thus failed to produce any support from those he considered his main backers, and this had a decisive effect on the shape of the war. Placed under the Imperial Ban for his challenge to Imperial authority, Frederick's territories could legitimately be occupied. For the Spanish, contemplating the renewal of war with the Dutch in 1621, the strategic benefits of controlling the Rhineland Palatinate were considerable. The vital 'Spanish Road'—the military corridor connecting Spanish Milan with the Netherlands—would be strengthened at a key point. In the autumn of 1620, Spanish troops from the Army of Flanders invaded Frederick's main territory and swiftly occupied all but a handful of fortified cities.[21]

The involvement of Frederick was also the factor which drew Duke Maximilian of Bavaria into the conflict on the Emperor's side. Faced with a challenge from the rival branch of the Wittelsbach family, Maximilian saw not only territorial advantages to be gained at Frederick's expense—the Upper Palatinate also adjoined Bavarian territory—but the possibility of supplanting the senior status of the Palatine branch by claiming the electoral vote. The transfer of an electorate to a loyal branch of a family had a precedent under Charles V, when in 1547 the Saxon vote was shifted from the Ernestine to the Albertine branch of the Wettins.[22] The potential to fulfil both territorial and dynastic ambitions decided Maximilian on open support for Ferdinand.[23]

RESISTING THE PAX AUSTRIACA, 1621–9

The strategic significance of the collapse of Bohemian resistance following the battle of the White Mountain (November 1620) and the occupation of all of the Elector Palatine's territories took a little time to become fully apparent. The Dutch Republic was the first power to realize its full political and military significance. Following the impressive demonstration of military cooperation between the two branches of the Habsburgs in Bohemia and the Palatine territories, the Spanish-Dutch truce expired, and from 1621 the Spanish moved into action on the frontiers of the Republic. The Dutch were aware of the strategic significance of a Spanish military foothold within the Holy Roman Empire, and also saw that there was a good chance that the debt incurred by Emperor Ferdinand for Spanish support in crushing the Bohemian revolt might be repaid by active military assistance against the Dutch. Moreover, Maximilian of Bavaria, shortly to gain the Electoral seat by Imperial transfer, was concerned to erase all traces of military resistance by his Palatine rival, and this brought his own army deep into the north-west German territories abutting the Republic as he pursued the remnants of the Palatine's Protestant forces.[24]

If the Dutch Republic was one European state that had now recognized the significance of Habsburg strategic cooperation for future policy, the other was France. French diplomats operating in the Empire in 1618–19 had initially thrown their weight behind a negotiated solution to the Bohemian revolt, and had helped to neutralize a large part of the Protestant support for the Palatine Elector. However, the Habsburg powers read this as an indication of political weakness and division within France. For Spain, tighter control of the Alpine passes—principally the Valtelline, connecting Lombardy and the Austrian lands—was a prerequisite of closer cooperation with the Austrian branch of the family, and Spanish troops from Lombardy deliberately flouted France's interests by an opportunistic military occupation of these passes during the early 1620s.[25] Though France's initial responses were confused, and her ultimate military intervention in 1625 was ineffectual, it provoked a shift in strategic perception that was embodied in the unexpected return to political favour of Armand-Jean du Plessis, Cardinal de Richelieu.[26] Until his death in 1642, Richelieu's explicit priority as French First Minister, and the basis of his support from the king, was to reverse the political and military changes that in his view had brought the Habsburgs to a position of European hegemony.

But what principally determined the 'slow burning', gradualist character of the war was that neither the Dutch Republic, now engaged in a protracted war of sieges on the frontiers of the Spanish Netherlands against a resurgent Army of Flanders, nor France had any wish to commit to an open military conflict against the Habsburgs in the Holy Roman Empire. Aware that open war would hugely increase the financial and governmental burden on the king's subjects, Richelieu gambled until 1634–5 on being able to coordinate and exploit opposition to the Habsburgs that would allow France to gain strategic advantages from her position without the risks and costs of direct engagement in the struggle. Yet, both the Dutch and the French appreciated that a Habsburg reshaping of European politics would be disastrous for their strategic interests. If they were not prepared to oppose it outright themselves, they would need to find other states prepared to take up arms more directly to try to prevent a Habsburg settlement within the Empire.

The search for a resilient, committed set of military allies with common strategic priorities was to prove extraordinarily difficult. The continuation of the Thirty Years War reflected more the result of step-by-step, combatant-by-combatant diplomatic persistence than the working out of great and ineluctable forces of state or confessional interest. From 1622 to 1623, it was apparent that the capacity for resistance from within the Empire was crippled both by the magnitude of the Elector Palatine's defeat and by continuing loyalty to the constitutional framework of the Empire. Many Catholic states in the Empire, such as Bavaria and the Rhineland bishoprics, had made common cause with the Habsburg campaigns, while others such as Lutheran Saxony had explicitly not given their support to Bohemia and the Palatinate, and had no wish now to take issue with Imperial authority.

The attempt to gather together allies from outside the Empire proved initially little more successful. The greatest absence from these diplomatic efforts were the Ottomans. Ironically, from 1623 to 1640 the Ottoman Empire was under the control of Murad IV, one of the most militarily able and ruthless Sultans of the early modern period. However, the fall of Baghdad in 1624 to the Safavid ruler Shah Abbas presented an overriding political and religious threat to Ottoman authority. From

1624 until the final recapture of Baghdad in 1638 and peace with the Safavids in 1639, Murad would not be induced to break the peace settlement negotiated with the Habsburgs back in 1606.[27]

This Ottoman reluctance to join an anti-Habsburg alliance contributed in turn to the relatively weak and intermittent support that could be gained from the Transylvanian rulers, whether Bethlen Gábor or, from 1630, György Rákóczi. As vassals of the Ottoman Sultan, their ability and willingness to act independently of the political interests of the Porte was limited, and for much of this period the Ottomans had no wish to see their client provoking an escalation of hostilities with Vienna. Aside from this, it was clear that the interests of the Transylvanian princes would always rest more in trying to make territorial gains at the expense of Habsburg Hungary than in pursuing war on behalf of Protestant powers in the Holy Roman Empire. Subsidies to raise and maintain Transylvanian forces in the Empire in the mid-1620s usually proved money wasted, as the real nature of Bethlen Gábor's military and political interests became clear.

As a result the Dutch and French found themselves coordinating military supporters closer to hand. The failure of Protestant military forces in Germany left the way clear for the two previously unaligned Baltic powers, Denmark and Sweden. One apparent advantage of intervention by Christian IV of Denmark was that he was also duke of Holstein, a prince of the Empire, and a member of the Lower Saxon Circle, and was therefore more likely to attract support from German princes. The potential gains from Christian's intervention were not merely the negative ones of countering the build-up of Habsburg influence across the Empire; his participation also offered the possibility of consolidating a far stronger position amongst the German princes and cities on the Baltic, especially the Hanse cities, which had traditionally sought to hold the Scandinavian powers at arm's length. Yet, positive strategic goals had less impact on Christian's thinking than the concern that if he did not take up the challenge of intervention, his rival, Gustavus Adolphus, King of Sweden, might do so, and thereby reap the benefits of successful resistance to Habsburg power in the north German territories.[28]

But Christian's assumptions that his own ambitions to consolidate a Danish presence in North Germany would mesh with German princes' concern at growing Habsburg authority proved entirely misguided. He failed to grasp the ambivalence among rulers within the Empire towards armed resistance and the subversion of the Imperial constitution. Despite his membership of the Lower Saxon Circle, he failed to mobilize significant local support and was left isolated and outgunned by the armies of the Habsburgs and of the Catholic Liga led by Bavaria. His frantic efforts, assisted by the Dutch, to raise an additional army of private military contractors under the veteran Protestant campaigner, Ernst von Mansfeld, proved unavailing, and by early 1629 Denmark had withdrawn from the conflict.[29]

STRATEGIC OVERSTRETCH, 1629–34

A consequence of the Habsburg triumph against Denmark was the ratcheting up of their own strategic ambitions. One aspect of this was the Spanish decision to launch a war in North Italy to oppose the claims of Charles de Nevers to the duchy of Mantua, representing Nevers as a French client whose accession would allow French political and military influence into North Italy.[30] The result was a conflict which not merely drew large Spanish forces from other theatres but also activated the agreement with the Austrian Habsburgs and drained Imperial troops from Germany down into North Italy. Despite initial military success, the Habsburgs nonetheless abandoned the struggle when it became clear that France, in the narrow context of a war in North Italy, would be prepared to maintain and steadily increase her military support for Nevers.[31]

Even more striking evidence of political overconfidence was provided by Emperor Ferdinand's decision to make a far-reaching change to the Imperial constitution by promulgating the notorious Edict of Restitution (1629), which reviewed and rescinded all of the transfers of Catholic ecclesiastical territory which had been made since 1552. The edict represented a decisive shift in strategic thinking from what had previously been presented by the Emperor as policing operations, maintaining peace in the Empire against internal and external threats, and punishing only those rulers and territories who overtly resisted Imperial authority or who allied themselves with external enemies. The Edict represented a sweeping attack on all of the German Protestant powers, even those such as Electoral Saxony that had hitherto been scrupulously loyal to the Emperor. It had the potential to extend Habsburg and Catholic authority in the Empire to an unprecedented level, and to alter the balance of power as drastically again as the events of 1620–1. But it achieved what no event or decision from the outbreak of the Bohemian revolt had managed: the alienation of moderate Protestant opinion in the Empire from the Imperial constitution and from Imperial authority. When this was combined with an additional Habsburg project to establish a Baltic navy as a means to place direct pressure on the Dutch Republic and implicitly to assert control over Baltic maritime activity, circumstances suddenly seemed again propitious to launch a further challenge to overambitious Habsburg strategies.[32]

Gustavus Adolphus's own motives for challenging the Habsburg settlement in the Empire were mixed and certainly did not add up to a single, clear-sighted strategic vision. Most immediately, French and Dutch diplomacy seeking to get Sweden involved in the Empire could be used to extricate Gustavus from a war with Poland, fought in Polish Prussia, which was running into serious military problems.[33] Moreover, the establishment of a Habsburg navy in the Baltic was as immediate a threat to Sweden's strategic interests as to the Dutch.[34] Much of the rhetoric of Swedish expansionism in preceding decades had presented successive military operations and acquisitions around the Baltic as a means to ensure lasting Swedish security by drawing on the notion of *dominium maris Baltici*, easily expanding from control of Baltic waters to control of the territory around the sea.[35] Thus, not just the Baltic fleet but the more general issue of much-expanded Habsburg power in the Empire could be presented as a long-term threat to Swedish security that should be confronted before the political changes in train consolidated unprecedented power in the hands of the Emperor.

Gustavus's strategic calculation was that the alienation of the German Protestants and their concern at the implications of the vast growth in Habsburg authority provided a narrow window of opportunity for Swedish intervention in which they would either fight alongside the Swedish army or at least provide resources to support the war effort. He nearly repeated the mistakes of Christian

IV by overestimating the extent to which Protestant alienation would translate into direct military support for the Swedish invader. For the majority of the German Protestant princes, Sweden's military threat was seen only as a bargaining counter, a means by which the Emperor might be persuaded to back down from his latest demands and negotiate over the Edict of Restitution and the scale of his military forces.[36] Gustavus's response to this lukewarm support was an uncompromising demand that the German princes should either join the Swedish war effort or pay the price in the form of territorial occupation and heavy 'contributions' to the costs of the armies.[37] If they would not serve as Swedish allies, then they would be compelled to act as auxiliaries and a resource base for military operations.

For a while this approach worked. In the aftermath of the battle of Breitenfeld in September 1631, the threat of a Habsburg-dominated Empire seemed in full retreat. The limited strategic goals of ensuring security and restoring the *status quo ante bellum* had seemingly been replaced by a vast project that would permanently transform the balance of power in Europe with the destruction of Habsburg and Catholic influence north of the Alps. Yet the decisive strategic initiatives which might have consolidated this political transformation were not forthcoming. After the death of Gustavus in 1632, the Swedish Council of Regency underwent what was to be nearly a decade of doubt and debate about the nature of their strategic interests in the Empire and the long-term costs of becoming an Imperial power.[38]

Even before the Swedish started to question their military commitment, neither the French nor the Dutch had been prepared to join a victorious Swedish assault in a common strategy based upon a substantial increase in their own military commitment against the rest of the Habsburgs' European and overseas territories. Indeed, France, for confessional reasons, grew uneasy about the prospect of an outright Swedish triumph, which might open the way to a Protestant Empire strongly under the thumb of a Lutheran Emperor. The German princes were also concerned at these developments, and the conflict in the Empire began to take on the form that it resembled until 1648. It became a German civil war, in which overt supporters of Swedish power and committed defenders of the Habsburg hegemony battled out the successive campaigns over a middle ground of variously occupied territories, reluctant allies on both sides, and a handful of states and major cities who were fortunate enough to be able to maintain genuine neutrality.

LIMITED GOALS, PROTRACTED CONFLICT, 1635–48

The last moment at which this process could have been reversed was 1634–5, when the overwhelming defeat of the Swedish and their Protestant allies at Nördlingen in South Germany at the hands of a combined Spanish-Imperial army transformed the situation again in favour of the Habsburgs. This time the Emperor was prepared to sacrifice the potential political and territorial gains offered by the Edict of Restitution, and to negotiate what became the Peace of Prague, a settlement to which the vast majority of the German princes, Protestant and Catholic, subscribed. The Emperor's authority over the Empire had been enhanced, but to the majority of the princes this was a reasonable price for the recovery of internal stability and the return to the constitutional framework of the Empire so violently disrupted by the years of Swedish military activity and Imperial counter-measures.[39]

Yet, such a transformation threatened what Dutch and French diplomacy had sought to avoid since the early 1620s: the consolidation of Habsburg power in central Europe. In 1635, France negotiated a military alliance with the Dutch and declared war on Spain, and then the Emperor. Though historians have traditionally applauded Richelieu's statesmanship in avoiding open war until 1635, and have presented this as a premeditated strategic decision to hold back French resources until the decisive moment, the reality was that the events of 1634–5 left him with little choice but to change policy if France's interests in Europe were to be maintained. Far from being a military and political masterstroke, French intervention came close to producing total defeat in 1636 and thereafter remained plagued with setbacks and by an inability to transform material superiority into military results.[40] Nevertheless, at a basic level it achieved its strategic purpose. It almost certainly saved the Swedes from being pushed out of the Empire, and allowed them to make a gradual military and territorial recovery through the later 1630s and 1640s.

The extent to which the French, Swedes, or Dutch shared positive political goals that could underpin strategy was negligible, but they did have a basic negative concern: to prevent the consolidation of Habsburg authority on the basis of the Peace of Prague. This one shared goal could bind them loosely into an alliance with a strategic purpose, but did nothing to reach out to the major German territories and princes, the majority of whom after 1635 continued to see the war as an undesired and intrusive challenge to the political and constitutional structures that they had reaffirmed at Prague. With regard to the great majority of German princes, the most that Swedish and French military power could achieve was their enforced neutralization, most notably Brandenburg (1641), Saxony (1646), and Bavaria (1647). What is in fact remarkable through this last decade of warfare, and which illustrates the inherent stability of the idea of the Empire, is just how little military-strategic opportunism took place between the German states. There were exceptions like the territorial struggle between the two houses of Hessen-Kassel and Hessen-Darmstadt, but in the main the war did not open up a mass of local conflicts. In the aftermath of the Peace of Westphalia, hundreds of cases of contested rights relating to religious and territorial jurisdictions that had arisen during the war were duly and peacefully arbitrated by the Reichshofrat or the Reichskammergericht.[41]

THE WAR OF THE GENERALS?

Why should a war that enjoyed such limited levels of support from the territories over which it was being fought, and where the involvement of external powers was so hesitant and uncoordinated, have dragged on for thirty years before reaching a final resolution? Answering this question takes us from strategy seen in the broadest political terms to strategy placed in its military context. It requires a re-evaluation of those assumptions that the war, because of the prevalence of sieges, the self-interest of military enterprisers who regarded their troops as a financial investment, and the insuperable challenge of supply, was almost devoid of strategic purpose.

In fact, what is striking about the military conduct of the war, above all as it was waged in its second half, is how effectively limited military means were deployed towards strategic ends. It might seem that a war in which the belligerents lacked an overarching and consistent political strategy would be militarily slow-moving and indecisive, constantly threatened by logistical failure, and primarily motivated by territorial occupation and extortion. The historical facts tell a different story. For example, far from withering away in the latter part of the war, pitched battles remain integral to the campaigns of the Thirty Years War. Moreover, these battles were not fought with ever-diminishing commitment by unmotivated and reluctant soldiers; as the war continued, battles became harder fought between ferociously resolute opponents. Some of these, notably Rheinfelden (1638), Freiburg (1644), and Jankow (1645), lasted for more than a single day, and almost all directly involved, in vicious forms of close-quarter combat, a high proportion of all those soldiers who were serving in these field armies.[42] In 1642 the second battle of Breitenfeld had been, by contemporary consensus, the most savage battle in memory, with 50 per cent of the Imperial army dead, wounded, or prisoners, and 30 per cent dead and wounded amongst the Swedes.[43] But, in fact, casualty statistics of this order were not uncommon across the later 1630s and 1640s.

Of itself the continued prevalence of hard-fought battles proves no more than that the commanders in the field were doing something more than simply occupying and plundering territory within the Empire. What makes the large number of these hard-fought battles significant is not that they were sporadic graspings at the mirage of the 'decisive battle', but the degree to which they can be seen as part of larger, integrated strategic plans, developed by military commanders over extended and often sequential campaigns and sustained by motivated officers and men.[44] Far from being a period of strategic indecisiveness, the second half of the war saw some of the most creative military thinking of the seventeenth century. In a remark that deserves wider attention, the eighteenth-century military theorist the Comte de Guibert spoke of the period of the war *after* the death of Gustavus Adolphus as 'an age of great generals, commanding small armies and achieving great things'.[45]

STRATEGY AND THE MILITARY ENTERPRISER

To understand this positive military context, a more realistic view has to be taken of the effects of military enterprise, which was an all-pervasive and deliberate response of most seventeenth-century governments to the administrative burdens and unsustainable costs of trying to set up their own armies and navies. Military enterprise in this period should not simply be dismissed as the last gasp of a terminally defective *condottiere* system. Colonels and senior officers had certainly invested heavily in their military forces, but this did not make them risk-averse or reluctant to think in strategic terms. Many of the commanders were hybrids: both investors in the military system and holders of military commands granted them by their ruler, with whom they had a relationship that would determine their own and their families' political and social status. Even as military investors, they could not afford to ignore the progress and the ultimate outcome of the war. In the case of the Swedish colonels and high command, for example, it was obvious that only a Swedish-dictated peace settlement would provide them with the vast sums that they considered were outstanding on their financial commitment to the war effort, and which the Swedish monarchy would never be able to provide from its own resources.[46]

However, the presence of enterpriser investors did ensure a very different attitude to the waging of war: one in which military operations were characterized by far more instrumentality in the linking of means to ends than in traditional 'state' warfare organized, funded, and waged directly by rulers. Instead of war as a dynastic process, part of the public assertion of the prince's status and the defence of princely honour and reputation, military operations outsourced to enterprisers were seen as the pursuit of objectives that would heap up the pressure on an enemy, but at realistic cost and risk. Forcing a battle that could destroy some of the fighting potential of an enemy army was a means to assert this pressure, but it would be a costly and wasteful success if it was not backed up by operational capacity—the ability to keep the army in being and enabled to pursue objectives through the rest of the campaign.

The strategic significance of sustained operational capacity as the primary means to achieve military goals was recognized by a succession of capable commanders in the field. In this respect, the assertion that the logistical problems involved in supplying armies necessarily prevented operational effectiveness in the Thirty Years War is simply unconvincing. The evidence of the activities of successful commanders of Bavarian, Imperial, and Swedish armies tells a different story. If logistical support determined the ability of armies to pursue coherent operational goals, to follow up military engagements, and to exploit opportunities as they opened up throughout a campaign, then a level of success in supplying these armies must have been achieved.

How was this done? Simply to summarize the key factors, the most important was an intuitive, problem-solving approach to maintaining the strategic capability of armies, a shaping of military means to ends.[47] In the first part of the war, the large campaign forces of, for example, the Imperial commander and military enterpriser Albrecht Wallenstein, and of Gustavus Adolphus, did indeed suffer immense problems in amassing and providing logistical support—problems that threatened the destruction of the armies, or turned military operations either into simple territorial occupation or the cumbersome pursuit of crude, easily antici-pated campaign objectives. The primary responses to the problems of keeping armies sufficiently supplied to maintain high levels of mobility and operational initiative were a systematic scaling down of the size of campaign armies and a shift in the numerical relationship between troops engaged in garrisoning and tax extraction and troops operating in the field. This was a deliberate decision, not some unintended consequence of the war as demographic disaster.

Drastic downsizing of field armies was accompanied by a change from tradi-tional infantry predominance to higher proportions of (more expensive) cavalry. The 1631 battle of Breitenfeld had been fought between 42,000 troops led by

Gustavus Adolphus against 32,000 Imperials and Bavarians; at the battle of Jankow in 1645, around 15,500 Swedish and German troops engaged with Imperial and Bavarian forces of around 16,000. The Swedish army contained 9,000 cavalry, the Imperial around 11,000.[48] Mobility was being prioritized, as was the generally smaller logistical 'footprint' created by scaled-down, cavalry-dominated field armies. And while numbers of troops were reduced, their quality, indicated by the ever higher proportions of experienced veterans in their ranks, increased. These armies contained strikingly large proportions of long-serving soldiers, resilient both in their ability to continue operating despite irregular and variable food supplies and in their epidemiological resistance, a much-neglected factor in military effectiveness. They fought hard and ruthlessly, whether in terms of taking and inflicting casualties in battle, sustaining the rigours of campaigns that might involve force-marching hundreds of miles, or exploiting circumstances that involved tactical flexibility, such as campaigning into the winter months, when armies were traditionally rested and reconstituted.

In ensuring a basic level of food and munitions supply, the commanders of these small armies benefited from administrative decentralization. Financial resources were usually collected by widely dispersed garrison troops who occupied specified territories and exacted war taxes, or 'contributions' that had been agreed with the populations as the (high) price of providing protection from predatory enemy forces and the otherwise random demands of the troops. Accepting this financial burden and garrisoning was the cost of remaining neutral, or at least not being directly involved in military activity. Just as garrisoned territories such as Mecklenburg, Pomerania, and Brandenburg provided the financial support for the main Swedish campaign army, the territories of the Westphalian Imperial Circle contributed substantially to keeping the Imperial field armies operational.[49] The monies collected were paid directly to the commanders, who themselves negotiated with suppliers and merchants to provision the army in the light of plans for the forthcoming campaign.

These relationships, like those between the commanders and their bankers and financiers, who could be persuaded to anticipate revenues and provide loans at short notice, were direct and personalized. Direct experience left the commanders acutely aware of what could and could not be achieved in supplying the armies, and led to a careful structuring of campaigns around supply networks, especially waterways and interior lines. When Bernhard of Saxe-Weimar, one of the most successful commanders of a 'downsized' army composed of colonel investors, decided to undertake the siege of Breisach on the Rhine in 1638, the key to the decision was his confidence that his financier and supply agent Marx Conrad Rehlinger would acquire sufficient grain and other provisions in the Swiss cantons against Saxe-Weimar's credit, and would maintain a steady shipment of these supplies down the Rhine from his base in Basel for the duration of the siege.[50]

In fact, one of the consequences of this emphasis on small, mobile armies was a reluctance to engage in large-scale sieges. Many of these armies had abandoned a cumbersome siege train of heavy artillery and focused on much lighter, more mobile field guns. Siege guns would need to be called up to undertake a siege, and in most cases a cost-benefit analysis of the logistical and manpower costs would militate against this style of campaigning.[51] This stood in obvious contrast to the style of traditional, directly controlled armies like those of the French and the

Spanish operating on the Flanders frontier, where sieges were still explicitly identified with the status and prestige of rival monarchs and undertaken regardless of costs and the commitment of resources. The armies operating in the Holy Roman Empire were more likely to use surprise, trickery, or intimidation to try to capture a fortified town. In many cases, they simply left such places alone, focusing on what seemed more likely to bring about operational benefits: the ability to outmanoeuvre rival forces and cut deep into enemy territory, bringing the pillage and destruction associated with the *chevauchées* of the Hundred Years War.

It was the destructiveness of a coordinated sweep into Bavaria by the Swedish army and the French army in Germany that forced the Bavarian Elector into the ceasefire of Ulm in early 1647.[52] Battles had their place in this type of operational thinking, but they had to be part of a wider set of campaigning goals. In 1645 the Swedish commander Lennart Torstensson determined to force a battle with the Imperial field army as early in the year as possible; if he was successful, it would leave the rest of the campaign to pile up pressure on Habsburg territory. His decisive victory at Jankow in early March 1645 was followed by a fast-moving, hard-hitting campaign that took his army to within one day's march of Vienna by 6 April.[53]

Commanders in this period did have a coherent grasp of strategy in the sense of an ability to relate military means to ends. It depended on maintaining operational capability throughout entire campaigns, and from one campaign to the next. The changing size and shape of the armies and the approach to warfare was a clear reflection of this priority. The aim, shared by commanders as diverse as Banér, Hatzfeld, Piccolomini, Mercy, and Wrangel, was to pile up incremental advantages brought by rapid mobility, territorial devastation, attrition of enemy veteran troops, and the concentration of the direct burden of supporting armies more and more on the territory of their opponents. The problem was that such an incremental approach was slow to achieve strategic results, especially when the belligerents were quite evenly matched in terms of operational capability and the capacity to frustrate the projects of an enemy.

If Swedish command and control frequently gave their troops the advantage on the battlefield, in the larger operational context they could be outmanoeuvred and defeated in detail by their enemies. Although the victory at Jankow and Torstensson's subsequent sweep into Habsburg territory in early 1645 might seem the opening act of a knock-out blow to the Austrian Habsburgs' military capability, the events of the rest of the summer showed the Imperial armies' ability to re-form and to put up such effective resistance that by the end of the year the Swedes were all but expelled from Habsburg territory.[54] Making due allowance for the military capacities and effectiveness of both Habsburg and anti-Habsburg military coalitions, it was nonetheless clear that the capacity of the Bavarian and Habsburg armies to hold back the Swedish-French military alliance was starting to weaken from 1646 onward. Both the 1647 Bavarian ceasefire at Ulm, which was abandoned later in the year and led to a second, devastating incursion into Bavaria in 1648, and the instructions from the Viennese Court, to their negotiators at Westphalia to move towards a settlement regardless of the price to be paid in terms of Habsburg authority in the Holy Roman Empire, were indicative of that realization.[55]

Yet, up to this point the war had been fought by military forces that were far more evenly matched than has usually been allowed. Their ability to protract the war reflected not inertia and strategic nullity, but a focused and clear-sighted ability to mobilize and deploy very similar styles of military force to overcome the obvious limitations of logistics and mobility and to counter the creative and resourceful operational plans of their opponents. The style of campaigning, as recognized by the Comte de Guibert, had much in common with the mobile, adaptable, hard-hitting strategic theories of irregular or 'small' warfare as they were to re-emerge in the mid-eighteenth century.[56]

Adapting to the demands and opportunities of this approach to warfare was possible above all because the actual campaigning armies were more and more made up of a professionalized cadre of career soldiers. The vast majority of them, whether in the Swedish, Imperial, or French army operating in Germany, were drawn from the territories of the Holy Roman Empire. Their status and remuneration reflected the heavy premium placed by unit and army commanders on getting and retaining soldiers with military experience.

It was thus a final irony that a war fought to its lengthy, destructive conclusion largely as the struggle by external powers to prevent a Habsburg-shaped political settlement within the Holy Roman Empire was actually waged by a universal soldiery overwhelmingly drawn from the states of the Empire. Both the Swedish and French armies were filled with German soldiers, even when the high command and some of the regimental colonels were native Swedes or French. Little separated these men in experience or motivation, not even religion: both the Imperial and Bavarian armies included soldiers representing opposing religious beliefs. While individual long-serving soldiers may have felt no ideological commitment to the war aims of the power for which they fought, they had a strong sense of group identity and *esprit de corps* which underpinned their fighting effectiveness and made capricious changing of sides and re-enlistment in other armies far rarer than popular views of the war have often suggested. Despite the professional similarity of the forces, and the common approaches to ensuring military effectiveness, the commanders were committed to military goals that would underwrite the aims of their political masters, though the military means by which these aims were pursued were heavily determined by the strategic decisions of the commanders. Field Marshal Torstensson had discussed with the Chancellor Axel Oxenstierna the plan for a lightning strike against Denmark in the winter of 1643/44, but the feasibility and military practicalities of what is known in Baltic history as 'Torstensson's War' were in the hands of the commander.[57] Conversely, Cardinal Mazarin's attempt to order the French army in Germany—largely made up of German colonel contractors—to campaign in 1647 beside the main royal French army on the frontiers of the Spanish Netherlands produced the outright mutiny that had been predicted by its commander, Turenne.[58]

CONCLUSION

The Thirty Years War emphasizes the importance of two very different conceptions of strategy that run through much of the discussion in the present book. 'Strategic theory'—the manner in which war is actually fought and the relationships among the tactical and operational levels and available military resources—

is vital to understanding the character of the struggle. Army commanders fighting the Thirty Years War shared a set of strategic conceptions that successfully matched military and ultimately political aims to military resources. Contrary to a historical tradition based on the unprecedented length of the conflict, this was not a meaningless war in which the armies and their commanders lacked any strategic purpose beyond sustaining themselves, and stumbled into battles when attempts to plunder and extort from occupied territory brought them into contact with other forces trying to do the same thing. Nor was it a strategic theory shaped by dramatic tactical innovations: the advent of modern war based on the 'decisive battle'—a concept attributed to Gustavus Adolphus and elevated into the theory of a 'military revolution'—which for several decades from the 1950s onward established a paradigm for the direct relationship between battlefield tactics and the formulation of strategy. The military campaigns during the Thirty Years War demonstrate a characteristic of strategic theory that is universal, but is too often overshadowed by an approach to warfare which sees 'great battles' in themselves as the building block of strategy.

The successful waging of wars is not primarily about the tactical but rather the operational dimensions of combat, and the operational dimension depends on mastery of the logistical possibilities and limitations of a given military environment. Winning a battle, or indeed successfully capturing a single fortress or city, will not contribute to winning a war unless it is integrated into a larger operational plan which is capable of following up and building upon these individual tactical advantages. While this may appear obvious, success depends to some extent on the freedom of the commander to formulate and pursue objectives as the contingencies of combat and manoeuvre best permit. Above all, it depends on the extent to which the logistical needs of the army can be adequately sustained beyond the 'first base' of an initial tactical success.

The Thirty Years War throws all of this into sharp relief. Its uninterrupted duration, in contrast to a pattern of wars consisting of a handful of successive campaigns that had characterized most combat before 1550, forced commanders to think operationally. A battlefield victory or a captured city might be a useful bargaining counter when peace negotiations followed the end of the campaign, but when no settlement was in sight their individual significance was transient and easily marginalized. Building upon and consolidating individual tactical advantages became the only route to winning a war, and this involved systematically devastating territory close to the enemy heartlands, threatening communications and supply lines, cutting off isolated forces, or making recruitment and supply of enemy campaign armies impossible. The armies of the Thirty Years War not only needed to develop this type of operational effectiveness but were well adapted to doing so, above all because the commanders were able to rationalize army organization in a way that was well adapted to the apparently all-pervasive logistical limitations of the period.

Winning in a military sense thus had meaning in the Thirty Years War, and by the mid-1640s the coalition of the Habsburg's enemies was clearly accruing a consistent and cumulative operational advantage. This was to bring them to the gates of Munich (1646) and Prague (1648), and would have brought them to Vienna had not the Emperor been prepared to make concessions at the Westphalia conference to buy peace at the price that the allies had sought since 1635:

the dismantling of direct Habsburg hegemony in the Holy Roman Empire. Had the Habsburgs refused to make peace on these terms, more and more of their territory would have been occupied, devastated, and fought over by enemy armies. It would have grown ever more difficult to raise and sustain even the most residual forces on the territory that remained, and the pattern of defeats and operational setbacks would have intensified.

It is easy to see in this a pattern for future wars based on *Ermattungsstrategie* (strategy of exhaustion): not the pursuit of the decisive, annihilating battle capable of transforming the course of a war in a few hours, but the gradual accumulation of operational advantages over successive campaigns, closely matched to both military means and limitations. Though concealed to some extent in earlier conflicts by the reluctance or inability to sustain wars for more than a few consecutive campaigns, something of this pattern can be seen in the *chevauchées* of Edward III or innumerable other military operations that had sought, albeit less systematically than the armies of the Thirty Years War, to wear down the enemy's resources and will to resist.

This, however, takes us to the broader meaning of strategy in its relationship to policy and statesmanship. If the military commanders pursued strategic goals, to what extent did the rulers and their statesmen have a 'grand strategy' or a strategic vision that justified the initial decision to go to war and the burdens of the conflict once begun? As the discussion above sought to emphasize, the tragic irony of the Thirty Years War was that suffering and devastation on an unprecedented scale were imposed on Europe by rulers who in the period up to and even after 1618 were more inclined to negotiate than to fight wars, and were profoundly conservative in their strategic vision of a political status quo.

It is too easy to point to the Habsburg powers as the 'villains' of the conflict: to argue, as did their most implacable enemy, Cardinal Richelieu, that the two branches of Austria and Spain had concerted a grand strategy that sought universal monarchy and European hegemony. In reality, the 1617 Habsburg family pact was a localized agreement that lacked wider political dimensions: its concerns were with stabilizing the Austrian Habsburg territories against internal dissent, strengthening the geopolitical position of Spain—at Austrian expense—for a resumption of her own 'internal' conflict with the Dutch, and maintaining the traditional Habsburg possession of the Imperial title. These were aims which, in the main, the other European powers were not prepared to resist by resorting to warfare, as the rapid dissolution of support for the Bohemian revolt demonstrated. Sweden and France pursued policies that were initially limited. Even after the great victory of Breitenfeld, it was striking that Gustavus Adolphus may have wished to see himself elected Emperor and to undermine Habsburg influence in Germany, but more profound constitutional and territorial changes were not on his strategic agenda.[59] Only in the millenarian ambitions of confessional extremists, most notably Frederick V of the Palatinate and his advisors, was there a vision of a 'Calvinist' grand strategy that sought profound political change and that was prepared to gamble everything to achieve it.

Two further motors of strategy as conceived by rulers and statesmen were predictable and universal. First was the fear for long-term security brought about by contingent political and military developments. While the impetus to maintain the political status quo was remarkably strong, fears that the political situation was turning in ways that threatened long-term security and vital interests were, as ever in history, instrumental in justifying the mobilization of resources and a commitment to military action. Such actions would in many cases, of course, further undermine an existing political order. Both the Habsburg intervention in Bohemia and the Swedish intervention in Germany were justified in these terms of vital interests, and both, initially narrow in their strategic conception, had a huge impact on the concerns and perceptions of other powers.

The concern over preserving security in an uncertain future was one universal factor that played its part in shaping action by statesmen in the Thirty Years War. The other stimulus to strategic thinking was military success itself. It is tempting for historians to imagine that strategic vision determines and shapes military action. Yet, in many cases it was unprecedented and unanticipated military success—notably the Imperial successes against the Danes and the German Protestants in the later 1620s, or the Swedes' triumph at Breitenfeld—which seemed to open a range of political options that had not previously seemed attainable or even desirable. Conditioned to see military action as hazardous and unlikely to bring rapid or decisive results, windfall military successes could encourage hitherto prudent rulers to formulate extensive and ambitious strategic goals, which survived only as long as their transient military advantages. By the mid-1630s, both the Emperor and the Swedish Council of Regency were disabused and realistic in their assessment of the strategically possible, in which preserving existing interests loomed far larger than reshaping either the map of Europe or the Imperial constitution. As the struggle settled into its pattern of operational attrition, 'winning' for the principal belligerents was seen in these narrower terms. If France and Sweden emerged from Westphalia with territory gained at the expense of the Empire, that territory was relatively modest in scale and explicitly held on terms that respected the larger Imperial constitution. It might seem a small gain for three decades of unprecedentedly destructive war, but it was in keeping with a struggle in which grand strategy had played its part more as a conservative than a transformative force in shaping the actions of Europe's rulers.

NOTES

1. C. V. Wedgwood, *The Thirty Years War* (London, 1938), 459–60.
2. S. H. Steinberg, *The Thirty Years War and the Conflict for European Hegemony, 1600–1660* (London, 1966); and N. Sutherland, 'The origins of the Thirty Years War and the structure of European Politics', *English Historical Review*, 107 (1992), 587–625.
3. M. Roberts, 'The Military Revolution, 1560–1660', in id., *Essays in Swedish History* (London, 1967) and numerous reprints; specific detail on Breitenfeld in Roberts, 'Gustav Adolf and the Art of War', in ibid.; and id, *Gustavus Adolphus. A History of Sweden, 1611–1632*, 2 vols (London, 1958), ii. 169–271.
4. G. Parker, *The Military Revolution. Military Innovation and the Rise of the West, 1500–1800*, 2nd ed. (Cambridge, 1996), 24–44.
5. M. van Creveld, *Supplying War. Logistics from Wallenstein to Patton* (Cambridge, 1997), 5–39.
6. See P. H. Wilson, *Europe's Tragedy. A History of the Thirty Years War* (London, 2009), 622–3, which both draws attention to historians' negative presentation of the later war

as crude, uncontained violence, and emphasizes the extent to which this impression had been deliberately fostered by post-war German princely governments to justify peacetime military establishments to their tax-paying subjects.

7. K. Repgen, 'Über die Geschichtschreibung des Dreißigjährigen Krieges: Begriff und Konzeption', in id (ed.), *Krieg und Politik, 1618–1648* (Münster, 1988).

8. The key works in English on this subject are P. H. Wilson, *The Holy Roman Empire 1495–1806* (London, 1999); and id, *Europe's Tragedy*, 12–48. The magisterial study by K. O. von Aretin, *Das Alte Reich, 1648–1806*, 4 vols (Stuttgart, 1993), provides an overview of Imperial institutions and their workings (i. 9–154).

9. M. Hüther, 'Der Dreißigjährige Krieg als fiskalisches Problem: Lösungsversuche und ihre Konsequenzen', in *Scripta Mercaturae*, 21 (1987), 52–81; and J. Burkhardt, *Der Dreißigjährige Krieg* (Frankfurt am Main, 1992), 90–125.

10. A. D. Anderson, *On the Verge of War: International Relations and the Jülich-Kleve Succession Crisis, 1609–1614* (Boston, 1999), esp. 211–40.

11. M. Rodríguez-Salgado, *The Changing Face of Empire. Charles V, Philip II and Habsburg Authority, 1551–59* (Cambridge, 1988).

12. G. Parker, *The Grand Strategy of Philip II* (New Haven, 1998), 1–114.

13. S. Ehrenpreis, *Kaiserliche Gerichtsbarkeit und Konfessionskonflikt. Der Reichshofrat unter Rudolf II (1576–1612)* (Göttingen, 2006), 125–34.

14. C. S. Dixon, 'Urban Order and Religious Coexistence in the German Imperial City: Augsburg and Donauwörth, 1548–1608', *Central European History*, 40 (2007), 18–33.

15. P. Brightwell, 'The Spanish Origins of the Thirty Years War', *European Studies Review*, 9 (1979), 409–31; and G. Parker, *The Thirty Years War*, 2nd ed. (London, 1997), 35–8.

16. H. Ernst, *Madrid and Wien, 1632–37* (Münster, 1991), 13–19.

17. R. J. W. Evans, *The Making of the Habsburg Monarchy, 1550–1700* (Oxford, 1979), 44–5, 67–70.

18. P. Brightwell, 'Spain and Bohemia: the decision to intervene, 1619', and 'Spain, Bohemia and Europe, 1619–21', *European Studies Review*, 12 (1982), 117–41, 371–99.

19. P. Wolf, 'Eisen aus der Oberpfalz, Zinn aus Böhmen und die goldene böhmische Krone', in id. et al. (eds), *Der Winterkönig. Friedrich von der Pfalz. Bayern und Europa im Zeitalter des Dreißigjährigen Krieges* (Augsburg, 2003), 65–74; and B. Pursell, *The Winter King* (Aldershot, 2003), 66–86.

20. J. Polisensky, *Tragic Triangle: The Netherlands, Spain and Bohemia, 1617–21* (Prague, 1991), 93–112.

21. A. Egler, *Die Spanier in der linksrheinischen Pfalz, 1620–32: Invasion, Verwaltung, Rekatholisierung* (Mainz, 1971), 43–90.

22. Wilson, *Europe's Tragedy*, 356.

23. D. Albrecht, *Maximilian von Bayern, 1573–1651* (Munich, 1998), 539–80.

24. A. de Villermont, *Ernest de Mansfeldt*, 2 vols (Brussels, 1866), ii. 116–67.

25. J. H. Elliott, *The Count-Duke of Olivares. The Statesman in an Age of Decline* (New Haven, 1986), 62–3, 222–9; and S. Externbrink, *Le Coeur du Monde. Frankreich und die norditalienische Staaten (Mantua, Parma, Savoyen) im Zeitalter Richelieus, 1624–35* (Munich, 1997), 69–86.

26. R. Pithon, 'Les débuts difficiles du ministère du cardinal de Richelieu et la crise de Valteline, *Revue d'histoire diplomatique*, 74 (1960), 298–322.

27. C. Imber, *The Ottoman Empire 1300–1650: The Structure of Power* (London, 2002), 71–83.

28. P. Lockhart, *Denmark in the Thirty Years War, 1618–48. King Christian IV and the Decline of the Oldenburg State* (Selinsgrove, 1996), 106–30.

29. Ibid. 155–205.

30. D. Parrott, 'A *prince souverain* and the French crown: Charles de Nevers, 1580–1637' in R. Oresko, G. Gibbs, H. Scott (eds), *Royal and Republican Sovereignty in Early Modern Europe* (Cambridge, 1997).

31. J. H. Elliott, *Richelieu and Olivares* (Cambridge, 1984), 86–112.
32. E. Straub, *Pax et Imperium. Spaniens Kampf um seine Friedensordnung in Europa zwischen 1617 und 1635* (Paderborn, 1980), 288–314.
33. Roberts, *Gustavus Adolphus*, ii. 357–425; and R. Frost, *The Northern Wars 1558–1721* (London, 2000), 104–114.
34. G. Mann, *Wallenstein. His Life*, trans C. Kessler (London, 1976), 401–17.
35. M. Roberts, *The Swedish Imperial Experience, 1560–1718* (Cambridge, 1979), 15–18.
36. Wilson, *Europe's Tragedy*, 454–7; and Mann, *Wallenstein*, 496–536.
37. Roberts, *Gustavus Adolphus*, ii. 452–64.
38. M. Roberts, 'Oxenstierna in Germany, 1633–36', in Roberts, *From Oxenstierna to Charles XII* (Cambridge, 1991).
39. H. Haan, *Der Regensburger Kurfürstentag von 1636/37* (Münster, 1967), 15–53.
40. D. Parrott, *Richelieu's Army. War, Government and Society in France, 1624–42* (Cambridge, 2001), 110–63.
41. Wilson, *Europe's Tragedy*, 762–9.
42. Ibid. 602–5, 679–84, 693–6; and W. Guthrie, *The Later Thirty Years War. From the Battle of Wittstock to the Treaty of Westphalia* (Westport, CO, 2003), 79–86, 203–12, 131–41.
43. Guthrie, *The Later Thirty Years War*, 116–22.
44. This integrated approach seeks also to challenge the traditional 'decisive battle' argument with its focus on chosen, decontextualized encounters such as the first battle of Breitenfeld or the Franco-Spanish battle of Rocroi (1643).
45. Guibert, *Essai Général de Tactique (1772)*, ed. J-P. Bois (Paris, 2004), 29.
46. T. Lorentzen, *Die Schwedische Armee im Dreißigjährigen Kriege und ihre Abdankung* (Leipzig, 1894), 105–34.
47. The author's forthcoming book, *The Business of War. Military Enterprise and Military Revolution in Early Modern Europe* (Cambridge), will examine these issues in more detail.
48. Guthrie, *The Later Thirty Years War*, 132–4.
49. Lorentzen, *Schwedische* Armee, 73–4; H. Salm, *Armeefinanzierung im Dreißigjährigen Krieg. Der Niederrheinisch-Westfälische Reichskreis, 1635–1650* (Münster, 1990), 106–54.
50. R. Hildebrandt (ed.), *Quellen und Regesten zu den Augsburger Handelshäusern Paler und Rehlinger, 1539–1642*, 2 vols (Stuttgart, 2004), ii. 222–34.
51. For an example of such an approach in the Breisgau in 1644: J. Heilmann, *Die Feldzüge der Bayern in den Jahren 1643, 1644, 1645 unter den Befehlen des Feldmarschalls Franz Freiherrn von Mercy* (Leipzig, 1851), 157–60.
52. E. Höfer, *Der Ende des Dreißigjährigen Krieges. Strategie und Kriegsbild* (Cologne, 1997), 54–9; and G. Immler, *Kurfürst Maximilian I. und der Westfälische Friedenkongreß. Die bayerische auswärtige Politik von 1644 bis zum Ulmer Waffenstillstand* (Münster, 1992), 308–23, 398–431.
53. L. Höbelt, *Ferdinand III* (Graz, 2008), 231–35; and P. Broucek, *Der Schwedenfeldzug nach Niederösterreich, 1645–46* (Vienna, 1967), 6–8.
54. Wilson, *Europe's TragedyYears*, 696–8.
55. K. Ruppert, *Die kaiserliche Politik auf dem Westfälischen Friedenkongreß (1643–48)* (Münster, 1979), 119–228.
56. J. Kunisch, *Der kleine Krieg. Studien zum Heerwesen des Absolutismus* (Wiesbaden, 1973), 5–24.
57. P. Englund, *Die Verwüstung Deutschlands. Eine Geschichte des Dreißigjährigen Krieges* (Stuttgart, 2001), 330–82.
58. J. Bérenger, *Turenne* (Paris, 1987), 241–9.
59. M. Roberts, 'The Political Objectives of Gustav Adolf in Germany, 1630–32', in id. *Essays*, 99–102.

7

Britain and the 'Long' Eighteenth Century, 1688–1815

Jeremy Black

INTRODUCTION

A discussion of British strategy in the 'long' eighteenth century focused on the Seven Years War (1756–63), the American War of Independence (1775–83), and the French Revolution and the Napoleonic wars (1793–1815) at the turn of the century calls into question the value of employing the concept of strategy when the terms to describe it were different or nonexistent. It also raises the issue of shaping into a false coherence the often disparate discussion, limited planning, and fragmented points of evidence that exist. These problems underline the additional difficulties of aligning the situation in one state in one (lengthy) period with that in other states in other periods—always a task for which historians lack the enthusiasm of social scientists, and also the problems entailed in the search for a 'unified theory of strategy'.

Britain in the 'long' eighteenth century warrants special attention in the field of strategy and policy, as it witnessed the interaction between a new form of political system, an imperial representative monarchy, and the myriad international and domestic challenges of power politics in a highly competitive situation. A key element in eighteenth-century Britain was the lack of any unpacking of strategy and policy. This lack reflected the absence of any institutional body specifically charged with strategic planning and execution, as well as the tendency, in politics, government, and political discussion, to see strategy and policy as one necessarily indivisible concept.

THE NATURE OF STRATEGY

The very existence of strategy, strategic culture, and strategic policy in the eighteenth century is highly problematic as far as some well-informed scholars are concerned.[1] The delay in the development of the idea of strategy is held to have reflected conceptual and institutional limitations. Certainly, compared to the formal, institutional processes of strategic discussion and planning in recent decades, strategy was, at best, limited and ad hoc, lacking both structure and doctrine. Despite repeated experience of war, especially during most of the years between 1689 and 1720 and again between 1739 and 1763, and despite continued concerns that war might recur, there were serious deficiencies in the administration of the British war effort (e.g. the separate administration of the Ordnance), let alone in military planning.[2] These deficiencies related largely to structures, not least the lack of a General Staff, although it is worth noting that the most significant structural problem, that of army-navy coordination,[3] persisted as recently as the Falklands War of 1982. Whatever the theory, modern joint structures and doctrines face the reality of continued hostility between the services.

Alongside these flaws, it is worth underlining the issue of comparative capability. If British war-making had deficiencies, not least in strategic planning, so also did that of other powers. Indeed, the greater emphasis in most Continental states on the role of the sovereign created serious problems. Monarchy was no guarantee of competence, as Spain clearly demonstrated in the 1800s, while the delegation of royal powers provided opportunities for factionalism, as happened in France under Louis XIV (1643–1715) and Austria under Charles VI (1711–40). This factionalism may have lacked the public contention seen in Britain, but was nonetheless serious as a consequence.

However, treating the existence of strategy as highly problematic mistakes the absence of an articulated school of strategic thinking for the lack of strategic awareness, a key point throughout the history of strategy. For example, as far as the British navy—the key external arm of the state throughout this period—was concerned, there was considerable experience of balancing between tasks. This need and experience can be seen in the detachment of squadrons from home waters for service in the Baltic and the Mediterranean, which remained a recurrent feature in naval planning and, with a different geographical span, is still pertinent today. Moreover, a strategy of naval commercial interdiction played a role in operations against the Dutch in the late seventeenth century and in the Anglo-Spanish crisis of 1725–7, where it included a powerful transoceanic dimension. The planned use of naval power in international crises, as in 1730, 1731, and 1735, can be seen as wide ranging and reasonably sophisticated given serious limitations in communications and institutional support.

The same was true of planned operations on land, although here Britain encountered a degree of greater complexity because such operations involved coalition warfare. Thus, there was an intertwining of military planning and diplomatic exigencies, and whatever is interpreted as strategy cannot be separated from coalition diplomacy. Each, indeed, was an aspect of the other. This intertwining can be seen with the Nine Years War and the War of the Spanish Succession, in which Britain was involved from 1689 to 1697 and 1702 to 1713, respectively, and again in the War of the Austrian Succession, in which Britain was involved from 1743 to 1748.

Thus, an important background to the issue of strategic culture during the Seven Years War and the American War of Independence is an appreciation that strategy existed as a concept, even if the word was not used in English until about 1800, when it was borrowed from the French. The earliest citation in the second edition of the *Oxford English Dictionary* is from 1810. However, as much of the scholarly discussion of the eighteenth century uses terms not employed by con-temporaries—such as 'the Enlightenment'—it is difficult to see why this approach should not be employed in the military history of the period.[4]

Ideas of Power

If that recognition is one context for the subject, a second is provided by an understanding of strategy in the widest sense, namely, as it related to the health and strength of the country as a whole. From this perspective, the British role in the Seven Years War was a symptom, albeit a very significant one, of a wider anxiety about the country. This point may seem far removed from the habitual consideration of the conflict, but it repays attention because it helps to explain the contours of contemporary public political concern. These, in turn, helped drive the politics of the conflict.

That anxiety reflected the extent to which organic theories of the state were important. In contrast, there is a tendency, when considering the eighteenth century, to emphasize mechanistic themes, not least because of the intellectual thrall of Newtonian physics, and the extent to which notions of the balance of power were regarded as important. This importance was accorded to both inter-national relations and domestic constitutional issues. As far as the former were concerned, states were seen as sovereign, but linked, like the components of a machine. This system was viewed as being self-contained, and as part of a static and well-ordered world: an efficient machine that enabled its parts to conduct activities only in accordance with its own construction. The mechanistic concept of the system of states was well suited to the wider currents of thought at the time, specifically Cartesian rationalism and its successors.

These currents of thought provided not only an analytical framework but also a moral context for international relations. For example, balance-of-power politics, as generally presented, appear as selfishly pragmatic, bereft of any overarching rules, and lacking any ethical theoretical foundations. In practice, however, the situation was somewhat different. Britain had a widely expressed theory of the balance of power, and rules for its politics were outlined in tracts, pamphlets, doctoral dissertations, and explanations of the reasons for the resort to war. The relationship between such theories and rules on the one hand, and decision-making processes on the other, is obscure, and it clearly varied by ruler and minister, but such discussions set normative standards that helped shape policies and responses.[5] Strategy, in short, drew on widely diffused concepts of how power should operate, and the elements of political placing and cultural conditioning were crucial.

Without denying a central role for the notions bound up in the balance of power, it is necessary to complement them by an awareness of organic assump-tions. These were important not so much at the level of the international system (until the nineteenth century), but at the level of individual states. Moreover, these assumptions helped provide a dynamic component that is generally lacking in the more structural nature of the mechanistic themes. This dynamic component was vitalist in intention. In particular, there was a sense of a state as the expression of a nation, of the nation as linked in a national character, and of this character as capable of change and prone to decay. The dynamic view rested in part on cyclical accounts of the rise and fall of empires, which drew much of their authority from the commanding role of classical Rome in the historicized political thought of the period, but there was also a strong input from ideas of health. Thus, a traditional sense of the nation as akin to a person remained important.

This idea translated into the international sphere with a sense of nations as competitive, and as under threat from challenges whose causes and mechanisms were both foreign and domestic. Looked at from one perspective, the importance of these issues, and the very value of terms such as 'balance of power', 'overreach', 'limits', 'revolution', or 'enlightenment', are products of their varied applicability and conceptual flexibility. This is also true for strategy. Looked at differently, this very flexibility makes contemporary conceptualization of limited value because the idea of strategy was imprecise. Aside from the problem of assessment, there is also the contrast between the use of the concept in a descriptive or in a prescriptive fashion.

Strategy and Limits

In terms of strategy, notions of balance encouraged action on the part of a Britain—which was France for most of the period—opposed to hegemonic power. Yet they also acted as a restraint, not least because of anxieties about the possible domestic consequences of such action in terms of an overmighty state and an overexpanded state. As such, restraint only guided strategy up to a point. In particular, in normative as well as prudential terms, war and imperial expansion, insofar as the two were possible, appeared feasible, successful, and necessary for most of the period up to 1945. Churchill pursued colonial gains for Britain as late as the Second World War at the expense of the Italian colony of Libya. Within Europe, states sought simultaneously to consolidate authority and to gain territory, each goal that involved normative and prudential valuations. To opt out would not have seemed sensible. With its stress on honour and dynastic responsibility and its concern with *gloire* and the normative values of combat, the dominant political culture of continental Europe was scarcely cautious or pacific.

Owing to domestic circumstances, as well as to its island position, Britain was different from other nations as far as European expansion is concerned, but this difference has to be handled with care, not least due to the transoceanic dimension. At one extreme, for Britain not to have resisted the American Revolution (1775–83) would have appeared as bizarre as for Philip II of Spain not to oppose the Dutch Revolt two centuries earlier. More generally, as far as expansion was involved, the issue was a prudent defence of interest, not overreach. This was true whether the case was advancing Spanish goals in Italy (from the 1490s to the 1740s) or pursuing British objectives in the Ohio Valley region in the early 1750s.

For either Spain under Philip II or Britain in the long eighteenth century to respond to rivals by trying to avoid conflict and, instead, defining mutually acceptable spheres of influence through diplomatic strategy was difficult, if not impracticable. Such a policy would have been politically and ideologically problematic. It would also have been a serious signal of weakness. Lastly, for Spain as far as the Ottomans, the French, or the Dutch were concerned, as for Britain in

1689–1815 as far as France was concerned, there seems little reason to believe that compromise could have been reached and sustained short of large-scale conflict. The same can be said regarding the War on Terror.

Thus, strategic reach could only be defined as part of, and yet also responsive to, what others might see as overreach. Indeed, far from being alternatives, reach and overreach were part of the same process. Moreover, the very success of both Spain and Britain makes it clear that overreach is a difficult, although still useful, concept. The conquest of large areas by relatively small forces, and the successful laying of claims to others, did not demonstrate the value of limits. A desire to avoid risk would have prevented Britain from responding to French moves in 1754–5 and 1792–3, or would have kept the Spaniards in the Caribbean, offshore from the American mainland, in the early sixteenth century. Neither policy would have appeared prudent in hindsight, and, in the British case, such a course would have been impossible.

Furthermore, the element of perception central to the apparently objective notion of strategic overreach also reflects the ideological and cultural assumptions of the perceiver—assumptions that are frequently subliminal but nonetheless very significant. This applies to historical appraisals of both Britain and Spain. In the case of Spain, there is a long-standing perspective that can be described as Whiggish or liberal. This perspective reflects critical views of Catholicism and, correspondingly, the customary association of progress with Protestantism. Aside from being anachronistic, the Spanish empire appears in this account as something that had to be defeated in order to usher in the future. Given this perception, it is not surprising that many historians apply the idea of overreach to Spain, and judge its strategy accordingly.

Strategy and Dynasticism

Comparison with Britain then comes to the fore.[6] First, it is important to stress the role of contingency and thus apparently imminent limits on Britain during the period 1688–1815. If Spain suffered rebellions during the period 1560–1660, so also did Britain in 1688–1815. Moreover, in Britain there was a rival dynasty, with all the issues that posed for stability and loyalty, a situation that did not occur in Spain until the 1700s and then again in 1808–13. Britain, moreover, faced a threat that Spain did not confront in 1560–1660: that of foreign invasion. In 1688–9 the male line of the Stuart dynasty was overthrown. Subsequently, invasion attempts on behalf of the Stuarts were mounted on a number of occasions, including 1692, 1708, 1719, 1744, 1745, and 1759. Each was backed by France, apart from the 1719 attempt, which was supported by Spain. Thereafter, France mounted invasion attempts during its wars with Britain, including in 1779, 1798, and 1805. Britain could launch nothing comparable against France. The frequency of the French attempts, and the even more insistent level of threat, brings forward the question of appropriate strategy, both for the state and, more problematically, for the dynasty.

Thus, the question of strategic grasp and overreach can be reconceptualized to ask whether rule of Britain represented overreach for the Orange and Hanoverian dynasties. In the former case, the reign of William III was short (1689–1702), and he was already in opposition to Louis XIV of France. If becoming ruler of Britain opened up another military front for William, and tied up Dutch and allied troops that might otherwise have been deployed against France on the Continent in 1688–90, it did so in a way that also weakened France. The war against Britain became a major military and naval commitment for Louis XIV. After that state of war had ceased, William III benefited greatly from British resources, both in the war that continued until 1697 and in the subsequent post-war negotiations. Indeed, there was an instructive contrast between William's failure to sustain a strong enough alliance to limit Louis XIV after the French-Dutch War ended in 1678 and the greater success shown after 1697. William succeeded both in negotiating a European settlement with France through the partition treaties of 1698 and 1700, and, after Louis rejected the partition of the Spanish empire in 1700, in preparing a Grand Alliance for the forthcoming war.

The question of shared strategic interests is more problematic as far as the Hanoverian dynasty was concerned. Initially, the British connection, which began with the accession of George I in 1714, appeared a way to advance Hanoverian dynastic claims to territory and status, not least in the partition of the Swedish empire as a result of the Great Northern War (1700–21). George II (1727–60) continued this policy, with hopes of gains for Hanover in Germany: notably, but not only, the territories of Hildesheim, Osnabrück, and East Friesland. Yet, these hopes were not realized and, instead, the vulnerability of Hanover was repeatedly demonstrated, whether by the threat of Prussian attack (1726, 1729, 1753, 1801, and 1805) or of French attack (1741, 1757, 1803, and 1806). The Electorate was devastated by the occupying French forces in 1757, and Hanover's participation in the Seven Years War proved very costly. Indeed, the difficult consequences led Hanoverian ministers to speculate about ending the dynastic link with Britain,[7] a situation that, indirectly, presaged Hanoverian neutrality in 1795–1804.[8] The British commitment could be regarded as the cause of Hanover's plight in 1757, not least as George II, under pressure from his British ministers, rejected the option of neutrality.

Conversely, strategic limits can be seen in another aspect of the relationship. The attempt to pursue what could be presented as shared Anglo-Hanoverian interests in Europe ran up against several hindrances: first, the dynastic rivalry of the ruling houses of Hanover and Prussia; second, the Austrian defence of the authority of the Holy Roman Emperor and the interests of the Catholic Church against Protestant rulers such as Hanover; and, third, the expansionist schemes of Russia.[9] The result was repeated Anglo-Hanoverian failure, albeit a failure overshadowed by transoceanic British expansion.

Strategy and the Limits of Imperial Power

As with Spain in 1560–1660, or indeed with the entire eighteenth century, this point opens up the question of where emphasis should be placed in strategic analysis and, again, whose emphasis. It might be suggested that this is a simple question of contrasting contemporary with modern values, but even that is not clear-cut. For example, there is an important debate about the extent to which eighteenth-century Britons were committed to transoceanic goals,[10] which represents the dominant view in the literature of the 1990s, or, rather, European ones, an argument increasingly prominent in more recent years.[11] Similar debate attaches to Britain at the present moment, while there is likely to be a strengthening of debate in the United States, not least as the Republicans seek to define a new policy in response both to the Bush legacy and to the Obama presidency. Such debate underlines the problematic nature of the thesis that interests are clear—a point that must be stressed in any discussion of strategy. Indeed, the very discussion of strategy is largely a matter of the debate over interests, however defined: national, state, dynastic, class, and so on. This point makes the debate more, not less, important.

Returning again to eighteenth-century Britain, there is a parallel between the American Revolution and the revolution against Philip II in the Netherlands, and the question of how far the two indicated limits of strategic capability. Here, limits can be seen as much, if not more, in terms of policy as of the geography of strategy. Indeed, a focus on the latter may seem to represent a militarization of strategy and the question of limits that is disproportionately important in the literature. In contrast to this militarization of issues of policy and strategy, other policies would certainly have led to very different situations, affecting the possibility of rebellion, the likelihood of support within the areas that rebelled, and the prospect for a reconciliation short of revolution. This issue cuts to the heart of the discussion about strategic effectiveness—a discussion that takes the form of 'Thus far is appropriate, but more creates problems of overreach'—because it removes this discussion from the realm of mechanistic theories of the state or empire.

Instead, it is the very driver of the system that is in question when policies and the pressures for obedience and order are considered. Partly for this reason, there is a need to include domestic policy as a key aspect of strategy. Indeed, as noted earlier in the examination of limits, the value of a flexible definition for strategy emerges. It is conventional to restrict the term to the military, but this practice is not terribly helpful from the perspective of the pursuit and limits of power as discussed in this chapter. Strategy emerges as primarily political in background, goals, and indeed means, with the use of force simply an aspect of the means, and frequently one that is only to be employed as a substitute. Thus, strategy should be understood in terms of a process of policy formation, execution, and evaluation in which military purposes are frequently secondary.

In recent decades, the definition and discussion of an operational dimension to war provided a key opportunity for reconceptualizing strategy, separate from its usual military context, and, instead, seeking an understanding of the concept that centres more on the political realm. In any event, even at the operational and tactical levels, political considerations play a key role. Indeed, they can be seen as aspects of the political character of warfare, notably again the sense of limits in means as well as goals.

This point is not a semantic play on the notion of limited war, instructive as that is in this context. Instead, it places an emphasis on the extent to which warmaking involved limits or their absence—for example, in the treatment of prisoners and civilians, or the extent of scorched-earth policies—depending on whether conflict was designed to retain and/or incorporate territory or was more focused on battle with, or even the destruction of, opposing forces.

The Tone of Strategy

As far as Britain was concerned, limits can also be debated in such terms as the extent to which territorial expansion was pursued from the centre, or largely by colonial lobbies and proconsular generals and officials. This contentious political question is directly germane to questions concerning the appropriateness of the use of armed force at particular junctures and, indeed, the extent to which limits were a matter of debate and nuance, rather than being clear-cut. This was also the case with such 'ethnic violence' as the controversial expulsion of the Acadians from Nova Scotia or indeed the contested policies followed towards Native Americans. Limits in tone thus overlap with limits in policy, the two influencing and also expressing each other.

Variations and limits in tone bring up key cultural elements that act as a qualification to the ready ahistorical transference of example for analytical purpose, for example, from ancient Rome to the modern United States. Thus, although religion was important to the various aspects of the character of British imperialism,[12] it can be suggested that it did not have an equivalent impact to that of Catholicism under Philip II of Spain and, indeed, his two successors. This view can be qualified and debated, but that very process underlines the extent to which the cultural or ideological dimension, and everything it entailed for an understanding and telling of interests and limits, has to be understood in terms of a specific historical context and cannot be readily reduced to, or by, any form of structuralism and determinism.

THE SEVEN YEARS WAR

For example, as far as the Seven Years War (1756–63) was concerned, anti-Catholicism was crucial in affecting British attitudes.[13] This point is worth underlining, because it encouraged a sense that Britain should persist in the struggle even in the face of very negative news, as was the case in the early days of the war.[14] Anti-Catholicism led to a sense of existentialist and meta-historical struggle. Thus, policy and strategy rested on a clear ideological commitment.

British war-making in this conflict was greatly affected by the possibilities and exigencies of alliance politics, as indeed had been the case throughout the years of war with France from 1689, and many, but not all, earlier conflicts, for example the Third Anglo-Dutch War of 1672–4. Britain alone could hold off attack, but, despite the hopes of 'blue-water' power exponents, could not overthrow its opponent. This was a lasting problem in British strategic culture. In the Seven Years War, Britain's ally Frederick II (the Great) of Prussia possessed the resources (just) and skill simply to put up a good resistance to Austria, France, and Russia. Britain had only been able to defeat France (and Spain in 1762) in the sense of capturing colonies and sinking warships (and blocking the Spanish invasion of Portugal). Coastal raids on France had accomplished little, and the loss of the Austrian and Dutch alliances in 1756 had ensured that there was no war in the Low Countries.

The strategy of the war was a complex mixture of taking initiatives and responding to those of Britain's enemies: France and, from 1762 onwards, Spain. The relationship between initiative and response was framed in the contexts of domestic and international politics, and these took precedence over the actual conduct of war. There was scant debate about the latter. Instead, the key questions arose from the impact of both the entry into senior office of William Pitt the Elder and the alliance with Frederick II.

The former led to an emphasis on transoceanic operations as a result of Pitt's linkage with Patriot and Tory political groupings and themes. As such, the policies advocated in 1757 by William, Duke of Cumberland, George II's son and the head of the army protecting Hanover, were pushed to one side. Pitt had had experience as a peacetime cavalry cornet, but had no real view on the conduct of war other than that he wanted it to be vigorous. Thus, in operating in North America, Pitt pressed for the defence of the British colonies and the conquest of France's Canadian territories, but the extent to which this entailed battles or sieges was up to the commanders on the ground and to circumstances. The same was true of naval operations. Britain, British trade, and British overseas operations had to be protected from attack, but it was difficult to force battle on opponents unless they left the fleet, and therefore the blockade of France's ports came foremost. As far as British policymakers were concerned, the war had been forced on Britain by French aggression in the Ohio Valley region, and the extent to which the conflict was intended to yield additional gains only became clear with success. Prior to that, it was likely that the war would end, as the War of the Austrian Succession had done in 1748, with the exchange of gains. The latter was the norm, and was not the basis for any strategy focused on conquest.

THE AMERICAN WAR OF INDEPENDENCE

The political context was very different in the American War of Independence (1775–83). This underlines the extent to which any focus on war-winning involves understanding strategy or, rather, operationalizing it, in terms of military activity when, in fact, the key to strategy is the political purposes that are pursued. In short, strategy is a process of understanding problems and determining goals, and does not simply consist of the details of the plans by which these goals are implemented by military means.

British strategy in the American War of Independence has to be understood in this light because it was very different in type from strategy during the Seven Years War. In the latter case, the British focus had been on conquering French possessions in North America and not on pacification in those territories. The latter aim was very much subservient to the former, although different policies were pursued for the purpose of pacification. These included an eighteenth-century equivalent of ethnic cleansing in the expulsion of the Acadians from Nova Scotia, as well as the very different post-conquest accommodation of the Catholics of Québec, which looked towards the Quebec Act.

In the War of Independence, by contrast, pacification was the British strategy, and the question was how best to secure it. The purpose of the war was clear: the return of the Americans to their loyalty. The method chosen was different from that taken in response to the Jacobite risings in Scotland and northern England in 1715-16 and 1745-6. In the latter cases, as happened later in the face of the Irish rising in 1798, the remedy had been more clearly military. However, in making that argument, it is necessary to note post-war policies for stability through reorganization, most obviously in the introduction of new governmental systems for the Scottish Highlands and Ireland.

Actions in the case of America did not involve this sequencing but, instead, a willingness to consider not only pacification alongside conflict but also new systems as an aspect of this pacification. Indeed, in one sense, pacification began at the outset, with the misconceived and mishandled attempt to seize arms in New England. The most prominent instances of pacification were the instructions to the Howe brothers in 1776 to negotiate as well as fight, and, even more clearly, the dispatch of the Carlisle Commission in 1778. Moreover, the restoration of colonial government in the South was a concrete step indicating, during the war, what the British were seeking to achieve.

Alongside that, and more central, were the practices of British commanders. Although the Americans were traitors, they were treated with great leniency, and suggestions of harsher treatment were generally ignored. This point underlines the extent to which conduct in the field both reflects strategy and also affects the development of strategic culture.

This focus on pacification provides an essential continuity to British strategy, but there were, of course, differences in emphasis. An attempt at evaluation faces the classic problem that history occurs forward, 1775 preceding 1776, but is analysed from posterity, with 1775 understood in light of 1776. This approach is unhelpful, however, not least because the course of the war was affected by two key discontinuities that transformed the parameters.

The usual one given is the internationalization of the war, with France's entry in 1778, but prior to that the declaration of American independence in 1776 transformed the situation. Alongside that came military unpredictabilities, such as the unsuccessful American invasion of Canada in 1775-6 and the British failures at Saratoga (1776) and Yorktown (1781). These events were not secondary to the military operationalization of strategy but, instead, helped direct it. The wider political dimension was also affected by events.

Thus, the Southern Strategy, both military and political, arose in large part from the impact of French entry into the war. This entry ended the unusual situation in which Britain was at war solely in North America and therefore able to concentrate attention and resources on it. Moreover, French entry essentially pushed Britain into a bifurcated struggle involving separate strategies. The struggle for pacification continued in the Thirteen Colonies (albeit complicated by the French presence there), while a straightforward military struggle began elsewhere, especially in the West Indies and India. Again, this apparently clear distinction can be qualified by noting that Britain had political options to consider in both cases.

The general impression is of progressive moves towards such a bifurcated war, but, in practice, the political dimension again came first, and was made more complex by the need to consider the goals and moves of various powers, including unpredictable responses to the actions of others. Thus, aside from Britain's relations with the states with which it eventually went to war—France, Spain, and the Netherlands—there were relations with neutral powers, both friendly and unfriendly. These relations were linked to the military operationalization of strategy, not least with the possibility that alliances in Europe would yield troops for North America: a key goal as, lacking conscription, Britain was short of troops. In some respects, this situation prefigured that of the United States in the Second World War. Furthermore, the European crisis of 1778, which led to the War of the Bavarian Succession of 1778–9 between Prussia and France's ally Austria, created diplomatic opportunities for Britain and indeed was seen in this light. There has since also been scholarly discussion along the lines that a more interventionist European policy would have distracted France from taking part in the American war, with key consequences for British options there.

This point highlights a fundamental aspect of British strategy in the 1770s. Britain was acting as a satisfied power, keen obviously to retain and safeguard its position, but not interested in gaining fresh territory. Representing a satisfied power, British ministers were also wary of becoming involved in European power politics. Here the American war fitted into a pattern that had begun with George III's rejection of the Prussian alliance in 1761–2, and had continued with a subsequent refusal to accept Russian requirements for an alliance, as well as with the rebuff of French approaches for joint action against the First Partition of Poland of 1772.

Thus, there was to be no recurrence of the situation during the Seven Years War, namely, war in alliance with a Continental power. However unintentional, this situation had proved particularly potent, or had been shaped thus by William Pitt the Elder with his presentation of British policy in terms of conquering Canada in Europe. In the American War of Independence, there would be no alliance with Prussia (or anyone else) to distract France, and, thus, in military terms, no commitment of the British army to the Continent, as had occurred in 1758.

Further, subsidized German troops, such as those deployed in 1757 in an unsuccessful attempt to defend the Electorate of Hanover, would not be used for 'German' or European power-political purposes. Instead, some troops would be retained in Europe—Hanoverians, for example, being sent to serve in the Gibraltar garrison—but most were sent to America, where, at peak strength, they comprised nearly 40 per cent of the British army. Britain's fundamental strategy thus rested on a policy cohesion that had military consequences: passivity in Europe combined with the preservation of status in America.

Was there an alternative? The thesis that, in order to gain a powerful ally, post-1763 Britain should have supported Russian demands on Turkey, with which Russia was at war from 1768 to 1774, or, subsequently, Poland, which Russia helped despoil in the partition of 1772, discounts the problems that would have been created by such an alliance. This thesis also exaggerates what the British state could afford to do, and that at a time when it was struggling with the burden of unprecedented debt and was facing serious political problems in Britain and North America over attempts to raise taxation.

Second, even had Britain allied itself with Austria, Prussia, or Russia after 1763, there is little reason to believe that it would have enjoyed much influence with its ally or allies, or even been consulted by them. This conclusion was suggested by

Britain's experience with Austria in 1731–3 and 1748–55, and with Prussia in 1756–63, and presages subsequent British problems with allies from 1914 onward.

Moreover, as the three major eastern European powers were at, or close to, war in 1768–74, 1778–9, and 1782–3, the caution of these British ministers was vindicated. Not only were these conflicts in which Britain had only limited interest, but it was also unlikely that these powers would have been able or willing to provide appropriate support to Britain in its confrontations with the Bourbons. Even had they done so, more auxiliaries backing Britain in North America in 1775–83 would have made little more difference than a greater number of French troops supporting Emperor Maximilian would have made in Mexico in the 1860s. In each case, there was a powerful opposition able to sustain resistance, so that output by the occupying power did not equate with outcome in the form of political success.

Reviewing the diplomatic strategies on offer, it is reasonable to consider the 'What if?' of Austrian or Prussian pressure on France, or the possibility that this pressure would deter the French from helping the Americans from 1778 onwards, and would thus justify interventionist British diplomacy. It is pertinent to ask, however, whether such an alliance would not have led, instead, to a highly damaging British commitment to one side or the other in the Austro-Prussian War of the Bavarian Succession (1778–9). The Seven Years War, in which Britain had allied with Prussia, was scarcely encouraging in this respect, as it was initially far from clear whether Britain's involvement in the conflict on the Continent then would work out as favourably as it actually did. Given the use made of this example, that point provides a key instance of the nature of strategic thought and culture as recovered memory.

In addition, had Britain allied with Austria or Prussia in the War of the Bavarian Succession, then Hanover would presumably have been exposed to attack by its opponents. Hanover was vulnerable, as was repeatedly demonstrated, and had it been overrun, as it was by the French in 1757, then its slow recovery might have jeopardized the military, diplomatic, and political options of the British government. Furthermore, the War of the Bavarian Succession was restricted to two campaigning seasons, but could have been longer, like the Seven Years War, or speedily resumed, like the two Austro-Prussian conflicts of the 1740s. Either outcome would have posed problems for Britain, limiting other strategic options.

There is another critique of the interventionist counterfactual, in this case specifically the argument that intervention could have deterred French action and thus ensured British victory. Prior to French entry into the war, the British had already failed to translate victories in North America into an acceptable political verdict. Thus, the 'What if the French had not entered into the war?' is of less moment than might be suggested by a focus on the major French role in the Franco-American defeat of the British at Yorktown in 1781. This point underlines the need to locate speculation about diplomatic and strategic options in a context of understanding strategic possibilities. This understanding is insufficiently pursued in the case of some work on the eighteenth century.

Goals also need to be borne in mind: it is always a problem if counterfactuals are not adequately grounded in an understanding of contemporary objectives. Britain was a satisfied power after 1763, and, as a consequence, it was difficult, if not dangerous, to try to strengthen the status quo by alliances with powers that wished to overturn it. There was also no significant domestic constituency for an interventionist strategy, and notably none for any particular interventionist course of action.

Aside from the practicalities of British power and the nature of British politics, the Western Question—the fate of western Europe, and more particularly the Low Countries, the Rhineland, and Italy—had been settled diplomatically in the 1750s, when the Austrian alliances with Spain and then France removed both the need and the opportunity for British intervention. This shift in power politics was crucial, for in Britain public support for interventionism on the Continent was fragile, if not weak, unless the Bourbons (the rulers of France and Spain) were the target. Indeed, the domestic coalition of interests and ideas upon which public backing for foreign policy rested was heavily reliant on the consistency offered by the resonant anti-Bourbon beat. Thus, British military strategy in the war cannot be separated from wider currents of political preference and engagement. This point underlines the problems that the extent of public engagement created for British strategy during the War on Terror in 2000.

What British strategy appeared to entail in North America, however, varied greatly during the conflict. Britain initially believed that opposition largely existed only in Massachusetts, and this suggested that a vigorous defence of imperial interests there would save the situation. This view led to British legislation in 1774 specific to this colony and to a concentration of Britain's forces in North America there. The first military operationalization of the strategy continued after the clashes at Concord and Lexington, both because the emphasis on Massachusetts appeared vindicated and because there were not enough troops for action else-where—a key failure in British preparedness.

In the event, this policy failed, both in Massachusetts and elsewhere. In the former, the military presence was unable to prevent rebellion or to contain it, and eventually, in March 1776, the British had to evacuate Boston when the harbour was threatened by American cannon. Elsewhere in North America, the lack of troops stemming from the concentration on Boston ensured that British authority was overthrown in the other twelve colonies involved in the revolution. Meanwhile, the Americans were able to mount an invasion of Canada that achieved initial success, bottling up the British in Québec.

As a result of the events of 1775–6, the second stage of the war—a stage expected and planned neither by most of the Patriots nor by the British government—led to a major British effort to regain control, a policy that entailed both a formidable military effort and peacemaking proposals. Here, again, it is necessary to look at the military options in terms of the political situation. The rebellion could not be ended by reconquering the Thirteen Colonies (and driving the Americans from Canada). The task was too great. Instead, it was necessary to secure military results that achieved the political outcome of an end to rebellion—an outcome that was likely to require both a negotiated settlement and acquiescence in the return to loyalty and in subsequent maintenance of obedience. This outcome rested on different politics from those of the conquest of New France (Canada) during the Seven Years War.

What was unclear was which military results would best secure this outcome. Was the priority the defeat, indeed destruction, of the Continental Army, as it represented the revolution, and not least its unity; or was it the capture of key American centres? Each goal appeared possible, and there was a mutual dependence between them. The British would not be able to defeat the Americans unless they could land and support troops, and, for this capability to be maintained, it was necessary to secure port cities. Conversely, these port cities could best be held if American forces were defeated.

The equations of troop numbers made this clear, not least the problems that maintaining large garrison forces posed for finite British military resources. Indeed, the latter point lent further military importance to the political strategy of pacification, as such a strategy would reduce the need for garrisons and produce local Loyalist forces, as well as diminishing the number of Patriots.

In an instance of a long-standing issue in both strategy and operational planning, the British emphasis possibly should have been on destroying the Continental Army, which was definitely a prospect in 1776–7. Instead, Britain placed emphasis on regaining key centres, not least as this policy was seen as a way of demonstrating the return of royal authority, particularly by ensuring that large numbers of Americans again came under the Crown. Indeed, from the period when the empire struck back, in the summer of 1776, the British gained control of most of the key American points, either for much of the war (New York from 1776, Savannah from 1778, Charleston from 1780), or, as it turned out, temporarily (Newport from 1776, Philadelphia from 1777).

Yet this policy still left important centres, most obviously Boston from March 1776, that were not under British control. This point indicated the fundamental political challenge facing the British and more generally applicable to strategic planning: whatever they won in the field, it would still be necessary to achieve a political settlement, at least in the form of a return to loyalty. The understanding of this issue was an achievement for the British, but also posed a problem, just as it was also both achievement and problem for the Patriots.

This point helps to explain the attention that Patriot leaders devoted to politics throughout the war, as political outcomes were needed to secure the persistence and coherence of the war effort. The British, in turn, could try, by political approaches and military efforts, to alter these political equations within the Thirteen Colonies. At times, they succeeded in doing so, as in the new political prospectus offered in South Carolina after the successful British siege of Charleston in 1780. Indeed, in tidewater South Carolina, British authority was swiftly recognized. This success appeared to be a vindication of the British strategy of combining military force with a conciliatory political policy, offering a new imperial relationship that granted most of the American demands made at the outbreak of the war. It was scarcely surprising that northern politicians, such as Ezekiel Cornell of Rhode Island, came to doubt the determination of their southern counterparts.

To treat this conflict, on either side, therefore simply as a military struggle is to underplay the key role of political goals. Indeed, these goals affected not only the moves of armies (a conventional, but overly limited, understanding of strategy) but also the nature of the forces deployed by both sides. The British use of German 'mercenaries' and, even more, Native Americans and African Americans, provided opportunities for political mobilization on the part of the hostile Patriots. The American reliance on France correspondingly increased domestic support for war in Britain and lowered sympathy for the Patriots, who could now be presented as hypocrites, willing to ally with a Catholic autocracy (two, when Spain joined in 1779), which was also Britain's national enemy.

These alliances brought the war to a new stage, as there was no inherent clarity regarding the allocation of British resources between the conflict with the Bourbons and that with the Americans. It was relatively easy for the Patriots to abandon the Greater American plan of conquering Canada after failure in 1776 was followed by British military efforts in the Thirteen Colonies that had to be countered, but there was no such agreement over policy in Britain. Partisan politics came into play, not least the politics of justification, with the Opposition pressing for a focus on the Bourbons and the ministry unwilling to follow to the same extent, not least because it neither wished, nor thought it appropriate, to abandon hopes of America.

This debate was not settled until Yorktown. The battle in October 1781 was less crucial than the political consequences in Britain, specifically the fall of the Lord North ministry the following March, and the fact that it was not succeeded by a similar one that followed royal views (e.g. a ministry under Lord Thurlow, the Lord Chancellor, a close ally of George III). Instead, the Opposition, under the Marquess of Rockingham, came to power.

As a result of the central role of politics in strategy, 1782 was a key year of the war. It was a year, ironically, in which the Patriots had singularly little military success, George Washington, in particular, getting nowhere with his plan to capture New York. Moreover, this failure was more generally significant, as it marked the decline in the Franco-American alliance. This decline reflected both the problems of pursuing very different military priorities and, far more significantly, war-weariness on the part of the French government that mirrored the priorities of European power politics. Furthermore, in 1782 the French fleet in the West Indies was defeated by Admiral Rodney at the battle of the Saintes—a key instance of the role of battle in determining strategic options.

Thus, militarily, the war was going Britain's way. New warships were being launched, public finances were robust, fears of rebellion in Ireland and of disaffection in Britain were largely assuaged, the Bourbons were increasingly unable to attempt another invasion of Britain, Gibraltar had been held, and the British position in both India and Canada was more resilient than had been feared. Yet the politics was now one of peace and settlement, rather than being focused on a return of America to its loyalty, and strategy was framed accordingly. The priority was the disruption, if not destruction, of the coalition of powers fighting Britain and, it was to be hoped, better relations with an independent United States (as it later became). Paradoxically, this strategy was to be successful in both the short and the long terms, which simply underlines the shortcomings of conceiving of strategy in terms of its military operationalization.

THE FRENCH REVOLUTIONARY AND NAPOLEONIC WARS

This point also emerges where the French revolutionary and Napoleonic wars are concerned, and it is instructive to compare this chapter with the next one, as it indicates how strategy can, and should, be approached in different lights. These conflicts proved key episodes in British strategy, not only because they were important in their own right for developments in the period but also because they served as the crucial frame of reference for British public discussion about strategy until the next 'Great War', that with Germany in 1914–18. This continuity, moreover, was maintained because, until the Entente of 1904, France was Britain's leading rival, a situation underlined as late as 1898 when the two powers came close to war in the Fashoda crisis. Indeed, Russia, which challenged British interests and views from the Balkans to the Far East in the nineteenth century, with a particular emphasis on the threat to the British position in India, could be subsumed into this Anglo-French enmity as a result of the Franco-Russian alliance that developed in the late nineteenth century in reaction to their joint antagonism to the alliance between Germany and Austria.

The French revolutionary and Napoleonic wars underlined a lesson learned from the challenge, variously from Spain and France, from the 1530s to the 1740s: namely, that the threat from a foreign power, the key element in reactive strategy, was linked to domestic issues, in the former case Catholicism and, from 1689, Jacobitism as well. In contrast, the ideological challenge from the French Revolution abated after Napoleon's seizure of power in France in 1799. This situation presaged the status that persisted throughout the nineteenth century, and, indeed, until intervention in the Russian Civil War at the end of the First World War: namely, a dissociation between international and domestic strategic threats.

This dissociation has played too prominent a role in the literature, as nineteenth-century strategy and policy have generally been seen in terms of realist power politics, but the suggestion here is that this analysis is misplaced. Indeed, the British governing elite fostered a strategic imagination that was set by domestic, rather than international, paradigms. Thus, for modern Britain a key factor is that, despite talk of the country's need to be on a war footing, for example against terrorism, no policy choices should entail conscription, as conscription is no longer acceptable either to public culture or to the government. The contrary view argues that threats drive domestic considerations, as happened in 1916, when Britain adopted conscription even though it clashed with the liberal and libertarian tendencies in British thought. Yet the French revolutionary and Napoleonic wars saw Britain confront serious threats without the introduction of conscription.

Comparative capability is a key issue in strategy that must be addressed with reference to the tasks that militaries were expected to execute, and here Britain had particular problems as a consequence of its island status and transoceanic interests. The British military was expected to dominate and ensure the security of the British Isles, to operate on the European continent, and to defeat both European and a wide range of non-European opponents across the oceans. These tasks entailed not only strategic commitments but also prioritization, which was the key issue in the public and governmental politics of strategy, for example colonies versus Europe in the 1790s.[15]

These politics were crucial to strategic formulation because the government was not partly insulated from political pressures by the institutionalization and secrecy that characterized strategic planning in the twentieth century and today. Furthermore, the politics of strategy helped to provide a considerable measure of continuity. Issues and problems were interpreted and debated in terms of what was by 1793, when Britain entered the French Revolutionary War, over a century of experience of conflict with France and also a long-standing background of conflict with Spain. In each case, experience was perceived through the perspective of collective (and contentious) public myths, such as the hopes invested in blue-water strategy: naval mastery and the consequent transoceanic conquests through amphibious operations.

The established treatment of strategy for the period, instead, is operational or combat orientated,[16] but it ignores the central role of the Home Front. The struggle with France was not, because of its ideological current, inherently a new type of war. Moreover, strategy, as before, related to two aspects of domestic politics: first, potential supporters of the foreign power, and second, conventional high politics. These overlapped, with George III very concerned about the loyalty of the Whig opposition and the extent to which their attitudes encouraged the French revolutionaries and Napoleon. Furthermore, George was worried that if the Opposition gained power (as it actually did in 1806), Britain's war goals would be jeopardized and the war abandoned, as it had been in 1782.

A key element of the war strategy was therefore the exclusion of the Opposition from power. This was very important to George III in his negotiations with politicians, as shown in 1804, when William Pitt the Younger returned to office. If the issue was not quite as central to George as that of preventing the extension of equal civil rights to Catholics (Catholic Emancipation), it was nevertheless of great importance to him. A continuity in strategy can indeed be seen between wartime planning and discussion over the terms to be offered in peace negotiations, both those in the 1790s and in 1806.

This was not the limit of the domestic dimension. There was also a concern about popular radicalism and its potential to recruit support. As a result, two major strands of wartime strategy consisted of acting against radicals, particularly through the trials and changes in the law that occurred in the 1790s, and fostering loyalism. The latter took the form of a spontaneous public movement, but one that was also sponsored and sustained by government action.

Loyalism had a direct military consequence in the shape of the massive increase in militia and Volunteer forces. These provided a key force for domestic security, not least against any action by radicals (matching the role of the American militia against Loyalists during the American War of Independence), and also were intended to strengthen the country against invasion. Of the 162,300 effective rank-and-file troops in Britain in 1798, only 47,700 were regulars: 60,000 were militia and 54,300 Volunteers.[17] As such, the militia and Volunteer forces made it possible to increase the number of regulars who could be sent on expeditions, anticipating the role of the Home Guard in the Second World War. Thus, loyalism illustrates the multiple overlaps of the domestic and foreign spheres of wartime strategy, overlaps of which contemporaries were well aware. There was a new emphasis on winning public support.[18]

At the same time, this military need indicated the extent to which strategy was in part a matter of reinterpreting the nuances of domestic power relations. Raising militia and Volunteer forces underlined the need for the state to cooperate with local interests in obtaining resources—an aspect of the long-standing balance between the Crown and local interests. Militia colonels regarded their regiments as fiefs, immensely valuable to them as county magnates and public men for both patronage and prestige. As a result, important changes in the militia laws had to be negotiated with the colonels, and even the practice of regular drafts into the army was carefully conducted to protect their interests.

The domestic dimension was most acute in Ireland, which Britain had seen during, and after, the American War of Independence as a potential site of rebellion. There was indeed one in 1798, which was followed by a French invasion. Another, far more minor, rising took place in 1803. Their failure should not direct attention away from the key role of defence in British strategy. This lay behind many military activities, including the construction of fortifications on the south coast of England in the 1790s and 1800s.

Domestic strategy was a matter also of national reform. This was similar to the position abroad, for example in Prussia after her defeat by France in 1806, and was not unprecedented in British history. Aspects of the Revolution Settlement, or governmental and political changes that followed the 'Glorious Revolution' of 1688–9, owed much to the pressures of war with France in 1689–97 and 1702–13. Not least among them were the establishment of the Bank of England in 1694 and Union with Scotland in 1707. The same was true in 1793–1815, just as the Liberal Unionists of the 1900s also pushed domestic regeneration as an aspect of a strategy of international confrontation. In each case, specific changes, as well as the process of change as a whole, were seen as strengthening Britain, and as key elements of the strategy for keeping the country resilient and competitive, and of directing the energies of society. As far as naval power was concerned, national strength was clearly important to an economic strategy of protecting trade and harming opponents, because this ensured the financial clout necessary to support operations abroad, both British deployments and the actions of allied forces.

Important reforms during the Napoleonic wars included the introduction of income tax (1799), which helped make possible a shift from financing war by borrowing to financing it through taxation. This shift was a response to the liquidity crisis of 1797, and made it easier to endure setbacks, as borrowing was very dependent on confidence. A focus on taxation also fulfilled the vital strategic goal of making public finances far less dependent on the inflow of foreign capital that had been a key feature of the borrowing regime. The French occupation of Amsterdam in 1795 had threatened this flow. Parliamentary union with Ireland (1800–1) was seen as a key way to reduce the vulnerability represented by Ireland, as it was regarded as making the link with Britain acceptable to Irish opinion. There was also a stress on the acquisition of information as a way to strengthen government. The first national census (1801) was important, but more immediate value was gained by detailed mapping designed by the Board of Ordnance to help operationally in the event of a French invasion.[19]

The focus of major reform initiatives in the late 1790s and early 1800s underlines the value of providing a chronological perspective. The sense of a domestic challenge, and the need for a corresponding strategy, was strongest in the 1790s and, in contrast, less pronounced after victory at Trafalgar over the combined Franco-Spanish fleet in 1805. The radicalism of the late 1800s and early 1810s did not seem revolutionary. Although there was some admiration for Napoleon in the British Isles, his abandonment of republicanism greatly tarnished his appeal and that of French political models. Napoleon also lost interest in the cause of Irish independence, which had always been peripheral to his concerns. Robert Emmet had received a promise of support when he visited Napoleon in 1802, but his preparations for a rising in Ireland in 1803 were correctly made without any anticipation of French backing, and the rising was ultimately unsuccessful.

If the chronological dimension provides an important perspective on the strategy of domestic preparedness, it also offers a crucial one for the very different issue of tasking. The latter might appear obvious: France had to be defeated. In practice, however, there were two separate, but related, strands that repay attention. First, there was the issue of determining the goal of the war with France, and, second, that of the range of opponents and allies, and how this interacted with the first strand. There was a crucial tension, one fundamental to strategy, between the argument that France had to be defeated in order to contain it, and the far more ambitious approach that containment could only be secured if the French political system were transformed, most clearly by a restoration of Bourbon rule. Even before serious hostilities began, there was a sense that this was to be a different conflict because of the ideological gulf separating the two sides, and that this would require new military measures.

CONCLUSIONS

Each of the wars entailed conflict between Britain and its traditional foes, France and Spain. Thus, there were important geopolitical and strategic continuities. However, there were also important political differences. The American War of Independence centred on a revolution in part of the empire, while the French Revolution posted the threat of revolutionary movement in the British Isles. As a result, domestic policy was pushed to the fore as a component of strategy.

British strategy was greatly affected by the presence or absence of two key resources: domestic stability and alliance partners. These requirements were not unique to British (and other) military history, but central to it: not only was tasking involved, and with it the political strategy crucial in terms of the dynamics and cohesion of coalitions, but also military strategy. There was a parallel in India, where the mastery won by Britain depended at least as much on the ability to gain allies, ensure stability, and benefit from the mutual enmities of the leading regional powers—Mysore, the Marathas, Hyderabad, Nepal, and the Sikhs—as from success in more conventional 'point of conflict' military history. This was also to be crucial in staving off the challenge of the Indian Mutiny in 1857–8: Britain then benefited greatly from Indian assistance, not least from Hyderabad, Nepal, and the Sikhs. In Europe, alliance with Austria and/or Prussia made it possible to intervene in the Low Countries and Germany, and led to pressure for such action, in particular to sustain the alliance. Strategy was as one with policy. Conversely, the collapse of such an alliance, as in 1756 with Austria and 1762–3 with Prussia, removed this option.

Blue-water rhetoric assumed no need for an alliance, but the tradition of the amphibious operation, of seizing particular points, not of engaging an army and defeating it, only worked well in transoceanic operations against vulnerable colonies, as the Seven Years War showed. As such (and prefiguring conflict with

Italy in North and East Africa in 1940–1), the indirect capability was more significant politically, in showing real and potential allies that Britain could, and would, challenge France on land, than militarily, in the shape of distracting French forces from fighting the allies.

The burgeoning economy of Britain and of the oceanic trading system, and the strength of her public finances, were crucial to the British war effort and thus set the parameters of strategy. Yet, politicians had to understand these parameters, and, more generally, parameters did not settle the issue of prioritization in tasking. Thus, the politics (both domestic and international) of strategy arise throughout as the key issue.

A similar point can be made for other states. Strategy as politics does not exhaust the subject, but it makes sense of a context in which public debate was more potent than institutional continuity. Furthermore, the absence of an equivalent, in terms of policy or royal power, to the messianic imperialism of Philip II of Spain resulted in a strategic debate in eighteenth-century Britain that was more open to political cross-currents.

NOTES

1. J. B. Hattendorf, *England in the War of the Spanish Succession: A Study of the English View and Conduct of Grand Strategy, 1701–1712* (New York, 1987); and N. A. M. Rodger, 'The Idea of Naval Strategy in Britain in the Eighteenth and Nineteenth Centuries', in G. Till (ed.), *The Development of British Naval Thinking* (Abingdon, 2006).
2. R. J. B. Muir and C. J. Esdaile, 'Strategic Planning in a Time of Small Government: The Wars against Revolutionary and Napoleonic France, 1793–1815', in C. M. Woolgar (ed.), *Wellington Studies*, 3 vols (Southampton, 1996).
3. R. Harding, *Amphibious Warfare in the Eighteenth Century: The British Expedition to the West Indies, 1740–1742* (Woodbridge, 1991).
4. For another instance, for a term advanced in 1899, see J. Black, *Geopolitics* (London, 2009).
5. H. K. Kleinschmidt, *The Nemesis of Power* (London, 2000), esp. 114–70, and id., 'Systeme und Ordnungen in der Geschicht der internationalen Beziehungen', *Archiv für kulturgeschichte*, 82 (2000), 433–54; and A. Osiander, *The States System of Europe, 1640–1990: Peacemaking and the Conditions of International Stability* (Oxford, 1994).
6. J. H. Elliott, *Empires of the Atlantic World: Britain and Spain in America, 1492–1830* (New Haven, 2006).
7. U. Dann, *Hanover and Great Britain, 1740–1760* (Leicester, 1991).
8. P. G. Dwyer, 'Prussia and the Armed Neutrality: The Invasion of Hanover in 1801', *International History Review*, 15 (1993), 661–87; and id., 'Two Definitions of Neutrality: Prussia, the European States-System, and the French Invasion of Hanover in 1803', *International History Review*, 19 (1997), 502–40.
9. A. C. Thompson, *Britain, Hanover and the Protestant Interest, 1688–1756* (Woodbridge, 2006); B. Simms and T. Riotte (eds), *The Hanoverian Dimension in British History, 1714–1837* (Cambridge, 2007); and B. Simms, *Three Victories and a Defeat: The Rise and Fall of the First British Empire, 1714–1783* (London, 2007).
10. K. Wilson, *The Sense of the People: Politics, Culture and Imperialism in England, 1715–1785* (Cambridge, 1998); and D. Armitage and M. J. Braddick (eds), *The British Atlantic World* (London, 2002).

11. T. Claydon, *Europe and the Making of England, 1660–1760* (Cambridge, 2007); and J. Black, *Debating Foreign Policy in Eighteenth-Century Britain* (Farnham, 2011).

12. C. G. Pestana, *Protestant Empire: Religion and the Making of the British Atlantic World* (Philadelphia, 2009).

13. M. Schlenke, *England und das friderizianische Preussen, 1740–1763* (Munich, 1963), 171–225.

14. G. Yagi, Jr, 'A Study of Britain's Military Failure during the Initial Stages of the Seven Years' War in North America, 1754–1758', Ph.D. diss., University of Exeter, 2007.

15. P. Mackesy, *War without Victory: The Downfall of Pitt, 1799–1802* (Oxford, 1984).

16. P. Mackesy, 'Strategic Problems of the British War Effort', in H. T. Dickinson (ed.), *Britain and the French Revolution 1789–1815* (Basingstoke, 1989).

17. 'State of Forces in Great Britain', Feb. 1798, British Library (BL), Add. MS 59281, fo. 15.

18. Thomas, Lord Pelham, 'Further Considerations on the Plan for a General Enrolment of the People', 2 July 1803, BL, Add. MS 33120, fo. 135.

19. W. Seymour (ed.), *A History of the Ordnance Survey* (Folkestone, 1980), 21–31; and W. Ravenhill, 'The South West in the Eighteenth-Century Re-mapping of England', in K. Barker and R. J. P. Kain (eds), *Maps and History in South-West England* (Exeter, 1991), 20–1.

8

Britain and the Napoleonic Wars

Charles Esdaile

INTRODUCTION

The English-language bibliography of the military history of the Napoleonic epoch is vast, but also deeply flawed. Operational histories abound—the classic English-language example is David Chandler's *The Campaigns of Napoleon* (1966)—while individual battles from Marengo to Waterloo have all received detailed treatments, some of them many times over. At the same time, there are many biographies of the major commanders of the epoch. In the last thirty years, there have also appeared a considerable number of works that look at one or other of the armies of the period, and, on occasion at least, seek to examine the relationship between them and their parent societies.

However, other approaches tend to be notable by their absence, all the more so when they demand an approach which is analytical rather than descriptive. For example, to the best of the author's knowledge, there is but one study of Napoleon's generalship (rather than of his battles or his military career). As for such treatment of this subject as can be found in works such as those of Chandler, it is pitched very much in terms of the operational level. We hear a great deal about in-theatre manoeuvres of one sort or another, but much less about broader patterns of statecraft and the role which making war played therein.

In short, one area which has come off particularly badly is grand strategy. In this respect, it is of no use turning to the pages of the various books that claim to discuss the art of war in the age of Napoleon either. While the authors concerned are very anxious to tell the reader about what happens on the battlefield, and, indeed, what happens in between one battlefield and another, they almost never raise their sights beyond such matters except, perhaps, to engage in yet another spot of potted history. This chapter, then, has been written with a view to filling the resultant gap in the historiography, though it is naturally recognized that it cannot be regarded as a substitute for a full-length monograph on the subject.

CLAUSEWITZ AND JOMINI

In any chapter devoted to the issue of strategy in the Napoleonic Wars, there is an obvious place to start. It was precisely this conflict that produced two of the most influential military commentators of the entire nineteenth century: men whose writings were to influence the conduct of war right down to 1914 and even beyond. We are talking here, of course, about Antoine Henri Jomini, the Swiss staff officer who served with the French armies in Spain and Germany, defected to the Allies in 1813, and in 1836 published *The Art of War*; and Carl von Clausewitz, the Prussian officer who, after prolonged service with both the Prussian and Russian armies in the Napoleonic Wars, went on to write *On War*. Given that these works were so influential—*On War*, indeed, remains one of the greatest works of military thought ever written—it seems appropriate that we should begin this discussion by referring to what they have to say on the subject.

Unfortunately, considerations of space do not allow us to write a detailed analysis of the work of either writer, but, while there are differences between them, it soon becomes clear that, as far as strategy is concerned, they have much in common. Thus, in brief, both see strategy as the business of deciding where and how to deploy the forces available to a belligerent power, judging what course of action is possible with those forces, and, finally, stringing one battle after another in a continuous process until the enemy's means and will to resist are overcome, if not broken. From this, then, it followed, that strategy was the chief means of obtaining this objective, and, further, that as the foundation of everything else it was the highest form of the military art. As such, it was also the most demanding, the fact being that strategy ought properly to be conducted only by men who were at the very pinnacle of their careers, not least because the personal pressures facing a statesman or commander in the council room were far greater than those experienced by a mere field officer.

That it was, to make use of a hackneyed phrase, 'tough at the top' is doubtless very true, while the same applies to many of the principles that have been sketched in this passage. Yet that does not mean that they are entirely satisfactory. Despite comments, some of them very famous, which suggest that both Jomini and Clausewitz were well aware that strategy had a wider dimension than just what a state did with its armed forces once it had decided to make war, neither of them ever clearly enunciated the idea that strategy—one ought, perhaps, to use the term grand strategy—was at all times an inherent part of statecraft. Instead, their analysis commenced at the moment that a country went to war. Yet, going to war might very well be a mark of strategic failure. Let us here take as an example the case of the campaign of the Hundred Days. Napoleon, it is generally accepted, did not want an immediate war in 1815 and sought frantically to present himself as a man of peace, but his proclamations fell on deaf ears, and thus it was that the *grande armée* found itself marching into Belgium.

Even more extraordinary, meanwhile were the *idées fixes*, first, that strategy necessarily revolved around battle, and, second, that it was an issue that could seemingly only be discussed in the context of marching and fighting by land. Jomini (Clausewitz, by contrast, is completely silent) admittedly included a chapter in his work on 'descents' in which he wrote at some length of the movement of armies by sea, and, more particularly, the use of this possibility to stage full-scale invasions of enemy territory, but such endeavours were clearly in his eyes at best very risky. In the first place, armies large enough to take part in full-scale campaigns of the type seen in Napoleonic Europe were simply too big to be transported by sea, and, in the second, the risks involved were too great. As ports, it is implied, could not be assaulted from the sea, so landings would have to be carried out on open beaches, and this in turn courted disaster, and all the more should the landings be resisted.

As even a cursory knowledge of the Revolutionary and Napoleonic Wars suggests, however, this view flies in the face of reality. Very large armies, certainly, could not be transported by sea with any ease, but the armies employed in this fashion did not necessarily have to be very big. Napoleon, for example, had subdued all of Egypt at the head of just 20,000 men. Equally, in 1808 the British liberated Lisbon, and with it the means to bring in unlimited reinforcements in perfect comfort, with forces that initially numbered just 13,000 men. As for the claim that amphibious operations were bound to fail, the Walcheren disaster, say, is more than counterbalanced by the capture of Copenhagen.

It is not, however, Jomini's dismissal of amphibious warfare that grates so much as his utter failure, like that of Clausewitz, fully to discuss the issue of sea power. In many respects, for Britain and France at least, control of the seas was absolutely at the heart of both the conduct and strategy of the Napoleonic Wars.

Let us begin with Britain. Traditionally no land power—if only for the simple reason that strong historical and political factors had ever since the seventeenth century militated against her maintaining a large army—Britain in 1803 as much as in 1792 would have preferred to embark on war with France with her naval power very much to the forefront. Indeed, it could be said that in the first instance her strategy centred on ensuring control of the sea. On both occasions she had been somewhat caught by surprise, with much of her fleet laid up in port, but if there was one part of the machinery of government that worked on oiled wheels in Britain it was the administration of the navy. The result was that very soon ever greater numbers of frigates and men-of-war were slipping out to sea. Moreover, to ensure that there were always new vessels to plug the holes left by shipwreck or general wear and tear, and to meet any fresh challenges that might arise, all around Britain shipyards were put to work building new frigates and men of war. Many of these vessels were constructed in accordance with simplified designs that reduced costs to a minimum. Be it noted that sea power counted in another fashion as well here: lacking adequate supplies of timber and other useful materials such as hemp, Britain depended on the Baltic trade to keep her navy and merchant marine going.[1]

As to what should be done with this force, there was little equivocation. While some squadrons settled down to blockade the chief French naval bases—Antwerp, Brest, La Rochelle, Toulon—others swept the seas of French trade. Still others convoyed small armies of British troops to conquer the colonies of France and her allies, thereby at one and the same time neutralizing them as potential enemy bases and adding them to the resources of Great Britain. Whether this strategy would ever have been enough to win the war on its own is another matter—indeed, in some respects it might even be reckoned counterproductive—but its short-term benefits were considerable. On the one hand, the vital colonial trade—the centre of Britain's financial well-being—was safeguarded from French interference and given a considerable fillip, while on the other France saw an exactly comparable drop in the value of her own commerce.

Nor was this the only economic boon that Britain received from her control of the seas. Setting aside the West Indies, there were other markets to which her ships now enjoyed what amounted to unlimited access, a very good example here being Spain's American colonies. In theory, all trade with Buenos Aires, Lima, Montevideo, and the rest had to be carried in Spanish bottoms and via Spanish ports, but the erosion of Spain's naval power and the blockade of her ports that was imposed as soon as Spain joined France as an ally in 1796 together threw the American empire wide open to British merchants. In short, as the great American proponent of naval power Alfred Mahan wrote, 'By the natural and almost unaided working of its intrinsic faculties, the sea-power of Great Britain sustained the material forces of the state.'[2]

Control of the seas, then, enabled Britain to keep the war going. At the same time, of course, it rendered her invulnerable to direct attack, while strengthening her against assaults of a more insidious nature. At various times, for example, the economic situation was extremely bleak, but there is no doubt that without the enormous quantities of wheat that Britain was able to ship in from the Baltic and the United States, it would have been a great deal bleaker. In short, sea power ensured that Britain could not be starved into submission. Equally, in a situation in which France seemed to be ruled by a veritable superman backed by an invincible army, the Royal Navy and its victories were a source of both pride and hope. And, finally, the enduring strength of the navy was also a source of social stability in that it shielded Britain from many of the harsher realities of conscription. There was impressment to the navy, certainly, but in practice this fell only on sailors and was sweetened by the considerable amounts of prize money that jack-tars could expect if they were serving under successful captains.

The army, however, was a different matter. In the wake of the failure of the Peace of Amiens in 1803, Britain decreed a limited levy of recruits to make up army ranks, but it was conceded that the men concerned should never be required to serve outside the British Isles, and this was in any case a one-off measure that was not repeated. For the rest, all the troops were volunteers, and this in turn ensured that the human burden of the war never became so great as to be insupportable. At various times, there might have been war-weariness and even open disaffection among the populace, but the destabilization of the regime that an impossibly heavy 'blood tax' produced in France in 1813 and 1814 never became much more than a cloud upon the horizon.

Next on the list of the many advantages conveyed to the cause of Great Britain by her ability to pursue a maritime strategy comes the way in which this acted as a force multiplier. Britain's disposable forces in terms of the regular army were far from great, and yet the ability to mount 'descents' frequently enabled Britain to have a far greater impact on the course of the war than would otherwise have been the case. In 1801, it was control of the seas that ejected the French from Egypt; in 1806, it was control of the sea that saved Sicily from conquest; in 1807, it was control of the sea that denied Napoleon the Danish navy; and in 1808, it was control of the sea that opened the new front in the Iberian Peninsula that was thereafter to play so great a role in British strategy.[3] Not all such expeditions were such a success, of course—in the period 1806-9, expeditions to South America, Sweden, Naples, and Holland all led to more-or-less embarrassing fiascos—but in the end it remains clear enough that without the Royal Navy, Britain would have been confined to a strategy that was purely colonial and economic.[4]

Last but not least, Britain's mastery of the sea brought her the additional advantage of forcing Napoleon, in the first instance at least, to do battle with Britain on her terms and in the process to court humiliation. From the beginning of the French Wars, British naval superiority had been very marked. To begin with, in 1792 the Royal Navy was much larger than its French counterpart with 141 ships of the line and 157 frigates to only 86 of the former and 78 of the latter. Admittedly, French ships were often better built and more heavily armed, but far fewer of them were ready for immediate service. The Revolution in any case wrought havoc with their fighting ability: large numbers of officers emigrated, discipline broke down among seamen, and the dockyards and arsenals were disrupted by political unrest. Despite France's considerable efforts to redeem the situation, the result was that the British, whose leadership, training, morale, and organization by contrast went from strength to strength, secured an advantage that the French were thereafter never able to make good. Hampered by long periods of confinement in port that left their officers and crews desperately rusty in terms of their seamanship, French fleets therefore suffered heavy defeats at the battles of the 'Glorious First of June' in 1794 and Abukir Bay (1 August 1798).

Nor was the support obtained from other navies of much help. Certainly, the sequestration of Holland as a client state known as the Batavian Republic in 1795 and the decision of Spain to re-enter the war as an ally of France in 1796 were potentially great blows to Britain: Spain had seventy-six ships of the line, including the largest in the world—the *Santísima Trinidad*—and Holland another forty-nine. However, in the event, the Spaniards and the Dutch proved no more capable of defeating the Royal Navy than the French: a Spanish fleet was heavily beaten at Cape St Vincent on 14 February 1797 and a Dutch one virtually destroyed at Camperdown on 11 October the same year.

By the time of the Peace of Amiens, then, Britain enjoyed complete naval superiority: thanks to captures and new construction, the Royal Navy now had 202 ships of the line and 277 frigates to French totals of only 39 and 35, few of which were in any condition to take the sea. Since 1793, indeed, Britain had sunk, burned, or captured eighty-four ships of the line alone. As for what remained of French, Spanish, and Dutch naval power, it was cooped up in half a dozen widely separated ports that could easily be blockaded. It was partly for this reason that Napoleon made peace in 1801, for peace would allow him to regroup his forces and embark upon a new programme of naval construction, and it was partly to forestall this same programme of naval construction that Britain resumed the war in 1803. Yet once she had done so, she quickly resumed the position of superiority which she had enjoyed in 1801, as witness, above all, the battle of Trafalgar.

Trafalgar did not quite put an end to the naval struggle. On the contrary, French squadrons continued from time to time to escape the British blockade in pursuit of one errand or another. Napoleon continued to pour huge resources into naval construction and to take such steps as he could to augment his forces, either by treaty or by force of arms, with foreign navies (specifically those of Russia, Denmark, and Portugal). However, although the Royal Navy was placed under great strain by the demands of the blockade, Napoleon was never again to offer a direct challenge to British naval power: indeed, it is interesting to note that Trafalgar was fought as a result of an attempt not to attack Nelson's fleet head-on but rather to support of French land operations in Italy. While the fact that the emperor maintained the proverbial 'fleet in being' ensured that the Royal Navy had to be kept at full strength and employed in long and costly blockades of every French naval base, how much greater would the pressure have been on British resources had Trafalgar never been fought? To paraphrase a famous quotation from Clausewitz, indeed, battle might well have been pursued to gain the end of war, but in this instance doing so had been bad strategy.

ECONOMIC WARFARE

From the beginning there had always been another option open to Napoleon: economic warfare, and, more specifically, a blockade of Britain by excluding her trade from the Continent. This was hardly a novel idea: a number of the measures the emperor eventually adopted in this respect had been prefigured under the Directory. In fairness, one of his very first moves on resuming hostilities against Britain in 1803 had been to send troops to secure the mouth of the River Elbe and thereby impede British access to central Europe. And, though commerce raiding was always more of an irritation than anything else, no sooner had war begun again than large numbers of French frigates and privateers were cruising the seas in search of British prizes.[5]

We come here to another problem with the view of the Napoleonic Wars espoused by Jomini and Clausewitz. Neither writer paid any attention at all to economic warfare, and yet economic warfare was not only eventually to form—on the surface, at least—the centrepiece of Napoleon's strategy against Britain, but also to come very close to bringing Britain to her knees. Indeed, whereas Britain could probably not hope to bring down Napoleon by economic means alone, the reverse was true of France. Although the emperor certainly underestimated Britain's resilience in the face of economic adversity, cutting her off from her continental markets had the potential to be absolutely devastating. In consequence, within a very short time of his promulgation of the decree of Berlin—the measure that barred France and her allies from trading with Britain and closed their ports to any neutral vessel that had put in to British ports before making landfall in Europe—Britain was plunged into crisis. Indeed, in the course of the whole war, there was probably no darker a moment.

Let us set aside the threat posed to naval construction, although this was bad enough: in 1805, 11,841 cargoes of naval timber arrived in Britain's ports, but in 1808 the number was just 27. Meanwhile, there was a corresponding increase in price: between 1807 and 1809 the price of wood imported from the ports of Danzig and Memel doubled.[6] More to the point, with the solutions to the problem—the acquisition of new markets in the wider world and the development of large-scale smuggling in Europe—at best in their infancy, the initial impact of the Continental Blockade on Britain's trade was very serious. By the end of 1808, for example, it was said that only nine of Manchester's eighty-four cotton mills were working at full capacity, and that forty-four had been shut altogether.

And, much as Napoleon had always planned, with the slump came unrest. Thus, in various industrial areas there were demonstrations in favour of peace. In Lancashire, the handloom weavers organized a general strike in protest at the fall in their pay that had been the consequence of the economic downturn; in Manchester, there were serious outbreaks of rioting, one of which culminated in the burning down of a local prison; and, last but not least, the press published a series of letters criticizing the war and denouncing the various measures imposed by the government in response to the blockade. For the moment, nothing was heard of a secret revolutionary movement in the style of the supposed 'black lump' conspiracy of 1802, but the general fear of invasion that had so much contributed to the mood of national unity of 1803–5 was no longer strong enough to swing all and sundry behind 'Church and Crown', and this in turn ensured that the calls for political reform that had been so characteristic of the previous decade also resurfaced.[7]

In fairness, the Continental Blockade was not the only factor underlying Britain's economic and political woes in 1808. In the first place, weary of the constant obstacles that Britain and France put in the way of its trade, the United States chose precisely this moment to impose a total ban on all commercial contacts with the two belligerents—the so-called Jefferson Embargo imposed in December 1807—with the result that bread prices registered a dramatic increase. In the second, this was also the period of the war when commerce raiding was at its most effective: in 1805, the British lost 507 ships in this manner; in 1806, 519; and in 1807, 559—the consequence being that there was a considerable rise in the cost of maritime insurance. However, beyond doubt, Britain was infinitely more vulnerable than France to a blockade. With the situation on the continent very dark indeed—at the beginning of 1808 the only allies Britain possessed in Europe were Sicily and Sweden—had Napoleon continued to apply pressure at the same intensity, it is entirely possible that Britain might have cracked.

Let us compare this situation with the effects of the continued pressure that was applied to France and her empire right through to 1814. This was not, of course, without impact: many coastal cities and their hinterlands were reduced to a state of absolute misery because of the blockade, while across the Continent the prices of colonial products of all sorts were artificially inflated. Thanks in part to harvest failure and in part to sudden changes in course on the part of Napoleon, there was also a serious slump in 1811–12, and all this was going on against a background of soaring taxation and conscription. However, against this we must contrast a series of points that do not give the unbiased observer much cause for confidence in arguments that the Royal Navy on its own could have won the war for Britain. Thus, popular risings were few and far between and had almost nothing to do with the impact of the Continental Blockade when they did occur; conscription continued to function relatively well as late as 1813; and almost none of the various satellite monarchs made any effort to throw off the emperor's rule until the latter's power was broken at the battle of Leipzig in October 1813. Curiously, the one exception was Napoleon's younger brother Louis, who, as King of Holland, became so desperate at the impact of the Continental Blockade on the Dutch economy that in 1810, with a French army bearing down on Amsterdam to enforce its provisions, he seriously considered mobilizing his own forces to defend the city until such time as help could be obtained from Britain.[8]

In the last resort, then, economic warfare could have brought victory to France in a way that it could never have done to Britain. Why, then, have so many commentators argued that the Continental Blockade was counterproductive? The answer, of course, is that they have in the first place been far too much guided by hindsight. Two centuries later, we know that Britain was able to find new markets that enabled her to outflank the Blockade, that even in Europe significant cracks opened in its execution, and that the British financial system was far stronger and more flexible than Napoleon believed. Equally, we know that the Continental Blockade generated such pressures in Russia in particular that it was likely that Russia would renege on the deal she had done with Napoleon at Tilsit and rejoin the ranks of his opponents. Also very clear to us is that the potential benefits of the Blockade were never extended to Europe as a whole (instead, France was shut off from the rest of the Continent by extremely high tariffs).

In the wake of Trafalgar, however, given that the emperor was determined to fight Britain—confronted in 1806 with a British government, the so-called Ministry of all the Talents, which contained many elements favourable to a compromise settlement, he had refused to make even minimal concessions—the Continental Blockade appeared the logical way forward. Victory, it was believed, would be rapid, while the policy also had the merit of tapping into the rampant anti-British prejudice that was so marked a feature of opinion in the *salons* and council chambers of Europe. The French Revolutionary War of 1792–1801 had not been good for Britain's standing beyond her frontiers. While substantial overall, British subsidies had not operated in a consistent fashion, with some countries (generally those, such as Austria, which the British believed would have to fight come what may) getting virtually nothing, and others (generally those, such as Prussia, which the British believed would have to be bribed into fighting) getting exorbitant sums. British troops had not come to the battlefields of Europe very often, and, when they had appeared, had neither particularly distinguished themselves nor come in great numbers. And, finally, British sea power had certainly captured many enemy ships, run up the Union Jack over many enemy colonies, swept most rival trade from the sea, and facilitated victorious military campaigns in India and Egypt—theatres for which there never seemed to be the same lack of troops as always appeared to pertain in Europe—but this seemed less a contribution to the war against France than a concerted push to expand the British empire and wipe out commercial rivals. Meanwhile, there were, of course, a number of states with long histories of rivalries with Britain that gave depth to these passing frictions. A policy, then, that at one and the same time promised to humble 'perfidious Albion' and, seemingly, to establish imposing barriers behind which nascent industries across Europe could 'take off', had much to offer.[9]

In principle, then, economic warfare was a highly attractive option as far as France was concerned, and from 1806 it duly lay at the forefront of her war effort. What is harder to justify, however, is the claim that it was the conscious centrepiece of Napoleon's strategy—that the emperor always planned to establish the Continental Blockade. The measure was inaugurated following the occupation of Berlin in 1806, but no one would seriously argue that Napoleon fought the campaigns of Austerlitz and Jena in order to secure a position strong enough that he could declare the whole of Europe to be in a state of blockade as far as Britain was concerned without immediately making himself a laughingstock.

Viewed in this fashion, the Continental Blockade appears in its true colours: essentially a gigantic piece of opportunism that might well yield significant results in due course, but that, above all, satisfied the emperor's need to strike a blow against an enemy whom he had thus far been unable to touch—who, still worse, had humiliated his forces at Trafalgar—and at the same time to indulge his own lust for glory. After all, such a pattern can certainly be observed at other moments in the emperor's career: for example, the invasion of Russia in 1812 was in part a petulant response to the failure of his armies to obtain victory in the Peninsula.

Once imposed, the Continental Blockade certainly became a useful alibi for the emperor. Almost every forward policy, whether it was the annexation of Tuscany, Rome, Holland, and the coast of northern Germany or the invasion of Russia, could henceforth be explained in terms of the need to enforce the Blockade. Ever afterwards, the emperor's numerous apologists could argue that at all times their hero had been driven by the demands of the struggle with England. This blithely ignores the fact that in 1810 the French ruler in effect abandoned the Continental Blockade as it was originally envisaged—that is, as an attempt to drain Britain of specie and thereby reduce her to bankruptcy—in favour of a policy that allowed British merchants to trade with Europe so long as they sent all their products via France and paid handsomely for the privilege.

THE CONTINENTAL SYSTEM

To argue that the Continental Blockade was the motivation for Napoleon's every *démarche* in the period 1807–12 is therefore very difficult. However, as I have argued elsewhere, it is very difficult to discern any coherent strategy in Napoleon's actions at all.[10] All that one can truly observe, indeed, is a determination to overawe the whole of Europe by force and to mete out condign punishment to all those who dared to oppose his will. Given that the chief means of doing this was by winning great battles that could in turn lead to savagely punitive peace treaties, it is certainly possible to argue that battle was at the heart of Napoleon's strategy. This, however, is so blindingly obvious that it seems hardly worth stating.

What is far more interesting is to examine the steps that the emperor took to ensure that his empire was always of such a nature in geographical and political terms that such punishment could be meted out. Here and here only can one genuinely observe a consistent strategy. On the one hand, the utmost ruthlessness was to be observed in ensuring that the French army and its satellites were kept up to strength by means of conscription. On the other, the empire was on no account to be allowed to be stripped of the territories that might be counted as its strategic heartlands. Writing in another context, the British historian Michael Broers has argued that the Napoleonic empire can be divided into two zones: namely, the inner empire and the outer empire.[11] This concept can be applied to the strategic as well as the political. In brief, around the periphery of the empire were a fringe of territories—the Grand Duchy of Warsaw, the Illyrian provinces, and the kingdoms of Naples and Spain—that could *in extremis* be sacrificed for the good of the whole. This does not mean to say that Napoleon was ever happy to order strategic retreats: on the contrary, as the frontiers of his rule contracted in 1813, he sacrificed thousands of veteran troops to garrison fortresses in Poland, Germany, and Spain that he hoped might one day provide the key to their recapture. The fact remains that, when matters reached a state of desperate crisis in the wake of the battle of Leipzig, Napoleon abandoned his claim to the Spanish throne and turned loose the captive Ferdinand VII in the hope that this might somehow put an end to the Peninsular War.

With the inner empire, however, it was very different. The territories that this composed included, in addition to the greatly expanded France of 1812, the Confederation of the Rhine and the Kingdom of Italy. These could not be sacrificed on any account. So long as he continued to hold Holland, Belgium, the so-called 'third Germany', and Lombardy and Venetia, Napoleon could hope one day to dictate his will to Europe once more. For this reason, just as the ever-loyal Prince Eugène was ordered to defend Milan to the end, he himself hung on at Leipzig until long after all hope of victory had gone. Equally, offered Austrian support by a Metternich frantic to avoid a Prusso-Russian-dominated peace settlement in exchange for concessions in Germany and Italy, the French ruler would not concede an inch of the territories concerned. In the end, then, curiously enough, Napoleon's strategy was much more closely linked to issues of territory than has hitherto been recognized.[12]

THE LONG ROAD TO COALITION

So much, then, for Napoleon, but what of his opponents? Taking Britain, first of all, as we have seen, in the first instance her strategy in both 1792 and 1803 centred on the establishment and exploitation of naval supremacy. However, as has already been implied, while Britain might be mistress of the sea, she could not win the war solely with her ships. Colonial expansion was all very well—though in fact the general view was that British interests were best served by trade rather than conquest—but it could not meet Britain's security concerns in Europe and in some ways multiplied her problems.

Let us here consider the course of events in the eighteenth century. In a succession of wars in which France had always been Britain's chief opponent and Britain's goal the defence of the balance of power—the War of the Spanish Succession, the War of the Austrian Succession, and, finally, the Seven Years War—Britain had prospered through a strategy that had combined colonial and maritime warfare with an alliance with one or more of the powers of continental Europe. Conversely, in the one war that she had lost—the American War of Independence—she had found herself fighting not only the American colonists but also a highly dangerous alliance of France, Spain, and the United Provinces. Britain having lost control of the Channel and only narrowly escaped invasion, it was an instructive lesson and one that was to ensure that successive British governments only rarely lost sight of the need to couple colonial and economic warfare with a continental commitment, whether this was expressed in troops or subsidies or both.

Herein lay the danger of relying solely on a combination of blockade and what the leading Whig Charles James Fox once scornfully referred to as 'filching sugar islands'. Such a way of war, as we have seen, had its benefits, but in the long term it was inclined to breed bitter resentment. Not only did French claims that Britain was only fighting to swell her trade and colonies alike—even that she was deliberately prolonging the war to augment the profits she was making from it—come to sound all too plausible, but the countries that were having to bear the brunt of the land war—above all, Austria—also increasingly came to resent the fashion in which the redcoats rarely made an appearance on the battlefield. Added to this was another problem in that there was but little faith in the British army even when it did appear.[13] In short, if she was to have any hope of securing victory against France, Britain had no option but to engage with continental warfare. Indeed, it is no coincidence that the potentially disastrous alliance between Russia and France that was negotiated at Tilsit in July 1807 came in the wake of the irritation and disillusionment generated in Europe by the 'Ministry of All the Talents'—of all the cabinets of the Napoleonic Wars, the one that paid least heed to Britain's interests in Europe. It was, of course, under the Talents that substantial forces of British troops were dispatched to take part in the futile attempt to establish a bridgehead in South America.[14]

The problem, then, was clear enough, but what was not so clear was the solution. To put it another way, there was policy in plenty but no strategy. Had Britain been fighting an opponent other than Napoleon Bonaparte, her situation would have been grave indeed. It is a measure of the desperation of the Portland administration—the government that succeeded the Talents—that the first months of 1808 found it putting together an expeditionary force to embark on a fresh South American adventure. This time it was an invasion of Venezuela, undertaken at the behest of the renegade adventurer and sometime general in the army of the French Revolution, Francisco de Miranda. What saved Lord Portland and his fellow Ministers—and with them the unfortunate general who had been deputed to lead the attack (none other than Sir Arthur Wellesley)—from the fresh catastrophe that this scheme promised was that in effect, as argued above, the emperor had no strategy. Driven by a variety of factors—vainglory, the need for constant action, and a sudden necessity to increase his control of Spain's ports and naval resources in anticipation of the Balkan campaign that Russian ambitions in that area were making ever more likely—in January 1808 he suddenly resolved to overthrow the Spanish Bourbons and install a puppet Bonaparte monarch in their place.[15]

With hindsight, of course, this decision has been much criticized, not least by Napoleon himself, but it would have taken extraordinary foresight to anticipate the situation to which it gave rise. It should be noted, indeed, that it took the British as much by surprise as it did the French. This, however, is by the by: what matters here is rather, first, that a giant hole was immediately ripped in the Continental Blockade that could never be repaired short of total French victory in Spain. Indeed, the blockade was from that moment as good as dead. Second, Britain at last found the theatre that she needed to demonstrate her military good faith. There had been no want of understanding of the need to achieve this goal under previous administrations (always excepting the Talents). In the autumn of 1805, for example, William Pitt had dispatched an expeditionary force of 14,000 British troops to Hanover under Lord Cathcart, but the relatively small field armies that were all that Britain could send to the Continent could not hope to sustain themselves against the might of the *grande armée* in the plains of northern Germany. Nor did descents on the coast of, say, the Low Countries offer much more hope, the lesson of the Anglo-Russian expedition of 1799 having very much been that such expeditions could easily be contained.

The Iberian Peninsula, and, above all, Portugal, were different, however. It would, of course, be very wrong to think that the Portland administration had a clear view of the possibilities that had suddenly been opened from the moment the news of the Spanish revolt first arrived in London in the first week of June 1808. In large part through the influence of Sir Arthur Wellesley, who from September 1808 onwards produced a series of memoranda in which he laid out the methods that would allow the British to maintain a permanent presence in Portugal, over the course of the next eight months there emerged the strategy that successive Cabinets were to follow for the rest of the war. In brief, sustained and protected by the continued application of naval power, and reinforced by a reformed Portuguese army, a British expeditionary force was to base itself in Lisbon and by its operations both embarrass Napoleon and demonstrate that Britain was sincere in its determination to oppose the emperor and was a reliable military and diplomatic partner.[16]

Initially, Britain's new strategy was at best conceived of as a holding operation: when he was finally confirmed as British commander in the Peninsula in April 1809, Wellesley's orders were confined to the defence of Portugal, and he was not given permission to switch over to an offensive strategy until March 1811. Nor, meanwhile, was there any attempt to pursue the formation of a fresh coalition, it being felt that the state of Europe was such that all that this would do would be to hand Napoleon fresh victories as was, in fact, proved all too graphically when Austria went to war with France again in 1809. Rather, the objectives of the game were, first, survival; second, the maintenance of British naval superiority (hence the expedition to Walcheren in August 1809); third, the disruption of Napoleonic rule by economic means; and, fourth, the creation of a positive image that would serve Britain well in the event of some dramatic change in the circumstances of the Continent. Putting matters very crudely, while not being allowed to secure an advantage at sea or in the colonies, Napoleon was to be given enough rope to hang himself.

In all this, meanwhile, it will be seen that battle figured but little. It was accepted that Wellesley, or, as we may now call him, Wellington (he was made Viscount Wellington in August 1809) might on occasion have to fight battles to achieve his objectives, but on the whole, and particularly after the narrow escape of the Talavera campaign of July 1809, it was much preferred that he not take risks. This, meanwhile, was a principle with which the British commander was all too willing to concur. However much risking a fresh confrontation with the enemy might have seemed desirable for political reasons, throughout the period August 1809–August 1810 he therefore remained deaf to all entreaties to come once more to the aid of the Spaniards. The two largest armies in Spain were allowed to go down to smashing defeats at Ocaña and Alba de Tormes. Rich and populous Andalusía—the very heartland of the Patriot cause—was suffered to fall to enemy invasion without the British army firing a shot in its defence; and the important border fortress of Ciudad Rodrigo was left to surrender to the French even though it was only a few miles from the British outposts. Only when the French invaded Portugal in July 1810 and marched on Lisbon was a battle risked, and then in so strong a position that the risks involved were minimal. Whether Wellington hoped to stop the French at the action that resulted—the battle of Buçaco—is a moot point, but he was certainly prepared for failure. Thus, as the French advanced, so the countryside through which they would have to move was devastated and its population forced to leave their homes, and the Portuguese militia and home guard set to harry their communications. As for Lisbon, meanwhile, it had been given a massive belt of fortifications called the Lines of Torres Vedras. Unable to get through, the French commander, Marshal Masséna, in consequence found himself trapped in a man-made desert, and, though he hung on for six dreadful months, in the end, exactly as Wellington had foreseen, he had no option but to retreat.[17]

Battle, then, at best played an auxiliary role in Britain's strategy during the long period of waiting to which she was now committed. If Wellington had given battle at Buçaco, it was not to save Lisbon, which was perfectly safe anyway, but rather to blood the newly reorganized Portuguese army and to conciliate a Portuguese government that, understandably, was ever more distressed at the appalling suffering being visited upon the populace of Beira. When the time came for Wellington to advance into Spain in the spring of 1811, matters were very different, of course: if the Anglo-Portuguese army was indeed to thrust the French beyond the Pyrenees, then at some stage or another battle would become inevitable. To return to Clausewitz, battle would have to be used to gain the end of war.

In the event, 1811 proved to be a year of false hope in that the French forces in Spain, which outnumbered those of Wellington by a factor of over three to one, proved strong enough both to continue with their ongoing operations against the Spaniards and to concentrate on the Portuguese frontier in sufficient number to check the British commander, who was further hampered by a want of adequate siege artillery. However, it is important to note that, on the operational level, the French were increasingly unable to live up to Clausewitz's dictum. Already in 1810 Marshal Masséna had, understandably enough, baulked at the thought of launching a direct attack on the fortifications that Wellington had erected to defend Lisbon, and this caution now spread to field actions. In May 1811 were fought the battles of Fuentes de Oñoro and Albuera. In both instances, French armies attacked detachments of Wellington's army, and in both instances they were repelled with heavy losses.

This did not mean that Wellington henceforth had the Portuguese frontier to himself. On the contrary, in June a much bigger concentration of French troops forced him to abandon a somewhat abortive attempt to besiege Badajoz, while in September an attempt to reduce Ciudad Rodrigo by blockade led to a similar conclusion. Thus, in both instances, Wellington deployed such troops as he had to hand in imposing defensive positions, and, in both instances, the French commanders concerned declined to give battle. In short, the Anglo-Portuguese army had established a moral superiority over its opponents, and so, for the rest of the Peninsular War, except in instances where circumstances allowed the French to achieve massive local superiority, we generally find the latter seeking to achieve their objectives not through battle but through manoeuvre.

From the end of 1811 onwards, provided with a proper siege train that allowed him to deal quickly and efficiently with the Spanish border fortresses that blocked his way, Wellington had no such qualms. In two great battles—Salamanca (22 July 1812) and Vitoria (21 June 1813)—the British broke the French hold on Spain.

Worth highlighting here, however, is that in neither case were the offensives that produced them predicated solely on marching forward in a single mass and forcing the enemy to fight a decisive battle. On the contrary, in both instances, elaborate diversionary operations were mounted to ensure that large parts of the French armies were kept fully occupied elsewhere.

In this respect, much nonsense has been written about Wellington consciously following a strategy that combined regular and irregular warfare, it being argued that at all times he coordinated his operations with those of the Spanish guerrillas.[18] If the term 'guerrillas' is taken to mean 'bands of irregulars', this is certainly not the case: Wellington appears to have had no contact with even the semi-regular commands of chieftains such as Francisco Espoz y Mina until the operations of 1812–13. However, what is true is that he liaised with the commanders of the regular Spanish armies that, in however attenuated a form, were still hanging round the flanks of the French zone of occupation. He persuaded them to attack the enemy troops in their vicinity at the same time as his own men were moving forward, while simultaneously organizing a series of amphibious operations in both the Bay of Biscay and the Mediterranean. In these diversionary operations, it was certainly hoped that the guerrillas would play their part as in many instances they did, but no reliance was ever placed on them. What was therefore combined was not so much regular and irregular warfare as grand campaigning and the so-called *guerre des postes*.[19]

It would be unwise to go too far down this road. Ever eager to prove the value of his theory of the indirect approach in the wake of the First World War, the British military theorist Basil Liddell Hart tried very hard to argue that what had mattered in Spain had not so much been Salamanca and Vitoria as the use of these diversionary tactics and the constant attrition suffered by the French forces at the hands, or so he supposed, of the Spanish guerrillas.[20] Such arguments are unconvincing, however. While the methods so much admired by Liddell Hart may have ensured that Salamanca and Vitoria were fought under optimum conditions, in the end it was Salamanca and Vitoria that broke the French position in Spain, and, for that matter, Salamanca and Vitoria that gave Britain the diplomatic and military credibility that she had so lacked in 1808.

ENDGAME

In discussing Wellington's victories, however, we should remember that they were not just the product of that commander's genius, undoubted though it was. On the contrary, they were also the product of Napoleon's shortcomings. One here returns to the issue of whether the emperor ever had a clear strategy. If his priority really was to defeat England, then logic dictated that, once the Iberian Peninsula had risen in revolt, every nerve should be strained to reduce it to submission. In the first place, this was the only way to repair the terrible damage that had been done to the Continental Blockade, and, in the second, the presence of a British army in Portugal afforded Napoleon an opportunity he could ill pass by. Had Wellington's army ever been caught and forced to surrender in a replay, say, of the battle of Bailén, the political and military repercussions would have been so dramatic that even the determined Tory administrations that ruled Britain after 1807 might well have been forced to make peace.

Fortunately for Britain, however, unity of strategic aim once again proved to be Napoleon's Achilles heel. Once war had broken out in the Peninsula, it behoved the emperor to do all that he could to maintain peace everywhere else, and, above all, to do all that he could to conciliate Alexander I of Russia. To put it bluntly, Tilsit held the keys to Spain and Portugal, but the French ruler threw the settlement negotiated there away, so alienating the tsar as eventually to transform him into one more overmighty rival who had to be put in his place by means of war. In this decision there were other factors as well: once again one thinks of Napoleon's constant need to demonstrate his prowess as a military commander. As far as the situation in Spain is concerned, all that matters is that from the end of 1811 the constant flow of reinforcements and replacements that had kept the war going hitherto was suddenly reduced to a trickle, with the added complication that, determined to safeguard his prestige, the emperor continued to urge his commanders to keep on advancing.[21]

The results, of course, were Salamanca and Vitoria. By 1813, meanwhile, Europe had been transformed. Thanks to Napoleon's invasion of Russia and its aftermath, the great coalition that had been the sine qua non of victory as far as Britain was concerned had come together. Now headed by Lord Liverpool, the British government was able to reap a further fruit of British command of the sea. Thus, such was the wealth that this dominance had brought her that she was able to provide Austria, Russia, Prussia, and Sweden with subsidies of a size that had never been seen previously. Meanwhile, thanks to Wellington's victories, Britain was able to play a substantial part in the final campaigns of the war. Having broken through the Pyrenees in November 1813, Wellington blockaded Bayonne at the head of an army of 75,000 men, and in February 1814 swept across the River Adour to defeat the French forces defending south-western France.[22]

Yet, while the history of the war was certainly now a litany of battles, even now it is perhaps worth pointing out that the campaigns of 1813–14 did not quite correspond to notions of campaigns consisting simply of massing overwhelming numbers on the decisive point. We can here comfortably set aside that, particularly in the operations that culminated in the battle of Leipzig, Napoleon himself did not conform to such dictums, that his 'operations . . . consistently reverted to a strategy of manoeuvre rather than annihilation'.[23] The implication here is that, had the emperor maintained his old focus on his enemy's armies, he would have won, but much more to the point is that the Allies themselves employed a strategy that was much more complex than the post-war commentaries appear to recognize.

The first question to examine here is that of 'national war'. In Spain, Wellington had not sought to build popular insurrection into his strategy.[24] In Germany in 1813, however, it was a very different matter. How far Alexander I and Frederick William III were serious in their intent is hard to say, but the exiled Stein and those around him were eager to call Germany to arms in a great crusade against Napoleon. By the end of 1812, the nucleus of what Stein appears to have conceived of as a new national army had been organized from German prisoners in the form of the so-called Russo-German Legion. No sooner had Frederick William declared war on Napoleon in March 1813 than he issued a proclamation calling on 'his' people—a group that could be interpreted to mean the inhabitants not just of the rump state that he now ruled over, but also of the many territories Prussia had lost at Tilsit—to mobilize for war. To supplement such appeals, which were buttressed by the busy pens of nationalist writers, flying columns of volunteers were formed whose task it was to fan out across the country, engage in guerrilla warfare against the French, and whip up popular revolt. The impact of this activity was beyond doubt disappointing, but that is not the point: unlike in Spain and Portugal, we see a conscious effort to wage war by revolutionary means. To quote Alexander I, 'The time has come for going beyond the normal conventions of warfare.'[25]

Mention of Alexander I also brings us to the question of how the Allies waged the final campaigns of the war. What is interesting here is that a tendency emerged to seek a way of fighting the French on terms other than those set by Napoleon. Thus, much influenced by Wellington's defence of Lisbon in 1810, the tsar initially pursued a defensive strategy whereby Napoleon would be enticed to attack a great fortified camp deep inside Lithuania at Drissa on the River Dvina, while a field army manoeuvred against his communications. Frustrated by the sheer size of the *grande armée*, this plan had to be abandoned, but in the end the effect of the Russians' actions was much the same: Napoleon was drawn still deeper into Russia—as far as Moscow even—and was eventually forced to retreat by Russian armies menacing his communications, these last having already come under constant harassment by raiding forces of Cossacks and light cavalry (as much as Buçaco, then, Borodino appears above all as a battle fought for political reasons).[26] And then in 1813 there emerged the famous Trachtenberg Plan—the idea that the Allied commanders should refuse to give battle when Napoleon was present on the field and rather concentrate on defeating his subordinates. This still envisaged an offensive campaign with one last great battle as its goal—initially, it was believed that this would come at Dresden rather than Leipzig—but the climax was in effect to be delayed until the French had been worn down by a long process of attrition.[27]

CONCLUSION

To conclude, strategy in the Napoleonic Wars embraced a far greater range of options than those covered by the remarks with which this chapter opened. In fairness to Clausewitz and Jomini, they even recognized that this was so. Taking Jomini as an example, for instance, he explicitly recognized 'national war' as a means of defending a country against invasion, indeed 'as the most formidable of all'. However, at the same time, it was also the most dreadful: 'the consequences are so terrible that, for the sake of humanity, we ought to hope never to see it'. Rather like Wellington, he was inclined to banish the concept from his military lexicon and, 'as a soldier preferring loyal and chivalrous warfare to organised assassination', went so far as to express the hope 'that wars of extermination may be banished from the code of nations'.[28]

What we see in the views of both Jomini and Clausewitz is a view of strategy that was coloured very much by their personal experiences: both served in continental armies whose business was essentially the decisive battle. Meanwhile,

Jomini fought in Spain and emerged with a horror of guerrilla warfare, while Clausewitz was an eye-witness to the chaos of the Jena campaign and was therefore inclined to stress the problems posed by divergent views in the high command, not to mention the general concept of friction. So far as they go, their views are true enough, but to believe that either of these commentators offers the whole truth is therefore at the very least unwise. To quote Liddell Hart, 'War has not the simplicity that single-minded strategists have too readily assumed.'[29]

Quite so, though coming from an observer determined to prove that the key to winning wars was the indirect approach and the indirect approach alone, this is, perhaps, a little rich. There remain, however, two questions that ought to be discussed further. First, what goals did the various methods we have discussed seek to achieve? Second, to what extent did the conduct of the Napoleonic Wars conform to generic notions of what strategy consists of, and, by extension, how wars should be conducted?

Taking victory first, it should first be stressed that the author rejects out of hand the notion that the Napoleonic Wars were an ideological struggle that could not be settled without one side or the other being completely broken. Far from seeking to overthrow the old monarchies, Napoleon was looking rather to join their ranks, while almost to the very end France's opponents would have been willing to entertain a compromise peace that would have left the emperor on the throne. For neither side, then, did victory have to be total.

That said, for Britain and her allies victory was much more straightforward and, indeed, much more attainable than it was for France. In brief, what was required was a settlement that would see France confined either to the borders of 1792 (Britain's preferred option) or the natural frontiers (the option generally accepted as a fall-back position by the other powers) and expelled from the rest of Europe. Beyond this, there were two issues. First, all the powers wished to reorder the Continent and the erstwhile colonies of France and Holland in such a manner that the defeat of Napoleon would bring with it an advance in their wider foreign-policy interests. And, second, there was also general agreement that France had to be contained in such a fashion that she could never again disturb the peace of Europe. This was again bound up with the distribution of the spoils (one thinks here of the decision to establish both a greater Holland and a greater Piedmont as bastions against French aggression). In the end, however, all this mattered little, everything depending on driving Napoleon back to at least the Rhine and then persuading him to accept defeat. That this in the end took what amounted to total victory is neither here nor there.

For France, however, the problem was much greater. Insofar as can be judged, Napoleon did not aspire to rule the whole of Europe, nor, still less, the whole of the world, directly from Paris. If we ignore the utterly implausible claims that he made on St Helena to the effect that what he wanted to see was a united Europe made up of federal states, we may judge his goal to have been a continent in which a greater France stood supreme surrounded by a cluster of satellite states organized on the French model. Beyond them, an outer ring of *ancien-régime* monarchies would be allowed to go their own way in terms of domestic policy so long as they remained utterly subservient to the imperial will in matters relating to the ordering of Europe and their place in it. This, however, was a much more difficult objective. Victory still did not have to be total—Austria, for example, was reduced to what was pretty much the status that Napoleon envisaged for her without the Habsburg state having actually to be overthrown—but the scale of what was required was still very great. Even then, it would be all but impossible to prevent one or other of the powers from re-arming and rising against the French dominium.

On the one side, then, was a goal that was rational and finite—a goal that even included the possibility of a France with expanded boundaries, revolutionary institutions, and Napoleon as ruler—and, on the other, a goal that lacked all reason and, in effect, had no bounds. At any time, of course, Napoleon could have settled for less, but that, alas, would have required the emperor to have recognized the limits of his power—to have accepted, in fact, that there was indeed such a word as 'impossible'.

How, then, does all this fit in with wider concepts of strategy? In this book, strategy is defined as the art of winning by purposely matching ends, ways, and means. In this respect, the Napoleonic Wars seem very much to fit the common pattern: Napoleon lost because he did not match ends, ways, and means, while the Allies won because, in the end, they did. Moreover, that much in the course of the struggle prefigures later conflicts, and, indeed, reflects earlier ones, suggests that a pattern of war had emerged in Europe that was, in effect, timeless. Thus, in effect, on the one hand there was a Britain that for her own sake could not allow any power to dominate the entire continent, and on the other a succession of polities that wanted to achieve just that.

In each instance, meanwhile, the answer for both the British and their enemies was the same. Thus, for Britain the task was to construct a powerful alliance in Europe—something that usually took confidence-building measures (the Peninsular War may here be regarded as akin to the campaigns in the Western Desert or even the Battle of the Somme) and financial assistance. From the Napoleonic Wars onwards, Britain also had to mobilize the resources of the wider world, while France or Germany had to exclude British influence from the Continent and make use of land power to neutralize or even break British control of the sea. That said, there were obviously factors that were purely situational, a good example being the extent of industrialization (economic warfare, then, was of no account in 1700, of great account in 1800, and of incalculable account in 1900), and one can envisage circumstances that would seriously have challenged the pattern which we have discussed. In the end, however, those circumstances never really emerged—the one exception being the Crimean War of 1854–6, but this was settled too quickly to have much of an impact in strategic terms. Thus, it is that we may say that, whatever else they did, the Napoleonic Wars settled the patterns of modern war.

NOTES

1. For all matters naval relating to Great Britain in the Napoleonic epoch, the best general introductions by far are P. M. Kennedy, *The Rise and Fall of British Naval Mastery* (London, 1976), 123–48; and N. A. M. Rodger, *The Command of the Ocean: A Naval History of Great Britain, 1649–1815* (London, 2004), 426–574.
2. A. T. Mahan, *The Influence of Sea-Power upon the French Revolution and Empire*, 2 vols (London, 1892), ii. 383–4.

3. The role of British sea power in the Peninsular War was, in fact, far greater than these brief lines give it credit for. Setting aside that the Royal Navy played a vital part in the famous 'little war' by putting ashore raiding forces of Spanish and Anglo-Portuguese troops, landing consignments of arms for the forces of such commanders as Francisco Espoz y Mina, and, on occasion, stiffening the local insurgents with landing parties of sailors and Royal Marines, it was British ships that saved Sir John Moore's army in January 1809, British ships that kept Lisbon and Cadiz supplied with food when the French blockaded them in the period 1810–12, and British ships that allowed Wellington to transfer his chief base from Lisbon to, first, Santander and then Pasajes in 1813. For all this, see C. D. Hall, *Wellington's Navy: Sea Power and the Peninsular War, 1807–1814* (London, 2004).

4. The expeditions to Naples, Sweden, and Walcheren may be studied in W. H. Flayhart, *Counterpoint to Trafalgar: The Anglo-Russian Invasion of Naples, 1805–1806* (Columbia, South Carolina, 1992); C. J. Esdaileand R. Muir, 'Strategic Planning in a Time of Small Government: The Wars against Revolutionary and Napoleonic France, 1793–1815', in C. W. Woolgar (ed.), *Wellington Studies I* (Southampton, 1996); and G. Bond, *The Grand Expedition: The British Invasion of Holland, 1809* (Athens, GA, 1979).

5. The subject of commerce raiding is discussed at length in P. Crowhurst, *The French War on Trade: Privateering, 1793–1815* (London, 1989).

6. For a discussion of the impact of the Continental Blockade on the Baltic trade, see C. D. Hall, *British Strategy in the Napoleonic War, 1803–1815* (Manchester, 1992), 89–90.

7. For the economic depression of 1808, see C. Emsley, *British Society and the French Wars, 1793–1815* (London, 1979), 135–8.

8. For the impact of the Continental Blockade on Holland, see S. Schama, *Revolution in the Netherlands, 1780–1813* (London, 1977), 555–610.

9. For the hostility with which Britain was viewed in Europe, see A. D. Harvey, 'European Attitudes to Britain during the French Revolutionary and Napoleonic Wars', *History*, 63/209 (Oct. 1978), 356–65.

10. See C. J. Esdaile, 'De-constructing the French Wars: Napoleon as Anti-strategist', *Journal of Strategic Studies*, 31/4 (Aug. 2008), 515–52.

11. See M. Broers, *Europe, 1799–1815* (London, 1996), 180–230.

12. For a highly critical discussion of Napoleon as a strategist, see J. Riley, *Napoleon as a General: Command from the Battlefield to Grand Strategy* (London, 2007), 19–42.

13. See W. Napier, *History of the War in the Peninsula and the South of France from the Year 1807 to the Year 1814* (London, 1828–1840), i. 7.

14. For a particularly pithy analysis of Britain's strategic position and the choices open to her, see P. Mackesy, 'Strategic Problems of the British War Effort', in H. T. Dickinson (ed.), *Britain and the French Revolution, 1789–1815* (London, 1989), 147–64. See also J. Black, 'British strategy and the struggle with France, 1793–1815', *Journal of Strategic Studies*, 31/4 (Aug. 2008), 553–70.

15. It will be objected here that Napoleon had in fact been planning to overthrow the Bourbons since at least October 1806, if not all along, but, whatever a variety of circumstantial evidence might suggest, there is every indication that the decision was taken at the last minute in response, above all, to the deteriorating situation in the Balkans.

16. For a general discussion of the policies of the Portland administration and its successors, see R. Muir, *Britain and the Defeat of Napoleon, 1807–1815* (London, 1996).

17. For a recent discussion of Wellington's defence of Portugal, see J. Grehan, *The Lines of Torres Vedras: The Cornerstone of Wellington's Strategy in the Peninsular War* (London, 2000).

18. See D. G. Chandler, 'Wellington and the Guerrillas', in id. (ed.), *On the Napoleonic Wars: Collected Essays* (London, 1994), 166–80.

19. For a revisionist discussion of the part played by guerrilla warfare in Wellington's strategy, see C. J. Esdaile, 'Wellington and the Spanish Guerrillas: The Campaign of 1813', *Consortium on Revolutionary Europe Proceedings*, 21 (1991), 298–306.

20. See B. H. Liddell Hart, *The Decisive Wars of History* (London, 1929), 106.

21. It is often argued that Napoleon invaded Russia in 1812 to enforce the Continental Blockade. This, however, is not so: when he issued his famous ukase in October 1810, Alexander made no mention of the Blockade and in fact continued to take a very hard line in respect of British commerce. Instead, what was imposed was a heavy tariff on all goods emanating from France, the bulk of Russia's luxury imports in this respect being products such as silk, scent, and furniture.

22. For the campaigns of the Anglo-Portuguese army in 1813–14, see C. Oman, *A History of the Peninsular War*, 7 vols (Oxford, 1902–1930), vii. 158–512.

23. M. Leggiere, *Napoleon and Berlin: The Napoleonic Wars in Prussia, 1813* (Stroud, 2002), 286.

24. Cited in Earl of Stanhope, *Notes of Conversations with the Duke of Wellington* (London, 1889), 69.

25. Cited in G. Best, *War and Society in Revolutionary Europe* (London, 1982), 163.

26. There is a useful summary of Russia's initial strategy in 1812 in C. Duffy, *Borodino and the War of 1812* (London, 1973), 53–5. Mention of Cossacks here brings up the need for a clarification: Cossacks are sometimes envisaged in this context as peasants-in-arms—the spearhead, indeed, of the Russian people-in-arms. This interpretation, however, is utterly at odds with reality: Cossacks were free peasants settled in what had once been the borderlands of the east and south-east who held their land and personal freedom in return for military service in time of war. Organized into temporary regiments of light cavalry and militia, their tactics were irregular, certainly, but they can in no respect be regarded as guerrillas.

27. See J. P. Riley, *Napoleon and the World War of 1813: Lessons in Coalition Warfighting* (London, 2000), 118.

28. A. H. Jomini, *The Art of War* (West Point, 1862), 26–7.

29. B. H. Liddell Hart, *The Ghost of Napoleon: A History of Military Thought from the Eighteenth to the Twentieth Century* (London, 1933), 170.

Part III

Modern and Contemporary

9

The American Civil War

Williamson Murray

INTRODUCTION

One must begin an examination of grand strategy and the American Civil War with an understanding of what the term itself suggests. The problem is that there are innumerable usages of the term 'strategy': military strategy, diplomatic strategy, political strategy, business strategy, complex game strategies, ad infinitum. All of these usages entangle the analyst or historian in their web, muddying the water and confusing the issue. This chapter will attempt to focus on two particular aspects of strategy: obviously, first and foremost, grand strategy, but secondly, with considerable attention, the military strategy of the conflict.

We might begin with a short examination of these two concepts, their crucial relationship and interactions, and the difficulties involved in intertwining them into an effective national response to the challenges they confront. Only then will we turn to an examination of these two aspects of strategy in terms of how they influenced or failed to influence the American Civil War.

Above all else, the world of grand strategy is one of uncertainty and ambiguity. It is a world of hard choices, where political realities must cancel out military necessity and where, as the conqueror of Canada in 1759, James Wolfe, so aptly noted, the conduct of military strategy inevitably involves 'an option of difficulties'. Thus, grand strategy is about balancing risks and ensuring that the balance of politics and force is right in those areas that matter most. As my colleague Allan Millett and I suggested in an article examining the *Military Effectiveness* volumes the two of us edited in the late 1980s:

> No amount of operational virtuosity...redeemed fundamental flaws in political judgment. Whether policy shaped strategy or strategic imperatives drove policy was irrelevant. Miscalculation in both led to defeat, and any combination of politico-strategic error had disastrous results, even for some nations that ended the war as members of the victorious coalition. Even the effective mobilization of national will, manpower, industrial might, national wealth, and technological know-how did not save the belligerents from reaping the bitter fruit of severe mistakes [at this level]. This is because it is more important to make correct decisions at the political and strategic level than it is at the operational and tactical level. Mistakes in operations and tactics can be corrected, but political and strategic mistakes live forever.[1]

Grand strategy is not necessarily a matter of war, although military power is always a major factor in peace as well as in war. But it has always been about adapting national focus in times of great stress on those areas of overstretch that threaten the polity. In other words, it combines a wide variety of attributes into a coherent effort to achieve some larger goal. And it is important to remember that some of its constituent parts are often in tension, if not outright opposition.

What distinguishes those who have achieved a modicum of success in developing and executing a grand strategy has been their focus on acting beyond the demands of the present; that is, they have taken a longer view beyond simply reacting to the events of the day. Nor have they concentrated on a single aspect of the problem. Instead, they have focused on the goals towards which they have reached, but have always proved flexible in executing the path towards the future. There has been, one must admit, considerable confusion between grand strategy and policy, military strategy, and strategies to achieve this or that specific goal. Grand strategy is none of these, but to one extent or another it consists of all of them. It demands a recognition of and ability to react to the ever-shifting environments of war and peace. Thus, the goals of grand strategy must be intimately intertwined with the day-to-day decision-making processes of policy and military strategy. In other words, grand strategy must envelop military strategy as well as diplomatic strategy and political strategy.

No simple, clear definition of grand strategy can ever be fully satisfactory. The closer one comes to what it entails, the more uncertain and complex are the aspects that encompass its making and use. One might adapt a comment by Clausewitz to our purposes to develop a sense of what a theory of grand strategy might be:

> theory need not be a positive doctrine, a sort of *manual* for action ... [Instead] it is an analytic investigation leading to a close *acquaintance* with the subject; applied to experience—in our case [strategy]—it leads to thorough *familiarity* with it. The closer it comes to that goal, the more it proceeds from the objective form of a science to the subjective form of a skill.[2]

Grand strategy involves a willingness and ability to think about the future in terms of the goals of a political entity. Those who have been most successful at its practice have also recognized that 'the future is not foreseeable'.[3] Consequently, they have been willing to adapt themselves and their policies to the political, economic, and military conditions as they are rather than as they wish them to be. Above all, grand strategy demands an intertwining of political, social, and economic realities with military power, as well as a recognition that in nearly all cases politics must drive military necessity.[4] Thus, developing a concept for grand strategy demands not only a deep understanding of the past, but also a comprehensive and realistic understanding of the present.

Grand strategy must also rest on a realistic assessment and understanding not only of one's opponents, but of oneself as well. As Sun Tzu so aptly commented, 'if you know the enemy and know yourself, you need not fear the results of a hundred battles'.[5] Here the nature and goals of one's opponents are essential components of the calculations on which grand strategy must rest. Thus, it exists in a world of constant flux, where incalculable factors, driven by the truculence and unpredictability of human nature, dominate the landscape. Therefore, there is rarely clarity in the effective casting of grand strategy, because by its nature it exists in an environment of constant change, where chance and the unexpected are its constant companions.

Finally, grand strategy throughout history has depended to a great extent on individual leadership for better or for worse. Others can make a major contribution, but the responsibility for displaying the flexibility and adaptability that grand strategy has always required has in the end devolved onto the shoulders of the individual leader. Themistocles in Athens at the beginning of the fifth century BC, George Washington during the American Revolution, Abraham Lincoln during the American Civil War, Otto von Bismarck in creating a united German polity, Franklin Roosevelt and Winston Churchill during the Second World War, and Harry Truman and Dwight Eisenhower during the cold war, all brought together the qualities of leadership and foresight. As a result, they were able to create strategic visions that allowed for the success, or at least survival, of their states in difficult and dangerous environments, where incompetent strategic leadership might well have led to catastrophe.

GRAND STRATEGY AND THE OPENING
OF THE CIVIL WAR

Abraham Lincoln became the sixteenth president of the United States on 4 March 1861. He found the nation in desperate straits, confronted by a crisis that lay at the very heart of how Americans viewed their government. The states that comprised the Deep South had seceded from the Union to form what they regarded as an independent nation.[6] Moreover, the slave states to their north teetered on the brink of secession. His predecessor, James Buchanan, perhaps the most disastrous president in American history, had stated that the act of secession was illegal, but almost in the same breath had declared that the federal government possessed no powers to suppress what was an out-and-out rebellion. In taking office, Lincoln had to slink into Washington in disguise—such was the popular feeling in favour of the break-up of the United States as far north as Baltimore, Maryland.

From his first day in office, Lincoln's goal towards which his grand strategy aimed was nothing less nor more than the preservation of the Union with its form of government, which he was later to term 'the last best hope of mankind'. In discussing his goal at the time, he issued the Emancipation Proclamation that freed the slaves, he commented, 'If I could save the Union without freeing *any* slave I would do it, and if I could do it by freeing *all* the slaves I would do it; and if I could do it by freeing some and leaving others alone I would also do that.'[7]

Lincoln's problem in evolving a grand strategy to achieve his goal of reuniting the nation was that the states in the South had to do nothing if there were no response from the North. However, to reverse the situation, the North would have to use force to bring its recalcitrant sister states back into the Union. And to use force would inevitably upset the delicate political balance in those slave states that had so far remained loyal to the Union. The operative phrase is 'so far' because the states in the middle South were clearly unwilling to see any force used against their sister states, and if they had not yet chosen secession, they were poised on the doorstep.[8] Then, there were the four border states, whose adherence would prove crucial to the military geography of the war, because they were vital to the projection of Northern military power into the South's heartland.[9]

Lincoln also confronted the knotty problem in March 1861 that much of the North's population remained ambivalent about what to do about the crisis of secession, with many taking the attitude of 'good riddance to bad rubbish'. As a leader of a democratic nation, Lincoln had to pay close attention to popular opinion. Thus, the treatment of the political consensus in terms of relations with the Congress as well as the Congressional elections of 1862 and the presidential elections of 1864 were major factors that had to influence the overall approach that the president would take in managing the conflict. In every respect, those political concerns, as we shall see, assumed a dominant position in his handling of the war.

In the months of March and April 1861, Lincoln played a complex and difficult political hand with consummate skill. He manoeuvred to resupply Fort Sumter without being seen to take military action.[10] His opponent, Jefferson Davis, who proved a disaster as the South's political leader and chief strategist, blinked first, and by ordering the bombardment of Fort Sumter created a fire-storm of outrage in the North. With popular support in the North behind him, Lincoln then called for troops from the loyal states to confront the outbreak of a war the South had started. That in turn tipped Virginia, North Carolina, and Tennessee into the Confederacy, but they had already proven to be weak reeds on which to base a policy of reknitting the political fabric of the United States. The test was then on whether Lincoln and his advisers could keep the border states within the Union. In each case, Lincoln used a variety of means to keep those states loyal: a minimum of effective force in Maryland and Delaware; diplomacy and political savvy in Kentucky; and ruthless surrogates in Missouri.[11]

The problem now was that the North was going to have to crush the rebellion with military force. No one was prepared in either of the two warring camps to wage a major war, much less the great conflict into which the 'war between the states' turned. That demanded the mobilization of financial, economic, and industrial resources on a scale never before seen in the Western world. And that mobilization in turn had political and social consequences of immense importance in the running of the country.

In other words, in casting his grand strategy, Lincoln confronted a whole host of problems that demanded as much, if not more, attention than the development of the military required to defeat the Confederate armies in battle. Here Lincoln was ably served by a first-class Cabinet consisting, for the most part, of men of extraordinary capabilities. Significantly, he had picked his major rivals for the 1860 Republican nomination, where they not only contributed to the Union cause, but, as Lyndon Johnson so expressively put it in another era in commenting about the critics of his policies within the administration, 'they were inside the tent pissing out, rather than outside pissing in'.[12]

On the surface, the North possessed enormous advantages in its larger population, superior industrial capacity, and vast railroad network. In fact, those advantages led a whole generation of historians, in explaining why it took the North four long years to defeat the Southern states, to create the myth of the superiority of the manpower that made up the Confederate armies—soldiers drawn from the farms of the South, fighting against Union armies largely drawn from the riff-raff of the North's cities. Nothing could be further from the truth, because both armies drew their manpower largely from rural populations—approximately 85 per cent of the North's population lived on farms and small towns in 1861.[13]

The real explanation for the length of the war lies in two major factors, which were not readily apparent either at the time or to many of those who later wrote about the conflict. The first was that the North confronted the problem of projecting military power over *continental* distances. The Confederacy spanned distances that are hard for most Europeans to comprehend.[14] For example, the distance from Richmond to Atlanta is equivalent to that from East Prussia to Moscow. Moreover, the terrain over which much of the war in the west took place was at the time thick, overgrown wilderness, complicated by swamps and bayous along most of the course the Mississippi River takes from St Louis to the Gulf of Mexico. Furthermore, the great Appalachian mountain chain separated the eastern and western theatres of war and presented major difficulties in coordinating efforts, let alone transferring forces from east to west.

The second factor was that a revolution in military and social affairs was occurring: the fourth in a line of revolutions that were propelling the West towards dominance of the world. That fourth revolution involved the coming together of the French Revolution and the Industrial Revolution.[15] The former provided both North and South with the popular enthusiasm to wage a war of huge casualties and suffering to the bitter end. The latter, particularly the transportation revolution with steamboats and railroads, allowed the North not only to project its power over the immense distances of the South but also to support its armies logistically. For example, in September 1863, faced with the defeat of the Army of the Cumberland at the battle of Chickamauga, the Union high command transferred two corps of the Army of the Potomac (20,000 soldiers and all their equipment) to Tennessee, a distance of over 1,200 miles by railroad, in less than a week. Nothing equivalent to that move was to happen in Europe until the First World War.

Complicating the picture for the North's military strategy was that no one in either the North or the South understood how to wage a war of such magnitude.[16] In 1861, Lincoln himself, as he confronted the stark reality of war, requested that the Library of Congress send over to him the major books on war that it possessed so that he could read up on the issues he would confront. Moreover, most political and military leaders on the opposing sides believed that the conflict would be of relatively short duration.

For the most part, Southerners believed that the North would not be able to put effective military forces in the field, since most of its inhabitants consisted of money-grubbing shopkeepers. Most Northerners, including Lincoln, severely underestimated the well of passion driving Southerners to secession and believed that pro-Union sentiment would soon lead the South back into the United States. Thus, both took the view that the coming war would be of short duration, punctuated by a few short and glorious battles that would settle matters between the sections. They could not have been more wrong in their estimates.

We might note here that the South's approach to the war stood in stark contrast to the flexibility and adaptability that Lincoln and his advisers displayed. Jefferson

Davis consistently refused to adapt to the changing political and strategic circumstances that the war threw up. He treated his fellow Southern politicians with contempt, sought quarrels when he might have assuaged frayed tempers with a few well-chosen words, supported ill-chosen commanders in the west, where the South was to lose the war,[17] and let the operational concerns of his commander in the eastern theatre, Robert E. Lee, outweigh the strategic necessities of the hour, the prime example being the decision not to reinforce the west in May 1963. In effect, Davis had no grand strategy, except to hope first that the South would win a decisive victory, then that the North would tire of the conflict, and thirdly that the Europeans at some point might show up. Never did Davis examine these basic assumptions; Southern politicians who questioned them he cast into the outer darkness.

Moreover, the South's military strategy was equally inept. In the east, Lee sought a Napoleonic 'decisive' victory that would drive the North out of the war in a single battle. Lee's aggressive approach also added immensely to the casualty bills the South could not support in the long run. In Lee's 'greatest' victory, the battle of Chancellorsville, the Army of Northern Virginia suffered almost as heavy losses in killed and wounded as the Army of the Potomac.[18] The North could absorb such losses; the South could not. In the west, the South's military strategy was disastrous, particularly in 1862 and 1863. In 1862, Confederate forces attempted to defend everything and consequently lost control of the Cumberland and Tennessee rivers, which in turn meant the loss of most of the state of Tennessee. In 1863, Davis's meddling and the absence of an overall command to coordinate military strategy in the west resulted not only in the loss of Vicksburg but also in the capture of John Pemberton's whole army.

The first concern, if one were to have a war, was to put some semblance of military force together. That turned out to be no easy matter. Here the North appeared to have the advantage, because the Army of the United States remained under its control. In fact, that state of affairs was not so advantageous. The army in its bureaucratic wisdom determined to keep its regulars, including most of the officers, separated from the volunteer regiments that appeared in enormous numbers in both western and eastern theatres.[19] The result was that the volunteer regiments in the North, with the few exceptions of those lucky enough to possess an experienced officer, learned the painful lessons of discipline and tactics on the battlefield.

On the other hand, the South, with no regular army, took those officers who had resigned from the Army of the United States and spread them throughout the Confederate army, where they had a leavening effect in the training and disciplining of the South's military forces in preparation for combat.[20] That advantage only lasted into 1862, by which time Union regiments, as a result of their combat experience, were equally effective and disciplined killing machines as their opposite numbers in the Confederate armies. But they had to develop that effectiveness by filling the 1861 equivalent of body bags.[21]

The politics of calling forth the great armies to defeat the Confederacy also required a close connection with the political realities of the North as a democracy. Essential to winning the war would be the ability of the Republican Lincoln to persuade large numbers of the Democratic Party to support the cause of Union. In the early days of forming up regiments, Ulysses S. Grant, not yet in the army, found himself engaged in the organizational processes of enlisting men into the volunteer regiments raised by the state of Illinois. Two democratic politicians, McClernand and Logan, requested permission to speak to the prospective volunteers. Grant records the following about his feelings at the time:

> I had some doubt as to the effect a speech from Logan might have; but as he was with McClernand, whose sentiments on the all-absorbing questions of the day were known, I gave my consent. McClernand spoke first; and Logan followed in a speech which he has hardly equalled since for force and eloquence. It breathed a loyalty and devotion to the Union which inspired my men to such a point that they would have volunteered to remain in the army as long as an enemy of the country continued to bear arms against it.[22] They entered United States service almost to a man.[23]

Both Logan and McClernand would themselves enlist and rise to the rank of major-general, although they would have quite different military careers, the first as an enormously effective corps commander, the second to be dismissed by Grant for insubordination. Lincoln would appoint a number of other Democratic politicians to important military positions, some with disastrous results, but, as we shall see in discussing the military strategy of 1864, the political importance of keeping a significant part of the Democratic Party adhering to the goal of Lincoln's grand strategy of reuniting the country far outweighed the question of their military effectiveness.

In developing the North's grand strategy beyond mobilizing its political and military strength, Lincoln confronted the problem of preventing foreign intervention in the conflict on the side of the Confederacy. In the early months of the war, the British and especially the French displayed considerable sympathy for the South. The Union blockade of the South only served to exacerbate relations with those two European powers, although the British blockade of France during the revolutionary and Napoleonic wars made Her Majesty's government somewhat leery of protesting too loudly about Northern actions off Confederate ports.[24]

On 8 November 1861, the USS *San Jacinto* stopped the British mail packet *Trent*, and its captain, Charles Wilkes, seized two Confederate diplomats on their way to Britain. Public opinion in the North was delighted; the British press demanded war. In the face of this international crisis, cooler heads prevailed. As Lincoln commented, 'one war at a time'.[25] The president and James Seward, secretary of state, eventually worked out a compromise that satisfied the public at home and the British abroad. Nevertheless, throughout the next two years, Lincoln had to keep a wary eye on the Europeans, at least until the conflict began to turn irrevocably in the North's favour.

GRAND STRATEGY AND MILITARY STRATEGY, 1861–2

How to win the war while achieving the president's goal of a reunited nation was the wider problem that confronted the Union leadership in spring and summer of 1861 as hundreds of thousands of young—and middle-aged—men answered the president's call to the colours. Nevertheless, only the army's decrepit and ancient commander Winfield Scott came up with anything that resembled an overarching military-strategic approach to the conflict. First of all, unlike the rest of the Northern leadership, Scott recognized that the conflict was going to be a long one. Consequently, he articulated a strategic approach aimed at isolating and strangling the South without doing irreparable damage that would make reunion politically impossible. Thus, the North, in his view, should impose a blockade, open up the Mississippi River, and maintain a firm hold over the border states.

Within Scott's plan, which would be termed the Anaconda Plan, were elements of what eventually formed portions of the Union's grand strategy, but what was notably absent was a willingness to take the war to the South. The latter component rested on Scott's misconception about the degree to which pro-Union sentiment existed in the South and the belief that any measures that involved an invasion would make reconciliation extremely difficult. In that respect, Scott was clearly correct. Reconciliation would truly not occur, ironically, for over a hundred years.

However, the political pressure on Lincoln was such that he had to demand that the armies of the republic that were forming take military action as soon as possible against an enemy who was incapable of serious resistance.[26] The result was the disaster at Bull Run and the rout of Union forces in northern Virginia. To a certain extent, defeat was a clear warning to the North that the war was going to prove far more difficult than most believed. And it certainly helped the Lincoln administration to undertake further mobilization measures to prepare for a longer conflict. Nevertheless, the belief among leaders as well as the general population in a short war, and that the pro-Union population in the South would eventually win out, would persist well into 1862.

In his eloquent and simple memoirs, Ulysses S. Grant noted that, until his bloody victory at Shiloh, Tennessee, in April 1862, he too had believed that a few salient victories would bring the South to its senses:

> Up to the battle of Shiloh I as well as thousands of other citizens believed the rebellion against the government would collapse suddenly and soon, if a decisive victory could be gained over any of its armies. Donelson and Henry were such victories. An army of more than 21,000 men was captured and destroyed. Bowling Green, Columbus and Hickman, Kentucky, fell in consequence, and Clarkesville and Nashville, Tennessee, the last two with immense amounts of stores, also fell into our hands. The Tennessee and Cumberland Rivers, from their mouths to the head of navigation, were secured. But when confederate armies were collected which not only attempted to hold a line farther south ... but assumed the offensive and made such a gallant effort to regain what had been lost, I gave up all ideas of saving the Union except by complete conquest.[27]

It would take most of the rest of 1862 to convince the population of the North of the nature of the titanic struggle on which they had embarked. Clausewitz's description of what had occurred in his own time and which had entirely upset the European order in the cataclysm of violence that lasted from 1792 to 1815 best captures what now enveloped the American people:

> Suddenly war had become the business of the people ... all of whom considered themselves to be citizens.... The resources and efforts now available for use now surpassed all conventional limits; nothing now impeded the vigor with which war

could be waged.... War, untrammeled by any conventional constraints, had broken loose in all its elemental fury.[28]

The year 1862 began with considerable promise for the Union. Grant's stunning victories at forts Donelson and Henry had basically broken in the back door of the Confederacy to Northern armies, opening up not only much of Tennessee but Alabama and Mississippi as well. At the same time, Major-General George McClellan had launched the Army of the Potomac against Richmond in the Peninsula Campaign, which took his army to the gates of Richmond. In the aftermath of Bull Run, Lincoln had appointed McClellan as head of what was to become the Army of the Potomac, and soon thereafter appointed him as Scott's replacement as commanding general of all Union armies.

McClellan was to prove ineffective in both roles. As commander of the Army of the Potomac, he did bring organization, order, and discipline to the mob of volunteer regiments that had descended on Washington and then run away from the Confederates at Bull Run. But 'Little Mac'—an apt characterization— was neither a strategist nor a combat general. Lincoln suggested to him early in 1862 that, if Union armies advanced at the same time, they might place such pressure on the Confederates that they would crack at some point. McClellan, in a series of appalling letters to his wife, poured scorn on what he termed Lincoln's complete ignorance of strategy and military matters.[29] In retrospect, Lincoln was exactly on the mark, but while he paid the closest attention to military matters, he rarely intervened to order his generals to undertake specific courses of action. He provided the resources and the guidance, but he expected them to get on with the business of running the war against the Confederates in the field.

With the exception of Grant's brilliant strokes at forts Donelson and Henry early in 1862, the remainder of the year consisted of one setback after another for the North, as the Union's generals proved almost completely inept at the larger strategic or operational issues raised by the war.[30] McClellan launched an invasion of the Peninsula (formed by the confluence of the York and James rivers) as a means of escaping the need to fight his way overland to Richmond. That campaign foundered on Little Mac's incapacity to display any sort of command leadership. With McClellan and his forces bogged down in the swamps outside of Richmond, Lincoln found himself thoroughly discouraged by Little Mac's distinct unwillingness to fight. The president's first move was to replace McClellan as the overall commander-in-chief of the Union army and bring Major-General Henry Halleck from the western theatre as his replacement. He would then wait until two months after the drawn battle at Antietam finally to fire McClellan as the commander of the Army of the Potomac for the general's congenital caution—a caution that bordered on moral cowardice in his consistent overestimation of the Army of Northern Virginia's strength and his unwillingness to fight.

There is some considerable irony in Halleck's appointment because he was no improvement over McClellan in terms of the overall direction of the war. In effect he was a glorified paper-pusher, who at times played politics at the expense of the Union cause. He had been less than impressive in the field after Shiloh and had made considerable efforts to get rid of Grant, most probably because of jealousy of his subordinate's competence. In effect, Halleck's removal to Washington opened up the western campaigns to far more competent officers, but it did nothing to improve on the North's ability to come up with a coherent military strategy that would complement and support Lincoln's grand strategy.

By summer 1862, Lincoln recognized what Grant had realized at Shiloh: the war would have no simple, quick end, but rather was going to involve a long, terrible slogging match. In July the president began working on what became the Emancipation Proclamation to free the slaves. Such an action would represent an out-and-out war not only on the South's economic system but on its culture as well. It would represent an escalation of the war while making any reconciliation between the states impossible except through total victory over the South. It was Lincoln's calculation that that was already the case. But the emancipation of the slaves would also raise delicate political problems in segments of the North's population as well as portions of the army. In the end, Lincoln solved the former problem—here the political generals were of great importance in keeping the Northern population solidly behind the war effort—while the appearance of regiments of black soldiers who quickly proved they were willing to fight for their freedom convinced most Union soldiers that blacks who fought in Union blue deserved their freedom.[31]

Lincoln was not able to issue the Emancipation Proclamation until after the terrible killing battle of Antietam—a battle that saw more Americans die in a single day of combat than any other day in history through to the present. Shortly after the battle, the president issued the proclamation, which announced that all blacks in states that were in rebellion would receive their freedom on 1 January 1863. Thereby, Lincoln created the impression that emancipation was a measure of military and economic expediency aimed at undermining the ability of the Confederacy to maintain the struggle. At the same time, the North gained considerably by the proclamation in terms of attitudes abroad, particularly in Great Britain. From this point on, in the war there was no chance that the British would intervene in the conflict on the side of the Confederacy.

1863: THE TURNING POINT IN THE WAR

By the spring of 1863, three great Northern armies confronted the Confederacy with what should have been overwhelming force. In the east, the Army of the Potomac under Major-General Joseph Hooker, the third commander of that organization in a year, confronted Robert E. Lee's Army of Northern Virginia; in central Tennessee, Major-General Rosecrans's Army of the Cumberland was poised to drive into the south-eastern portion of the state and attack Chattanooga; and in the west, Grant's forces were ready to manoeuvre past the defences of Vicksburg and attack that crucial bastion, which, much as West Point united the colonies during the revolutionary war, protected the river that tied the states of the Confederacy together. But there was still no guiding military command at the centre. Thus, Grant and Hooker moved at nearly the same time in late April. But Rosecrans dithered away the spring and early summer to get everything ready for his push. Lincoln wished for all three armies to move at the same time, which would have placed intolerable strain on Confederate resources, but Halleck, clucking away at his desk in Washington, was not about to provide serious direction or guidance to the North's field commanders.

Grant succeeded beyond the administration's wildest dreams.[32] He moved his forces south of Vicksburg and crossed the Mississippi. At that point, he cut himself loose from his supply lines and determined to live off the countryside. As he crossed the Mississippi, he informed Halleck of his actions, knowing full well that the pedant in Washington would forbid his approach. But, considering the state of communications, Grant knew that by the time he received Halleck's order to desist, he would have either succeeded, making the orders overtaken by events, or dismally failed, in which case it would not matter. Indeed, when he received orders from Halleck to return to his starting point, his troops were smashing the rebel position along the Big Black River and driving them pell-mell back into the Vicksburg fortifications.[33]

By 19 May, after the most brilliant campaign in the civil war, Grant had besieged Major-General Pemberton's army in Vicksburg with every prospect of capturing both that army and the city within the next month and a half. However, in the east, Lee, ably supported by his brilliant lieutenant Stonewall Jackson, had narrowly defeated Hooker at the battle of Chancellorsville.[34] Confronting disaster in the west, the Confederate leaders met in Richmond on 16 May 1863. Jefferson Davis argued that a portion of the Army of Northern Virginia be dispatched to the western theatre to save Vicksburg. Nevertheless, the Confederate president yielded to Lee's urging that the South pursue the Napoleonic mirage of decisive victory in the east by invading Pennsylvania rather than provide reinforcements from the Army of Northern Virginia to the west to restore the desperate situation in the western theatre of war. Among other arguments, Lee expressed the idle hope that the hot, humid summer weather of central Mississippi would so debilitate Grant's forces that the Northerners would have to abandon the siege. No more disastrous strategic mistake was to occur during the course of the war.

The result of that decision was the devastating defeat at the battle of Gettysburg, which ended on 3 July with Pickett's charge.[35] Meanwhile, in the west, Grant easily fended off efforts to relieve the Confederate forces he had trapped in the Vicksburg defences. On the day after Meade's troops had sealed their victory in Pennsylvania, Grant received the surrender of the city of Vicksburg and an entire Confederate army.[36] As Lincoln so eloquently expressed it, 'The father of waters again goes unvexed to the sea.'[37]

Immediately upon Vicksburg's surrender, Grant proposed to Washington that his forces move on Mobile. Halleck would have none of it. In his clerk's mind, he saw only difficulties, and, whether because of jealousy of Grant's success or his inability to understand the larger issues of military and grand strategy, he parcelled out much of Grant's victorious army to Rosecrans and other more dubious endeavours in the western theatre. Thus, Grant spent the remainder of the summer mouldering on the banks of the Mississippi.

Finally, on 24 June, nearly two months after the other two great Union armies had attacked, Rosecrans moved. In two months, his army drove the Confederates out of central and then southern Tennessee into northern Georgia and captured Chattanooga. In this desperate situation, Davis overruled Lee and ordered the Army of Northern Virginia to transfer two of its divisions under James Longstreet to reinforce Braxton Bragg's Army of Tennessee. With the help of these reinforcements, the Confederates were able to win a major victory over Rosecrans and chase the Army of the Cumberland back to Chattanooga, where they besieged it. Lincoln described Rosecrans in the aftermath of the battle being 'stunned like a duck hit on the head'.[38]

Lincoln's first response to this setback in the west was to send two corps from the Army of the Potomac under Hooker to redress the balance in the west. As Edwin Stanton, Lincoln's highly competent secretary of war, acidly noted, 'they weren't doing much in Virginia, so they might as well go west'. Not surprisingly, Meade took the opportunity to get rid of two of his less competent corps commanders, Major-General O. O. Howard, whose XI Corps had been outflanked at both Chancellorsville and Gettysburg, and Major-General Henry Slocum, who had spent the first day of Gettysburg 5 miles away at Cashtown without moving an inch, because his orders did not specify reinforcing the troops at Gettysburg.[39]

But Lincoln's most important move came three weeks after the battle of Chickamauga, when he created the Division of Mississippi, which incorporated every scrap of territory between that great river and the Appalachian Mountains, and appointed Grant to that command. The new commander in the west met with Rosecrans on his way to the battle-front in south-east Tennessee, and, as he commented in his memoirs, 'we held a brief interview in which he described very clearly the situation in Chattanooga and made some excellent suggestions as to what should be done. My only wonder was that he had not carried them out.'[40] Not surprisingly, Grant fired Rosecrans and replaced him with Major-General 'Pap' Thomas, the hero of Chickamauga.

Grant did carry out Rosecrans's suggestions. As one officer commented about Grant's arrival, 'we began to see things move'.[41] By the end of November, the forces under his command had inflicted a crushing defeat on Bragg's army and completely restored the situation in the west. Thus, over the course of 1863, Grant had managed not only to capture Vicksburg and open up the Mississippi River for Northern commerce, while cutting the South off from the sustenance of its western states, but had also solidified the North's strategic position in Tennessee. Union armies were now poised to begin the invasion of the Deep South and carry the war into its heartland. Lincoln was about to find the general who could execute the military portion of his grand strategy.

THE DECISIVE YEAR

Grant's brilliant performance in 1863 led to his promotion to commander of Union armies. Had he received that appointment shortly after his victory over Bragg at Chattanooga in November 1863, the overall preparations of Northern armies and the coordination of military strategy for the upcoming campaigns might have been better. But Lincoln hesitated until February of 1864 to appoint Grant to this position. What the president clearly wanted to discover was whether Grant had any presidential ambitions. Simply put, Lincoln had had enough of the political machinations that had characterized all too much of McClellan's time in command. When Lincoln was assured of that point, he appointed Grant to

Halleck's position, while Halleck became the paper-pushing army chief of staff, which had been his conception of the position all along.[42]

On 4 April 1864, the new commander-in-chief of all Union armies made clear his overall military strategy for the year in a short, pithy, and eloquent directive to Major-General William Tecumseh Sherman, who now assumed command of Union forces in the western theatre:

> It is my design, if the enemy keep quiet and allow me to take the initiative in the spring campaign, to work all parts of the army together, and somewhat toward a common centre. I have sent orders to Banks ... to finish up his present expedition against Shreveport with all dispatch ... To [his force] I will add five thousand men from Missouri. With this force he is to commence operations against Mobile as soon as he can. It will be impossible for him to start too early. Gilmore joins Butler with ten thousand men, and the two operate against Richmond from the south side of the James River. This will give Butler thirty-three thousand men to mount operations with ... I will stay with the army of the Potomac ... and operate directly against Lee's army wherever it will be found. Sigel collects all his available forces [for operations in the Shenandoah]. You I propose to move against Johnston's army, to break it up and to get into the interior of the enemy's country as far as you can, inflicting all the damage you can against their war resources. I do not propose to lay down for you a plan of campaign, but simply lay down the work it is desirable to have done and leave you free to execute it in your own way ... From the expedition from the department of West Virginia, I do not calculate on any great results ... if Sigel can't skin himself, he can hold a leg while some one else skins.[43]

In every respect Grant's military strategy for 1864 echoed the strategic ideas which Lincoln had suggested to McClellan two years before, but which the commander of the Army of the Potomac had so contemptuously dismissed.

Had Grant's generals followed the directions of their commander-in-chief, the war would have been over by the end of 1864. But they did not. Sigel, a political general, went into the Shenandoah valley and came back out even faster than he had entered it. Butler, a political general commanding 33,000, had gotten himself 'bottled up like a cork' in Bermuda Hundred, south-east of Richmond, in a position of complete uselessness. And Banks, a political general, found himself so tangled up in the Red River that he almost lost his army and presented no threat to the port of Mobile. Thus, the Shenandoah valley remained a substantial threat to Washington; Lee felt no threat to Richmond or his supply lines that ran through Petersburg; and Johnston was able to recall Polk's corps from the defence of Mobile to defend Atlanta.

Significantly, in his memoirs, Grant never blamed the difficulties into which his military strategy ran in 1864 on the fact that the Lincoln administration had saddled him with a large number of political generals who were not up to the tasks that confronted them. Certainly, Sherman, who was unwilling to appoint political generals to senior positions, would have had little difficulty in blaming the failures on Butler, Sigel, and Banks.[44] Why Grant's reticence? My opinion is that Grant understood that the political generals were absolutely necessary to maintain political support for the war in the North. What good would it do for Union armies to win major victories in summer 1864 while the political consensus at home broke down and McClellan was elected president of the United States—a man who in every likelihood would give the South much of what it had failed to gain on the battlefields of the war?

Thus, it all fell to Grant and Sherman to break the South at far greater cost by defeating the main Confederate armies in the field. For Grant there were the terrible killing battles of the Wilderness, Spotsylvania Court House, North Anna, Cold Harbor, and Petersburg, which forced Lee finally into the desperate defence of Petersburg and Richmond.[45] At every step of the 1864 campaign, Grant found himself hindered by the culture of the senior officers of the Army of the Potomac, who proved incapable of reinforcing success, rarely if ever displayed initiative, and consistently placed caution over aggression. At times it seemed as if no senior officer in the Army of the Potomac possessed a simple watch.[46] Nevertheless, by the time the siege of Petersburg began in summer 1864, Grant had robbed Lee of his ability to take the initiative. The only thing that the Confederate leader could do was to hang on for dear life and hope that something would turn up in the west to mitigate the desperate circumstances into which his army and the Confederacy had fallen.

In the west, Sherman also faced great difficulty in his campaign against Joe Johnston's army defending Atlanta. Nevertheless, by July, Sherman had man-oeuvred his armies to the outskirts of Atlanta despite the effective defensive tactics of the Confederates. At that point, Davis blinked and fired Johnston for his lack of aggression and replaced him with John Bell Hood, who still believed the date was 1862. Lee described Johnston's replacement aptly as 'all lion and no fox'.[47] Hood immediately launched a series of ferocious attacks on Sherman's troops, all of which were crushed with heavy losses.

July and August of 1864 were the darkest months the Union cause was to suffer over the course of the conflict. Even Admiral Farragut's triumph in running his ships past the forts that guarded Mobile Bay—'Damn the torpedoes! Full speed ahead'[48]—failed to dispel the gloom in the North. The stalemates in front of Petersburg and Atlanta appeared to be unending, while the casualty bill, especially in the eastern theatre, seemed almost unimaginable. Major-General Gouverneur Warren, one of the heroes of Gettysburg, commented, 'For thirty days it has been one funeral procession past me and it has been too much.'[49] Lincoln himself felt that there was every prospect that he would lose the upcoming election to McClellan, now in the role of a politician as the candidate of the Democratic Party.

But the dawn came in early September, when Sherman managed to cut the main rail lines behind Atlanta, and Hood was forced to abandon the city. On 19 September, Major-General Philip Sheridan, as ferocious and driving a commander as Stonewall Jackson on the other side, broke the Confederate forces of Jubal Early in the Shenandoah. As the war turned, so too did the political consensus in the North. Buoyed by increasing Union successes, Lincoln cruised to re-election, winning the Northern states by as big a margin as he had four years earlier.

GRAND STRATEGY AND THE HARD WAR

At the beginning of the conflict, Union commanders had made considerable efforts to treat civilians in the South with civility and certainly with what was regarded as the proper behaviour towards non-combatants and their property.[50]

But by the summer of 1862, such attitudes had begun to alter in fundamental ways. For Union soldiers, the overt hostility of the Southern population soon disabused them of the notion that they were dealing with fellow countrymen eager to rejoin the Union. Moreover, Northern commanders quickly encountered the problem of what to do with the slaves who had run away from their masters and sought asylum with the Union army. In one case in 1861, a Southern plantation owner showed up behind Union lines and demanded that his slaves be returned under the conditions of the Fugitive Slave Act. The response of the Northern commander, Ben Butler, was to point out that since Virginia had proclaimed itself no longer part of the Union, the laws of the United States no longer applied. Thus, he declared the slaves were 'contraband of war' and put them to work as labourers supporting his troops.[51]

By 1863, Grant in the west had moved to an open policy of confiscating the food and fodder for his army directly from the civilian population. In his retreat to Holly Springs, Tennessee, in late 1862 after Confederate raiders had destroyed his supply lines, Grant had been astonished at how easily his quartermasters had been able to keep the army supplied with sustenance from the farms and plantations throughout northern Mississippi. The insight that he gained from that experience led him to plan his campaign against Vicksburg in spring 1863 on the basis that, when he moved his army south of Vicksburg on the western bank and then crossed to the eastern bank, he would be able to cut his lines of supply and live off the countryside. At the time, such an approach to campaigning drew considerable criticism from Sherman. But the results soon convinced him that Grant had been correct. It would represent a lesson that he would not forget.

By 1864, it had become clear to the political and military leaders of the North that they were going to have to break the will of the Southern people if the Union cause were to prevail in the conflict. Thus, the 'hard war' emerged in all its ferociousness in that year. In every respect, the campaigns to break the Southern will represented a precursor to the war on civilians, especially the strategic bombing campaigns of the Second World War, that conflicts in the twentieth century were to bring in their wake.[52] And in some ways, the efforts of Union commanders were more successful in their impact on the conflict, because the presence of Northern troops on the ground was a direct indication of military defeat that Southerners could not ignore. Not surprisingly, the destruction of the South's heartland had a direct and palpable impact on the Confederate armies in the field. By the fall of 1864, desertion had become a major problem, to which neither the Confederate military nor government had a response.

The full nature of the hard war emerged in the campaigns of Sheridan and Sherman in the last half of 1864. In the eastern theatre, Virginia's Shenandoah valley had represented a nightmare for the Union cause. It had seen Stonewall Jackson's forces wreck the reputations of a large number of Union generals in 1862. It had made way for Lee's invasion of Maryland in 1862 and Pennsylvania in 1863. As late as July 1864, it had provided the path for Jubal Early and 15,000 rebels to reach the outskirts of Washington.[53] Moreover, the valley had afforded large amounts of sustenance for the soldiers of the Army of Northern Virginia and fodder for its horses throughout the conflict. And finally, it was the home of guerrilla bands that caused Union logistics and supply depots no end of difficulties.

Grant now ordered Sheridan to get rid of the Confederate forces in the Shenandoah valley. This Sheridan did with a vengeance by winning two decisive victories, first at Winchester on 19 September and then at Cedar Creek on 16 October. But Grant had another task for Sheridan, and that was to destroy the valley from one end to the other. As the commander of the Union's army made clear in a message to Halleck, Sheridan's mission was to create a 'barren waste [in the valley] . . . so that crows flying over it for the balance of the season will have to carry their provender with them'.[54] Sheridan's comment on his instructions was that 'the people must be left nothing but their eyes to weep with over the war'.[55]

But Sheridan's assault on the South's landscape was small potatoes compared to what was about to happen farther south. After capturing Atlanta, Sherman had sparred with Hood, but was unable to pin the Confederates down. Sherman then proposed to Lincoln and Grant that he divide his army: a portion of it to pull back to Tennessee and cover Hood's army, while he and 60,000 of the toughest troops in his command cut their lines of supply and marched through Georgia to destroy everything that might be of use to the Confederacy. As he expressed it in his inimitable fashion, 'If we can march a well-appointed army right through [the heart of the Confederacy], it is a demonstration to the world, foreign and domestic, that we have a power which [Jefferson] Davis cannot resist . . . I can make the march and make Georgia howl.'[56] And that is precisely what Sherman and his army proceeded to do.

One week after the presidential elections, Sherman abandoned Atlanta—after destroying everything that was of any worth—and began his march to the sea. Hood refused to follow him, but instead set off on an ill-fated invasion of Tennessee, which ended in two disastrous defeats at Franklin and Nashville. Meanwhile, Sherman's troops burned their way through the heart of Georgia. What they did not eat or find some use for, they burned, derisively placing placards renaming the towns they passed through 'Chimneyville'. One Union major, ironically born in Alabama, recorded his feelings in the following fashion:

> while I deplore this necessity daily and cannot bear to see the soldiers swarm as they do through fields and yards . . . nothing *can* end this war but some demonstration of their helplessness . . . This union and its government must be sustained, at any and every cost; to sustain it, we must war upon and destroy the organized rebel forces,— must cut off their supplies, destroy their communications . . . [and] produce among the *people of Georgia* a thorough conviction of the personal misery which attends war, and the utter helplessness and inability of their 'rulers,' State or Confederate, to protect them . . . If that terror and grief and even want shall help paralyze their husbands and fathers who are fighting us . . . it is a mercy in the end.[57]

Sherman arrived at Savannah just before Christmas to make Lincoln and the North a 'present' of the city. Little remained of Georgia's riches behind them: towns and villages smashed; foodstuffs seized for the army's use; what was not used destroyed; and behind the army masses of slaves eager to abandon their thraldom, putting paid to the myth that the South's slaves were happy with their lot.

But the travails of the South were not at an end. By the end of December 1864, with the Union victories in the Shenandoah, Tennessee, and Georgia, it was clear that the Confederacy was dead. But, like the Germans in 1945, the Confederate leadership determined to fight the war to the bitter end.[58] Thus, Davis and Lee ensured that Union armies would ravage what portions of the South still remained largely untouched by Northern armies. In January, Sherman began his drive through South Carolina. His troops, fully mindful that its inhabitants had been the most rabid of the secessionists, destroyed the portions of the state through which they passed with a vengeance. By March, the western armies had reached North Carolina. Meanwhile, in April 1865, Major-General James H. Wilson, a mere lieutenant at Antietam in 1862, took 13,000 cavalry in a massive raid through northern Alabama to lay waste to one of the few areas of the South still untouched by war.[59] As Sherman put it eloquently in his memoirs, 'We cannot change the hearts of these people in the South, but we can make war so terrible ... [and] make them so sick of war that generations would pass away before they would again appeal to it.'[60]

CONCLUSION

Lincoln's approach to grand strategy achieved its goals. The cost was immense in both lives and treasure, but there was, in fact, no cheap, simple solution that would reunite the country as so many, including the new president, had hoped in 1861. In spite of their deep bitterness—a bitterness that persisted in many portions of the South well into the mid-point of the twentieth century—no one in what had been the states of the Confederacy was going to attempt to reverse the verdict that 'the United States *is* a country', not that 'the United States are a country', the latter being the terminology that had been the case until 1865. In that sense, Lincoln's grand strategy had succeeded completely.

Above all, there was a close relationship between the evolution of Northern grand strategy and the evolution of its military strategy. By 1864 the military strategy was not just to destroy the Southern armies but to destroy the South to the point where the civilian population would no longer support the war. The ferocity of the Union approach matched anything that 'Bomber' Harris was to dream up during the Second World War. As Sherman remarked in early 1864:

> If they [the Southerners] want eternal war, well and good; we accept the issue, and will dispossess them and put our friends in their places ... Three years ago by a little reflection and patience, they could have had a hundred years of peace and prosperity, but they preferred war; very well. Last year they could have saved their slaves, but now it is too late. ... Next year their lands will be taken; for in war we can take them, and rightfully, too, and in another year they may beg in vain for their lives ... To those who submit to the rightful law and authority, all gentleness and forbearance; but to the petulant and persistent secessionist, why, death is a mercy, and the quicker he or she is disposed of the better. Satan and the rebellious saints of Heaven were allowed a continuous existence in hell merely to swell their just punishment. To such as would rebel against a Government so mild and just as ours was in peace, a punishment equal would not be unjust.[61]

Sherman would prove to be a prophet not only of the war but also of its aftermath. In the period after the civil war and the deliberate destruction wrought by Union armies, Southerners certainly did accept the results of reunion. They would not try rebellion again. But they certainly did not accept the implications of the freeing of the blacks. The result was a virulent, racist, murderous insurgency during the period of reconstruction. In the 1870s, that insurgency broke the willingness of the North to impose some sense of justice and equal rights for the newly freed slaves that took place under the rubric of states' rights.[62] Not only did Northern politicians refuse to take a stand, but the North's own racist beliefs, embodied in the attitudes of the Democratic Party, exacerbated the difficulties that American blacks confronted. Thus, for over 100 years, Americans refused to deal with the other consequence of Lincoln's grand strategy, namely the ending of slavery.

NOTES

1. A. R. Millett and W. Murray, 'Lessons of War', *National Interest* (Winter 1988–9).
2. C. von Clausewitz, *On War*, ed. and trans. M. Howard and P. Paret (Princeton, NJ, 1976), 163.
3. I am indebted to Colin Gray for this line in a speech he gave at Joint Forces Command in Norfolk in June 2008.
4. The German military in the First World War consistently rejected strategic and political concerns because of what its leaders posited as 'military necessity'—a concept which they used to override all political and strategic concerns. In this regard, see particularly I. V. Hull, *Absolute Destruction: Military Culture and the Practices of War in Imperial Germany* (Ithaca, NY, 2005).
5. Sun Tzu, *The Art of War*, ed. and trans. S. B. Griffith (Oxford, 1963), 84.
6. Those states were Florida, Georgia, Alabama, Mississippi, Louisiana, South Carolina, and Texas.
7. Quoted in S. W. Sears, *The Landscape Turned Red: The Battle of Antietam* (New York, 1983), 166.
8. The middle states were North Carolina, Virginia, Tennessee, and Arkansas.
9. The four border states were Missouri, Kentucky, Maryland, and Delaware.
10. The resupply effort was unarmed.
11. Kentucky had attempted to stay neutral in the conflict, and Lincoln appeared willing to allow it to maintain that stance, all the while waiting for the South to make the first move. Once again Davis and his advisers made the mistake of following the path of military necessity. By taking the high road, Lincoln ensured that Kentucky fell into the Union camp like a ripe plum.
12. For a first-class discussion of the relationship between Lincoln and his Cabinet and how he used its most effective members, see D. Kearns Goodwin, *Team of Rivals: The Political Genius of Abraham Lincoln* (New York, 2006).
13. For a further examination of these issues, see W. Murray, 'What Took the North So Long?', *Military History Quarterly* (Autumn 1989).
14. Or, for that matter, current-day Americans whose cars and airplanes span their continent at speeds that citizens in the nineteenth century could not have comprehended.
15. In this respect, see M. Knox and W. Murray, *The Dynamics of Military Revolution, 1300–2050* (Cambridge, 2000), ch. 1.
16. Nor did anyone in Europe.
17. The prime examples are John Pemberton and Braxton Bragg, both of whom Davis kept in their positions for far too long a period.
18. For a clearly thought-through criticism of Robert E. Lee's generalship, see J. F. C. Fuller, *Grant and Lee: A Study in Personality and Generalship* (Bloomington, IN, 1982).

19. See the discussion in U. S. Grant, *The Personal Memoirs of U. S. Grant*, 2 vols (New York, 1885), i. 282–3.

20. The twentieth Maine, perhaps one of the most combat-effective regiments in the Army of the Potomac, was lucky enough to have Adelbert Ames as its first commanding officer in August 1862. Ames had graduated from West Point in 1861, had been wounded at the battle of Bull Run, and had risen steadily in the ranks of the Army of the Potomac in the fighting in early 1862. He had then accepted the colonelcy of the twentieth Maine in August 1862. Not only did he train the regiment into one of the finest regiments in the Union army, but he also educated the deputy commander of the regiment, Joshua Chamberlain of Gettysburg fame, into an officer whom Grant regarded as the finest combat brigade commander in the Army of the Potomac by war's end.

21. This largely involved dumping the dead into unmarked graves spread higgledly-piggledly over the countryside.

22. They were being asked to enlist for three years.

23. Grant, *The Personal Memoirs of U. S. Grant*, i. 244–6.

24. Not surprisingly, during the First World War, when Woodrow Wilson's government complained about British blockade measures aimed at the Central Powers, the British were able to use American actions during the civil war as justification for their blockade measures.

25. J. M. McPherson, *Battle Cry of Freedom: The Civil War Era* (Oxford, 1988), 390.

26. The situation was similar to that which confronted the American polity in 1942 and which led the president, Franklin Roosevelt, to order an unwilling U.S. military to undertake Operation Torch, the November 1942 landings in Algeria and Morocco.

27. Grant, *The Personal Memoirs of U. S. Grant*, i. 368–9. Shiloh was the first great killing battle of the civil war; its casualties had totalled almost as much as all the other major battles in the war thus far. It was, in fact, however, to prove no bloodier than the subsequent battles that would occur over the next three years. Nevertheless, it came as a terrible shock to the Northern and Southern populations and contributed considerably to the unjustified reputation that Grant has enjoyed among some historians as a butcher.

28. Clausewitz, *On War*, 592.

29. One might note that few military leaders have condemned themselves to posterity in their letters to the extent that McClellan managed to do.

30. On the tactical side of matters, by summer 1862, Union troops were every bit as effective in combat as their Confederate opponents. The problem was that in almost every theatre their commanders were being out-generalled by their Confederate opponents.

31. And at the same time increased their own chances of survival.

32. For the Vicksburg, see, among others, J. R. Arnold, *Grant Wins the War: Decision at Vicksburg* (New York, 1997).

33. Grant records in his memoirs that Halleck's message for him to desist in his campaign reached him as he was about to thrash Pemberton's troops along the Big Black River. To the horror of the major who delivered the message, Grant simply pocketed the message and paid it no attention. Grant's final comment is that he never saw the major again during the course of the war. Grant, *The Personal Memoirs of U. S. Grant*, i. 524–6.

34. Far and away the best study of the battle of Chancellorsville is S. W. Sears, *Chancellorsville* (Boston, 1996).

35. The best book on the battle of Gettysburg is also by Stephen W. Sears: *Gettysburg* (New York, 2004).

36. It is worth noting in terms of Grant's military reputation that he was the only general in the civil war to defeat and then capture an enemy army, in his case *two* enemy armies.

37. Quoted in McPherson, *Battle Cry of Freedom*, 639.
38. Ibid. 675.
39. Slocum's nickname among some of the veterans of the first day was 'slow come', an apt description of a general who reflected the Army of the Potomac's culture that placed rigid obedience to orders above any desire to display initiative.
40. Grant, *The Personal Memoirs of U. S. Grant*, ii. 28.
41. B. Catton, *Grant Takes Command* (Boston, 1969), 56.
42. Halleck may well have also contributed to the delay in appointing Grant to the position of commander of the Union armies, but there is no evidence that he took any action in supporting or attempting to thwart Grant's appointment.
43. Grant, *The Personal Memoirs of U. S. Grant*, ii. 130–2. Grant got the final comment about Sigel holding a leg from Lincoln during a briefing he gave the president on his overall conception of Union military strategy for the upcoming year.
44. When Major-General James McPherson, commander of the Army of Tennessee, was killed in July 1864, Sherman refused to appoint General 'Black Jack' Logan, an outstanding volunteer officer, as his replacement, but rather chose the thoroughly undistinguished O. O. Howard. Later that year, however, Grant selected Logan to replace General Thomas at Nashville, should the latter not attack Hood's army in front of that city.
45. For a clear discussion of the campaign in northern Virginia in 1864, see M. Grimsley, *The Virginia Campaign, May–June 1864* (Lincoln, NE, 2005).
46. I am indebted to Colonel Richard Hart Sinnreich, US Army (Retd), for this point.
47. McPherson, *Battle Cry of Freedom*, 753.
48. Ibid. 761.
49. Ibid. 742.
50. The ground-breaking study on this topic is M. Grimsley, *The Hard Hand of War: Union Military Policy towards Southern Civilians, 1861–1865* (Cambridge, 2008).
51. McPherson, *Battle Cry of Freedom*, 355.
52. Nevertheless, it is worth underlining that the Royal Air Force's bombing campaign against Germany in the Second World War did have a direct and significant impact on the morale of Germany's population.
53. This was the famous occasion when the future Supreme Court Justice Oliver Wendell Holmes, Jr, yelled at Lincoln, who was trying to see what was happening by raising his head above the fortifications: 'Get down, you damn fool, before you get shot.'
54. Quoted in McPherson, *Battle Cry of Freedom*, 778.
55. As an observer of the Franco-Prussian War six years later, Sheridan was to suggest to the Prussians that they were being much too kind to the French and then repeat the above remark.
56. Quoted in McPherson, *Battle Cry of Freedom*, 808.
57. Ibid. 811.
58. And over the same period of months: January to May.
59. At Antietam as a lieutenant, Wilson went to the wounded Hooker and suggested that the general lead a charge of the right wing to finish off the Confederate army.
60. W. T. Sherman, *Memoirs* (New York, 1875).
61. Quoted in S. Foote, *The Civil War, a Narrative*, ii: *Fredericksburg to Meridian* (New York, 1963), 941.
62. See the examination of this period in J. M. McPherson, 'War and Peace in the Post-Civil War South', in W. Murray and J. Lacey (eds), *The Making of Peace: Rulers, States, and the Aftermath of War* (Cambridge, 2009).

10

The First and Second World Wars

Martin van Creveld

INTRODUCTION

The purpose of this chapter is to explore the conduct of strategy during the two largest and most 'total' wars that have ever been fought or are likely to be fought—World Wars I and II. Unlike Gaul, this chapter consists not of three parts but of four. The first is general, seeking to show the broad similarities between the First and Second World Wars at the highest level on which those conflicts were waged: to wit, the one where national policy and politics, strategy, diplomacy, economics, and mobilization meet and interact. The second part provides a brief discussion of the strategy of each of the principal belligerents separately. The third focuses on the differences between the two wars, the most important being the large-scale use of armoured forces—which made for much greater operational mobility in the Second World war than in the First—and the far more extensive employment of air power. Yet, insofar as war is a continuation of, and supposed to be subordinate to, politics, these military differences were less significant than the similarities. The final part is an attempt to pull the various threads together and draw some conclusions. As a result, looking back the two wars are best understood as parts of a single conflict. To history, that conflict presents a Janus face: one face, looking backward, marks the culmination of centuries of 'great power' wars; the other, looking forward through the debris left by two nuclear explosions, opened the period in which we live.

SIMILARITIES

In many ways, the Second World War was a repetition of the First. Above all, in both wars the most important actors by far were a small number—no more than seven or eight—of mighty political organizations known as states or, to use the terminology of the period, 'great powers'. Compared with those states, their hundreds of thousands or millions of square miles of territory, their millions upon millions of citizens or subjects, their million-strong armed forces, and the vast economic resources at their disposal, any other kind of organization hardly counted. Contemporaries understood this very well; when Stalin famously asked how many divisions the Pope had, he had more of a point than most historians are willing to admit.[1] It is true that the war also saw the emergence of very large 'partisan' movements, some of which numbered in the hundreds of thousands. Yet compared to the number that states mobilized and sent to the battlefields, even hundreds of thousands did not matter that much; furthermore, insofar as they did not fight on their own behalf but either assisted states or fought against them, they hardly change the overall picture.

In both wars, the states in question formed two vast coalitions, the largest that have ever existed. Those two coalitions engaged one another and fought one another tooth and nail. In fact, they systematically beat one another to pulp, not desisting until one triumphed and the other broke down. In both wars, each of those states, or belligerents, was organized along what, in my book *The Transformation of War*, I called 'trinitarian' lines.[2] Referring to Carl von Clausewitz's 'remarkable trinity',[3] that means that each had a government, armed forces, and a civilian population. Inside each state, a clear division of labour existed. It was the task of the government to mobilize resources and to conduct the war at the highest level: that of the armed forces to fight their opposite numbers, killing and getting killed if necessary; and that of the civilian population to pay and to suffer. So well understood was this division that it had become rooted in international law as understood from Hugo Grotius on. In both wars, violations of this 'trinitarian' division of labour, especially military operations that crossed the boundary between soldiers and civilians, were considered war crimes—which did not prevent millions of such crimes from being committed by all sides.

In both wars, the majority of belligerents were either located in Europe or had the centres of their power in that continent. Accordingly, though the importance of conflicts in other parts of the world should not be underestimated, it is not surprising that both conflicts broke out in Europe and that Europe, as the epicentre from which the evil spread, witnessed the largest military operations by far. Yet in neither war were operations limited to Europe alone; the fact that a number of the most important belligerents owned colonies in other continents, or drew their supplies from them, ensured that hostilities should spread over much of the world. In both wars, the only continent that remained immune, more or less, was Latin America. All the rest—Europe, Asia, Africa, North America, Australia—were involved in one way or another. So, by necessity, were most of the world's seas and oceans that linked those continents.

The above paragraphs by no means exhaust the list of parallels between the two wars. Both also had this in common that, contrary to the expectations of many of the men (there were no women among them) who started them, they lasted for years, not days, weeks, or months. In 1914, almost all the senior statesmen and commanders in the various capitals were unanimous in their belief that modern conditions made a long conflict impossible and that the troops would be home by Christmas. In 1939–41, Hitler, Mussolini, and Tojo all hoped for a short conflict that would be quickly decided in their own country's favour. In this respect their enemies—that is, first, the British Prime Minister, Chamberlain, and the French premier, Daladier, and then Stalin and Roosevelt—were more prescient. All four expected a long conflict; once it had broken out, they conducted it, or at any rate tried to conduct it, accordingly. In the event, the First World War lasted a little over four years, whereas the Second took up the best part of six.

By definition, at the grand strategic level, a long war necessarily meant that the defence was stronger than, or at least as strong as, the attack. This fact was even more apparent in the First World War than in the Second; at the operational level, the latter witnessed a much greater number of much more mobile campaigns. Since the defence was at least as strong as the attack, in both wars the issue was finally decided by attrition. In neither conflict was there a single climactic battle of the kind nineteenth-century people had come to expect: neither an Austerlitz, nor a Wagram, nor a Waterloo, nor a Solferino, nor a Königgrätz, nor a Sedan. This explains why different works on the Second World War provide quite different lists of supposedly 'decisive' battles.[4]

In both 1914–18 and 1939–45, the onset of attrition led to the victory of the bigger battalions. Backing up the bigger battalions were the greater populations and the larger gross domestic products. In 1913, according to the best available figures, if we put the industrial potential of the United States at 3, then that of the runner-up, Germany, stood at 1.4; that of the British empire stood at 1.3, that of Russia at 0.76, that of France at 0.6, that of Austria at 0.5, that of Japan at 0.25, and that of Italy at 0.22. Overall, the gap between the Entente and the Central Powers stood at 3.2:1. Twenty-five years later, Austria-Hungary had dropped out; the new figures were 3, 1.2, 1, 0.8, 0.5, 0.3, and 0.24, the balance between the Allies and the Axis Powers 2.4:1.[5] Add a good dosage of hindsight and stir well. Doing so, it appears that the gamble the losers took in 1914 was even more hazardous than that of their successors a quarter of a century later.

Prolonged wars, the triumph of the defence, and attrition all meant that the belligerents had ample time to attract allies and mobilize resources. In both 1914–18 and 1939–45, the outcome was what is often called total war.[6] In one sense, total war was nothing new; to convince oneself of that one need only read Thucydides's account of the Peloponnesian War or Livy's description of the Second Punic one. In a different sense, it was only made possible by modern industry, modern means of transportation, modern methods of administration, and a modern system of mobilization. In both wars, the result was conscription on a vast scale never attempted before or after. To adduce just one figure, the number of those who wore Red Army uniforms in 1941–5 reached 34,700,000,[7] yet even this only constituted the tip of the spear.

It was one of the outstanding, and most commented-upon, characteristics of total war that it reached backward behind itself, so to speak, from the fronts into the rear and from the battlefields into the offices, the factories, and the fields. For every soldier who fought, several civilians had to toil, providing him with the food, clothing, transportation, weapons, equipment of every kind, and shelter he needed. In 1915–16, total war came as something of a surprise; in 1939–45, almost everybody except Germany and Italy expected it and prepared themselves for it.

Yet it is interesting that, in both of these desperate struggles, when even the most free and democratic countries resorted to coercion to mobilize manpower, one group, comprising half of the population, remained largely exempt. Women certainly worked in all countries; still, even at the height of the conflicts they did so in much smaller numbers than men.[8] Furthermore, it was only in the Soviet Union during the Second World War that women were obliged to work and that any real measures were taken against them if they refused. Though a few women fought, mainly in the resistance movements, not a single one was compelled to bear arms or, failing to comply, was punished or executed. To put it in another way, women were exempt from the duty to kill and be killed;[9] in the whole of social life, if there is a greater privilege, I would dearly like to know what it is.

Finally, in both world wars a large percentage of the resources of several belligerents, and several of their allies, was located not in Europe but overseas. The outcome was that, in both world wars, it was the coalition with the largest navy and merchant fleet that ultimately triumphed.[10] In this sense, it might be said that, though the numbers involved were relatively small, the struggle at sea was as important as the one on land; sea power, in the form of the hilt, provided the leverage to land power, which represented the blade. To this, the Second World War added a large number of strategically very important seaborne landings, or, to use the lingo of a subsequent age, cases when power was 'projected' from the sea to the land. In both wars, naval blockades, whether imposed from the air, on the surface of the sea, or under the sea, played an extremely important role. In both wars, it was the side that imposed the more effective blockade, and was also able to use its command of the sea in order to import weapons, raw materials, and vast numbers of troops, that emerged victorious.

THE STRATEGIES OF THE INDIVIDUAL BELLIGERENTS

While this is hardly the place to enter on the famous question of 'war guilt', it would be hard to deny that, both in the First World War and in the Second, the real dynamo during the first part of the hostilities was Germany. Whether coming under the Kaiser or under Hitler, it was Germany that held the military initiative and acted, the rest reacted as best as they could. Accordingly, this survey will start with German strategy in both wars.

Germany

In both 1914 and 1939, Germany was dissatisfied with the current geopolitical situation and hoped to change it, using force if necessary. Both times, it was conscious of fighting a coalition of enemies that, collectively, were stronger than itself in terms of both military power and economic resources. Both times, it had some allies but none that was even remotely as powerful as itself. Turkey and to some extent Austria-Hungary in the First World War, and Italy in the Second, proved to be liabilities; instead of supporting Germany, they had to be supported, opening additional fronts and draining off men and *matériel* that could probably have been put to better use against Berlin's principal enemies. Both times, German commanders, enjoying unrivalled though perhaps somewhat exaggerated prestige that went back to the Great Moltke and the Wars of Unification, exercised considerable influence over their allies' armed forces and even found themselves commanding parts of those forces. Yet, never did the coalitions whose centre was Germany succeed in setting up a unified command structure of any kind—a fact that played a key role in their eventual defeat.[11]

To compensate for this disadvantage, both in 1914 and in 1939, Germany built up armed forces that were qualitatively superior to those of its adversaries. Indeed, its advantage in this respect may have been even more pronounced during the second war than in the first.[12] In 1914, the Kaiser and the Oberste Heeresleitung (the Supreme Army Command) put their faith in the Schlieffen Plan for a short war against the main enemy, France; in 1939, Hitler and the Oberkommando der Wehrmacht hoped to knock out their country's enemies by means of a series of short campaigns that were later called *Blitzfeldzüge*.[13] Both times the gamble failed. Both times, perhaps, it had always been doomed to fail. Germany became involved in a prolonged war on several fronts. Yet, operating on internal lines, with communication lines that were much shorter than those of its enemies, it was able to mobilize as efficiently as, and probably fight better than, anybody else.[14]

Like France, Austria-Hungary, and Russia (the Soviet Union), but unlike Britain, the United States, and Japan, both in 1914–18 and in 1939–45, Germany was primarily a land power.[15] Both in 1914–18 and in 1939–45, it supplemented its army with a navy, without, however, being able to prevent the British from blockading it. The German navy's most important tasks were to safeguard its own coasts on one hand and to try to knock Britain out of the war by means of a submarine blockade on the other. Both in 1914–18 and in 1939–45, when it was much assisted by the occupation of France and Norway, it came perilously close to achieving its goal, only to see submarine warfare play a major role in causing the United States to enter the war against it. In both 1917 and 1941, once the United States had joined the war, there could be no more question of Germany's winning it.

In 1944–5, even more than in 1917–18, the Germans, fighting desperately against much of the remainder of the world, saw their rather few, rather feckless, allies fall away one by one. In 1944–5, even more than in 1917–18, they held out against overwhelming odds until their world collapsed around their ears and they simply could do no more. A master strategist might conclude that, in both world wars, German strategy at the highest level was incredibly stupid: twice on end, the sacrifice of millions resulted in nothing better than defeat. A dramatist might add that, given how hard and well German troops fought, the way its rulers set out to run the war was a tragedy or, perhaps, a crime.

Austria-Hungary

In this context, little needs to be said about Austria-Hungary. In 1914, the Danube empire had at least as much to do with the outbreak of the war as its stronger ally, Germany, did; in 1939 it no longer existed. Unlike Germany, Austria-Hungary was a status quo power. Throughout the nineteenth century, it had lost one province after another, and surely it would have been happy if the rest had left it alone. With only very limited access to the sea, even more than Germany it was primarily a land power. Like Germany, it found itself fighting on several fronts: the Serb one, the Russian one, and, later, the Italian and the Romanian ones as well. Austria-Hungary's population was comparable to those of Britain and France (excluding their empires). However, it did not really have the industrial resources to wage a war on this scale. Whereas Austrian output of artillery rounds never reached 1 million a month, as early as 1916 Germany was producing

7 million and the Russians more than 4 million.[16] As a result, on each of the various fronts it ended by asking for, and receiving, German assistance, whether to save itself from defeat or to attack and vanquish its enemies.

As was only to be expected, Vienna paid a heavy price for its military-industrial weakness and for the aid it received. The longer the conflict, the more powerful the German stranglehold and the more limited the freedom of action that the Dual Monarchy still enjoyed. Had this not been so, then it is quite possible that Vienna would have dropped out of the war much earlier than was actually the case. Like their German comrades in arms, the Habsburg armed forces fought bravely, a feat made all the more remarkable by their extraordinarily heterogeneous ethnic composition. Like them, in the end they simply could do no more even though their homeland remained unoccupied.

Italy

Italy, too, is of little interest on these pages. In both 1914 and 1939, Italy was a Great Power only by courtesy. In both 1914 and 1939, its strategic options were very limited owing to its being confined to its 'Mediterranean prison', as Mussolini at one point put it. As he also put it, the bars of that prison were Gibraltar, Malta, and Alexandria. Poorly endowed with raw materials and in energy, Italy was as dependent on imports as any of the belligerents. Industrially, it could not compete with any of the big boys.

In both 1915 and 1939, Italy entered the war totally unprepared. In 1915, under a policy that its foreign minister, Sidney Sonnino, called 'sacro egoismo', it chose to violate its alliance with Germany and Austria-Hungary and to join Britain and France instead.[17] In return it was to receive South Tirol, or the Alto Adige as the Italians insisted on calling it, as well as some bits and pieces of colonial territory elsewhere. In 1915, the war proved to be a disappointment almost from the beginning; eleven offensives on the River Isonzo, aimed at breaking through to the Ljubljana Gap, failed to make any progress and merely resulted in vast casualties. In October 1917, a combined German-Austrian offensive came within a hair of driving the country out of the war and could only be halted by the so-called Miracle of the Piave, when the enemy was standing at the gates of Venice.[18] At sea, where the Italians enjoyed a huge geographical advantage, things went a little better for them. Even so, throughout the war they needed constant Allied military and financial assistance. Still, in favour of the Italian government of the day it must be said that, thanks to the incipient disintegration of Austria-Hungary and the last-moment victory at Vittorio Veneto, their country did achieve its major objective in Europe as well as gain a few pieces of land elsewhere.

Looking back on Italy's performance in the First World War from the perspective of the Second, one can only say that the men of 1915–18 were geniuses. In 1939, as in 1914, Italy was allied with one of the warring sides but chose to violate its commitment at the last moment (in response, Berliners claimed that the Italians were 'sh-ng on the Axis'). Both times, within less than a year the country's rulers, hoping for easy pickings, entered the conflict nevertheless. The 'strategic' objective, as Mussolini put it, was to generate a few thousand dead so that he could take his place at the peace conference. The difference was that, in 1940, the Italians chose the wrong side. Twenty years of Fascist propaganda notwithstanding, the Italian armed forces turned out to be even less prepared than they had been in 1915. The men lacked motivation; their equipment was insufficient and often second rate. Accordingly, they went from defeat to defeat, failing to make any headway on the border with France, driven back by the Greeks, almost chased out of Libya by the British, and thrown out of East Africa into the bargain. Early in 1941, the series of military disasters compelled the Germans to step in. Still, in the end, overwhelming Allied superiority in North Africa turned the scales against the Axis and resulted in the loss of its foothold on that continent.

Two months later, in July 1943, first Sicily and then Italy itself were invaded and turned into battlefields. By that time, there was not one government but two. One, in the south, came under the former chief of staff, Field Marshal Pietro Badoglio; the other, in the north, was formed by Mussolini after the Germans had rescued him from Italian captivity. Divided into two, occupied by its 'allies' on both sides, the country ceased playing any active role in the war. In the end, though it had to relinquish all its colonies, it was lucky to escape with as little territorial loss in Europe as it did.

France

To return to more serious matters, Germany's 'hereditary enemy', its *Erbfeind*, as the Germans liked to say, was France. Some historians even traced the rivalry between the two nations all the way back to the division of Charlemagne's empire among his offspring. France being the first to form a national government and a national state, from the time of Louis XIV to that of Napoleon inclusive, it was almost always French-speaking forces that invaded and devastated Germany. However, from 1813 on, the boot was on the other foot. The Franco-Prussian War of 1870–1 cost France the twin provinces of Alsace and Lorraine. From that moment on, the one overriding objective of French foreign and military policy was to recover them. The negative result of this was that it put most of its resources into the army, whereas the navy suffered; the positive one, that relatively few French forces were diverted to secondary fronts.

In 1913, the industrial potential of France compared to that of Germany was 1:2.3. Too weak to take on its powerful neighbour on its own, France sought allies. It found them first in the form of Russia and then, from about 1908 on, in that of Britain as well. In case of war, the French planned to take the offensive in Alsace and Lorraine. As it turned out, nothing could have been more foolish. The French troops who tried to invade the two provinces during the first weeks of the war were massacred by their tens of thousands. Meanwhile, the French General Staff saw the heart of the country threatened by a massive German juggernaut aiming straight at Paris. Only heroic improvisation, plus some British assistance, enabled the French to stop the German advance at the Marne. Even so, much of the most industrialized part of the country was occupied.

Mobilizing its human and industrial potential, France continued to fight back. Again with British assistance, most of the time it succeeded in holding its own, as at the ferocious battle of Verdun. However, the offensives it undertook during those horrible middle years of the war fared no better than those of 1914. The so-called Nivelle Offensive of April 1917 alone cost the French army some 187,000 casualties for no visible gain. With some of its units rising in mutiny, the High Command wisely decided to stand on the defence and stop offensive action until its newly won American allies could arrive in force.[19] The miracle is that, notwithstanding its relatively small demographic base and the horrendous losses that it suffered, France was somehow able to put more troops into the Western Front than either Britain or the United States. It also provided the American Expeditionary Force with most of its weapons and equipment. Paris's allies appreciated this fact; when an Allied supreme commander was finally appointed in 1918, it was a French officer, Field Marshal Ferdinand Foch, who got the job.

After 1918, France's attempts to compensate for the loss of its Russian ally by setting up the so-called Little Entente were a complete failure. Twenty years later, its industrial potential in relation to Germany had deteriorated slightly so that the balance now stood at 1:2.4. Much more serious than this shift—if a shift it was, for such figures are notoriously unreliable—was a changed mentality. In 1914, the French army had marched into battle under the twin mottos of *élan* and *furor franciscus*. By 1939, influenced partly by pacifist propaganda and partly by the belief, in the words of Field Marshal Henri-Philippe Pétain, that 'fire kills', it had adopted an almost purely defensive strategy based on the famous Maginot Line.[20] Perhaps the term 'strategy' itself is inappropriate, given that all the army did, or apparently was capable of doing, was to cower in its fortifications and tremble with fear. The casualties France suffered in the First World War—which, on a per capita basis, were much heavier than the German ones—as well as a certain spiritual malaise probably contributed to this. Not for nothing was Jean-Paul Sartre's book *Nausea* published just a year before hostilities broke out.[21] Whatever the cause, the outcome was the 'strange defeat' of 1940, as it has been called.[22]

Britain

In both world wars, France's principal ally, without which it might not have survived as a 'great power' and perhaps not even as an independent country, was Britain. As the Fashoda Incident of 1898 reminded people, since 1700 or so the two countries had been enemies at least as often as they had been friends. However, by the time war broke out in 1914, things had undergone a considerable change. Though no formal treaty bound Britain to any other power, the build-up of German naval power had driven London into the arms of Paris. As had been the case at least since Henry VIII in the first half of the sixteenth century, it was one of 'perfidious Albion's' principal goals, perhaps its most important goal of all, to prevent the Continent from falling under the sway of a single power. As had been the case at least since then, the way to accomplish this was to form an alliance with some kind of Continental 'sword'.

Meddling in Continental affairs is one thing, looking after one's own existence, another. Smaller than three of the four powers discussed so far, Britain is an island off the European coast. Densely populated, for several centuries before 1914 it had been unable to feed itself and was compelled to import food as well as many different kinds of raw materials. The decision to switch the Royal Navy from coal to oil, which was made by Winston Churchill in his capacity as Lord of the

Admiralty just a few years before the First World War, increased this dependence still further;[23] the growth of motor transport during the years 1919–39 was to make oil absolutely indispensable. All this made Britain even more dependent on control of the sea lanes, and more determined to maintain that control at any cost, than it had been in earlier times.

Under such circumstances, it was inevitable that the navy should retain its traditional position as the senior service—to the navy goes the gravy, as the saying went. In both world wars, it proved itself one of the greatest fighting organizations the world has ever seen: tough, resourceful, determined, and courageous. In both world wars, it kept a strong enough force always at hand, mainly at Scapa Flow, to make sure that the Germans would not even try to invade. In both, it kept open the empire's communications, though in 1939–45 in particular it was a close call. It also imposed a blockade on Britain's main enemy, Germany, though this worked considerably better in 1914–18 than it did in 1939–45, when Hitler controlled a much greater part of the European continent than the Kaiser had.[24] In both world wars, the centre of gravity was the Atlantic Ocean, where German submarines did their utmost to sink more British and Britain-bound ships than their enemy, and later their enemies, could build.

British control of the sea also enabled the country to do what its enemies could not; in other words, send its armed forces to fight at whatever place around the world where, in its leaders' opinion, the enemy might be damaged and there were pickings to be had. While it was attempted during both world wars, on the whole this strategy, which has a centuries-long history of using the opportunity provided by a continental conflict to take away other people's colonies, worked considerably better in the First World War than in the Second. Indeed, it could be argued that, had Britain forfeited its empire in 1945 in the same way as Italy did, it would have saved itself no end of trouble. Nevertheless, in both world wars, the most important theatre was clearly France. But whereas the British army in France maintained itself throughout the four years of the First World War, in the Second World War it was defeated almost as soon as serious fighting got under way in the spring of 1940 and had to be evacuated from Dunkirk.[25]

This early defeat had very serious strategic consequences. It cost the British their only real ally as well as their foothold on the Continent; with Germany in a much stronger position than it had ever been in the First World War, it became very questionable whether there was *any* method by which they could wage the conflict and emerge victorious. To make things worse—or, depending on one's point of view, better—from Churchill down, few people in Britain had any wish to repeat the experience of 1914–18, with its trench warfare and horrendous casualties. The outcome was constant attempts, lasting from 1940 to 1944, to find 'soft spots' where the British army, transported and supplied by the navy, could inflict more damage on the enemy than the enemy could inflict on them. This line of reasoning led first to the abortive attempt to invade Norway so as to cut off the supply of nickel from Norway in April 1940, then to the equally abortive attempt to assist Greece, in February-April 1941, then to the invasion of north-west Africa in late 1942, and then to that of Italy in mid-1943; had it been up to Churchill, British and American forces would have invaded the Balkans too. The strategy made the British operate on external lines, whereas their enemy could rely on much shorter internal ones. No wonder that, on the whole, it was but a mediocre success.

During the First World War, Britain, thanks to the fact that it was never in danger of being occupied, its command of the sea, and its financial strength, had been the real hub of the Entente. Not so during the Second, when, facing bankruptcy, it was increasingly overshadowed by its much more powerful Soviet and American allies. The longer the conflict, the clearer it became that, fighting side by side with these two behemoths, Britain's days as a first-class imperial power were numbered. By 1944, the country was chock-a-block with American troops—'overpaid, oversexed, and over here', as the natives used to say. With every additional US division and squadron of aircraft, with every Soviet success in rolling back the German tide, its role in helping determine Allied strategy as a whole declined. By 1945, wits had begun calling the country 'Airstrip I'. This was exaggerated, to be sure, but not by very much.

Russia (the Soviet Union)

In both world wars, standing at the opposite pole from Britain was its large ally Russia (the Soviet Union). Whereas Britain was democratic, Russia (the Soviet Union) was autocratic. Whereas Britain, 'the whale', was a naval power, Russia (the Soviet Union), 'the bear', was a land power above all. British manpower was always limited and used with relative care, though this was much more evident in the Second World War than in the First. By contrast, Russian (Soviet) manpower was unlimited or seemed to be; in both 1914–18 and 1939–45, it was often squandered in the worst imaginable ways.

Starting in 1893, Russia had been allied with France. Straddling two continents, its chief objective in Europe was to maintain the status quo in the Balkans and the Dardanelles and extend its influence over them if possible. At the same time, it also found itself competing with Japan in the Far East. In July 1914, Russia was the second power to mobilize after Austria-Hungary did. Faithful to his commitments, the Tsar launched his forces at his ally's enemies, that is, Germany and Austria-Hungary, as soon as he could and perhaps even sooner than he should have. Though Russia's armies were badly defeated at the battles of Tannenberg and the Masurian Lakes, it is just possible that the pressure they exerted on Germany's rear ruined the latter's chances of taking Paris and, perhaps, putting a quick end to the war almost before it had even begun. When Turkey opened hostilities in November of the same year, Russia found itself engaged in a war on three fronts: one against Germany, one against Austria-Hungary (over which its armies continued to win victories until 1916 inclusive), and one against the Ottomans in the Black Sea and the Caucasus.

Like Italy and Austria-Hungary, Russia was industrially ill-prepared for war.[26] Like Britain, it relied on enormously long lines of communications. Accordingly, instead of making the best of its internal lines, in effect it found itself waging three separate wars while at the same time having to keep an anxious eye on the Far East. Poorly commanded and manned by hordes of conscripted, often illiterate, peasants, Russia's armies turned out to be no match for the Germans; whenever the two sides met, the outcome for Russia was heavy defeat. The situation was made even worse by constant shortages of weapons, spare parts, and supplies of every kind. In the end, owing partly to these factors, partly to extraordinarily high desertion rates, and partly to the October Revolution and the civil war that followed it, Russian military power collapsed.

In 1941, as in 1914, Russia (the Soviet Union) possessed the world's largest armed forces.[27] Some of the weaknesses that had done so much to bring the country to its knees during the First World War had been corrected. The government was much stronger; educational standards had improved markedly; and the country now possessed an enormous, if often not very sophisticated, military-industrial base capable of turning out very large numbers of serviceable weapons. Governed by Stalin, this colossus was ready for expansion and had already annexed eastern Poland, parts of Finland, the Baltic states, and northern Bukovina. Not content with this, in his conversations in Berlin in November 1940, Stalin's foreign minister, Molotov, made no bones of the Soviet desire to dominate the straits, both the Dardanelles and those of Denmark.[28] Some authors have argued that, at the time Hitler attacked him on 22 June 1941, Stalin was within weeks, perhaps less, of launching his own offensive against Germany.[29] That is probably exaggerated; on the other hand, had the war between Hitler and Britain, perhaps joined by the United States, gone on, and had Germany shown signs of weakness, sooner or later Stalin would probably have stabbed it in the back.

When it came, the German attack quickly exposed Soviet shortcomings. The most important of them was probably a clumsy command system—Soviet middle-ranking officers did not have nearly as much freedom of action as their German counterparts, and probably would have been incapable of using it even if they had been granted it. Also, much Soviet military equipment was not really up to par. For months on end, disaster followed disaster; probably no other country in history has sustained such blows and survived them. Strategically, it was a question of mobilizing every man, every woman (though few women actually fought at the front), every piece of equipment, and every industrial plant to throw them at the enemy. Fighting a 'total' war par excellence, the Soviets, assisted by the sheer size of their country, were able to mobilize unprecedented numbers of men and *matériel*.[30] These they used to deliver a series of increasingly powerful blows at the enemy. As Soviet commanders gained experience, their style of waging war became more and more sophisticated. Yet the Red Army never achieved quite the finesse displayed by the Wehrmacht at its best; as a result, though it could take the credit for three out of every four German troops who lost their lives in the conflict, its own casualties were enormous.

Listening to Truman tell him of the atom bomb at Potsdam, Stalin was convinced that it was aimed at him as much as at the Japanese.[31] He therefore sent his legions to invade Japanese-occupied Manchuria while the going was good. For a few days, Stalin's commanders did as they pleased, storming forward at a pace not exceeded by any general since Alexander the Great. Thus, they proved, if proof was still needed, that the Soviet war machine had overcome its difficulties and become second to none, a position it would maintain throughout the coming cold war.

The United States

In both world wars, the United States was the only belligerent that was never occupied, whose territory was never invaded, and whose capital was never bombed.

Compared to the size of its population, it also suffered the smallest number of casualties by far. In part, this extraordinarily favourable balance was due to the foresight shown by its leaders, who, to the extent that it was their choice, only entered the conflict when the other belligerents were approaching exhaustion and the tide was turning. To a greater extent, though, it resulted from America's unique geographical position as a global island.

As no less an enemy of the United States than Adolf Hitler once said, the very idea of mounting an invasion across the Atlantic Ocean could only occur to a disturbed military imagination.[32] Both in 1914 and in 1941, it was not the United States that started the war. Both times, to use a phrase coined by the famous anthropologist Margaret Mead, it displayed its character as the 'chip on the shoulder nation'. By this she meant that, although Washington DC did not initiate hostilities, it did challenge, some would say almost force, the other side to attack it first. In 1914, its chosen instrument for this purpose was the assumed right to provide the Entente, Britain in particular, with all it wanted in terms of money, raw materials, equipment, and weapons; in 1941, in addition to escorting British convoys across the Atlantic and firing at German submarines that tried to interfere with their progress, the United States pressed Japan to the point where the latter could only choose between starting a shooting war or the abject surrender of all its conquests since 1937. Surely, some would condemn America for its hypocrisy; yet the policy had the advantage of gaining and keeping the moral high ground. In a democracy, where everything depends on the population's willingness to join the colours and fight, the importance of doing so cannot be overestimated.

In both 1917 and 1941, the United States, while already in possession of a very powerful navy, did not at first have ground forces to match its huge resources. Accordingly, in both 1917 and 1941, its first task was to mobilize those resources. So gigantic was the task that, in 1917–18, the enemy collapsed and the war was brought to an end before it could be completed. Thus, America's most important contribution to the victory over the Central Powers was the economic muscle it provided as well as the million and a half or so men it sent to Europe. Arriving, those men were equipped mainly with French arms; however, they came too late to intervene in the decisive battles of March-May 1918. After the Armistice, the United States was the only one among the victorious powers that did not seek territorial aggrandizement. All it received were a few islands in the Pacific; nevertheless, after 1919, nobody in his sound mind should have misunderstood the country's ability to build and use a gigantic war machine if so required.

In 1941, the same task—building up military power and transporting it to the places where it could be used—was even more difficult. Yet in the end it was accomplished even more successfully. As President Eisenhower once put it succinctly, America's greatest advantage was Detroit.[33] Detroit and its sister concentrations of industry in New England, on the West Coast, and, increasingly, in Texas enabled the United States to out-produce everybody else. To return to the above-mentioned figures pertaining to the industrial potential of the powers, the United States, at 3, was bigger than its two main allies, Britain and the USSR, combined. It even came within measurable distance, 3:3.3, of equalling all four other main powers together. As the war went on and the Axis Powers grew weaker, if anything the US advantage increased until, in 1950, its gross national product exceeded that of the next-largest power, the USSR, by a factor of more than 3:1. It also exceeded that of the USSR, Britain, France, West Germany, Japan, and Italy combined.[34] Not only was Washington able to supply its own forces with a flood of weapons and equipment greater than anything in history before or since, but it used Lend-Lease to support its allies too.[35] To focus on one small detail only, whenever Stalin or his magnates flew, or prepared to fly, from one Soviet city to another, their favourite means of transport were American-built DC-3 passenger aircraft.[36]

Having been forced into the struggle by Japan's attack on Pearl Harbor on the one hand and Hitler's declaration of war on it on the other, America's first problem was to decide which of these two fronts should be given priority. Early on, the decision was taken to focus on the Atlantic and Germany first; in the event, it turned out that the United States could mobilize more than enough men and resources to wage two large wars across two huge oceans at once. On both fronts, the US strategy was to substitute machines and firepower for manpower. As the relatively small number of casualties suffered shows—just 300,000 dead, incomparably smaller than that of the USSR, Germany, and Japan, and proportionally about a third as large as the British figure—the strategy worked. In Europe, where its main instrument consisted of massive, recently established, ground forces, the US military performance was fairly conventional and, compared to the brilliant German campaigns of 1940–1, fairly mediocre. In the Pacific, where it relied on an increasingly effective combination of aircraft, surface ships, and submarines, its performance gradually improved until it got to the point where it became very good indeed. Even so, the war had to be ended by dropping two atom bombs on Japan—not because it could not have been done otherwise, but in the hope of saving casualties, shortening the war, and teaching Stalin a lesson all at once.[37]

Japan

Finally, Japan. Except for taking over some German possessions in Asia and the Pacific, Japan did not participate in the First World War. By contrast, its role not only in conducting but also in originating the Second World War was considerable, and indeed it could be argued that the train of events that led to the latter was started by the Japanese occupation of Manchuria in 1932. Of all the major belligerents, it was Japan that developed the worst—one is tempted to say most idiotic—strategy. By the second half of 1941, that strategy had created a situation where, in one way or another, it was at loggerheads with all its most important neighbours: China, Britain, and the United States. Only with the Soviet Union did it have a non-aggression treaty; yet given that, as recently as 1939, the two countries had fought a war over their border in the Far East, to trust that Stalin would not break the treaty as soon as it suited him was preposterous. To make things worse still, Japan's allies—Germany and poor little Italy—were so far away as to rule out almost any form of effective economic and military cooperation.

Given the enormous and well-known difference in industrial potential between Japan and the United States, strategically speaking, for the former to attack the latter was an act of madness. If it nevertheless took the gamble, then this was because its rulers, most of whom were high-ranking officers, had convinced themselves of their own forces' qualitative superiority. Japanese troops, they believed, were determined to fight and die; 'Western' ones, they thought, were soft and rooted in even softer civilian populations.[38] To the extent that the generals had any strategy at all, it seems to have consisted of invading and occupying as many foreign countries and islands as possible. The countries, most of them located in South-East Asia, were supposed to provide Japan with raw materials and oil, of which it was desperately short. The islands, most of them in the Pacific Ocean, were supposed to constitute a sort of outlying barrier to protect it against American counterattack. The entire gigantic complex, stretching over millions of square miles, was to be tied together by the Imperial Japanese Navy and protected by the Imperial Japanese Naval and Army Air Forces.

To the extent that its troops fought like men possessed—towards the end of the war several thousand of them even mounted specially built aircraft and, turning themselves into human bombs, hurled those aircraft at Allied warships—the Japanese commanders got things right. To the extent that even the most determined fighters were no match for Allied firepower, though, they merely took numberless unnecessary casualties. After mid-1942, following its defeats at Coral Sea and Midway, Japan was left without any strategy at all. Engaged in war on many fronts, all that the generals and their armed forces could still do was to try and hold onto their newly acquired empire at all costs, however great the odds. This they did, often to the world's amazement. Yet even so, they had to watch the ring closing irresistibly on them.

While the US Navy imposed a blockade and brought Japan to the edge of starvation and social chaos, the US Army Air Force bombed its cities. Even before atomic weapons entered the picture, it succeeded in killing perhaps 1 per cent of Japan's entire population and rendering another 10 per cent or so homeless.[39] In the end, the Americans, by dropping two atom bombs on Japan and giving Emperor Hirohito and his paladins the excuse they needed 'to endure the unendurable and suffer what is insufferable',[40] probably did the country a favour. This is because the bomb, for all its tremendous horrors, brought the war to an end before the planned Allied invasion, which would have resulted in vastly greater casualties still.

DIFFERENCES

Having got this far, what were the most important differences between the two world wars? We have seen that the coalitions fighting one another, though in some respects similar, were not the same in both cases; there is no point in repeating this discussion here. Instead, I shall focus on two factors, both military. Being military, they are by definition less important than the politics of which they are supposed to be the continuation.

The first factor I have in mind is the role of armoured formations. Large numbers of tanks had been produced and used during the First World War, especially by the Allies. As the conflict approached its end, their importance was growing all the time. During the years that followed, while all countries continued to develop armoured formations, from 1933 on it was the Germans who took the lead. Their objective was to endow the forces with sufficient mobility to turn them from siege engines into something akin to the cavalry, both heavy and light, of old. Guided by the likes of General Heinz Guderian, in this endeavour they succeeded beyond their wildest dreams.[41]

Come the campaigns of 1939–41, and the Wehrmacht's Panzer divisions proved their superiority over all the rest. In a series of brilliant operations that have few equals in history, they easily smashed their enemies, forcing the latter to copy them.[42] Their success, and later that of their Soviet, British, and American opponents, created a situation where the fronts, instead of being stationary as had been the case in 1914–18, were often fluid. This was most evident in France, Russia, North Africa, and north-western Europe; less so in Italy, where the difficult terrain impeded large-scale armoured operations.[43] Yet in some respects the change was illusory. The logistic requirements of armoured formations were two to four times larger than those of their infantry predecessors. This greatly limited the distance the formations in question could advance before stopping and waiting for the railways to catch up. Depending on the state of the roads, the amount of motor transport available, traffic discipline, and similar factors, by and large their maximum range was about 200 miles.[44] Early in the war, 200 miles proved sufficient to bring down countries such as Poland, the Low Countries, France, Yugoslavia, and Greece. Later on, they did not prove sufficient to do the same to huge, continental-size powers in the form of the USSR and Germany itself.

The other factor that distinguished the two wars from one another was the role played by air power. To be sure, air power had been introduced even before 1914. It was used in the war between Italy and Turkey as well as during the Balkan wars. Its importance in the First World War was considerable.[45] By the time that conflict ended, one belligerent or another had attempted almost all the various missions air power is capable of carrying out. At times, this was done on a very large scale indeed. About the only exceptions were air transport and airborne operations. Even these tasks were clearly envisaged by some of the officers of the period, though the available aircraft were not yet sufficiently capable of carrying them out. During the inter-war years, the speed with which the technology of air power advanced almost certainly exceeded that of developments on land and, even more so, at sea. As a result, when war broke out again in 1939, the role of air power was destined to be much greater than it had been in 1914–18.

Used over land, the most important roles of air power consisted of air-to-air combat, close support, interdiction, 'strategic' bombing, transport, and mounting airborne operations, employing either paratroops or gliders behind the enemy front. Used at sea, its principal roles were air-to-air, sea-to-sea, air-to-sea, and sea-to-land combat (what was later called 'power projection'), escorting convoys, anti-submarine warfare, and mining operations. Depending on geographical circumstances, industrial capacity, organization, and doctrine, different belligerents put different emphases on these roles. For example, island nations such as Britain, the United States, and Japan naturally invested very great resources in naval air power, both land- and carrier-based. By contrast, land powers such as Germany and the Soviet Union only did so to a much more limited extent, and indeed the German failure to build up a proper naval air arm became one of the principal reasons why the attempt to starve out Britain by means of submarine warfare did not succeed. Neither the Soviet Union nor Japan ever developed a true 'strategic' bombing force. Britain and the United States did so, putting their forces to use first against Germany and then against Japan with such effect as to turn their enemies into seas of rubble. Having decided to put most of its resources into fighters, close-support aircraft, and light bombers, Germany did not really have a 'strategic' bomber force suitable for bringing its enemies to their knees. During the Blitz, this fact did not deter the Luftwaffe from pressing ahead and trying its hand in this game. Fortunately for the world, it failed.[46]

CONCLUSIONS

The more time passes, the clearer it becomes that, for all the differences that separated them, the two world wars were, in reality, but two parts of a single protracted struggle. Both wars, as we saw, were waged by states against one another. Both were total in the sense that they were waged on the basis of all available resources—military, economic, technical, and scientific—and, especially in 1939–45, in disregard of the difference between front and rear. In both, the defence ultimately proved stronger than the offense, with the result that, after the first few weeks, months, or years, there developed a vast struggle of attrition which was ultimately decided in favour of the side with the greater resources at his disposal. A struggle of attrition meant that, in 1939–45 as in 1914–18, the side that won was the side that commanded the sea and was thus able to husband and transport resources from all over the world to where they were needed.

At the time it got under way in 1914, the First World War represented the latest round in a long series of 'great power' conflicts that went back all the way to the Treaty of Westphalia in 1648 and, in some ways, even as far as the middle of the sixteenth century. At the time it ended in 1945, the Second World War represented both the climax of those conflicts and their end. During the six-and-a-half decades since 1945, there have been no occasions when first- or even second-rate powers engaged in major hostilities against one another. To put it in a different way, the Second World War alone cost the lives of perhaps 2 per cent of the human race as it then was. Nothing similar has taken place since; we must hope that nothing similar will take place in the future either.

In my view, the principal, indeed almost the only, cause behind the change is the introduction and subsequent proliferation of nuclear weapons.[47] To echo the greatest nuclear strategist by far, Thomas Schelling, nuclear weapons have cut the link between victory and survival. In a nuclear world, it is quite possible, indeed probable, that the 'victor' would suffer as much destruction as the loser.[48] Under such circumstances, war between nuclear-armed states has ceased to make sense. Conversely, humanity has long reached the point where every state worth its salt—and quite a few that are not worth their salt—are capable of joining the nuclear club. These developments have relegated large-scale inter-state warfare, of which the First and Second World Wars formed the culmination, to the dustbin of history. There, it is to be hoped, it will forever remain.

NOTES

1. The story originates with Winston Churchill, who attributes it to a conversation between Stalin and the French foreign minister Pierre Laval that allegedly took place in 1935; see W. S. Churchill, *The Second World War*, i (London, 1948), 105.
2. M. van Creveld, *The Transformation of War* (New York, 1991), 33–62.
3. C. von Clausewitz, *On War*, ed. M. Howard and P. Paret (Princeton, 1976), 89. It is only fair to add that not everyone accepts my interpretation of this passage.
4. H. Jacobsen and J. Rohwehr, *Decisive Battles of World War II* (New York, 1965); and B. Young (ed.), *Decisive Battles of the Second World War* (London, 1967).
5. Calculated on the basis of P. Kennedy, *The Rise and Fall of the Great Powers* (New York, 1989), 201, table 17.
6. See R. Chickering and S. Foerster (eds), *Great War, Total War* (Cambridge, 2000).
7. S. S. Montefiore, *Stalin: The Court of the Red Tsar* (New York, 2003), 502.
8. For example, even in 1918, while millions of men were wearing uniform, almost two-thirds of Britain's workforce was male; see A. W. Kirkaldy, *Industry and Finance: War Expedients and Reconstruction* (London, 1921), vol. e, sect. 1.
9. On the role of women in 1914–45, see M. van Creveld, *Men, Women and War* (London, 2001), 126–48.
10. For 1914–18, see P. G. Halpern, *A Naval History of World War I* (London, 1994); and for 1939–45, R. Hough, *The Longest Battle: The War at Sea, 1939–1945* (London, 2003).
11. For a good example of how things worked and did not work and could have worked and should have worked, see J. Corum, 'The Luftwaffe and its Allied Air Forces in World War II and the Failure of Strategic and Economic Cooperation', *Air Power History* (Summer 2004), 6–19.
12. For some of the factors that made for German qualitative superiority in the First World War, see D. Showalter, 'From Deterrence to Doomsday Machine: The German Way of War, 1890–1914', *Journal of Military History*, 64/3 (July 2000), 679–710. For the Second World War, see M. van Creveld, *Fighting Power: German and US Army Performance, 1939–1945* (Westport, CT, 1982).
13. The most detailed exposition of 'blitzkrieg' as a strategy remains A. Milward, *The German Economy at War, 1939–1945* (London, 1965). For the opposite view, see J. Mosier, *The Blitzkrieg Myth* (New York, 2003).
14. For some calculations to this effect, see N. Ferguson, *Der falsche Krieg: Der Erste Weltkrieg und das 20. Jahrhundert* (Stuttgart, 1998), 307–10.
15. From 1939 to 1945, the share of the ground forces in the Wehrmacht declined from 84 to 67 per cent; van Creveld, *Fighting Power*, 66, table 7.1.
16. N. Stone, *The Eastern Front, 1914–1917* (London, 1975), 121.
17. See A. Répaci, *Da Sarajevo al 'maggio radioso': L'Italia verso la prima guerra mondiale* (Milan, 1985).
18. The latest account is A. Monticone, *La battaglia di Caporetto* (Udine, 1999).
19. On these efforts, see D. Stevenson, 'French Strategy on the Western Front, 1914–1918', in Chickering and Foerster (eds), *Great War, Total War*.
20. On the pacifist propaganda, see M. L. Siegel, *The Moral Disarmament of France: Education, Pacifism, and Patriotism, 1914–1940* (Cambridge, 2004); and on the Maginot Line, see J. M. Hughes, *To the Maginot Line* (Cambridge, MA, 2006).
21. J.-P. Sartre, *Nausée* (Paris, 1938).
22. M. Bloch, *Strange Defeat* (Oxford, 1949).
23. See G. Gareth Jones, 'The British Government and the Oil Companies, 1912–1924', *Historical Journal*, 3 (1977), 642–54.
24. See A. Offer, 'The Blockade of Germany and the Strategy of Starvation, 1914–1918', in Chickering and Foerster (eds), *Great War, Total War*.

25. Among the endless accounts, see B. Bond, *France and Belgium 1939–1940* (London, 1979).

26. See Stone, *The Eastern Front*, 144–64, 194–211.

27. For a discussion of its order of battle, see A. Seaton, *The Soviet Army, 1918 to the Present* (New York, 1986), 113–16.

28. See *Documents on German Foreign Policy*, ser. D, vol. ix (London, 1956), nos. 326, 328, 329, 348.

29. See V. Suvorov, *Icebreaker: Who Started the Second World War?* (New York, 1990).

30. Almost twice as many men passed though the Red Army as through the Wehrmacht, the second-largest force; for the figures, see V. Suvorov, *Den-M* (Moscow, 1994), 476; and B. Mueller-Hillebrand, *Das Heer*, 3 vols (Darmstadt, 1954–69), iii. 253.

31. Montefiore, *Stalin*, 502.

32. *The Speeches of Adolf Hitler, April 1922–August 1939*, ed. N. Baynes, 2 vols (London, 1942), ii. 1650.

33. A. P. N. Edrman, "War No Longer Has Any Logic Whatever": Dwight D. Eisenhower and The Thermonuclear Revolution', in J. L. Gaddis, P. Gordon, E. May, and J. Rosenberg (eds), *Cold War Statesmen Confront the Bomb: Nuclear Diplomacy since 1945* (Oxford, 1999).

34. Kennedy, *The Rise and Fall of the Great Powers*, 369, table 36.

35. For the achievements and limitations of Lend-Lease, see A. Milward, *War, Economy and Society, 1939–1945* (Berkeley, 1979), 50–2, 71–3, 272–3, 351–2.

36. Montefiore, *Stalin*, 412, 425, 463, 496.

37. The most detailed recent account is S. J. Walker, *Prompt and Utter Destruction: President Truman and the Use of Atomic Bombs against Japan* (Chapel Hill, NC, 1997).

38. For what passed as Japanese strategy, see H. P. Wilmott, *Empires in the Balance: Japanese and Allied Pacific Strategies to April 1942* (Annapolis, MD, 1983).

39. For some figures on Japanese losses, see J. W. Dower, *War without Mercy: Race and Power in the Pacific War* (New York, 1986), 297–300.

40. The text of the imperial surrender, broadcast on 15 August, is available at <http://en.wikisource.org/wiki/Imperial_Rescript_on_Surrender>, accessed 17 February 2011.

41. On the rise of armoured forces in the inter-war period, see M. R. Habeck, *Storm of Steel: The Development of Armor Doctrine in Germany and the Soviet Union, 1919–1939* (Ithaca, NY, 2003).

42. On the way it was done, see C. Messenger, *The Blitzkrieg Story* (New York, 1976).

43. See D. Graham and S. Bidwell, *Tug of War: The Battle for Italy, 1943–1945* (New York, 1986).

44. See M. van Creveld, 'World War I and the Revolution in Logistics', in Chickering and Foerster (eds), *Great War, Total War*, 69–71.

45. Much the best work on this subject is L. Kennett, *The First Air War* (New York, 1991). See also J. Morrow, *The Great War in the Air* (Washington, DC, 1993).

46. The best work on the use of air power in the Second World War remains R. J. Overy, *The Air War, 1939–1945* (London, 1980).

47. See, most recently, M. van Creveld, *The Culture of War* (New York, 2008), 270–89; for a different view, see J. Mueller, *The Remnants of War* (Ithaca, NY, 2004).

48. T. C. Schelling, *Arms and Influence* (New Haven, 1966), 18–26.

11

The Nuclear Age and the Cold War

Colin S. Gray

INTRODUCTION

Is nuclear strategy an oxymoron? Was the great cold war between the United States and the Soviet Union just another historical example of great power antagonism and competition? And how did the answers to these distinctive questions interact, both at the time and now with a little historical perspective? It is my working hypothesis that the subject of this chapter is the same in nature as every other case study examined in this book, notwithstanding the nuclear revolution. My subject is not nuclear strategy; rather it is strategy. The fact that it is judged by a massive consensus to be strategy-defined by a particular weapon technology must not be permitted to mislead. The *Schwerpunkt* of this story is the strategic rivalry of two superstates that came to be armed, indeed over-armed, with weapons that were eventually as near absolutely potent in destructiveness as they were, *ipso facto*, hard if not impossible to tame with strategy.

Naturally, the course of the cold war was influenced by burgeoning nuclear realities, but the Soviet-American rivalry did not have its origins in those realities; once launched (by 1947), it was by no means wholly driven by them, either directly or indirectly. Those caveats duly granted, there is no escaping the shadow of the eponymity that a certain military technology has long secured imperially over the period 1945–91. Less inclusive dating of 1947–89 for the cold war also is readily defensible. With the small but still-valuable benefit of hindsight now exploitable, one can begin the scholarly mission of locating the Soviet-American cold war both as yet another episode in history's *longue durée*, and as a distinctive but nonetheless familiar example of strategy in action—as actual historical strategies.

So habituated did people become to casual reference to the nuclear age, and to nuclear strategy, that strategic thought and behaviour worthy of the descriptor were bound to be victims of such dominant and seemingly self-evident eponymity. The problem is that when agent and purpose are intellectually compounded in favour of the former, the generic logic of strategy is denied.[1] At least in principle, weaponry should support politics, not vice versa. As a descriptor, the adjective 'nuclear' is fair enough as a reasonable, if greatly oversimplified, characterization of the post-1945 world. However, aside from the banality of its obviousness, the 'nuclear' tag is as likely to confuse as it is to provide necessary focus for historical understanding. Although the destructiveness of nuclear weapons created what seemed to be a novel challenge to statecraft, the weapons were and could only be policy instruments, albeit admittedly somewhat contestably. The military-historical discontinuity effected by the nuclear fact did not occur in isolation, and its meaning is by no means entirely self-evident, even from the vantage point of today. Such is the purpose of this chapter: to consider the novelty and the lack of novelty in the complex strategic history of 1945–91, with particular reference to the eternal and universal function of strategy.

The plan of attack opens with identification of the important contextual factors that helped shape and give meaning to the strategies considered and arguably pursued in this forty-six-year period. From contextual conditioners and pressures, we move to a historical narrative. The narrative sets the stage for an attempt at explaining strategy.

THE CONTEXTS OF STRATEGY

It is a curse of history that historians cannot deprive themselves of knowledge—understanding is another matter—of the past, of what led to what. It matters considerably for this study whether or not one chooses to go with the flow of popular and scholarly usage and regard the cold war as a Long Peace or a Long Virtual War.[2] Possibly, one might pick none of those close variants, but choose rather to see Soviet-American or East-West relations from the mid-1940s to the end of the 1980s as simply the most recent case of intense rivalry between great powers. Admittedly, the rivalry was unusual in modern times for being essentially bipolar, rather than multipolar, and there is no denying the unique qualities of nuclear armament. However, even with those concessions made, the extraordinary great cold war of 1945–91 arguably was historically less unusual than it appeared at the time to those who were there and at extreme risk.[3] It may seem obvious to people today that because of mutual nuclear peril the cold war had to be a long peace. This was not so readily apparent to prudent political and military leaders during most of those years.

It is appropriate to identify seven categories of contextual matter: political, social-cultural, economic, technological, geographical-geopolitical, historical, and military-strategic. Unfortunately, to unpack context into seven sub-contexts is as convenient for reflective scholarly analysis as it is crucially unfaithful to historical circumstance. The cold warriors of 1945–91 were obliged to work within the framework of a single all-embracing context. Expressed graphically, the context of strategy at any time in history is best comprehended by means of a petal-patterned Venn diagram, with strategy at its centre. Referring to the 'elements of strategy', Clausewitz warned wisely against an attempt

> to try to develop our understanding of strategy by analyzing these factors [five 'types' of elements: 'moral, physical, mathematical, geographical, and statistical'] in isolation, since they are usually interconnected in each military action in manifold and intricate ways. A dreary analytical labyrinth would result, a nightmare in which one tried in vain to bridge the gulf between this abstract basis and the facts of life.[4]

In an effort not to lose the nuances in the complexity, we will identify the main contextual facts that shaped the contingent behaviour of cold war strategists.

The political context (I will drop the 'sub-' prefix henceforth, to avoid pedantry) for the grand and military strategies of the superpowers was plain enmity—antagonism—far beyond mere rivalry. Enemy identification was in all senses and forms complete by late 1950. Even though this hostility matured and became institutionalized from 1945 to 1950, it was thoroughly unavoidable.[5] The manner of expression and the particular dynamics of the hostility were very much the products of political and strategic choice, but the enmity itself was, if anything, overdetermined. At least three factors combined malignly to produce the cold war.

First, the conclusion to the Second World War left just two major state players still standing. Those states were condemned by the eternal logic of politics to be rivals or worse. Thucydides explained for all time why this had to be so, with his brilliant triptych comprising 'fear, honour, and interest'.[6] The cardinal rule of prudence in statecraft identified for each superstate only one credible worthy adversary in 1945–7.

Second, in addition to enduring anxiety over the balance of power, after 1945 the two great states still standing shared a highly ideological cast to their political cultures—only the ideologies happened to be profoundly antagonistic. Soviet and American leaders held quasi-religious political views that defined each other as deadly foes. These views could be, and were, subordinated to temporary tactical necessities, as in the few years of the not quite Grand Alliance of the Second World War. But, there was never a serious possibility that the United States and the Soviet Union would enjoy a political peace worthy of the name in their relations.

Third, on the contingent individual, group, and even broad social-cultural human level, the cold war was triggered and then driven by paranoia on the part of Stalin as a Soviet tsar, as well as by the personality of the extraordinarily mid-Western president Harry Truman. This analysis is not interested in debating who, if anyone, began the cold war. It is sufficient for our purpose to insist that Thucydides explains why the superpowers could only be enemies, with the detail of that emergence being important for historical accuracy, but not really for explanation and understanding. The point is that there was no path to a true political peace open in the mid- and late 1940s. On both sides of the Iron Curtain, after early 1947 for Americans and their friends and allies, and throughout for the Soviet Union and its dependent satraps and allies, strategists were not confused about their master political context.

The social-cultural context for cold war strategy was important, but most probably redundant. Of the elements in Thucydides's triptych, interest alone, in the form of balance-of-power anxieties, would have sufficed to guarantee Soviet-American rivalry and worse. The superstates were not rivals only because they were banner carriers for contrasting ideologies, but the cultural antagonism undoubtedly added potent fuel to the fire. Legitimizing theory, the quasi-religion of 'communism', told Stalin that the United States was a deadly enemy. Alas for clarity in education, Marxist ideology, as adapted and interpreted by its murderous Soviet disciples in the twentieth century, also informed Stalin that the leading capitalist states were lethal foes of each other.

The economic context to the cold war does not suffice to explain the courses taken competitively in strategy, but it goes a long way towards providing a credible answer to the basic question 'Why did the United States win the contest?' In truth, there is much to be said in support of the thesis that the cold war was the third great war of the industrial era, a period during which the belligerent(s) most amply blessed with material (and human) resources enjoyed an advantage in quantity that should be decisive. This somewhat simple proposition happens to be verifiably accurate enough. Imperial Germany and its allies, Nazi Germany and its allies, and the Soviet Union were each in turn defeated vitally by much larger economies.

One must hasten to advise that there was far more to the famous victories cited than just the imbalance in resources. Indeed, Germany might have won both world wars, while the Soviet Union could have enforced an awesomely complete mutual defeat. However, when all the caveats concerning the influence of wisdom, cunning, and skill in strategy—grand and military—as well as the ever-lurking role of chance, are accorded their due, there is no escaping the overall judgement that the cold war was a struggle that the Soviet Union was never likely to win, at least not by any reasonable definition of victory. America enjoyed a decisive advantage in the sources of economic strength that generated the wealth that prudent policy could, and typically (though naturally not invariably did), use to purchase superior leverage in international relations.

The scale, and especially the persistence, of the US-led Western economic competitive advantage was by no means self-evident until the 1960s, transparently obvious though it is in retrospect. Moreover, the US economic lead genuinely was under-recognized and unpredicted by Soviet policymakers. For our story, while we cannot help but be educated by some hindsight-foresight, it is necessary to attempt a useful empathy for the decision-makers of the 1940s and 1950s, in particular, who believed sincerely that the Soviet Union was well on the way to becoming truly competitive economically with the United States.

Unfortunately for Stalin's successors, strategic history, as noted already, is a Venn diagram of hugely overlapping interdependent sub-contexts. The Manhattan Project of 1942–5, and the Soviet counterpart launched in deadliest earnest under Lavrenti Beria in September 1945, yielded the dominant, indeed eponymous, theme to the grand narrative of cold war strategy.[7] The political struggle fuelled the military competition that witnessed and exploited at least three military revolutions from 1945 to 1991: nuclear, missile, and information. Strategic, tactical, and technical choices and experience mattered, but the three revolutions just cited were unavoidable. Policy and strategy had no option but to cope with the opportunities and dangers that modern science and technology provided. The superpowers could not choose to ignore nuclear, missile, or information technologies.

Because international politics inherently is competitive as well as contingent, political and military leaders needed to decide what the golden rule of prudence meant for them in the historical circumstances in which most of them found themselves. Above all others, the necessity to cope with the military-strategic challenge posed first by fission, then by fusion, weapons soon came to dominate the strategic history of the cold war. Alas for Soviet competitive prospects, America's unmatched strength in material and human resources, managed and exploited by a society committed ideologically to the virtue of wealth creation via personal initiative and risk-taking, and generally enabled by a permissive political system, could afford to invest in the technologies that built decisive grand-strategic advantage. The economic asymmetry favourable to the United States promoted, and almost effectively dictated, a technological leadership over the Soviet Union that was both broad (civilian and military) and deep. Moscow simply was outclassed, even though it did succeed in competing in niche areas well enough to promote acute American strategic anxiety as late as the beginning of the 1980s.

Geography is not the sole engine of destiny, but in its political meaning as geopolitics it is not implausibly portrayable as the most basic of the contexts of strategy. The geographical context to the cold war and its rival strategies saw the world's greatest continental power pitted against the world's greatest maritime and air power. The geopolitical cockpit of this sea/air-land struggle was peninsular Europe, most especially Germany. The overall stake in the contest was—certainly at the time was believed to be—global primacy, whatever that might mean, but the more proximate stakes were the 'Rimlands' of Eurasia. The rival centres of power literally were oceans apart (Atlantic, Pacific, Arctic), a geostrategic fact of profound significance for strategy, including nuclear strategy.

Characterized metaphorically, if unoriginally, the cold war was a contest between the tiger and the shark. The continental-size, effectively insular, US superpower strove successfully for nearly half a century to confine the mighty land power of the Soviet imperium to its Eurasian 'heartland'—to contain it well within Eurasia, not to limit it to Eurasia. Strategically in military terms, the cold war was a great duel between land-led and sea-led powers, an epic struggle overlaid by nuclear-armed air and then missile power, which in their turn were overlaid, not superseded, by the emergence of space and cyber power.

The geographical, geopolitical, and geostrategic asymmetries between the superpowers motivated and somewhat enabled each superpower to exploit its particular structural advantages to offset its disadvantages. Through four decades and beyond, the United States sought to provide compensation in technology for the vulnerability of its Rimland dependents in Europe. On the other side, the Soviet Union menaced America's friends and allies in Eurasia with its seemingly unmatchable military land power. At the tip of the Western spear for the military containment of a Soviet Union assumed to be committed to expansion was a US design in nuclear strategy always questing after the not wholly incredible range of threats that could nullify the proximity of deadly menace to the North Atlantic Treaty Organization (NATO) in Europe and Western interests in the Middle East (pre-eminently the oil of the Persian Gulf region).

The geographical, and hence geopolitical and geostrategic, stage(s) was given and stable throughout the cold war. One strategically stable exception to the broad claim just registered was the de facto strategic alliance of convenience between the United States and China in the late 1970s. In US-NATO strategic perspective, China comprised a large and useful source of distraction for Soviet land and tactical air power. Beijing did not need to read Niccolò Machiavelli or Kautilya to know that the enemy of its enemy was its friend of expediency.[8] The critical geographical context—the geopolitics and geostrategy—of the cold war was explained well enough in the classic geopolitical texts of the British geographer Sir

Halford Mackinder and the Dutch-American political scientist (based at Yale) Nicholas J. Spykman.[9] Their ideas were popular currency in the early and mid-1940s, and assuredly were familiar to the American leaders of the period.

It impoverishes (at best) understanding to analyse the cold war and its strategy in a manner essentially unconnected from its past. All events have a history, occur in history, and contribute to the future, which in its turn eventually will be history also. The political systems, societies, and military organizations that played leading roles in the lengthy drama of the cold war had their roots, and indeed many of their visible features, in the past. In the most obvious sense, the geographical stage-set for the most direct and enduring confrontation of the struggle was established by the military geography and geopolitics of Axis defeat and war termination in 1945. And the geographical facts of East-West military demarcation (most especially the Elbe) were all but conclusively predetermined by political and military decisions, and subsequent performances, in 1943–4. The most fundamental of all reasons for the Soviet-American cold war lay in the total ruin of Axis pretensions to empire in Europe (and Asia, secondarily). Arguably, the mighty European civil war that drove strategic history's mainstream from 1914 to 1945, or again contentiously just the second round in 1939–45, shaped the geopolitics, picked the leading state players and demoted or eliminated the rest, and effectively wrote the outline and more of the script for the conflict to come.

Finally, the military-strategic sub-context to the cold war was both a compounded net product of the whole context of the contest, as well as a dynamic variable supporting statecraft. Rather obviously, the meaning of this factor for analysis of strategy in the cold war was always potentially critically important as a political and strategic enabler. At all times from 1945 to 1991, there was extant and anticipated to be a particular state of military balance between the belligerents. This balance was in one sense existential, but equally, if not more, significant were perceptions of the balance and its strategic and political implications. As just one example, throughout the 1970s in America it was commonplace, if not quite mindlessly orthodox, to believe that the Soviet achievement of parity, and arguably a realistic prospect of parity-plus, in strategic nuclear forces would have consequences in Soviet policy choices unpleasant for the West. Even if the Soviet Union prudently could not directly cash strategic nuclear parity or marginal superiority in for the coin of military, or political, advantage, at the least might not competitive success serve to neutralize most of the nuclear menace that was central to NATO's strategy for war prevention, as well as for its contingent conduct should pre-war deterrence fail?

HISTORY AS USUAL

It aids understanding to segment the history of the cold war after the fashion of Caesar's Gaul, into three parts, or periods. The periods are 1945–50, 1950–62, and 1962–89/91. This periodization is far from arbitrary, but its massive inclusivities are eminently challengeable. From Germany's capitulation on 8 May 1945 to the literal disappearance of the Soviet Union on 25 December 1991, I elect to identify just three strategically 'decisive moments': the outbreak of, and US-led reaction to, the war in Korea (25 June 1950); the Cuban Missile Crisis of October (especially the 27th) 1962; and the collapse of the Soviet imperium in (June–December) 1989, an unravelling that was complete by Christmas 1991.

This periodization is expedient only for exposition. There were no great discontinuities in the course of the cold war, no matter what some histories may assert to the contrary. Identification of an alleged second cold war at the end of the 1970s and the early 1980s is unsound. History is ever a story of change and constancy, continuity and discontinuity. All happenings, anticipated or not, have origins, causes, and triggers. For example, the atomic bombs that devastated Hiroshima and Nagasaki in August 1945 were the material products of decisions and behaviours specific to the circumstances of 1942–5. But, they were also the products of a century and more of progress in physics, chemistry, metallurgy, and mathematics, *inter alia*, as were the B-29 Superfortresses that delivered them. Much as the diplomatic achievement of the incredibly complex Treaty of West-phalia in 1648 did not abruptly create the modern states system, recent orthodox teaching notwithstanding, so the cold war was not caused by some particular event or events in 1945. Even to select 1950, 1962, and 1989 as dates of exceptional significance is more problematic than typically is appreciated.

First, what do we know for certain? We know that there was a cold war between the United States and the Soviet Union that emerged slowly from the ashes of the German defeat in 1945, and that it faded precipitately when the Soviet imperium, then empire, imploded. No single mighty happening launched the struggle, and no portentous event, military or diplomatic, concluded it. Also, we can be certain that the Soviet Union lost the contest. In a vital sense the United States was victorious, in that it was the only superpower still standing as such in the 1990s. In addition, of the highest significance, we can claim with absolute conviction of our correctness that the nuclear-armed states that waged the cold war succeeded well enough in coping with the novel perils inseparable from a nuclear context.

We do not know whether the US-led West won, even though the Soviet Union definitely lost (did it fall rather than being pushed?), or why the cold war was a long peace rather than an awesomely dreadful nuclear war. It is commonplace among social scientists and historians to claim that nuclear weapons kept a 'technological peace', just as it is popular to assert that the Soviet implosion in the late 1980s was a necessary, inevitable result of its internal contradictions. It is tempting to read history backwards from outcomes to presumable causes. It is elementary to argue with complete plausibility that the cold war peace was overdetermined principally by the nuclear danger that nearly everybody who mattered (there were exceptions), everywhere, could not and did not fail to appreciate sufficiently. Despite the obvious reasons why nuclear warfare is mas-sively undesirable, and notwithstanding the internal problems and competitive disadvantages systemic to the Soviet Union and its imperium, there are good reasons to question the common-sense judgements just cited. Empires always decline, but they do not have to fall at any particular time, or for certain peacefully. The strategic logic of a nuclear-policed condition of peace (non-warfare, if not quite non-war) was never in much doubt, but policy and strategy are practical endeavours that have to be undertaken in conditions of significant uncertainty, not least about the adversary's intentions. And, need one add, strategy has to be resilient in face of friction of all kinds.[10] The possibility of an unintended, highly nuclear Third World War between East and West is apt to be judged far less probable in retrospect than it appeared at the time over four decades.

From Yalta to the Yalu

It is useless, not only for the strategically focused purpose of this work but also, far more generally, to pose the question 'Who caused the cold war?' The cold war was caused pre-eminently by the structure of world politics at the close of the Second World War, which is to say, by the post-war distribution of power. Precisely, how the conflict evolved was of course notably contingent on personalities and events.

The cold war emerged slowly, though in retrospect nonetheless inexorably, from late 1944 until December 1950.[11] To risk oversimplification, this period can be 'bookended' by the Big Three (Roosevelt, Stalin, Churchill) conference of Grand Alliance leaders at Yalta (4–11 February 1945) and the NATO Council Meeting on 18–19 December 1950. The former seemed to set the political stage for inter-Allied cooperation, though actually it achieved the reverse. The latter in-stitutionalized a US-led NATO alliance that would have a Supreme (Military) Allied Commander Europe (SACEUR)—American of course, and no one other than Dwight D. Eisenhower was a serious candidate to return to his former duty— a multinational military staff, a multinational military posture in Europe, a single strategy (though with some national opt-out aspirations), and in due course (May 1955) West German membership and military contribution of note. With the new (after 20 September 1949) Federal Republic of Germany joining NATO, the Alliance had little practical strategic option other than to provide some story for continental European defence east of the Rhine. How did it come to pass that an America that in 1945 anticipated a complete military withdrawal from Europe within two years, by the close of 1950 had so far transformed its national security strategy as to commit itself, as leader of an anti-Soviet military alliance, to indefinite garrisoning of west-central Europe? The transformation had been extraordinary yet gradual.

It is clear enough to see from today's perspective that neither belligerent sought the cold war. What happened was that American desires for a return, post-war, to a substantially militarily disengaged stance in world affairs were overtaken by a lethal combination of the eternal driving features in statecraft—which is to say again, Thucydides's 'fear, honour, and interest'—and history's ever-rich supply of contingent happenings (events).

The course of the Second World War brought the victorious and vengeful Soviet army into central Europe. That was the most dominant of strategic facts in 1945. At Yalta, the Western Big Two may have believed that they had extracted from Stalin a promise to behave respectfully towards the local political wishes of the societies in eastern Europe that his army had just conquered/liberated or was in the process of conquering/liberating. For his part, it is possible, even fairly plausible, to hold that Stalin was convinced at Yalta that his wartime co-belligerents/allies understood that the Soviet Union would behave more or less as Stalin chose in those areas that it occupied militarily. Paraphrased, Stalin may have thought he had been given a green light to turn his hard-earned military supremacy in eastern Europe into lasting political advantage.[12] Great powers tend to believe that they have a right to dominate their geopolitical neighbourhood. Stalin assuredly believed this, and it is plausible to hold that he believed that his American and British peers both understood and shared this precept. Whether Roosevelt and Churchill conceded cynically but realistically that which they were unable to prevent or reverse, we cannot know. What we do know, however, is that Roosevelt's death very early in his fourth term, on 12 April 1945, bequeathed the American presidency to a Harry Truman who, as vice-president for only eighty-two days, had not been at all privy to his principal's deeper beliefs and intentions vis-à-vis world affairs in general and the Soviet Union in particular.[13]

The advancing Soviet army misbehaved with a spectacular cruelty towards the people it was liberating. By the time of Yalta, the Soviet record in Poland and elsewhere was already thoroughly incompatible with the moral high ground upon which the Grand Alliance and its soon-to-be United Nations professed to be standing (the Atlantic Charter, signed on 12 August 1941). Churchill did not yield much in cynical opportunism to Stalin, but even he was embarrassed by Stalin's treatment of the peoples that his army was liberating from the Nazi yoke. Poland was a source of special embarrassment for London, given that its political integrity had been the occasion for Britain's declaration of war on 3 September 1939, and that quite large Polish forces were fighting with the Allies in the West. Americans, though long unfriendly to what they understood as 'communism', were vulnerable to political shock through the US domestic agency of the country's Polish immigrants, and by the reality check inescapable from thorough national immersion in the nasty business that is international politics. The shock may have been even greater because of the torrent of wartime propaganda that cynically, or naively, had whitewashed 'Uncle Joe' (Stalin). Roosevelt and Truman were eminently realistic in their tolerance of domestic American political sins and other malpractices, and were far from naive about human nature, but 1945 posed challenges to interwoven issues of moral integrity and prudential statecraft for which Americans most typically were seriously under-prepared.

Between 1945 and 1950, the two superstates drifted from a condition of uneasy and hugely incomplete cooperation as co-victors over Germany (and its allies), and then Japan, to one that could be characterized plausibly as war without direct warfare. This process of evolving antagonism beyond mere, fairly usual, great power rivalry to near-warfare was the product of some genuine misunderstandings of initiatives by both sides, and it was highly interactive.

The United States had to be taught that the Soviet Union was a deadly enemy. Also, it had to learn what kind of grand strategy would be needed if the new enemy were to be beaten or otherwise outlasted. In retrospect brilliantly, in truth probably fortunately, the Truman administration actually had won the cold war by 1949, even though the history books seek to resist such a confident, even outrageous-seeming, judgement.[14] Substantially, because of Stalin's gross errors in grand strategy and tactics, Moscow succeeded in turning an only suspicious and wary, though angrily critical, United States that was proceeding full-throttle with post-Second World War military demobilization, into the leader of a peacetime alliance (America's first such) committed to resist any geopolitical advance by Soviet influence, let alone control, around the Rimlands of Eurasia.

To Stalin, the United States was an enemy by geopolitical, ideological, and personal definition. He could not be other than committed to a struggle with the

United States, but he might, just possibly, have behaved strategically with sufficient cunning as to provide great, perhaps insurmountable, political difficulties for an America striving to mount effective resistance. Stalin had ample rationales for caution. He was hugely outnumbered in the resources that create wealth; his empire, though ultimately successful in war, had been obliged to secure a near pyrrhic victory over Nazi Germany; the new principal enemy enjoyed the strategic benefit, hopefully only temporary, of the atomic bomb; and his Marxist-Leninist ideology told him that History was on his side.

From 1944 to 1950, the Soviet Union proceeded with some caution to secure totally and then consolidate politically a strategically defensive geopolitical glacis in east-central Europe. Also, Stalin sought advantage to the south in Turkey and Iran, to which he felt entitled by virtue of victory in war and status in world politics, and with the blessing of the correct doctrine of historical change. This process of political consolidation naturally was as ambiguous geopolitically to Western observers as they found its grim practice morally objectionable. In response to what American (and British and some French) leaders believed initially was a political, but later—by 1950 certainly—also a military threat, Washington designed and implemented a grand strategy that, incredibly, stood the test of time for four decades.

Once persuaded that the Soviet Union was either an actual or a potential deadly menace, the United States (with much British urging and assistance) effected what unfolded as a three-stage grand strategy. The authorizing policy was the decision, really more of an emerging consensus than a single strategic moment of choice, to arrest what was seen as the Soviet bid for dominance in Eurasia. In 1945–7, the Truman administration slowly, but irreversibly, committed itself to the 'containment' of Soviet power and influence, a power and influence that was deemed indissolubly connected to the spread of communism. In order to pursue the policy goal of containment, US grand strategy sought so to help devastated Europe recover economically from the war that it would thereby be inoculated against political capture by the Soviet-owned and -directed communist virus. This was the grand-strategic logic behind the Marshall Plan (the European Recovery Program, ERP) launched in 1947. Congress was asked to vote $16.5 billion to restart the stalled European economic engine. In today's terms, the ERP delivered a value worth $200 billion. The ERP was a great success, no less psychologically and then politically as economically, as was intended. The ERP was launched and managed as an extraordinary anti-Soviet measure, and it did enable the authorities in central and western Europe to resist the fools' gold of communism. It is well to recall that France and Italy, in particular, seemed vulnerable in the immediate post-war years to takeover by their indigenous communist, and communist-sympathetic or compliant allied, political parties.[15]

Ironically, as is so characteristic of strategic history in all periods,[16] Stalin responded to Secretary of State Marshall's ERP by accelerating and completing his process of imperial consolidation, most especially in Soviet-somewhat-friendly Czechoslovakia. In so doing, Stalin provided the political fuel necessary to complete both American and west European threat identification. By an interactive process of move and counter-move, typically with the United States in the lead from the inauguration of the economic ERP onwards, American (and British) leaders invented the social-cultural, economic, political, and eventually the military-strategic concept of 'the West'. By December 1950, this West translated as a US-led military alliance of anti-Soviet democracies who had decided that they needed to be able to defend their national domains physically against a monstrous Soviet threat. After 1947, the most vital stimuli to the creation of the strategic West were the Soviet-organized Czech coup of 19–25 February 1948, the Blockade of Berlin (24 June 1948–12 May 1949), the first Soviet test of an atomic bomb (29 August 1949), Mao's victory in China (the new state was recognized by Stalin on 1–2 October 1949), and, last but not least, North Korea's invasion of South Korea on 25 June 1950.

By 1949 (4 April, with the creation of NATO), Stalin's endeavours to seize, hold, and exploit the geopolitical and strategic opportunity earned by victory in the Great Patriotic War had prodded the United States into erecting a containing alliance that simply outclassed the Soviet Union (even with the ambivalent assistance of a distinctly underdeveloped and dangerously independent communist China). American grand strategy in general was an outstanding success. The economic ERP enabled the political stability that would eventually enable the provision of military power. In the United States, Stalin had caught a tiger by the tail and he could neither let it go nor could he disable or kill it. Only accidental misfortune, poor statesmanship, or strategic incompetence by Americans could save the Soviet empire from ultimate defeat. But, in common with the West's erstwhile foes in imperial and then Nazi Germany, there was always the possibility that good fortune and skill might substitute for absent economic muscle.

The Korean invasion by the North triggered—actually hugely accelerated—the militarization of the West. Western reactions to the shock of the cross-border military happening enabled the US government to fund rearmament properly, with a threefold increase in the defence budget. It also yielded a context of alarm suitable for the closing of political deals with nervous European allies over plans for the revival of German military power. Such revival was politically feasible only within the safety framework of the new US-led, and -commanded, NATO alliance.

Given the outstanding, if painfully achieved, economic and then political success of US policy and grand strategy from 1945 to 1950, augmented though it was by Stalin's mistakes, it seems in retrospect that the danger of Soviet preventive military action in continental Europe ought to have been a greater source of Western anxiety than history reveals it to have been at the time.[17] Thus, in sharp distinction to the lengthy period 1950–89, although cold war history from 1945 to 1950 naturally had a military-strategic dimension, its leading edge was not military; rather it was successively economic and then political.

From Korea to Cuba

The cold war can be viewed as a protracted non-event, which means that historians of strategy can burn the midnight oil explaining why it was that direct warfare between the principal belligerents and their arrays of ally-clients did not occur. This can be portrayed as a fairly narrow military-strategic contest propelled most noticeably by a technological dynamic. Alternatively, or nearly so, the cold war can be regarded in comfortable retrospect as only a particular historical example of great power rivalry, characterized by a military-strategic dimension that quite early on all but mandated for both sides that there must be no overt direct violent clash between them. One should not even approach adoption of a dismissive approach to the cold war's novel nuclear feature, because the danger of a true multilateral catastrophe was both genuinely existential and literally incalculable.

What happened in the long peace that was the cold war from 1945 to 1989? By the historical standard of hostile behaviour, the simple answer is 'not much'. Naturally, it did not seem that way at the time.

World politics in the 1950s were dominated by the process and consequences of the retreat from empire effected often reluctantly by the erstwhile European masters of much of Asia and all of Africa. Those consequences included some real, though more often only apparent, opportunities for cold war statecraft.[18] America's near-visceral cultural-ideological antipathy towards colonialism was tested and somewhat expediently was found wanting when it came to alliance leadership. As the United States was torn between subversion and reluctant compliance with British imperialism during the Second World War, so it steered an uncertain course in the 1950s as its two major NATO-European allies, Britain and France, offered painful resistance to nationalist forces in Asia (including the Middle East) and Africa. But, although colonial devolution had some meaning for cold war statecraft in Washington and Moscow, that meaning proved to be rather less than had been anticipated. History's rear-view mirror shows us today that although the grand narrative of the cold war certainly was the dominant feature of world history from 1945 to 1989—indeed, it could effectively have concluded that history explosively—it was by no means controlling. Decolonization was happening and it proceeded for reasons that had little, in some cases nothing whatsoever, to do with the overarching East-West antagonism.

While Britain and France were submitting with more or less good grace to truly historical political forces whose advance they could only slow, not halt or reverse, the superpowers sought to come to terms with the nuclear novelty in great power rivalry. The Soviet Union chased the US atomic, then thermonuclear (1952–3), lead, with both states growing competitive nuclear arsenals of cumulatively impressive sizes. To illustrate: the United States is credited with a total atomic arsenal of some 299 weapons in 1950, to the Soviet 5; while by 1962 the respective figures had increased to 25,540 and 3,322.[19] Also, propeller-driven aircraft were replaced by jets, and jets were augmented by ballistic (and cruise) missiles. If the first nuclear revolution symbolized and demonstrated in August 1945 by Hiroshima and Nagasaki was understood to have profound strategic significance, the second, comprising the achievement of deliverable thermonuclear fusion weapons in 1952–3 (United States) and 1953–4 (Soviet Union), settled residual uncertainties over the true scope of the military-strategic discontinuity and the feasibility of military victory in nuclear war. Between 1950 and concluding with the Cuban Missile Crisis, the cold war had somewhat the character of a learning experience.

The atomic bomb was an extraordinary weapon of warfare. Its use, even its use in large numbers, could just fit, though uncomfortably, within the dominant paradigm of total industrial-age warfare which the century's history to date had bequeathed to both the West and East of the early cold war years. But hydrogen bombs, with energy yields unrestricted by science and technology, were something else entirely.

As the rival nuclear arsenals grew in the 1950s, and as the missile age layered over the still-extant air and nuclear ages, cold war statecraft had to cope strategically with its new-found military means. The political value of absolute, and arguably relative, nuclear power was unknown territory in these years. American officials in 1950 had feared that the Soviet achievement of effective atomic parity (in political terms), anticipated to be secured by 1954, would translate into a global military-strategic context that the Soviets would consider safe enough for the conduct of large-scale conventional warfare.[20] Increasingly, as each side's thermonuclear arsenal grew, it came to be recognized that nuclear warfare simply was not a viable option. This is an elementary conclusion to draw today, but it is rather less easy to grasp with suitable empathy the strategic challenge thus posed to statecraft in the 1950s. Whereas the very low hundreds of atomic bombs acquired by the United States by the late 1940s (about 170 by 1949) could have been employed in a precursor atomic campaign to a third great industrial-age world war, the same could not have been said of the US nuclear arsenal of 1960–2 vintage (18,638–25,540). Aside from the underappreciated environmental 'own-goal' problems derivative from massive nuclear use, there was the growing strategic and political problem that warfare on a large scale with the Soviet Union could not be won.

Intellectually, the problem for a deterrent strategy inherent in its ever-more robust mutuality could be solved by conceptual cleverness. Specifically, although the United States could not threaten credibly to take suicidal action, it could promise fairly credibly to take risks on the frontier of war that would leave the potential fall of the iron dice to chance. Thomas C. Schelling's brilliantly cunning theorizing thus seemed to square the circle of incompatible ends, ways, and means. The central problem that Schelling finessed and the US government chose to ignore was that American society was entirely vulnerable to enemy military action.[21]

For military-technical reasons of no great significance to this enquiry, it is at least possible, even probable, that the United States would have 'won' a nuclear war throughout this period, until at least the mid-1960s. However, and the caveats are huge, Soviet nuclear retaliation, assuming they did not strike pre-emptively, would have inflicted intolerable devastation on the United States and its European allies, and Soviet armies would have overrun a certainly (yet again) ruined NATO-Europe. A US military victory could not have so disarmed the Soviet Union that the Soviets would have been unable to effect some nuclear damage with the ragged and much depleted remainder of its forces. The concept and attempted practice of stable mutual deterrence was discovered and celebrated as the grand solution to the strategic dilemmas posed by the nuclear revolution(s). Unfortunately, though, the West had political need of a quality of strategic assistance that an apparently stable condition of mutual deterrence appeared uncertain to deliver, should the Alliance find itself *in extremis*.

That noted, the 1950s and early 1960s witnessed as much action by means of arms competition, arguably a surrogate for action, as it registered no shifts of great note on the political front. Episodically from 1958 to 1961, the Soviet Union experimented with coercive diplomacy in the form of nuclear-missile menace, keyed to Moscow's imperial political stability difficulties with its awkward dependant East Germany. The on-off-on crisis over Germany/Berlin in those years contained a genuine peril of an outbreak of warfare by misunderstanding, miscalculation, or accident. Tanks, gun barrel to gun barrel, at Checkpoint Charlie in the heart of Berlin were connected by an all-too-plausible powder trail to global nuclear war.

From Cuba to the Fall of the Wall

Over Cuba in 1962, the superpowers learnt by terrifying experience that the game of great power rivalry, even when apparently authorized by ideological inclination, if not quite command, was just too dangerous to play with their own military forces imminently in direct contact. The stakes had become too high. However, an under-answered strategic question persisted. What use were nuclear weapons? More to the point, since the weapons could neither be disinvented nor prudently retired from the arsenal unilaterally, what roles could they play in statecraft and how should the cold war's rival military machines plan contingently and responsibly to employ them? A central and inescapable conundrum for both sides was the enduring fact that while their rivalry mandated intense and multifaceted military competition, and called for military strategies for direction of the novel technologies that emerged, actual warfare could not be a live strategic option for policy. Plausible theories of military victory were vetoed physically by nuclear realities. Unfortunately, however, nuclear warfare was not at all prohibited by the course of historical events.

By the mid-1960s, the Soviet Union had succeeded in acquiring nuclear armed forces sufficient in number and diversity of delivery vehicles, and hence in a variety of deployment modes (land-based, sea-based, and on aircraft), as to preclude comprehensive and near-certain pre-launch suppression by all but the luckiest, not to say most reckless if brilliant, of American surprise attacks, and probably not even then.[22] Nuclear hazard could not guarantee the absence of political miscalculation, but certainly it encouraged a caution that was historically exceptional. The geopolitical containment perimeter remained rooted in barbed wire and concrete across central Europe, and close to the 38th Parallel in Korea. The post-colonial Maghreb and Middle East were somewhat in play between East and West, but even the open warfare in the latter between Israel and its Arab neighbours in 1956, 1967, 1969–71, 1973, and 1982 did not have much milestone significance for the great cold war. Conflict in the newly minted Third World, most especially in Vietnam, was believed to carry implications for the dominant struggle, but the connections transpired to be much less than had been anticipated. America's Vietnam War was not a proxy struggle with a Soviet, or even a Chinese, foe that prudently could not be engaged directly. It would seem to be the case that throughout the cold war the superpowers on balance may have been more manipulated for the advantage of their local dependent clients than vice versa.

Through the 1950s, the 1960s, and even the 1970s, the Soviet Union appeared, most likely even in its own optimistic net assessment, to be a worthy, if more than marginally asymmetric, adversary of the West. The consequences of Soviet limitations as a superpower competitor were delayed by the oil price rises of the early 1970s. Indeed, the Soviet Union's forward statecraft in Africa and its military modernization in that decade were financed by its gains from the global oil market. As for the course of the cold war struggle from its momentary plausible tipping point of panic in October 1962 until close of business for the Soviet Union on 25 December 1991, nothing by way of dramatic tectonic shifts occurred prior to the late 1980s. Mao's China became de facto a strategic partner of the West in the mid- to late 1970s, but its definitive geopolitical estrangement from a Soviet-led project for global influence had by then been registered for nearly twenty years. Soviet and American governments rented temporary ascendancy—rarely control—around the Asian and African Rimlands, but no political events in the 1960s, 1970s, or early to mid-1980s shifted the paradigm of the Soviet-American and East-West cold war conflict that was settled in its essentials in April 1949 with the founding of NATO.

The cold war concluded when it did, in the peaceful way that it did, because the leaders of the Soviet empire and imperium—one in particular, Mikhail Gorbachev—both recognized belatedly that their state was systemically ever more uncompetitive with the capitalist enemy and declined to resist forcibly the verdict of history rather than accept dishonourable political reorganization. Soviet arms failed expensively in Afghanistan in the mid-1980s, and embarrassingly and worryingly in Syrian hands over Lebanon in 1982. Prospectively in all military departments, presidents Jimmy Carter and Ronald Reagan's surge in defence investment, in good part exploiting Western civilian advances in information technologies, menaced every element of Soviet military power. Gorbachev sought by reform to save his Soviet inheritance, but this proved mission impossible. When the no-longer-affordable satrapies of the Soviet Union's East European imperium were told in 1989 that their political survival was strictly a domestic matter for them, the result was an accelerating and unstoppable cascade of political defection and collapse. From the Baltic republics seized by Stalin in 1939, throughout the imperium that the Soviet army had 'liberated' in 1944–5 and subsequently coerced into satrapy, the entire house of cards imploded.

Needless to say, since one must eschew determinism, the collapse of 1989–91, let alone its very largely peaceful character, was by no means predetermined. There were reasons attributable largely to relative resource disadvantages (of many kinds, quantitative and qualitative, material, ideational, and human) why the Soviet Union was always likely to lose the cold war. But, that granted, much work remained for the strategists on both sides from 1945 until 1989 to ensure that contingent disaster did not intervene to frustrate even powerful historical probabilities.

CONCLUSIONS: STRATEGY IN THE COLD WAR

This study of the cold war and the nuclear age has privileged the political plot of the cold war, especially during the early years in the late 1940s—a focus that inevitably tended to relegate military-strategic matters to a subordinate category of concern. In these concluding paragraphs, by way of contrast, the emphasis is more on the military-strategic dimension of the conflict, albeit with explicit political contextualization. The intention here is to conclude with an effort to identify the meaning of the cold war in strategic terms.

The seductions of nominalism. In common with the similar (mal)practice of reification, nominalism constructs a perception of reality that is to a degree, or more, fictional. In 1947, the eminent journalist Walter Lippmann popularized the idea that Soviet-American and East-West relations were in a condition of war without warfare that could be dignified as an abstract proper noun, 'the Cold War'.[23] The sobriquet was expedient as shorthand for a complex phenomenon. But potent ideas translated from the status of interesting propositions into claimed realities with names tend to oversimplify and mislead, as well as inform. We are so programmed in our thinking about recent history that it is a radical notion to suggest both that 'the cold war' was a severely flawed concept and that its firm authority, then and now, on balance probably impeded understanding, again both then and now.

One can object that the title 'the Cold War' was potentially dangerously misleading at the time, because while the conflict was ongoing, participants and bystanders-at-risk could not know that it would not become a hot war. Also, enculturation with the cold war paradigm was intellectually so imperial as to diminish markedly one's ability to recognize and identify those features of world affairs that were not, or at least were barely, dependants of the postulated overarching struggle. With reference to today's scholars of events from 1945 to 1989, there is much to be said in favour of demoting 'the Cold War' somewhat so that it is reduced to the still very important status of yet another of history's great power antagonisms.

The general theory of strategy is authoritative. Strategy (singular, as general theory) always plays historically as strategies (distinctly plural) that are widely variable in character. Many scholars, officials, and commentators who should know better have confused strategy's many actual characters with its enduring nature. The nuclear age did not mean that 'strategy hits a dead end',[24] only that the character of strategy suitable for polities with, and facing, nuclear armament is distinctive from the strategy appropriate to a context innocent of such weaponry. In fact, far from the nuclear dimension to the cold war's military-strategic context cancelling the relevance of the strategy function, rather was that function given a pragmatic significance higher than ever. The technologies that revolutionized great power warfare, had there been any, in the cold war decades required contemporary contextualization of the classic abstract elements of the strategic triptych of ends, ways, and means. The general theory of statecraft and strategy that lurks with variable ease of accessibility in the pages of Thucydides, Sun Tzu, and Clausewitz, for the first division of classic authors, can be demonstrated with no great difficulty to provide most of the fundamental education that strategists in the cold war needed when they sought to theorize, plan, and execute for a nuclear-shadowed strategic environment.[25]

Nuclear weapons probably contributed decisively to the cold war remaining cold. One can never prove a negative. It is not implausible to argue that the cold war superpower peace hardly needed keeping, because neither the United States nor the Soviet Union was ever strongly motivated to fight. We can never know why the cold war did not conclude with the once fearfully anticipated Third World War. Fashions in opinion have altered, as fashions must, but on balance it is plausible to argue that the nuclear revolution contributed more positively than negatively to the condition of non-war. It is worth remembering that, as recently as 1939, Britain and France chose to go to war, while Nazi Germany assuredly had risked, and was duly amply rewarded with, a fairly wide war when it chose to invade Poland. Foolishly optimistic or not, the Anglo-French alliance could devise a rational plan to defeat what they hoped was an out-resourced Germany in a lengthy armed struggle. Military victory won grand-strategically, of course, was judged reluctantly by sober and reasonable people in 1939 to be a feasible goal. The contrast with a nuclear-armed confrontation could hardly be more stark. The point certainly is not that war could not occur between nuclear-equipped states, but rather that war between them had ceased to be a reasonable and rational option for policy. The archives will never tell us whether the cold war would have turned briefly very hot were it not for sensible nuclear-related fears, but it is no great stretch to believe that those fears narrowed policy choice markedly, if not quite decisively.

A more contentious issue pertains to the quality and quantity of connection, if any, between the detailed management of the nuclear revolution by possibly interacting ideas, plans, and military postures, and the keeping of the peace. It is my most carefully considered opinion, as an erstwhile cold war theorist-warrior, that the cold war persisted and concluded as a long peace rather more by chance than by effort and cunning. A single nuclear torpedo launched on 27 October 1962 from a Soviet submarine not known by the US Navy to be so equipped could well have trumped a library of wisdom on the requirements of stable (nuclear) deterrence, to cite but one illustrative example that came alarmingly close to being actual and not hypothetical.[26]

Politics rules! With direct warfare between the principals rendered extraordinarily dangerous by the nuclear revolution, and with dependent or semi-dependent client states inclined to go off the reservation and behave unreliably, it is scarcely surprising that much of the action in the cold war took the form of a competition in armaments. So active were the so-called, though probably mislabelled, nuclear arms race, and the arms control diplomacy associated with it from 1969 (the Strategic Arms Limitation Talks, or SALT), that many contemporary officials, theorists, and commentators became more than a little confused about the relationships among ends, ways, and means. The episodic SALT process, as well as other arms control activities—one cannot accurately call every such venture 'negotiations'—were significant not, as publicly generally advertised, for their potential substantive military-strategic merits. Rather, arms control was important because there was not much other traffic in superpower political relations. In practice, SALT was about political, not meaningful military-strategic, advantage. Although both superpower governments bargained hard and long for a metric edge here or there, the strategic truth was that any such gain would be unexploitable in statecraft.

It is possible to praise cold war arms control diplomacy as a talking-shop useful for communication between enemies, but that is probably unduly generous a view. Ironically, the arms control process that may have contributed usefully to an otherwise unpromising political context on balance probably exacerbated political antagonism more than it relieved it. The technical debate over strategic arms control in the 1970s became ever more heated and accusatory. It was feared at the time in the West that even some nominal military advantage in strategic nuclear arms could encourage more adventurous foreign policy. Thus, the advent of an effective, if technically somewhat asymmetrical, condition of strategic nuclear parity, or of formal (simple metric) Soviet strategic nuclear superiority, was judged by some Americans in the 1970s to herald a period of growing peril for Western interests.

In practice, after the mid-1960s at the latest there never was a realistic prospect of either side achieving a politically exploitable advantage in the strategic arms competition. Of course, it is easier to state this judgement with high confidence today than it was then. None other than Thucydides's magic triptych of fear, honour, and interest mandated that both superpowers and their friends and allies should behave as if a politically and strategically meaningful advantage in nuclear arms might be attainable. A complacent, if well-founded, confidence in the denial of such a possibility could always be ambushed by the unexpected. Even rational statesmen are not guaranteed to be permanently reasonable. Both the political Left and Right in the West were wrong in regarding the arms race and nuclear weapons as the dominant problem for world peace. The basic problem was not military technology; instead it was the all-too-human dominance of human history. Whatever mixture of items the cold war was about, it was not about the nuclear arms race. Because politics ruled, as it always does, the arms race emerged, matured, and then faded and died for just one totally compelling reason: politics.

Three military revolutions. Nuclear weapons, ballistic missiles (which enabled the military and commercial exploitation of orbital space), and the computer, both individually and in combinations, had major consequences for grand and military strategies. Nuclear weapons, particularly when thermonuclear in character and carried by ballistic missiles, against which there was no defence, meant that pre-war deterrence as a goal was discovered to be the practicable limit of strategic ambition. Coercive nuclear diplomacy, explicit and less so, occasionally was a feature of cold war statecraft in the late 1940s, the 1950s, and the very early 1960s, but its decreasing military feasibility, in the context of a growing mutuality of technically not incredible nuclear menace, meant that it lost favour; it did not usually, and before long could not, work, given the risks to a would-be coercer.[27] However, the nuclear stalemate was never quite accepted to be such, at least not by the competing defence establishments.

Whereas the nuclear and missile revolutions cumulatively had the practical effect of denying any plausible prospect of military victory in all-out war, the third revolution cited, that inaugurated by the computer, almost certainly did carry a credible promise of delivering substantial, perhaps eventually decisive, military and economic advantage to one competitor, the United States. By way of grand-strategic competitive benefit, the information technology (IT) revolution of the 1970s and 1980s rendered the economic wealth-creating muscle of the United States in particular, and the Western world in general, massively unmatchable by an IT-challenged Soviet system. With respect to military-strategic feasibility, the IT revolution just might enable active US ballistic missile defences, while it seemed very likely to enable NATO to field smart stand-off weapons that would be able to massacre echeloned Warsaw Pact armored forces for a hundred miles and more behind the forward edge of the battle area. By the early 1980s, the Soviet military recognized that its wholesale modernization for successful land warfare against NATO on the Central Front in Germany most probably was about to be rendered obsolescent, while more distantly its US enemy might be able to defeat Soviet offensive missiles. In Europe, Soviet military mass no longer would compensate for technological deficiencies. NATO would be able to meet and defeat a Warsaw Pact conventional invasion conventionally.

This was a crisis for military strategy that could not be resolved by a systemically unreformed Soviet Union. Of course, Moscow would have the option of nuclear escalation, but the burden of leading such a perilously novel process would be on it, not, as previously, on NATO. And since the Soviet Union enjoyed no obvious nuclear or homeland defensive advantage that could be exploited at likely reasonable cost, the nuclear choice cannot have loomed as an attractive strategic future. Regarded overall, the Soviet Union was strongly competitive with the United States in nuclear weapon and offensive missile technologies in the later decades of the cold war, but its underlying economic deficiencies, keyed as they were to politics and culture, became alarmingly apparent to leading Soviet military professionals. Soviet inability to participate beneficially in the IT revolution that was gathering commercial and military pace in the 1980s proved to be a most significant nail in Moscow's imperial coffin.

Strategies, cultures, and geopolitics. Setting aside the IT revolution in the 1980s, the cold war principals shared access to a tolerably common scientific and technological menu of exploitable military options. In this important respect, as in many others, the superpowers' antagonism was reminiscent of the two world wars. The major belligerents of 1914–18 and 1939–45 shared a common technological context. Scholars of strategy have yet to engage satisfactorily with the challenge to explain wholly convincingly the relationship between strategic circumstance and strategic preference.

The 'cultural turn' in contemporary strategic studies can offer fairly plausible explanations for a rather distinctive American and Soviet-Russian 'way of war or way in defence preparation'. But such recognition of diversity among strategic cultures is apt to overemphasize differences. It is a reality of strategic history that belligerents, even only virtual military belligerents, both borrow from each other and all but cooperatively combine to produce a rather compounded strategic historical experience. The cultural-ideological antagonism between the superpowers added fuel, helped legitimize, but also adorned, the grand struggle. However, the real differences somewhat separating American (and NATO-European, which were never quite identical) and Soviet strategies were mainly all but mandated by political and hence strategic geography. Strategically approached, the cold war was a global containment effort on the part of the sole first-class superstate, which was a maritime-air, perhaps air-maritime, power, against a Eurasian continent-confined land power that was highly competitive in science, rocketry, and mass in conventional armed forces.

Since the proximate geopolitical stake was west-central Europe, with the focus on a divided Germany, the United States had to find a strategic solution to its competitive inferiority in land power in continental Europe. The history of US nuclear strategy from 1947 to 1989 is an evolving story of efforts to render credible American nuclear use options in the event of Soviet aggression on the ground. Thus it was that the US challenge always was to achieve the ability to extend deterrence over distant allies. This demand on America's military power was a political constant, as the superpower nuclear balance altered massively from a condition of US monopoly, through emerging parity, to an apparently arguable fragile parity. Strategies necessarily shifted in detail with the transformative change in military capabilities during the cold war. But after the early 1960s, there were no military shifts sufficient so to transform the military-strategic context that nuclear warfare on any scale could be judged a prospectively winnable enterprise. The military establishments of the United States and the Soviet Union would have striven mightily to wreak terminal damage upon each other, but as the doyen of American nuclear-age strategists, Bernard Brodie, sought to insist, nuclear weapons only had 'utility in non-use'.[28] Paradoxically, whatever their deeper convictions and suspicions, the military machines of both leading cold war belligerents, for want of anything better, were obliged to tilt at the windmill of a rational employment strategy for nuclear arms.

The challenge of nuclear strategy: possibly an oxymoron, but nonetheless inescapable. It is more likely than not that strategy cannot tame nuclear use by commanding, controlling, and exploiting it for worthwhile political objectives. However, for the first time in world strategic history, the cold war protagonists had no choice other than to seek to make strategic sense of a new class of weapon that was so potent in its destructiveness that it threatened to make a complete mockery of classical general strategic theory, prudence in statecraft, and ethically tolerable behaviour. Scholars have no difficulty demonstrating the improbability that nuclear weapons could have been so controlled bilaterally—not to say multilaterally—in their use to conclude the cold war explosively as to warrant description as an instrument of policy. But it is hard to deny the existential necessity for American and Soviet (*inter alia*) officials to do their best with the worst.

To be not incredible—the double negative of the litote is important—politically valuable nuclear menace had to be founded on at least some plausible appearance of actual military capability and serious contingent intent. Never in strategic history prior to the 1950s had rival polities been compelled to square the strategic circle by preparing rationally, if not entirely reasonably, to wage warfare of a character that almost certainly could have no tolerable, let alone net advantageous, outcome. Relatively attractive ideas for nuclear use by the United States, should all else fail, invariably foundered logically on the rocks of war's nature both as a duel and as a phenomenon extravagantly vulnerable to the unanticipated play of chance. For example, US-NATO aspirations for intra-war deterrence via flexibility, especially extreme flexibility, in carefully tailored nuclear use rested only on such authority as the Soviet enemy would choose, or more realistically would physically be able, to grant.[29] It takes two, and usually more, in some cooperation to shape the course of a violent duel. For more than forty years, strategic theory followed unenthusiastically, but doggedly in the wake of military capabilities that defied reasonable control by rational strategy.

Education by experience? All warfare is a learning experience for all participants, some close observers, and many interested others in the future. Because there was no nuclear, or other direct military, use during the cold war, nuclear-related strategic learning for the nuclear age had to derive more than a little from speculation. Much was learnt, albeit arguably, about warfare in a nuclear context, but knowledge of nuclear warfare itself, or even of large-scale conventional warfare between nuclear armed states, was entirely absent. The good news was so self-evident as to require no comment here, but the bad news was that poor or potentially catastrophically unsound strategic ideas and military practices most probably were adopted and persisted, with the world denied unmistakable evidence of error. Nuclear war was studied and planned during so many years, with such care and attention to fine-grained detail, and with so satisfactory an enduring (non-war) apparent consequence, that (intended deterrent) cause and (peace) effect were readily, if unwisely, identified and assumed.

Beyond almost unimaginable destructiveness in use, the mid- to late cold war nuclear arsenals have left no certain strategic knowledge for the guidance of future generations of policymakers and strategists. Would nuclear use have been controllable short of a full-scale 'exchange'? Could a 'process' of competitive coercive nuclear escalation have been either politically or technically feasible?—and how would it have been concluded?—leaving the nuclear gladiators, and the world at large, in what condition? The only accurate answer is that we do not know. Both sides developed high expertise in practicing the unilateral conduct of nuclear operations in peacetime, but because some indeterminable combination of factors kept the East-West peace, no one acquired reliable understanding of the sound practice of strategy in a war with nuclear weapons—even if such were indeed possible.

In part plausibly because of nuclear weapons, the West waged the cold war to more than a merely satisfactory conclusion courtesy of grand-strategic effect that had no need of direct and active military expression. Strategists on both sides had no practical choice other than to treat, perhaps to some degree pretend, that nuclear weapons were weapons that could be employed for worthwhile military and strategic effect. And similarly, policy and strategy on both sides could do no other than devise strategies for the contingent use of the gifts of science and industry in the form of weaponized technology.

Strategy in the cold war was usably grand, but unusable in military action between the principals. Indeed, the latter commanded a prudence in political choice that promoted an eventual decisive advantage to the far better resourced protagonist. Nonetheless, there was always some danger that contextually existential perils might leap alarmingly into acute inter-state crisis by miscalculation or the accidents of chance. Strategic historians cannot know how well the antagonistic blocs would have performed, and with what consequences, had the cold war erupted in large-scale warfare. Verdicts delivered on competing cold war military strategies will never be conclusive.

NOTES

1. See C. S. Gray, *The Strategy Bridge: Theory for Practice* (Oxford, 2010).
2. John Lewis Gaddis, a scholar who has made the cold war almost his own with a handful of important studies, was the creator of the concept of the long peace, though subsequently he wisely repudiated it. See Gaddis, 'On Starting All Over Again: A Naïve Approach to the Study of the Cold War', in O. A. Westad (ed.), *Reviewing the Cold War: Approaches, Interpretations, Theory* (London, 2001), 32; and id., *The Long Peace: Inquiries into the History of the Cold War* (Oxford, 1987), ch. 8.
3. Cold war history is a much contested field for scholarly combat, and it is certain to remain such for a very long time. Worthy efforts at balanced judgement are under way,

but they are hampered by both uneven access to archival sources and the lack of sufficient historical perspective. Signs of the times include M. P. Leffler and O. A. Westad (eds), *The Cambridge History of the Cold War*, 3 vols (Cambridge, 2010); and G. S. Barrass, *The Great Cold War: A Journey Through the Hall of Mirrors* (Stanford, CA, 2009).

4. C. von Clausewitz, *On War*, ed. and trans. M. Howard and P. Paret (Princeton, 1976).

5. In two 'long telegrams' home in 1946, an American diplomat (George F. Kennan) and a Soviet diplomat (Nikolai Novikov) explained to their respective political masters just why the other country was a permanent enemy. The American's telegram from Moscow was independently authored, the Soviet's one from Washington was most probably dictated or at least heavily supervised by higher authority. For Ambassador Novikov's telegram, see K. M. Jensen (ed.), *Origins of the Cold War: The Novikov, Kennan, and Roberts 'Long Telegram' of 1946* (Washington, DC, 1991), 'U.S. Foreign Policy in the Postwar Period, September 27, 1946'.

6. Thucydides, *The Landmark Thucydides: A Comprehensive Guide to 'The Peloponnesian War'*, ed. R. B. Strassler (New York, 1996), 43.

7. D. Holloway, *Stalin and the Bomb: The Soviet Union and Atomic Energy, 1939–1956* (New Haven, 1994), is excellent; and R. Dallek, *Harry S. Truman* (New York, 2008), 23–8, is convincing. See also M. P. Leffler, *A Preponderence of Power: National Security, the Truman Administration and the Cold War* (Stanford, CA, 1992), ch. 1.

8. Kautilya, *The Arthashastra*, ed. and trans. L. N. Rangarajan (New Delhi, 1992), 557, fig. 24: 'The Circle of States'.

9. H. J. Mackinder, *Democratic Ideals and Reality* (1919; New York, 1962); N. J. Spykman, *America's Strategy in World Politics: The United States and the Balance of Power* (New York, 1942); and id., *The Geography of the Peace* (New York, 1944).

10. See Clausewitz, *On War*, 119–21.

11. C. S. Gray, 'Mission Improbable, Fear, Culture, and Interest: Peace Making, 1943–1949', in W. Murray and J. Lacey (eds), *The Making of Peace: Rulers, States, and the Aftermath of War* (Cambridge, 2009), 265–91.

12. See S. M. Plokhy, *Yalta: The Price of Peace* (New York, 2010).

13. See C. S. Gray, 'Harry S. Truman and the Forming of American Grand Strategy in the Cold War, 1945–53', in W. Murray, R. H. Sinnreich, and J. Lacey (eds), *The Shaping of Grand Strategy: Policy, Diplomacy, and War* (Cambridge, 2011), 210–53.

14. The claim for US–Western victory by 1949 is advanced in V. Mastny, *The Cold War and Soviet Insecurity: The Stalin Years* (New York, 1996), 196.

15. The European narrative of the cold war is treated admirably in T. Judt, *Postwar: A History of Europe since 1945* (London, 2005).

16. See E. N. Luttwak, *Strategy: The Logic of War and Peace* (Cambridge, MA, 2001).

17. The severely adverse military imbalance of the early cold war years, notwithstanding the US atomic monopoly, is revealed with an almost appalling clarity in S. T. Ross, *American War Plans, 1945–1950* (London, 1996); and P. Cornish, *British Military Planning for the Defence of Germany, 1945–50* (Basingstoke, 1996).

18. See O. A. Westad, *The Global Cold War: Third World Interventions and the Making of our Times* (Cambridge, 2007), chs 1–2.

19. R. S. Norris and H. M. Kristensen, 'Global Nuclear Weapons Inventories, 1945–2010', *Bulletin of the Atomic Scientists*, 66 (2010), 77–83. The US number peaked at 31,255 in 1967, the Soviet figure at 45,000 in 1986: there was also a large decline in total megatonnage as weapon yields were reduced.

20. See the ground-breaking policy and strategy study document *NSC 68: United States Objectives and Programs for National Security*, 14 April 1950; repr. in T. H. Etzold and J. L. Gaddis (eds), *Containment: Documents on American Policy and Strategy, 1945–50* (New York, 1978).

21. See T. C. Schelling, *The Strategy of Conflict* (Cambridge, MA, 1960). By far the most satisfactory explanation of US policy and strategy for nuclear weapons, in the context of the evolving strategic theory developed for the nuclear age, is K. B. Payne, *The Great American Gamble: Deterrence Theory and Practice from the Cold War to the Twenty-First Century* (Fairfax, VA, 2008).

22. Both superpowers attended carefully, if distinctively, to the key military-technical/tactical issue of pre-launch as well as post-launch survivability of a fraction of its strategic nuclear force posture sufficient to impose unacceptable damage. Neither side planned long in advance to deploy its strategic forces triadically. But the three-way solution to pre-launch survivability, while preserving and enhancing options desirable in the war plans, was discovered to be usefully prudent by both countries. With stakes so high, the superpowers overpurchased strategic nuclear reassurance. That reassurance was restricted to confidence in the ability to strike back; it did not approach the competence to deny the enemy the ability to retaliate massively.

23. W. Lippmann, *The Cold War: A Study in U.S. Foreign Policy* (New York, 1947).

24. See B. Brodie, 'Strategy Hits a Dead End', *Harper's*, 211 (1955), 33–7; and L. Freedman, 'Has Strategy Reached a Dead-End?', *Futures*, 11 (1979), 122–31.

25. Gray, *The Strategy Bridge*.

26. See P. Ashdown, *Fate, Chance and Desperate Men: Six Studies of the Role of Chance in Twentieth Century History* (Brighton, 2009), 101–26. The US naval vessels that were harassing the Soviet submarine B-59 just outside the quarantine area did not know that it was armed with nuclear torpedoes. There is evidence that the responsible officers on B-59, who enjoyed pre-delegated release authority, disagreed on whether or not to launch a nuclear weapon at the USS *Beale*. The submarine's deputy commander, Vasily Arkhipov, won a heated argument and the torpedo was not fired. The Third World War might not have ensued—but it might.

27. See L. Freedman, *The Evolution of Nuclear Strategy*, 3rd edn (Basingstoke, 2003); and C. S. Gray, *Modern Strategy* (Oxford, 1999), chs 11–12.

28. B. Brodie, *War and Politics* (New York, 1973), ch. 9. Brodie had expressed this view as early as 1946.

29. See B. Heuser, 'Warsaw Pact Military Doctrines in the 1970s and 1980s: Findings in the East German Archives', *Comparative Strategy*, 12 (Oct.–Dec. 1993), 437–57; J. C. Hines, E. M. Mishulovich, and J. F. Shull, *Soviet Intentions, 1965–1985*, 2 vols (McLean, VA, 1995); and V. Mastny, S. G. Holtsmark, and A. Wenger (eds), *War Plans and Alliances in the Cold War: Threat Perceptions in the East and West* (Abingdon, 2006).

12

Modern Irregular Warfare: Afghanistan and Iraq

James D. Kiras

INTRODUCTION

Few words are as abused or misunderstood in discussions of contemporary conflict as the term 'strategy'. It has now become all things to all people. For example, strategy is often confused with policy, resource apportionment, and plans. Endless discussion in the mainstream press and the blogosphere has labelled as a 'strategy' the plan from General Stanley McChrystal's office for additional resources to regain the initiative from the Taliban.[1] Even the long-awaited speech by President Barack Obama on Afghanistan, delivered at the U.S. Military Academy at West Point, talked in the same breath about 'military strategies' and 'exit strategies'.[2] Perhaps the supreme abuse occurred in June 2003. In its lead story, *Jane's Defence Weekly* quoted Pentagon sources that suggested that campaign planning based on new methods and technology signalled 'the death of strategy'.[3] Five years later, that campaign planning method, effects-based operations, met an unceremonious end instead. As this chapter will make clear, the report of the death of strategy was very much exaggerated.

The profligate use and misuse of the term 'strategy' is only one symptom of this wider malady. Contemporary puzzlement regarding strategy and its relationship to the use of force reflects uncertainty and confusion about the type of wars currently being fought.

Current debate on Iraq and Afghanistan, and concerning groups of violent extremists globally, has highlighted the problems of what to call such violence. The latest terms on offer are 'compound warfare' or 'hybrid warfare', which allegedly capture the intricacies and interrelated problems of modern conflicts.[4] Proponents of hybrid warfare point to examples of sub-state groups mixing conventional attacks with irregular actions, as in the case of Hezbollah during the 2006 war in Lebanon. Others see hybrid warfare as encompassing the challenge of building capable security forces while simultaneously dealing with the interrelated problems of insurgency, terrorism, and communal conflict.[5] Still others suggest that the term 'irregular warfare' is sufficient. This umbrella term, defined as 'the use of violence by sub-state actors or groups within states for political purposes of achieving power, control, and legitimacy, using unconventional or unorthodox approaches to warfare owing to a fundamental weakness in resources or capabilities', suggests a difference in the form of warfare and the means and methods used.[6]

Critics take issue with both the adjective 'irregular' and the noun 'warfare'. They suggest, for example, that all wars are by definition 'irregular' in some respect. In addition, 'warfare' does not adequately capture what is essentially an internal struggle based on governance and popular support in which military force plays a supporting role.[7] Yet observers or even participants in contemporary conflicts are apt to view the modern wars as unlike anything previously seen. They interpret this as a clear signal that the character and even nature of war and strategy are changing. Retired British general Rupert Smith makes the case that interminable 'wars amongst the people', as opposed to wars between states that had definitive start and end points, are the norm today.[8]

This reaction to what each generation perceives as the novel conditions of its day is not unique. During the Second World War, officers within the British Special Operations Executive tried unsuccessfully to classify their missions of subversion and resistance as a distinctive 'fourth dimension of warfare' in an attempt to distinguish their organization.[9] Roger Trinquier, the French officer known for advocating a harsh approach to controlling the local population, argued in 1961 that the character of war had changed so drastically that it required an entirely different, even extreme, response.[10] What is often lost in attempts to come to grips with the 'the kind of [contemporary] war on which they are embarking' is the nature of strategy itself.[11] The idea that 'strategy at any level consists of ends or objectives, ways or concepts, and means or resources' is used here as a common vocabulary to make sense of the various contributing elements of strategy.[12]

This chapter is limited to exploring the nature and character of strategy in two contemporary conflicts: Afghanistan (2001–present) and Iraq (2003–present). Within the analysis of each conflict, a short narrative provides the necessary context for the subsequent examination of the strategy chosen and applied by various combatants. To limit the discussion, strategy is described from the perspective of a limited number of actors involved. For example, one focus of the Afghanistan section is on the strategy of the Taliban. Although al-Qaeda is an actor in the country and region, time and space simply do not permit an investigation of its strategy. This allows a more detailed investigation of Taliban goals, purposes, and conceptions of victory.

Although other conflicts can offer useful insights, reliable, objective sources for them may not be easily available. For Iraq and Afghanistan, a wealth of source material provides a clear portrait of how strategy was developed and conducted by the regular combatants. The same cannot be said for irregular opponents. For a variety of reasons, they rarely publicize their strategy or critique their conduct. Nevertheless, communiqués, video messages, captured and translated materials, as well as their actions, allow for informed speculation on the goals and priorities of irregular opponents. This imbalance of source materials resembles 'a football game in which the spectator sees one team in the sharpest detail but the other is largely invisible and can be perceived clearly only when in contact with the visible team'.[13]

Iraq and Afghanistan are fruitful grounds for analysis of strategy for another reason. These two campaigns are inextricably linked, and how they have been conducted demonstrates the impact and limitations on strategy imposed by politics, policy, and grand strategy. Untangling this Gordian knot illustrates many of the challenges faced by practising strategists today, especially given that the final outcome of both Iraq and Afghanistan lies in the future. This chapter concludes with a brief description of those attributes of strategy that influence its conduct while these wars are under way.

AFGHANISTAN

Background and Context

Although Alexander the Great had to deal with various warlike tribes in what is now Afghanistan during his march to the River Indus, there was no nation-state to speak of until the eighteenth century. In 1747, Ahmad Shah succeeded in freeing and forging together the various Pathan[14] tribes in the Durrani empire after the death of the Persian ruler Nadir Shah. Ahmad Shah Durrani, as he was subsequently known, went on to consolidate his power at the expense of the neighbouring Mughals, Marathas, and Sikhs and forge an empire that stretched from present-day Iran to India. After his death, a range of lineal descendants, some more inept than others, oversaw the decline in the emirate's territory and fortunes.

A representative from the British East India Company, Mountstuart Elphinstone, made the journey to Kabul in 1808 and entered into the first of many agreements and treaties with the rulers of Afghanistan. Successive wars with Afghanistan in 1839–42 and 1878–80 ended with much of the country under de facto British control. The wars were not entirely one-sided and Pathan tribes, such as the Ghilzai, earned a well-deserved reputation for their cunning, fighting ability, and cruelty. This reputation was cemented between December 1841 and January 1842, when an uprising led by Akbar Khan ended in the retreat, harassment, and eventual annihilation of British forces under the command of General William Elphinstone.[15]

The eastern and northern borders of present-day Afghanistan were delineated as a result of the contentious Durand Line agreement in 1893, which honoured British and Afghan interests at the time but artificially divided Pathan tribal land. The third and last Anglo-Afghan War (6 May–8 August 1919) resulted in British recognition of the ability of the emirate and later kingdom of Afghanistan, under Amanullah Khan, to negotiate relations with other nations. For this reason, 1919 is cited as the year Afghanistan gained its independence. Members of Amanullah Khan's family from the Pathan Barakzai tribe ruled the country, with brief interruption, from 1919 until 1973. The last and most successful king, Muhammad Zahir Shah, ruled Afghanistan for forty years. His numerous attempts to modernize the country succeeded only in establishing limited political reforms that did not threaten the power base of various tribal leaders.

In 1973, Afghanistan became a republic after King Zahir Shah was ousted in a coup. Subsequent infighting, coups, and counter-coups led to the direct intervention of the Soviet Union on 24 December 1979.[16] For the next nine years, Soviet forces, and those of their People's Democratic Party of Afghanistan (PDPA) proxies, waged an intensive but ultimately frustrating counter-insurgency war against a loose confederation of groups known collectively as the mujahidin.[17] 'Loose confederation' is perhaps the most accurate description for the resistance, as various groups and tribes, with few exceptions, switched allegiances among one another and between sides depending on the fortunes of war. At no point was the Democratic Republic of Afghanistan, the government supported by the Soviet Union, able to assert its power and control outside major cities such as Kabul and Kandahar.

The withdrawal of Soviet forces from Afghanistan, completed in February 1989, did not end the fighting between groups. The Democratic Republic of Afghanistan, under the PDPA leadership of Muhammad Najibullah, continued to fight against groups led by warlords such as Ahmad Shah Massoud and Gulbuddin Hekmatyar. The suspension of Russian aid following the collapse of the Soviet Union, combined with the defection of key warlords, led to the fall of the Democratic Republic of Afghanistan in April 1992. This event was followed by renewed civil war between various warlords until the arrival of a new actor on the scene in 1994: the Taliban.

The Taliban, comprising zealous students educated in *madrasahs* within Pakistan who followed an ascetic and narrow interpretation of Islam, managed in three years to break the power of a number of warlords and become the controlling authority in most of Afghanistan.[18] Although the Taliban had some modest success in implementing shariah law in areas it controlled, the harsh nature of their justice led to international criticism and dissatisfaction among many Afghans. The Taliban leader Mullah Muhammad Omar added to the controversy by offering sanctuary and protection to Osama bin Laden and other al-Qaeda leaders and followers after their eviction from Sudan in 1996. Al-Qaeda established numerous base and support camps throughout the country, trained recruits, and directed terrorist attacks in 1998 (Kenya and Tanzania), 2000 (Yemen), and 2001 (New York and Washington, DC).[19]

The 11 September 2001 attacks on the World Trade Center and the Pentagon provoked a response unanticipated by Taliban and al-Qaeda leaders. US military special operations and clandestine operatives, drawing upon Afghan Northern Alliance allies and US air power, conducted numerous offensives throughout Afghanistan from 19 October to 17 December 2001. These offensives destroyed or scattered Taliban forces, and al-Qaeda survivors, including Osama bin Laden, escaped to Pakistan.[20]

During their period of rule over the country, the Taliban had no better luck than presidents, emirs, or kings in welding Afghanistan into a cohesive nation. The reason why Afghans have defied such efforts is a function of both geography and culture. A landlocked country of more than 650,000 square kilometres, Afghanistan borders on Iran to the west, Pakistan to the south and east, China to the north-east, and Turkmenistan, Uzbekistan, and Tajikistan in the north. Although mostly arid, with formidable mountain ranges and deep valleys and gorges, especially in the Hindu Kush range, the country has plains in the south-west and north. Less than 15 per cent of its territory is arable, and only 3 per cent is irrigated. Under a third of Afghanistan's population of approximately 30 million is considered literate, which limits government avenues for both distributing its message and modernizing the country's economy and society. Many of the more educated members of society, who could serve as entrepreneurs, leaders, and bureaucrats, fled during the many periods of civil war. This loss of intellectual capital, an inability to replace it, and a lack of civil infrastructure and basic services in large parts of the country have posed significant challenges to Afghanistan's governance and development.[21]

Afghanistan's geography has had a considerable impact on its culture and ethnic groups. There are four main ethnic groups: Pathans, or Pashtuns (42 per cent), Tajiks (27 per cent), Hazaras (9 per cent), and Uzbeks (9 per cent), among others (Turcomans, Aimaks, Baluchis, etc.). More than three-quarters of the population are Sunni Muslim, while a further 19 per cent are Shia, although the vast majority of these are ethnic Hazara. The dominant, largely Sunni, Pathans can be divided into two or three main tribes: the Western Afghans, or Durranis (from whom the royal line derives), the Ghilzais, and the Eastern Yusufzais.[22]

Governance has only truly been sustainable throughout Afghanistan at the local and regional levels. Villages have largely organized along tribal, patriarchal, and economic caste lines. Local leaders, or khans, have sought to protect those within their territorial boundary, expand the wealth, power, and influence of their tribe, and defend the honour and integrity of their society. Put more bluntly, conflict for centuries has been driven by three primary motives: *zar* (gold), *zan* (women), or *zamin* (land). The adoption of the code of Pashtunwali, enforceable at the local or regional council (*loya jirga*) level, has provided basic justice and norms in the absence of any federal judicial system or national identity. Attempts to change this system of social, political, and economic governance, especially by national or outside authorities, are almost always met with suspicion, resentment, or rebellion.[23] The exception to this rule, of course, has been when tribes will gain at others' expense.

The net effect of culture and geography has been to create a people with 'a proud and aggressive individualism, practiced in the context of a familial and tribal society with predatory habits, a part feudal and part democratic ethos, an uncompromising Muslim faith and a simple code of conduct'.[24] The combination of Pashtun values, tribal divisions, suspicion of outsiders, and geography has had a considerable impact on the strategies of the various combatants in Afghanistan, as the next sections will show.

Taliban Strategy

One of the challenges of describing Taliban strategy is determining which Taliban is being discussed. For example, there are at least three distinct Taliban entities: the Afghan Taliban, controlled by the Quetta Shura Council under the direction of Mullah Muhammad Omar; semi-autonomous regional Taliban commands and commanders within Afghanistan; and Tehrik-i-Taliban Pakistan, operating in the autonomous Federally Administered Tribal Area (FATA) in the north-west of Pakistan and formerly under the leadership of Baitullah Mehsud.[25] Further complicating analysis is the diffuse nature of the Taliban organization. As the director of the Afghan Research and Evaluation Unit, based in Kabul, noted in 2008, 'What we generically refer to as "The Taliban" is a set of different individuals and groups who have differing grievances, differing motivations, differing attitudes—and take a hostile attitude toward the [Afghan central] government.'[26]

This has made estimating the rough size of the Taliban, to appreciate the scale of the problem, exceedingly difficult. One authoritative source suggests that there are 8,000–10,000 'full-time' and 22,000–32,000 'part-time' Taliban in Afghanistan.[27]

What is certain about the Taliban is that the Quetta Shura Council, which ostensibly speaks for its brethren in Afghanistan, has two primary strategic objectives: to force US and NATO forces to leave, and to regain much of their former power and control over the country. Power would allow the Taliban to replace tribal rule with the only law that they recognize: God's law, or at least, the strict and minimalist Taliban interpretation of Islamic shariah law. Some have speculated that the eventual goal of the Taliban is the creation of a new state, Pashtunistan, which will unite tribes currently separated by the border of Afghanistan and Pakistan.[28] With headquarters and operating bases in the mountains and towns of FATA, a renewable source of recruits coming from the *madrasahs* located there, and increasingly sophisticated methods of attack, including complex ambushes and improvised explosive devices, the Taliban appears to have the means to conduct their strategy. The ways in which the Taliban are going to use these means to achieve their ends are not at all apparent. Adding to the confusion are contradictory statements and proposed programmes that are apparent in Taliban media releases and products, as well as statements by other groups that purport to outline Taliban strategy such as al-Qaeda's Lashkar al-Zil, or Shadow Army.[29]

One author has suggested that the Taliban concept of operations for victory owes less to culture than to classic insurgency theory. Antonio Giustozzi posits that, after a period of recovery and consolidation, the reinvigorated 'neo-Taliban' launched an approach in 2003 based on Mao Zedong's ideas and writings on insurgency. In Giustozzi's assessment, the Taliban approach to the concept of operations from 2002 until 2006 had three phases: infiltrating the population (2002–3), consolidating their local hold on the population (2003–6), and a 'general offensive' (2006) designed to capitalize on the American diversion of forces, attention, and resources to Iraq.[30] In any event, the 2006 offensive, which saw Taliban units as large as 300 men operating in attacks on towns such as Kandahar, failed as a result of faulty assumptions and misjudgement of their opponents' capabilities.[31]

David Kilcullen, a noted counter-insurgency scholar and practitioner, offers a different opinion on how the Taliban believe they can translate their resources into success. He suggests that the Taliban theory for using their means can be summarized instead in three words: discredit, exhaust, and inherit.[32] *Discrediting* applies to the United States, the International Security Assistance Force (ISAF), and the government of Afghanistan and is accomplished by depicting their actions as unjust and unnecessary. US and coalition air and artillery strikes, some of which have resulted in heavy civilian casualties, provide propaganda fodder for the Taliban on this theme. Taliban propaganda also suggests that the legitimacy of the government of Afghanistan and its leader, President Hamid Kharzai, should be called into question. The result of the 2009 presidential election, with allegations of widespread voter fraud, played into this Taliban message. To some extent, this portion of the Taliban's strategy is passive in that it requires the enemy to make mistakes on which they then capitalize. One such example has been the dilemma confronting Kharzai and the ISAF over what to do about opium poppy cultivation and export. The Taliban have encouraged or coerced Afghan farmers to plant and harvest the lucrative crop to extract tax revenues. Western political leaders have responded by pressuring Kharzai and ISAF to take action against the drug trade. The dilemma is that Afghan farmers will be alienated if their crops are destroyed and not replaced by others that are equally lucrative.[33]

Exhausting requires the Taliban to continue their current pace of activities, replenish losses, harass ISAF and Afghan security forces, and force the coalition to repeatedly rebuild or retake positions. At some point, US and ISAF forces will return home after years of a lack of visible progress, and statements by some leaders about withdrawing some or all of their forces by 2010 or 2011 are encouraging signs for the Taliban.[34]

Inheriting does not mean that the Taliban will just sit back and wait to fill the power vacuum left by ISAF and the government of Afghanistan. Rather, regional Taliban leaders have been skilled in building local 'shadow governments'. Such governments, which may comprise only a few individuals, replace officials appointed by the Kharzai government from other distant tribes and provide local rule of law.[35]

The Taliban's strategy is not without its risks, vulnerabilities, and challenges. In particular, the Taliban must overcome residual hostility among large segments of the Afghan population to the excesses of their former rule. While many Afghans would like to see foreign troops leave, it is not certain that they want to see the Taliban return to power. Lack of significant popular support, and the added resources and protection it provides, call into question the ability of the Taliban to inherit anything in the country other than tribal resistance. Their approach, which accepts minimal strategic risks and counts on time and the mistakes of the enemy, cedes the initiative to ISAF and the government of Afghanistan. This illustrates one of the classic dilemmas insurgent opponents face in contemporary conflicts related to time and action. Take too little action and your adversary has the strategic breathing space to mobilize additional resources and institute reforms; take too much action and you risk losing your forces, alienating the population, and providing your opponent with the pretext for committing resources and carrying out reforms.

US and Coalition Strategy in Afghanistan, December 2002 until the Present

For the strategist, Afghanistan offers a perfect example of what management scientists and social planners have labelled as a 'wicked problem'.[36] The strategist seeks to apply means in certain ways to achieve one or more defined ends identified by policy. So-called wicked problems have no solutions, and therefore success can only be measured in terms of better or worse, and not failure or victory. The reason Afghanistan can be considered a strategically 'wicked problem' has to do with the set of intricately related problems that policymakers and planners must disentangle, clarify, and prioritize. This is not as easy as armchair strategists and pundits would have you believe. Consider the multiple factors and competing priorities faced by strategists today, which are summarized in the following four statements.

First, the Taliban and al-Qaeda are operating from bases in Pakistan, and within Afghanistan, with the former conducting an insurgency against the governments of both nations using insurgency and terrorist tactics financed by states, non-state organizations, and opium production. Second, the government of Afghanistan is racked by corruption, nepotism, and competing factions and has neither the resources nor the capability to enforce its authority within its borders or to provide essential services to the bulk of its population. Third, to force the Taliban and al-Qaeda out of their sanctuaries in Pakistan, the government of that country must take forceful action using its armed forces, whose members control a disproportionate share of wealth and influence, without driving tribally affiliated locals into the hands of either group and while maintaining the territorial integrity of its borders and ensuring control over its stock of nuclear weapons. Any deployment of troops to Pakistan, if only to provide training and support against a mutual enemy, must be done in such a way as not to inflame the Pakistani domestic population, which is very sensitive to foreign intervention in its sovereign state affairs.

Added to these interrelated problems are the dilemma of 'sunk costs', or time, effort, and resources already expended for purpose as yet unachieved, as well as the politics of coalition warfare and the need to maintain domestic support for actions. Which problems receive your immediate attention and resources, what problems can you defer, what are the risks in deferring them, and how will the enemy respond? This is not designed to excuse strategists from their responsibilities but rather to illustrate two points: the challenges confronting strategists are very real and rarely straightforward; and maintaining strategic focus, which requires hard choices to be made, limits your actions and prevents the problems with which you are confronted from expanding beyond your means.

Arguably, the United States failed to make some difficult choices regarding Afghanistan, and the strategy of US and coalition forces has suffered as a result. One clear manifestation of this has been an inability to maintain focus and unity of effort on a set of achievable goals in Afghanistan. After the 11 September 2001 attacks and even well into 2002, coalition unity against the Taliban and al-Qaeda remained strong. Such unity started on 12 September, when NATO invoked Article 5 of the Washington Treaty and pledged its members to respond collectively as if they had each been attacked. In a show of international support, the United Nations Security Council established ISAF and its headquarters in December 2001. The United States, in turn, expanded its operations with other coalition partners (the United Kingdom and Australia, among others) under the separate and largely independent line of command and control of Operation Enduring Freedom-Afghanistan. This US-led command conducted three main missions: to find and destroy holdout Taliban forces still in the country; to establish an Afghan national army and train, advise, and equip it to take over security duties; and to prevent Taliban and al-Qaeda forces from re-entering the country from Pakistan.

In the context of strategy, the immediate and obvious implication of these grandiose missions was that both ISAF and the US-led coalition had insufficient forces to complete them all. For example, the border with Pakistan stretches almost 2,500 kilometres and consists almost entirely of mountains, so securing it would require more than ten times the number of forces now assigned to

Afghanistan. Members of the US National Security Council realized that stabilizing the country and winning the 'hearts and minds' of the Afghan population in support of their government would require 'nation building on a huge scale'.[37] Nation-building thus needed to become exceptionally important to US and coalition strategy if the nascent government of Hamid Kharzai, who was elected as interim president of Afghanistan by the country's first national-level *loya jirga* in December 2002, were to stand any chance of success or even survival.

Rather than make the difficult decisions in late 2002, senior members of the Bush administration opted to expand nation-building actions in Afghanistan while also opting to invade Iraq. The latter decision, which remains the subject of controversy and state inquiry, had a number of adverse consequences for American and coalition strategy in Afghanistan. These consequences included strategic distraction in planning for and conducting a war in Iraq at a time when military operations were drifting away from the increasingly ill-defined and opaque ends of nation-building in Afghanistan, as well as the assumption that victory in Iraq would prove easy, thus relieving Afghanistan of the burden of being the litmus test for success in the 'War on Terrorism'.[38] Further, the decision put at risk the support in Afghanistan provided by a number of states whose leaders opposed the idea of invading Iraq. Such a diversion of resources also called into the question the credibility of the American commitment to Afghanistan within the country and abroad. In particular, President Bush's declaration that the United States would provide the people of Afghanistan with aid comparable to that provided to Europe under the Marshall Plan after the Second World War was challenged after the realities of insurgency and reconstruction in Iraq, described below, became apparent.[39]

One illustration showing how the ends of policy were inconsistent with the means used in Afghanistan is the Provincial Reconstruction Team (PRT) programme. The first PRT was fielded in early 2003. The concept behind the PRTs is sound. They are designed to 'improve security, support good governance, and enhance provincial development... [by utilizing a] combination of international civilian and military resources'.[40] The activities of PRTs, however, are only useful if they are integrated in a coherent manner with other means to achieve the ends of strategy. PRTs in Afghanistan are split between different commands, with fourteen operating under ISAF and the remaining twelve under separate US control.[41] In addition to reporting to different chains of command, PRTs have been used inconsistently because of competing national and bureaucratic interests and differences in opinion over how they should be employed. One potential indication that the means and ends of strategy are not well connected is found in a study evaluating the effectiveness of PRTs. The authors of the study concluded, among other things, that 'ISAF, lead nations, and the GOA [government of Afghanistan] need to develop a common vision and strategy to ensure ISAF PRTs meet the political-military objectives approved by the GOA and NATO.'[42]

In the absence of a coherent plan or feasible objectives, what occurred in Afghanistan from 2003 until 2009 can be described as different coalition and Afghan actors pursuing an ever-expanding range of missions and tasks in an uncoordinated manner. Four observations suggest that this has been the case.

The first is that the objectives within ISAF and Operation Enduring Freedom-Afghanistan change almost annually, as personnel, forces, and leaders are deployed in and out of the country in reaction to actual or anticipated Taliban offensives. This recalls the caustic observation about the conduct of the American war in Vietnam: 'the United States did not fight the war in Viet Nam for ten years, but fought one year at a time for ten years'.[43]

The second observation is that there are increasingly strained relations among ISAF partner nations. Such strains have occurred as a result of American unilateral reaction to a perceived lack of equitable burden-sharing among partners. German forces, in particular, have come under criticism for their unwillingness or inability to engage in combat operations or label their actions as anything but peacekeeping. Other friction has resulted from press allegations that Italian forces negotiated separate agreements with local warlords without notifying the French contingent sent to relieve them.[44] One method of dealing with such problems has been to divide command of ISAF regions according to willingness and ability, and keep combat-heavy areas, such as Regional Commands South and East, in 'trusted' hands.

The third observation is that a lack of clear and common set of objectives between allies has played into the hands of local Afghan leaders and power brokers. Tribal leaders constantly look for ways to enhance the power, prestige, and wealth of their tribe. They have been exceptionally skilled at playing off the US and coalition advisers against their government or Afghanistan counterparts.[45]

The fourth and last observation relates to the expansion of the strategy from one country, Afghanistan, to two. This strategy has been labelled by pundits and policymakers as 'AfPak', which is an acknowledgement of the complex and interrelated connections that exist between the countries. Increasingly, the strategy for Afghanistan is overshadowed by the emphasis placed on ensuring that Pakistan reins in internal stability problems, including the dual problems of Taliban and al-Qaeda recruiting grounds and sanctuaries.

It is too early to determine the impact that General Stanley McChrystal's change in approach, and more recently his replacement and General David Petraeus's appointment as ISAF commander, will have on strategy in Afghanistan. What is clear is that McChrystal's leaked assessment of the security situation in Afghanistan served a political purpose: it outlined, in direct terms, the gravity of the situation, the American appreciation of it, and a willingness to make the necessary changes to implement the ends of policy. Those ends, brought into sharper contrast by President Barack Obama in his speech at West Point, provide a clearer connection to the means and ways available. In particular, US forces will conduct a time- and resource-constrained campaign to improve the numbers and quality of Afghan security forces, stabilize the countryside, focus operations against al-Qaeda, and set the conditions for eventual withdrawal.[46]

IRAQ

Background and Context

Like Afghanistan, the modern state of Iraq was created at the end of the First World War. Unlike Afghanistan, Iraq was created by partition from the Ottoman empire. For four centuries (750–1258), the capital of Iraq, Baghdad, was the cultural and intellectual centre of the Abbasid caliphate, and the territory was at various times under the control by the Romans, Parthians, Sasanids, and Ottomans. Under a mandate provided by the League of Nations in 1920, Great Britain became the protector of the newly established country and a Hashemite Arab monarchy was established by plebiscite in 1921.

The formation of the state, and in particular of its government and boundaries, were not without controversy. The monarchy of Iraq established as king Faisal bin al-Hussein, a Sunni Arab, but this did not sit well with the majority Shia population. The borders of Iraq were created along geographic lines, with little consideration given to traditional tribal and ethnic territories and historic trade routes. In particular, the Kurdish population in the north found itself divided between Iraq and Turkey. Ethnic tensions, dissatisfaction with the government and its territory, and tribal responses to the presence of occupying British forces led to a number of revolts, among them tribal Shia and Kurdish uprisings, from 1919 until 1928. These revolts were almost exclusively local in scope and were dealt with by the British using a combination of 'air policing'—the use of air power to coerce and intimidate leaders and villages—and small expeditionary ground forces backed by armoured cars.[47] In 1932, Iraq gained its independence from Great Britain and the latter withdrew its forces. Other minor revolts flared up, including a brief military coup in 1941 and a Kurdish uprising in Baghdad in 1948, but their initial successes were short-lived.

The uprising that finally succeeded was the military coup in 1958 that resulted in changing the government of Iraq from a monarchy to a republic. As is often the case, the initial coup was followed by additional violence and changes in leadership as a revolving door of military officers assumed power through violence or guile. This period of flux, which lasted for almost a decade, saw the establishment of two predominant political forces in the country. The first was the installation of the pan-Arab Ba'ath Party as the dominant party from 1968 until 2003. Membership in the Ba'ath Party was not mandatory in Iraq but it provided opportunities and the potential for enrichment and advancement. Although only notionally socialist in outlook and platform, the Ba'ath Party was decidedly socialist in organization. From the lowest level of governance, the three-person party cell, up to the National Command, the Ba'ath Party implemented a high level of population surveillance and monitoring. Control was imposed by three state entities: the Mukhabarat (Jihaz al-Mukhabarat al-Amma), or General Intelligence Service; the Amn (al-Amn al-'Amm), or Directorate of General Security; and special military units including the Republican Guard. The Mukhabarat and Amn were the primary instruments of state control and terror, whereas the Republican Guard was used to protect the president of Iraq as well as to repress more sizeable internal rebellions.

Saddam Hussein was the second political force to be reckoned with in Iraq. Born in 1937 near the town of Tikrit, close to where he was captured in December 2003, Saddam had a turbulent upbringing. The troubles of his youth were quickly overshadowed by his rapid rise within the Ba'ath Party, combined with his role in consolidating a number of state security entities into the Amn. Saddam served as leader of the country from 1979 until 2003 and during his tenure shaped the government from a republic into a dictatorship. Like most dictators, he provided a mixture of incentives, repression, and bureaucratic reform designed to bind individual loyalty to him while ensuring suspicion of others and competition for favour. Through these measures, and the establishment of a cult of personality, Saddam managed to surmount a number of the social, economic, and political fault lines that existed within Iraq.[48]

In order to understand why the subsequent insurgency and civil war were so challenging for the US-led coalition, it is necessary to put these fault lines into context. Iraq is a country of more than 430,000 square kilometres bordering on Iran, Syria, Jordan, Saudi Arabia, Kuwait, and Turkey, with a population of almost 30 million. Although ravaged by war with Iran (1980–8) and economic sanctions, Iraq had experienced considerable infrastructure growth and modernization, financed largely through revenue from its oil production, and its population is highly literate compared to some of its neighbours.

Iraq's population is divided along a number of lines. The first dividing line is religious. Although the country is almost entirely Muslim, its population is roughly separated into two-thirds Shia and one-third Sunni. These religious partitions are by no means homogeneous between different sects of Sunni and Shia Islam. The population is further divided along ethnic and tribal lines, including Arab, Kurd, and Turcoman, as well as urban and nomadic ones. For example, great emphasis is placed on tribal or clan affiliation in a number of Sunni areas, led by the shaikh of the most influential tribe, whereas in Shia regions the imam is the source of authority. The fact that the Sunni Arabs largely controlled senior positions within the Ba'ath Party and took advantage of this to enrich themselves and expand their political power and the influence of their clans during the reign of Saddam Hussein, despite being the minority of the population, partially explains why the violence from 2003 to 2008 exploded as it did.[49]

Saddam Hussein's Strategy

Saddam Hussein had every reason to be confident on the eve of invasion in March 2003. He had survived assassination attempts, weathered a coalition air and ground campaign in 1991 (Operation Desert Storm), thwarted United Nations weapons inspectors, and withstood more than a decade of sanctions and the odd rebellion with his political power intact. In addition, he had strong political and economic ties with France and Russia. As permanent members of the United Nations Security Council, either country could veto any proposal by the United States to authorize the use of force. Saddam heard the rhetoric coming from the administration of President George W. Bush but had difficulty believing that the United States would invade. After all, international opposition to an invasion had been prominent and the United States had responded before with relatively ineffectual air and missile strikes.

In the event that a US-led coalition did invade, Saddam had a strategy in mind. He ultimately sought to remain in power as president of Iraq. In order to achieve that end, he hoped to rely on what appeared to the outside world as formidable military and paramilitary forces. These forces included two elite Republican Guard corps (each with three divisions), a special forces division (As-Saiqa), the Special Republican Guard, and seventeen regular army armoured, mechanized, and infantry divisions.[50] Added to this 375,000-strong army were additional state security and intelligence forces (32,000), the Ba'ath Party Popular Army (al-Jaysh ash Shaabi, 150,000), and the latest addition, the 60,000-strong fedayin.[51] Saddam had taken great pains to publicize the fedayin, including their capabilities, dedication to him, and commitment to martyr themselves if necessary.[52]

The plan of operations, or the way in which Saddam proposed to use these means, was relatively simple. Expecting to be invaded from the north, south, and west simultaneously, Saddam made Baghdad the centre of concentric lines of defence. This plan also reflected his concern about a coup.[53] The anchors of those lines of defence were the other cities of Iraq, including Mosul, Nasariyah, Karbala, Najaf, and Ramadi. The fedayin and other guerrilla forces would act as irregulars and harass the coalition forces while on the march or as they deployed into cities. By drawing US-led coalition forces into the cities and negating their dominance of air and space, Saddam hoped to inflict enough casualties on the ground forces to compel an end to the war. As a method of reinforcing this plan, he circulated copies of the book and movie *Blackhawk Down* to show that the Americans could be beaten and forced to retreat.[54] Should the US-led coalition actually break through these defences, the last bastion would be Baghdad itself. With the Special Republican Guard and utterly devoted intelligence, paramilitary, and fedayin forces, Baghdad would become an urban death zone for anyone foolish enough to enter. According to his own cost calculations, Saddam figured that at most he would lose additional territory in the south and perhaps have to allow United Nations weapons inspectors back into the country.[55]

US-led Coalition Strategy: Operation Iraqi Freedom

The strategy for the US-led coalition had two clear and related ends in mind: primarily to disarm Saddam Hussein of his stock of weapons of mass destruction (WMDs), including nuclear and chemical weapons, and secondarily to depose the leader. The way to meet those goals involved a campaign plan, code-named Cobra II, which went through numerous iterations.[56] The plan initially involved an air and space component designed to 'shock and awe' the Iraqi leadership and deny it the ability to command and control its armed forces in the field. The ground elements, comprising the 3rd and 4th Infantry Divisions, the 1st Marine Division, and other assorted brigades, regiments, and attached support elements, would advance along one northern (4th Infantry Division) and two southern (V Corps and I Marine Expeditionary Force, which included the British 1st Armoured Division) axes of approach.[57] In addition, special operations forces would secure oil platforms and other key infrastructure, as well as deny the Iraqis the use of territory in the west that had been used in the past to launch Scud missiles. The ground forces would manoeuvre on Baghdad and depose Saddam while WMD facilities were seized and their contents rendered safe for removal.

Almost immediately the plan had to be revised, as Secretary of Defense Donald Rumsfeld forced planners to do more with less and the recently elected Turkish parliament decided to deny port and entry rights to ships carrying the bulk of the 4th Infantry Division. The Cobra II plan took on a life of its own to account for all of these changes. As planning became more involved and detailed, the crucial consideration of what to do in Iraq after Saddam had been deposed was lost in the process. At the level of policy, the assumption was that the Iraqis so despised Saddam's regime that coalition forces would be welcomed as liberators.

In twenty-one days, Operation Iraqi Freedom achieved its secondary objective through bold tactics and innovative leadership, joint operations among land, sea, air, and special operations, and rapid manoeuvre. The net effect of this military operation was to deny Saddam both the ways and the means to conduct his strategy. US-led coalition forces largely skirted urban areas. Attacks on Iraqi command and control elements, including Saddam himself, prevented orders from being issued to units to manoeuvre and respond to the invading forces. Attacks in the west by Task Force Dagger and from the north by Task Force Viking Hammer, using special operations forces, locally raised militias, and attached conventional forces, succeeded in confusing senior Iraqi leaders about the main line of coalition advance.[58] In other cases, Iraqi leaders defected and men within units walked away from their equipment and returned home.

Strategy in Flux: Iraq 2003–4

While the US-led coalition succeeded in its strategic goal of deposing Saddam, the failure to find WMDs or to plan for consolidation and the transition of regime authority to another group within Iraq called into question the legitimacy of the invasion and jeopardized its strategic success. Failure to consider what should occur once Saddam was deposed was certainly a mistake, but not a fatal one strategically. A combination of bold action, clear direction, and a vision for the future of Iraq could have corrected it.

Unfortunately, three elements compounded the initial error. The first was the very rapid pace of victory, which exceeded the expectations of those involved, and the equally rapid collapse of the Ba'ath Party system. This led to a degree of what can only be described as military and policy disbelief and bewilderment. The second element was an almost universal change of senior military leadership shortly after the military victory was complete. This included the replacement of General Tommy Franks by General Ricardo Sanchez, and of several other key personalities involved in planning and executing Cobra II. This rapid change of command denied incoming leaders such as General Sanchez the benefit of their in-theatre knowledge, experience, and expertise and only added to the confusion. The third element was the strategically disastrous decision by the interim governing authority in Iraq, the Coalition Provisional Authority (CPA), to 'de-Ba'athify' the country. The CPA decision to disband the Ba'ath Party on 16 April 2003 was followed one month later by an order that stated, 'Full members of the Ba'ath Party holding [certain] ranks...are hereby removed from their positions and banned from future employment in the public sector.'[59]

The collapse of the Ba'ath state security apparatus and the lack of a suitable replacement led to a period of lawlessness and chaos in Iraq from mid-April until mid-May 2003. There was widespread looting of presidential palaces, government offices, hospitals, and the National Museum of Iraq in Baghdad, and US and coalition forces continued to take casualties from sporadic attacks. The senior leadership of the CPA suspected that the wave of sniper attacks, ambushes, and car bombings was part of a Mukhabarat resistance, sabotage, and subversion strategy.[60] Although some Ba'ath Party members living outside Iraq provided financial support to those fighting against the coalition forces, the initial violence was not coordinated or controlled to any degree. Therefore, it is difficult, if not impossible, to divine any strategy governing it. Nevertheless, within the first three months of irregular warfare, US forces had suffered as many casualties killed in action as they had during the twenty-one-day 'conventional' military campaign to topple Saddam. The combination of de-Ba'athification, sluggishness in restoring basic public services to the population, an inability to provide security against marauding bands of criminals and other thugs, and easy access to military weapons and explosives led to the next stage of the Iraq War, in which there was the hint of a strategy: the insurgency.

The Strategy of Insurgency, 2004–7

The insurgency within Iraq can be broken down into three discernible stages, the first two of which are discussed in this section. The third is inextricably linked with the reaction to the so-called 'surge' of American forces in 2007.

The first stage of the insurgency involved a backlash against the US-led coalition forces, who were perceived not as liberators but as occupiers out to pillage Iraq's natural resources. The de-Ba'athification order of 16 May 2003 prompted some former regime members, including many Sunni Arabs with specialized training and skills, to fight against those whom they perceived as having taken away their livelihoods. The power vacuum left in the wake of the collapse of the Ba'ath regime was also filled by a limited number of organizations that started with a local power base and expanded their influence regionally. One such organization, supported and sustained by the government of Iran, was the Shia Supreme Council for the Islamic Revolution in Iraq (SCIRI), which fielded its own private army (the Badr Corps). Another organization, the Mahdi Army, was the private militia of Muqtada al-Sadr and grew in power and stature into a political force to be reckoned with.

Attacks that took place from May 2003 until the following year, however, were almost exclusively local in nature and responsibility for many of them went unclaimed. From May 2004 onwards, groups within Iraq competed for attention and legitimacy among existing and potential supporters, and consolidated their power bases, as their communiqués and recruiting media make clear.[61] These groups included al-Qaeda in Mesopotamia (later Iraq), the Islamic Army in Iraq, Muhammad's Army, the 1920 Revolution Brigades, and the Army of the Mujahidin in Iraq. By 2005, identified groups and cells could be categorized along the following lines: Sunni Arabs, secular Ba'athists and Arab nationalists, Sunni tribes, religious groups, ultra-radical Salafis and Wahhabis, Shia groups, and al-Qaeda and other foreign groups.[62] Such categorizations obscure the fact that many cells and groups comprised aspects of more than one simultaneously, or, in the case of the first five, changed their primary orientation over time. Other attacks were perpetrated by loose networks of small cells, based exclusively on tribal and clan ties, which had no defined objective other than to inflict casualties on US and coalition forces, and later the Shia-dominated Iraqi security forces.[63]

Regardless of their political or ideological leanings, the estimated 15,000–20,000 insurgents from all groups shared a common purpose: to drive the Americans and their allies, including foreign aid and reconstruction workers, out of Iraq. Although a defined theory of operations, or way in which this goal would be achieved, is difficult to determine, cells and groups used their available means to that end in both isolated and coordinated local and regional attacks. Incidents such as the perceived US unwillingness to finish the first battle of Fallujah (4 April–1 May 2004), the online release of photographs of Iraqi prisoner humiliation and abuse at Abu Ghraib (30 April 2004), the drafting and ratification of a new constitution and the election of a parliament for Iraq (January–December 2005), and American patrolling and force protection measures, which were designed to minimize their vulnerability to ambush and attack, further cemented the purpose of cells and groups.

The bombing of the al-Askariya Mosque in Samarra on 22 February 2006 precipitated the second stage of the insurgency. The al-Askariya Mosque is one of the three most revered sites in Shia Islam (the others being the Mosque of Imam Ali in Najaf and the Shrine of Imam Husayn in Karbala). It contains the remains of several imams and other venerated founders, and is sacred ground for this denomination of Islam. The second stage of the insurgency saw the rise in notoriety and influence of al-Qaeda in Iraq and the unleashing of a bloody and bitter civil war. Although insurgents continued to target coalition forces for attack, the tension between rival Sunni cells and groups (moderates, nationalists, and fundamentalists) and Shia groups and militia exploded into bitter internecine fighting and reprisal killings and attacks after the bombing of the mosque. The number of Iraqis killed during this stage is difficult to determine, but a much-quoted source puts the figure at approximately 25,000 within the first year.[64] The bombing of the mosque and the subsequent fighting drove a wedge into Iraqi society, forcing families to choose sides, seek revenge for the death of family or community members, or move in fear of their lives. According to the United Nations High Commissioner for Refugees, more than 365,000 people were displaced from their homes as a result of attack and subsequent violence.[65]

The severe damage to the mosque by methodical demolition was ascribed to al-Qaeda in Iraq and its leader, Abu Musab al-Zarqawi.[66] Zarqawi, a Jordanian petty criminal and street thug who had once met Osama bin Laden in Afghanistan after the end of the Soviet-Afghan War, was converted to the extreme strain of violent radical Islam while in prison. Although many details of Zarqawi's career are sketchy, including his connection with the terrorist group Ansar al-Islam, the invasion of Iraq provided him with the venue and target to open up a new front against the Western 'crusaders'.[67] Zarqawi developed a reputation not only for religious zeal but also for brutal acts of violence, including the bombing of the United Nations headquarters in Iraq at the Canal Hotel and the videotaped beheading of Nicholas Berg, which brought him notoriety, resources, and additional recruits. Many rural, and in some cases nomadic, shaikhs in the western-most province of Iraq, al-Anbar, provided assistance and support to Zarqawi and al-Qaeda in Iraq as a means to remove American forces from their desert.

Zarqawi's methods may have served al-Qaeda in Iraq's immediate strategic aims, but they were counter-productive to the wider political objectives and strategy of al-Qaeda. Ayman al-Zawahiri, al-Qaeda's second-in-command, warned Zarqawi not to squander the potential victory in Iraq or forget its significance. He reminded Zarqawi that 'the two short-term goals, which are removing the Americans and establishing an Islamic amirate in Iraq, or a caliphate if possible', were only the first step in a strategy based on 'the strongest weapon which the mujahedeen enjoy... [which] is popular support from the Muslim masses in Iraq, and the surrounding Muslim countries'.[68] Zawahiri proved more prophetic than he knew. Within a year of receiving the letter, Zarqawi was dead, killed as a result of a nationwide manhunt, intelligence provided by interrogations, and an air strike.[69] More directly, Zarqawi's methods had alienated a large section of the population, and as a result the civil war had run its course and a number of shaikhs in al-Anbar province were disillusioned with the negative consequences resulting from their support for al-Qaeda in Iraq.

The Strategy of Counter-Insurgency, 2004–9

With more complete access to references, the passage of time, and knowledge of the outcome, historians will be able to render an objective judgement on the success or failure of US, coalition, and Iraqi counter-insurgency efforts. At the present time, the literature on the subject is dominated by works that seek to justify actions taken, to point fingers of blame at specific individuals, to restore personal or institutional reputations, or to enhance existing reputations.

Strategy is not the product of, nor is it determined by, an individual personality or a specific action, yet too often authors are quick to affix the labels 'decisive' to them. The success or failure of a strategy is the result of a range of subjective and objective factors that interact and influence each other over time. Most important, because strategy is the result of human interaction, mistakes occur in judgement or execution. Success goes to the side that commits fewer and less significant errors than its opponent, and therefore performs better strategically in relative terms. It is possible to say at this point that the US-led coalition and Iraqi forces performed better strategically than their most dangerous irregular adversaries, including al-Qaeda in Iraq.

The US-led coalition strategy from 2004 until the present, based on the simultaneous approaches of nation-building, security stabilization, and counter-insurgency, has seen its fair share of mistakes, especially in the early years. Some of these mistakes have already been outlined above. They include incorrect policy assumptions and a lack of guidance from civilian leaders, the absence of a coherent plan to stabilize Iraq after the completion of 'major combat operations', and the impact of various 'de-Ba'athification' orders, which suited ideological objectives in Washington but had grievous social and economic consequences in Iraq. Other disconnects between policy and strategy included rhetoric in presidential speeches unmatched by commensurate resources to achieve lofty goals. For example, the *Washington Post* noted in April 2006 that 'While President Bush vows to transform Iraq into a beacon of democracy in the Middle East, his administration has been scaling back funding for the main organizations trying to carry out his vision by building democratic institutions such as political parties and civil society groups.'[70]

Additional errors resulted from a listless political and military response by the coalition to growing violence, which reflected a substantial lack of knowledge about the political, economic, and social landscape of Iraq, as well as the nature, goals, and motivations of the irregular opponents arrayed against it. These errors manifested themselves in several ways. One such way was the mistaken belief in Washington and command headquarters that military transition teams (MiTTs) would succeed in creating competent and capable Iraqi military and police forces. The official US army history notes that on a functional level the 'learning curve [of MiTT advisers] was steep and time to build cohesion and trust [with their Iraqi counterparts before redeployment] was non-existent'.[71] At the level of policy and strategy, the number of Iraqis trained became a more important measure of success and improvement than their quality. Beneath the surface were significant problems, including pay rates and imbalances between military and police forces, the divided loyalties of Iraqi battalion and unit commanders, a lack of capable junior and non-commissioned officers, and little or no fiscal or material accountability, which promoted the creation of 'ghost' battalions.[72]

Friction between coalition partners compounded these troubles. Partners took issue with stringent security processes and rigid regulations and decisions that frequently denied them access to required information. More problematic were different national and individual opinions about the proper way to conduct counter-insurgency operations. Operations such as Phantom Fury, or al-Fajr (more commonly known as the second battle of Fallujah, 7 November–23 December 2004), were seen as a large-scale sweep of an insurgent stronghold with little attempt to win support of the local population. Other counter-insurgency actions billed as successes for their different approach, such as Operation Restoring Rights (Tal Afar, which began on 26 August 2005), were subsequently critiqued for a lack of sustained security and infrastructure reconstruction efforts.[73] One British brigadier went so far as to suggest that American problems in counter-insurgency resulted from 'cultural insensitivity, almost certainly inadvertent, [which] arguably amounted to institutional racism'.[74]

US-led coalition and Iraqi security forces were confronted by the traditional problem facing regular military forces fighting against irregular opponents. Irregular opponents can adapt more quickly on a tactical level, and frustrate their adversaries, by using their mobility among the population to retain the initiative and attack at a time and place of their choosing. Insurgents, terrorists, opportunists, and 'accidental guerrillas' possess significant advantages but are not without their vulnerabilities.[75] These vulnerabilities are most apparent at the level of strategy. Many irregular opponents believe that the combination of superior willpower, space to manoeuvre, and time is crucial to their success and victory. A greater challenge lies in consolidating their individual tactical victories through some sort of organizational controlling mechanism, or 'parallel government', which harnesses and mobilizes local resources to challenge the existing government and its backers for more substantial gains.[76] Ideology and local culture can strengthen norms, but they can also lead to biases and to underestimating the resolve, capabilities, and adaptability of their opponents in the constantly changing arena of strategy. In some cultural contexts, reflection and critique can be seen not as beneficial but rather as unhelpful criticism (of leaders and organizations) or loss of faith. This perhaps accounts for the relatively cool reception within radical

Salafi Islamic jihad circles to proposed strategies designed to correct perceived lost opportunities and mistakes, including Abu Musab al-Suri's *The Call for a Global Islamic Resistance* (2004), Abu Bakr Naji's *The Management of Savagery* (2004), and Muhammad Khalil al-Hukaymah's *Towards a New Strategy in Resisting the Occupier* (2006).

For some observers, the 'surge' of 30,000 additional US combat troops in Iraq, announced in President George W. Bush's speech on 10 January 2007, marked an entirely different strategy for the conflict. Some attribute the success of the US-led coalition strategy to the commitment of these extra means while overlooking the ways in which they were used and the ends to which they were applied. The groundwork for success began with the publication by the National Security Council of the *National Strategy for Victory in Iraq*, which clarified American policy objectives or the ends of the strategy.[77] Critics of the strategy pointed out that the means necessary to achieve the success of the national strategy were inadequate. Even if sufficient means were available, it was not entirely clear that they would be used in skilled ways.

The selection of General David Petraeus as the commanding general, Multi-National Force-Iraq (January 2007–September 2008), and later as the theatre commander (United States Central Command, September 2008–June 2010), solved this problem. In addition to being an accomplished soldier, General Petraeus is an intellectual who oversaw the development and writing of the army's much-publicized doctrine manual *Field Manual 3–24: Counterinsurgency*.[78] In addition to the arrival of a bright, energetic, and dedicated leader, qualitative changes were occurring in the means available in Iraq. Many armed forces, including the US army, had been criticized for failing to adapt to the realities of counter-insurgency. The additional numbers of the surge were useful, but proved secondary to the fact that organizations such as the US army could and did learn and adapt. Evidence of such adaptation included the promotion of senior leaders such as General Raymond Odierno to higher operational command, changes in pre-deployment training and more flexibility and innovative tactics, and acceptance of greater risk by forces on the ground, at sea, and in the air.[79] Many of these US means were dedicated to training, educating, and jointly sharing the risks, but gradually transferring local responsibilities to increasingly proficient Iraqi military and police forces.

The biggest shift that allowed the surge to succeed occurred within Iraq itself. Within the Iraqi government, senior leaders including President Nouri al-Maliki increasingly asserted their authority to ensure that those below them were accountable and to purge the Shia-dominated government of individuals with ties to insurgent and extremist groups and militias. After the al-Askariya Mosque was bombed a second time (January 2007), President al-Maliki fired local commanders who had previously assured him that Samarra was pacified.[80]

Within various elements of Iraqi society, fatigue set in after years of violence and internecine war. Some local Iraqi leaders also questioned how the violence improved the situation for them and their kinsmen. Friction also played a role during this phase of the campaign. In the case of al-Qaeda in Iraq, its members' indiscriminate violence, uncompromising ideology, and increasingly arrogant behaviour were contributing to the decision of shaikhs in the al-Anbar region to turn against the group and ally themselves with American and Iraqi government forces.[81] Perhaps as a result of the success of shaikhs in al-Anbar, but more likely because tribal leaders saw a way of disconnecting from the network of groups fighting and returning to normal (and not armed) politics, other so-called 'awakenings' have occurred in Babil, Baghdad, Diyala, and Saydiyah.

CONCLUSION

The examinations of strategy in Iraq and Afghanistan end rather abruptly without satisfying the reader of their outcome. It would be the height of folly to speculate on what will or will not happen. Predictions put forth are almost certain to be wrong given the range of unknown and unknowable information. Unlike the well-studied wars and campaigns of the past discussed in the preceding chapters, the outcome of the wars in Iraq and Afghanistan is still very uncertain. This chapter will conclude with some general observations on strategy as it is put into practice in contemporary conflicts.

Hindsight provides the scholar with the benefit of being able to place into context-specific decisions and their effects on the course of the campaign or war. For example, the decision of the Imperial Japanese General Staff to invade Midway Island in June of 1942 can be examined in light of the outcome of the battle and subsequent events. The effects on Japanese strategy of the disaster at Midway, considered the turning point of the Pacific war, included the loss of naval air supremacy; in the longer term Japan's action facilitated the American counter-offensive in the Solomon Islands and is even said to have led to the Japanese surrender in August 1945. Yet, both the Americans and the Japanese in 1942 acted according to a strategy that envisioned use of their available resources in a way that would achieve victory.

Regardless of the specific methods used, war has been and is still about the use of armed force to achieve specific political purposes, although the means and methods change.[82] As other chapters in this work have argued, strategy should connect the use of armed force to achieve the desired purpose in a manner that is both realistic and acceptable in political, social, economic, and military terms.

Three attributes of strategy are identifiable in all wars, but are especially apparent in contemporary conflicts. The first is that strategy does not exist in a vacuum. As a number of theorists periodically remind us, strategy is not an academic but rather a practical discipline.[83] Although strategy can be understood on a theoretical level, it must be *put into practice* to have any value. If all that were required in strategy was knowing what to do, and doing it, there would be no difficulties in executing it flawlessly.

The second and third attributes reflect the difficulties associated with conducting strategy in practice. The second attribute acknowledges that strategy is executed by, with, and through a number of actors. These actors include leaders, individual citizens, organizations, and society, and they can have a tremendous influence on how well or how poorly strategy is translated into action. Leaders, and US military leadership in particular, have been cited as the key to success in the American 'surge' of forces in Iraq. Actors with a role in planning and executing strategy should ensure that their actions do not occur in a vacuum or exist in isolation. Too often, casual observers make the mistake of assuming that once action has been agreed upon, a single strategy need only be put in motion to succeed, with all actors working in harmony towards a common purpose. As the Afghanistan example suggests, strategies or other actions may compete or work against one another within organizations and between allies, even if all the participants agree on a vaguely defined purpose. As General McChrystal noted, at one level of strategy 'ISAF's subordinate headquarters [the regional commands] must stop fighting separate campaigns.'[84] This competition or working at cross-purposes may be a function of expediency, different organizational or national preferences, or even the bureaucratic desire to control some or all of the strategy.[85] For example, one of the most significant challenges to the conduct of American strategy in Iraq and Afghanistan has been to reconcile its objectives and priorities with those of Nouri al-Maliki and Hamid Kharzai, respectively.

The third attribute reflects awareness that strategy is never static but is influenced dynamically by a number of sources. These influences include the actions and strategy of the enemy and changes in policy, among others. In discussions about contemporary strategy, too often attention focuses on one's own goals, interests, and resources as if these were constants. By some accounts, the only actor that matters in strategy is the United States or its Department of Defense. Views of the irregular adversaries against which the United States is struggling are often sketchy or grossly distorted. For example, in some accounts the Taliban, al-Qaeda, and various insurgent groups in Iraq appear to possess a unity of organization, thought, and purpose that they simply do not have. The preceding discussion of Afghanistan and Iraq should make clear that irregular adversaries are not immune from the very human influences of indecision, infighting, and misjudging their opponents.

The most dynamic influence on strategy has been and will remain the interaction between opponents as they seek to impose their will upon one another. Put simply, while you are trying to get the enemy to submit to your will, he is doing his best to thwart you and subject you to his instead. This dynamic interaction between opponents can challenge or ruin many of the assumptions, timelines, and schedules inherent in strategy. Such interaction forces changes to your strategy, just as your actions force changes on the enemy's.

The conduct of strategy is under still other pressures, which include shifts in the support base. This support base can include factors such as the much-desired but elusive 'popular support' sought after in classical works on counter-insurgency, as well as elements of power closer to home, including voters, financial backers, and other power brokers. Changes in the support base, as a result of discontent or disapproval, often lead to changes in policy or approach. As policy priorities change, strategy must account for them or it risks being conducted for its own sake.

NOTES

1. The redacted text of McChrystal's assessment, made available on 21 Sept. 2009, is at <http://media.washingtonpost.com/wp-srv/politics/documents/Assessment_Redacted_092109.pdf>, accessed 2 Dec. 2009.

2. See, e.g. the use by President Barack Obama in his much-anticipated speech of force levels in Afghanistan, 'Text: Obama's Speech on Afghanistan', *CBS News Political Hotsheet*, 1 Dec. 2009, <http://www.cbsnews.com/blogs/2009/12/01/politics/political hotsheet/entry5855894.shtml>, accessed 2 Dec. 2009.

3. N. Cook, 'The Death of Strategy: Effects-Based Air Operations', *Jane's Defence Weekly*, 39/24 (18 June 2003), 53–7.

4. T. Huber, 'Compound Warfare: A Conceptual Framework', in id. (ed.), *Compound Warfare: That Fatal Knot* (Fort Leavenworth, KS, 2002). On hybrid wars, see F. Hoffman, *Conflict in the 21st Century: The Rise of Hybrid Wars* (Arlington, VA, 2007); and J. Mccuen, 'Hybrid Wars', *Military Review*, 88/2 (April 2008), 107–13.

5. David Kilcullen offers the latter interpretation of 'hybrid warfare' in *The Accidental Guerrilla: Fighting Small Wars in the Midst of a Big One* (Oxford, 2009), 149–50.

6. J. Kiras, 'Irregular Warfare', in D. Jordan et al., *Understanding Modern Warfare* (Cambridge, 2008), 232. Forms of irregular warfare including terrorism, insurgency, *coup d'état*, revolution, and civil war, and such activities can be sponsored by states through sub-state groups.

7. See, e.g. B. Salmoni, 'The Fallacy of Irregular Warfare', *RUSI Journal*, 152/4 (August 2007), 18–24..

8. R. Smith, 'Trends: Our Modern Operations', in id., *The Utility of Force: The Art of War in the Modern World* (New York, 2008), 269–307.

9. Attempts to resurrect this classification in 1970 were unsuccessful; see M. Elliott-Bateman, *The Fourth Dimension of Warfare*, I: *Intelligence, Subversion, and Resistance* (New York, 1970).

10. R. Trinquier, *Modern Warfare: A French View of Counterinsurgency*, trans. D. Lee (1964; Westport, CT, 2006), 3–8.

11. C. von Clausewitz, *On War*, ed. and trans. M. Howard and P. Paret (Princeton, 1976), 88–9.

12. D. Jablonski, 'Why Is Strategy Difficult?', in J. Boone Bartholomees, Jr (ed.), *U.S. Army War College Guide to National Security Policy and Strategy*, 2nd rev. edn (Carlisle Barracks, PA, June 2006), 15. Jablonski warns of the dangers of such formulas. He adds, 'But those students also know from their experience in the field that there are limits to the scientific approach when dealing with human endeavors. As a consequence, they can also appreciate the art of mixing ends, ways, and means, using for each element the part subjective, part objective criteria of suitability, feasibility, and applicability—the essence of strategic calculation' (ibid.).

13. E. Reischauer, Foreword, in A. D. Coox, *The Anatomy of a Small War: The Soviet-Japanese Struggle for Changkufeng/Khasan, 1938* (Westport, CT, 1977), xii.

14. Depending on language, region, and preference, the term 'Pashtun', 'Pakhtun', or 'Pathan' is used. They all refer to the same ethnic group of Pashto-speaking people. For the purposes of this chapter, the term 'Pashtun' will be used throughout. V. Schofield, *Afghan Frontier: Feuding and Fighting in Central Asia* (London, 2003), 114.

15. For details leading up to the incident, see J. Waller, *Beyond the Khyber Pass: The Road to British Disaster in the First Afghan War* (Austin, TX, 1990). The classic popular history of the march to destruction remains P. Macrory, *The Fierce Pawns* (Philadelphia, PA, 1966).

16. For details, including the wider political context of global competition between the United States and the Soviet Union, see B. Rubin, *The Fragmentation of Afghanistan: State Formation and Collapse in the International System* (New Haven, 1995).

17. On why the Soviets failed in their counter-insurgency efforts, see S. McMichael, *Stumbling Bear: Soviet Military Performance in Afghanistan* (London, 1991), 38–44, 52–78. The Russian General Staff assessment of the mujahidin and their tactics is

contained in L. Grau and M. Gress (eds and trans.), *The Soviet–Afghan War: How a Superpower Fought and Lost* (Lawrence, KS, 2002), 53–72.

18. Abdulkader Sinno provides a theoretical explanation for why some mujahidin withstood Soviet and Taliban pressure while others collapsed; Sinno, *Organizations at War in Afghanistan and Beyond* (Ithaca, NY, 2008).

19. For details of al-Qaeda activities and US responses, and the often tense relationship between the intelligence, military, and national security policy communities, see S. Coll, *Ghost Wars: The Secret History of the CIA, Afghanistan, and Bin Laden from the Soviet Invasion to September 10, 2001* (New York, 2004), esp. chs 21–32.

20. The latter date marks the end of Operation Anaconda, more popularly known as the battle of Tora Bora, during and after which Taliban and al-Qaeda survivors made their escape. Details of the military special operations campaign are contained in the official history: C. Briscoe, R. L. Kiper, J. A. Schroder, and K. I. Sepp, *Weapon of Choice: U.S. Army Special Operations Forces in Afghanistan* (Fort Leavenworth, KS, 2003), esp. chs 3–4. A first-hand account by the Central Intelligence Agency team leader for the initial operations into Afghanistan is G. Berntsen and R. Pezzullo, *Jawbreaker: The Attack on Bin Laden and Al-Qaeda* (New York, 2005).

21. Figures derived from Central Intelligence Agency, *CIA World Factbook 2009*, s.v. 'Afghanistan' (updated 11 Nov. 2009), <https://www.cia.gov/library/publications/the-world-factbook/geos/af.html>, accessed 2 Dec. 2009.

22. Martin Ewans recognizes two main Pashtun divisions while Sir Olaf Caroe suggests there are three; Ewans, *Afghanistan: A Short History of its Peoples and Politics* (New York, 2002), 5–12; and Caroe, *The Pathans*, rev. edn (Karachi, 1985), xvi–xviii.

23. A useful if dated description of the political structure within Yusufzai Pathan villages is contained in F. Barth, *Political Leadership among Swat Pathans*, LSE Monographs on Social Anthropology, 19 (London, 1959), 9–30.

24. Ewans, *Afghanistan*, 7.

25. H. Abbas, 'A Profile of Tehrik-i-Taliban Pakistan', *CTC Sentinel*, 1/2 (January 2008), 1–4.

26. R. Synovitz, 'Afghanistan: Taliban Evolves into Network of Groups', *Radio Free Europe/Radio Liberty*, 26 Apr. 2008, <http://www.rferl.org/content/article/1109636.html>, accessed 2 Dec. 2009.

27. Kilcullen, *The Accidental Guerrilla*, 48–9.

28. S. S. Harrison, 'Beware Pashtunistan', *Newsweek* (12 Nov. 2007), <http://www.newsweek.com/id/67966>, accessed 2 Dec. 2009.

29. See International Crisis Group, *Taliban Propaganda: Winning the War of Words?* Asia Report, 158 (Brussels, July 2008); and B. Roggio, 'Al Qaeda's Shadow Army Commander Outlines Afghan Strategy', *Long War Journal*, 13 Apr. 2009, <http://www.longwarjournal.org/archives/2009/04/al_qaedas_shadow_arm.php>, accessed 2 Dec. 2009.

30. A. Giustozzi, *Koran, Kalashnikov, and Laptop: The Neo-Taliban Insurgency in Afghanistan* (New York, 2008), ch. 4.

31. Ibid. 127–9.

32. Kilcullen has used this phrase repeatedly in press statements and briefings. See, e.g. Australian Broadcasting Corporation, 'Counter-Insurgency Expert Joins *Lateline*', *Lateline* (21 Aug. 2009), <http://www.abc.net.au/lateline/content/2008/s2663455.htm>; and J. D. Leipold, 'Government Reform Key to Afghanistan says Kilcullen', *www.army.mil*, 27 Oct. 2009, <http://www.army.mil/-news/2009/10/27/29411-government-reform-key-to-afghanistan-says-kilcullen>, accessed 2 Dec. 2009.

33. For details on the opium trade, its relationship to the insurgency, and the challenges in stopping it, see G. Peters, *Seeds of Terror: How Heroin Is Bankrolling the Taliban and Al Qaeda* (New York, 2009). The International Council on Security and Development (ICOS) suggests that a way out of this dilemma is for poppy farming to continue under government control for production as medical morphine; ICOS, *Poppy for Medicine:*

Licensing Poppy for the Production of Essential Medicines: An Integrated Counter-Narcotics, Development, and Counter-Insurgency Model for Afghanistan (London, June 2007).

34. Two leading contributors to forces in the crucial southern theatre of operations, the Dutch and the Canadians, have publicly announced troop withdrawals in 2010 and 2011 respectively; see J. E. Barnes, 'U.S. Afghanistan Debate Curbs Gates on Canada Visit', *Los Angeles Times*, 21 Nov. 2009.

35. Described in more detail in Kilcullen, *The Accidental Guerrilla*, 50–1.

36. See, e.g. the characteristics of 'wicked' versus 'tame' problems in J. Conklin, *Dialogue Mapping: Building Shared Understanding of Wicked Problems* (New York, 2005), esp. ch. 1: 'Wicked Problems and Social Complexity', <http://cognexus.org/wpf/wicked problems.pdf>, accessed 2 Dec. 2009.

37. B. Woodward, *Bush at War* (New York, 2002), 193.

38. This argument was made by Secretary of Defense Donald Rumsfeld and Deputy Secretary of Defense Paul Wolfowitz in discussions on how to respond to the 11 September 2001 attacks; ibid. 83–4.

39. 'Afghanistan's Marshall Plan', *New York Times*, 19 Apr. 2002, <http://www.nytimes.com/2002/04/19/opinion/afghanistan-s-marshall-plan.html>, accessed 2 Dec. 2009.

40. US Agency For International Development, *Provincial Reconstruction Teams* (2 Dec. 2009), <http://afghanistan.usaid.gov/en/Page.PRT.aspx>, accessed 2 Dec. 2009.

41. Ibid.

42. US Agency For International Development, *Provincial Reconstruction Teams in Afghanistan: An Interim Assessment*, PN-ADG-252 (Washington, DC, June 2006), 11.

43. Quotation ascribed to Brigadier-General David Palmer, cited in (with reference) J. Etheridge, *Replacement Operations: The Use of CONUS Replacement Centers to Support the Warfighting CINC*, US Army War College Military Studies Program Paper (Carlisle Barracks, PA, 24 Jan. 1992), 4, 30.

44. T. Coughlin, 'French Troops Were Killed after Italy Hushed up 'Bribes' to Taleban', *The Times*, 15 Oct. 2009. The article, which caused a furore in France, has since been removed from the *Times* website. It was originally published at <http://www.timesonline.co.uk/tol/news/world/Afghanistan/article6875376.ece>, accessed 15 Oct. 2009). The text of the article is currently available at <http://www.militaryphotos.net/forums/showthread.php?166972-French-troops-were-killed-after-Italy-hushed-up-%91 bribes%92-to-Taleban>, accessed 8 Aug. 2010.

45. R. Synovitz, 'Afghanistan: Former Taliban Commander Advises U.S. Ambassador', *Radio Free Europe/Radio Liberty*, 16 Jan. 2008, <http://www.rferl.org/content/article/1079359.html>, accessed 2 Dec. 2009.

46. 'Text: Obama's Speech on Afghanistan'.

47. For details, see D. Omissi, *Air Power and Colonial Control: The Royal Air Force, 1919–1939* (Manchester, 1990), 18–38. Air campaigns and advisory efforts are covered in detail in J. Glubb, *War in the Desert: An R.A.F. Frontier Campaign* (London, 1960).

48. For details on Saddam's life and political role in Iraq, see S. Balaghi, *Saddam Hussein: A Biography* (Westport, CT, 2008).

49. Unless otherwise indicated, the source of figures is Central Intelligence Agency, *CIA World Factbook 2009*, s.v. 'Iraq' (updated 11 Nov. 2009), <https://www.cia.gov/library/publications/the-world-factbook/geos/iz.html>, accessed 2 Dec. 2009.

50. Years of sanctions had deprived these forces of replacements and spare parts necessary to rebuild after 1991 and Saddam diverted other equipment from the Republican Guard to the fedayin.

51. An excellent breakdown and comparison of available Iraqi and coalition forces, derived from publicly available information, is contained in A. Cordesman, *The Iraq War: Strategy, Tactics, and Military Lessons* (Westport, CT, 2003), 15–56.

52. See, e.g. N. Mackay, 'Saddam's Enforcers', *Sunday Herald*, 30 Mar. 2003, <http://www.freerepublic.com/focus/f-news/879603/posts>, accessed 2 Dec. 2009.

53. K. Woods et al., *The Iraqi Perspectives Project: A View of Operation Iraqi Freedom from Saddam's Senior Leadership* (Norfolk, VA, 2006), 27–8, <http://www.jfcom.mil/newslink/storyarchive/2006/ipp.pdf>, accessed 2 Dec. 2009. This report provides remarkable insights into how and why Saddam and regime responded to the coalition invasion as they did.

54. Mark Bowden, the author of *Blackhawk Down*, wrote that 'If Saddam Hussein wins his bet, then coalition forces could face fighting reminiscent of the 1993 battle of Mogadishu' in a bizarre case of life imitating art imitating life; Bowden, '*Blackhawk Down* Author asks 'Will Baghdad Fight to the End?'', *Rantburg*, 27 Mar. 2003, <http://www.rantburg.com:8080/poparticle.php?D=2003-03-27&ID=11969&HC=1>, accessed 2 Dec. 2009.

55. Woods et al., *The Iraqi Perspectives Project*, 28–32, and conversations with the report's authors.

56. The definitive work remains M. R. Gordon and B. E. Trainor, *Cobra II: The Inside Story of the Invasion and Occupation of Iraq* (New York, 2006).

57. Details of the various units, plans, wargames, and actions of US army forces are available in the official history: G. Fontenot, E. J. Degen, and D. Tohn, *On Point: The United States Army in Operation Iraqi Freedom* (Fort Leavenworth, KS, 2004). A more accessible history, which takes a broader perspective on the campaign, is W. Murray and R. Scales, Jr, *The Iraq War: A Military History* (Cambridge, MA, 2003).

58. Details of the contributions of British, Australian, and Polish special operations forces to these actions are difficult to obtain. The activities of American army special operations forces are available in its official history: C. Briscoe et al., *All Roads Lead to Baghdad: Army Special Operations Forces in Iraq* (Fort Bragg, NC, 2006).

59. Administrator Of The Coalition Provisional Authority, *Coalition Provisional Authority Order Number 1: De-Ba'athification of Iraqi Society* (16 May 2003), <http://www.iraqcoalition.org/regulations/20030516_CPAORD_1_De-Ba_athification_of_Iraqi_Society_.pdf>, accessed 2 Dec. 2009.

60. L. P. Bremer and M. McConnell, *My Year in Iraq: The Struggle to Build a Future of Hope* (New York, 2006), 126–7.

61. International Crisis Group, *In Their Own Words: Reading the Iraqi Insurgency*, Middle East Report, 50 (Brussels, 16 Feb. 2006), 7–13.

62. Categorizations used in D. Wright et al., *On Point II: Transition to the New Campaign: The United States Army in Operation Iraqi Freedom, May 2003–January 2005* (Fort Leavenworth, KS, 2008), 105–10.

63. M. Eisenstadt and J. White, 'Assessing Iraq's Sunni Arab Insurgency', *Military Review*, 86/3 (May–June 2006), 37–8.

64. See 'Year Four: Simply the Worst', *Iraq Body Count*, Press Release 15 (18 Mar. 2007), <http://www.iraqbodycount.org/analysis/numbers/year-four>, accessed 2 Dec. 2009.

65. Figures quoted in UNHCR, *UNHCR Worried About Effect of Dire Security Situation on Iraq's Displaced* (13 Oct. 2006), <http://www.unhcr.org/news/NEWS/452fa9954.html>, accessed 2 Dec. 2009.

66. For details of the attack, see *IED Attack on the Al Askariya Mosque in Samarra, 22 February 2006*, TRITON Quick-Look Report (Faringdon, 26 Feb. 2006).

67. For details on Zarqawi's early life before joining al-Qaeda, see J.-C. Brisand, *Zarqawi: The New Face of Al-Qaeda* (New York, 2005), 8–62.

68. Letter from al-Zawahiri to Zarqawi, 9 July 2005, trans. and released by the Office of the Director of National Intelligence (11 Oct. 2005), 3–4, <http://www.dni.gov/press_releases/letter_in_english.pdf>, accessed 2 Dec. 2009.

69. The details of how those closest to Zarqawi revealed his location are contained in M. Alexander, *How to Break a Terrorist: The U.S. Interrogators Who Used Brains, not Brutality, to Take Down the Deadliest Man in Iraq* (New York, 2008).

70. P. Baker, 'Democracy in Iraq not a Priority in U.S. Budget', *Washington Post*, 5 Apr. 2006, <http://www.washingtonpost.com/wp-dyn/content/article/2006/04/04/AR200604 0401626.html>.

71. Wright et al., *On Point II*, 463.

72. Iraqi commanders would submit false reports, including inflated rosters for units that only existed on paper ('ghost' battalions), to receive payrolls, weapons, and equipment for personal gain.

73. For a contemporary press account during the opening phase of the operation, see B. Roggio, 'After Action Report: Oil Spots and Tal Afar', *Long War Journal*, 14 Sept. 2005, <http://www.longwarjournal.org/archives/2005/09/after_action_re_1.php#ixzz0YqH9w v0h>, accessed 2 Dec. 2009. Ahmed Hashim, the cultural adviser to the commander conducting the operation, was much more pessimistic about its success two years later; see 'Police and Militants Gun Down Sunnis in Revenge Attacks', *PBS Newshour* transcript (28 Mar. 2007), <http://www.pbs.org/newshour/bb/middle_east/jan-june07/carnage_03-28. html>, accessed 2 Dec. 2009.

74. N. Alywn-Foster, 'Changing the Army for Counterinsurgency Operations', *Military Review*, 85/6 (November–December 2005), 3.

75. A common misperception is that irregular attacks are committed by dedicated members of terrorist organizations. David Kilcullen makes the case that responses of locals to external threats can be more cultural than political in nature; see *The Accidental Guerrilla*, p. xiv. Although aspects of this phenomenon were at work in Iraq, other opportunists had more personal motivations for conducting attacks. In particular, money flowing into Iraq from Sunni and Shia sources in the region and abroad financed improvised explosive attacks, and the 'going rate' to conduct an attack, despite the potential risks, was more than the monthly salary for service in the Iraqi military or police. Kimberly Kagan quotes a price of $500 to conduct an IED attack. On Shia funding and sources, see Kagan, *The Surge: A Military History* (New York, 2009), 160–8. For details on Sunni financial and material resources, see B. Fishman (ed.), *Bombers, Bank Accounts and Bleedout: Al-Qa'ida's Road In and Out of Iraq* (West Point, NY, 2008), esp. chs 3 and 4.

76. On the challenges of developing this 'clandestine infrastructure', see A. Molnar et al., *Undergrounds in Insurgent, Revolutionary, and Resistance Warfare* (Washington, DC, 1963), esp. chs 2 and 3.

77. National Security Council, *National Strategy for Victory in Iraq* (Washington, DC, November 2005), <http://www.washingtonpost.com/wp-srv/nation/documents/Iraq nationalstrategy11-30-05.pdf>, accessed 2 Dec. 2009. Other contributing factors included changes in senior policy leadership, especially within the Department of Defense.

78. On General Petraeus's background and role in the surge, see T. Ricks, *The Gamble: General David Petraeus and the American Military Adventure in Iraq, 2006–2008* (New York, 2009); and L. Robinson, *Tell Me How This Ends: General David Petraeus and the Search for a Way Out of Iraq* (New York, 2008).

79. This is the central theme of Kagan, *The Surge*.

80. Ricks, *The Gamble*, 228–30.

81. For a brief summary of events, see Kagan, *The Surge*, 60–80. A detailed assessment of tribal politics, relationships, and their influence in the awakening is contained in Kilcullen, *The Accidental Guerrilla*, 152–80.

82. A point made convincingly by Colin Gray, 'Irregular Warfare: One Nature, Many Characters', *Strategic Studies Quarterly*, 1/2 (Winter 2007), esp. 39–40.

83. Carl von Clausewitz was one of the first theorists to provide this corrective in his unfinished *On War*, but a more recent example, intended to remind those involved in teaching strategy in the curricula, is C. S. Gray, *Schools for Strategy: Teaching Strategy for the 21st Century* (Carlisle Barracks, PA, November 2009).

84. ISAF HQ, *COMISAF's Initial Assessment* (30 Aug. 2009), 2–14, <http://media.washingtonpost.com/wp-srv/politics/documents/Assessment_Redacted_092109.pdf>, accessed 2 Dec. 2009.

85. A point made succinctly, from a theatre commander-in-chief's perspective, by retired Marine General Anthony Zinni, in T. Clancy, with T. Zinni and T. Koltz, *Battle Ready* (New York, 2005), 322–5.

Conclusion

Colin S. Gray

INTRODUCTION

Every chapter in this book is a study of strategy. The entire political history of mankind, which is to say the whole history of relations of power among individuals and social groups, has a strategic dimension. Ironically, the extraordinary variety of the people, circumstances, motives, cultures, issues, relevant geographies, and technologies discussed in these case studies serves to strengthen recognition of strategic continuity. The continuity lies in the strategic function, obviously not in the strategies chosen, or pursued unselfconsciously by default, to meet the demands of the day expediently. The strategic function simply insists that ends, ways, and means should be mutually supportive, although the support need not be perfect. The author claims that:

1. The practice of strategy, singular, considered as a function, is an eternal, universal, essential, and therefore unavoidable feature of human life. Individually and variably collectively, people perform the strategic function as a competitive necessity for survival.

2. Because humans have always had to practice, or try to practice, strategy, it is inescapable to claim that a single, unified general theory must have pertained through all of history—past, present, and future.

These simple, but admittedly hegemonic, claims are not hard to support. Stated in the most basic form imaginable, all human beings, perhaps all life, must seek to match ends, ways, and means. Every human society has had purposes (survival, most significantly), more or fewer ways to advance or merely protect those purposes, and limited assets to employ. Whether societies performed competently or incompetently, and regardless of the particular words that they used to describe what they tried to do, they must therefore have sought to function strategically. This potent minimalist perspective on strategy in historical practice can accommodate any and all variations in specific detail as to ends (motives, purposes, goals), ways (strategies, methods, plans), and means (whatever assets, material, spiritual and other, are available and judged useful), as well as the assumptions, priorities, and theories of victory that specifically characterized strategy in action.

One cannot opt out of strategy's domain of practical historical authority. This argument ought not to be at all controversial, because it is difficult even to frame an alternative to it. Discipline has not been enforced by outraged military theorists and philosophers, but rather by the actual or anticipated pain of defeat. Failure, death, and damage is the price paid eternally for strategic incompetence or ill fortune.

STRATEGY: AN ENDURING FUNCTION

Scholars today cannot help but bring an early twenty-first-century lens to bear upon all of strategic history.[1] We are what we are, and we think as we think, in good part not only because of our place in time, geography, and experience (first-hand and as cultural legacy) but also because we are human, an all but timeless and universal complication. It is only rarely—perhaps never—possible to recover with complete and reliable assurance what the pre-modern historical figures prominent in this book thought about, and intended to effect, by the strategic choices that they made. Yet if the Romans, or Byzantines, did not function strategically—since strategy as we conceptualize it today would have been foreign to them—how else did they function to achieve their goals? Could pre-modern people have made and acted upon choices that we can reasonably label 'strategic', even if they understood those choices in other ways?

It might seem at first glance to be common sense, possibly even logically necessary, to hold that if military leaders in ancient or mediaeval times lacked the vocabulary of our modern strategic discourse in any contemporary language, they must have been unable to behave with strategic intent. Tersely rephrased: if they could not think it, because they lacked the ideas that the words would supply, they could not do it. Yet the evidence of pre-modern behaviour that we can recover with some confidence from words, and more persuasively from deeds and misdeeds, is scarcely less plausible as examples of strategic perspective than is generically like behaviour today. While this evidence usually calls for more or less creative translation to render tolerably 'modern', the decidedly thin written record of explicitly strategic ancient, mediaeval, and even early modern thought really is not a matter of great importance.[2]

For example, the Byzantines sincerely believed that the Virgin Mary, as protectress of their capital city of Constantinople, provided them great spiritual strength—and their faith was apparently confirmed by the failure of the great Arab siege of 717–718.[3] Did this, and similar beliefs throughout the centuries (*Gott mit uns*), mean that the believers in question put their trust in God rather than in their own strategic competence? Of course not. What it did mean was that devout Byzantines factored the anticipated strategic benefit of the Virgin Mary's intercession into their grand strategic triptych of ends, ways, and means, or at least as a potent source of confidence for morale.

Neither the Romans nor their Byzantine successors supported institutes for strategic and security studies that examined strategy from a theoretical perspective. They did not have professional associations for strategists and they lacked a dedicated strategic literature. However, there was an extensive military literature, some of which has survived, that speaks volumes plainly enough for us to render them comprehensible in our terms. Some of that literature explicitly addressed strategy, although the term presumably had different connotations for the writers than it does for contemporary theorists. For example, the author of *The Anonymous Byzantine Treatise on Strategy*, writing in the latter half of the reign of Emperor Justinian I (CE 527–565), advises as follows:

> [W]e have to speak of the science of strategy, which is really the most important branch of the science of government. By putting it into practice we shall be able not only to resist our enemies but even to conquer them. Strategy is the means by which a commander may defend his own lands and defeat his enemies. The general is the one who practices strategy... Strategy teaches us how to defend what is our own and to threaten what belongs to the enemy.[4]

The first sentence just quoted from the Greek of Byzantium of the 550s or 560s is more than slightly reminiscent of the first thought recorded in Chinese of Sun Tzu, writing either during the period known as The Warring States (453–221 BCE) or in the half-century immediately antecedent. Sun Tzu claims didactically that '[w]ar is a matter of vital importance to the state; the province of life or death, the road to survival or ruin. It is mandatory that it be thoroughly studied'.[5]

Closer to our own time, Clausewitz also wrote explicitly about strategy, although often today it is claimed that his was a military focus much narrower than the one popular now. Although he stated that 'tactics teaches *the use of armed forces in the engagement*' while strategy 'the use of engagements *for the object of war*',[6] he also noted that

> Strategy is the use of the engagement for the purpose of the war. The strategist must therefore define an aim for the entire operational side of the war that will be in accordance with its purpose. In other words he will draft the plan of the war.[7]

These examples are hardly exhaustive. The historical unity of strategic experience and contemplation thereon is readily appreciated if one compiles a short list of the more profound treatises on strategy faithfully recovered from all times past. Those treatises should pass the test of plausible tolerable fit with our contemporary thinking on what is, and what is not, strategic. Thus, this argument could be strengthened were we to add Thucydides's reconstruction of fifth-century Athenian and Spartan reasoning on what today is known as grand or national security strategy.[8] We could hardly expect an early nineteenth-century Prussian, a mid-sixth-century Byzantine, or a fifth-century BCE Chinese or Greek to explain what the strategic function meant for them in terms identical to those favoured today. The remarkable similarity among thoughts expressed across millennia, languages, and conditions of all kinds increases confidence in the claim that strategy as a function has not altered in its essential meaning or in its relevance over the course at least of recorded history (if often only recorded unreliably and in fragments).

Polities have always needed strategy—whether neutral–functional, grand, or military. When polities have not actually been at war, they have commonly anticipated the danger of war, certainly of some warfare, and as a reasonable consequence they have behaved strategically in preparing against that possibility, probability, or believed certainty. Discouraging though it may be for liberal optimism, with its faith in progress, the evidence obliges us to agree with Michael Howard when he wrote:

> If there are no wars in the present in which the professional soldier can learn his trade, he is almost compelled to study the wars of the past. *For after all allowances have been made for historical differences, wars still resemble each other more than they resemble any other human activity.* All are fought, as Clausewitz insisted, in a special element of danger and fear and confusion. In all, large bodies of men are trying to impose their will on one another by violence; and in all, events occur which are inconceivable in any other field of experience.[9]

It follows that polities differing greatly in character over millennia have needed to attempt to practice grand and military strategy purposefully. And therefore, because wars have exhibited such notable continuities, strategic theory has been as permanently relevant and necessary as its various applications. It is to the purpose, nature, and content of this theory that we now turn.

WHY THEORY?

People cannot function without theory. If repeated success in statecraft and generalship cannot be achieved through entirely spontaneous and probably near-random choices, such success is likely to be greatly in debt to some prior understanding of the kind and character of the problems that emerge. While competence in strategic practice does not correlate reliably with an intellectual grasp of strategy, strategic theory is not an optional extra for an idle hour. Practicing strategists have to make choices, and those choices must rest upon some anticipated flow from cause to effect. This, tersely put, is theory. We choose particular actions because we believe that they will bring about particular desired consequences; this is theory. All military plans provide explanations of how certain actions will achieve desired objectives; this, too, is theory.

Disciplines differ in their preferred definition of theory and its requirements. In the physical sciences, theory predicts, but in the social sciences one has to be content with a lesser standard. Approached from a social scientific perspective, strategic theory must provide explanation that is true in most, not necessarily all, situations, and it needs to be coherent and therefore systematic. The most perceptive and persuasive discussion of 'military theory'—which one can translate without difficulty *ab extensio* to strategic theory—known to us is provided by Harold R. Winton of the US Air University. Winton advises sensibly that theory should be required to perform four tasks: (*a*) 'to define the field of study under investigation'; (*b*) 'to categorize, i.e., to break the field of study into its constituent parts'; (*c*) to connect 'the field of study to other related fields in the universe' (Winton cites Clausewitz's success in relating war to politics); and (*d*) 'theory anticipates'.[10] The many and highly varied functional strategists discussed in this book have all required education of the kinds identified by Winton: (*a*) to know what it was that they needed to know; (*b*) to be able to identify and understand the parts of the challenges that they faced and how they interconnected; (*c*) to locate their issue-area in its relation to other subjects; and (*d*) to educate their guesses about the future.

If there is a unity to human strategic history, a single general theory of strategy must serve as one Big Tent that accommodates all strategic phenomena. A unified general theory of strategy exists, although it is frequently adapted to shifting contemporary taste in order to educate those who are or will be charged with the practice of strategy.[11]

The purpose of strategic theory is most easily explained by drawing the clearest possible distinction between *strategy*, singular, and *strategies*, plural. The former, which is the permanent nature of the strategic function, must be represented as one unchanging theory, while the latter gives expression to strategy in practice as strategies, keyed to the ever-changing character of perceived historical needs.

THE GENERAL THEORY OF STRATEGY IN TWENTY-ONE DICTA[12]

The sole purpose of a general theory of strategy is to prepare the strategist to practice competently whatever specific strategic tasks fall to his or her lot. The theory, and the pragmatic test of its every iteration, must simply explain what strategy is, what it does, and how and why it does it. Rephrased, general strategic theory explains to the strategist the structure and functioning of what it is that he or she is trying to do. It is up to him, or her, to apply the theory to the case at hand.[13]

The general theory of strategy thus performs essentially the same duty for the practice of strategy that pure mathematics does for the sciences. Both provide tools of understanding independent of local purpose, preference, and experience, but should help enable those who are educable to address specific problems. Unlike both pure and applied mathematics, however, applied strategic theory is almost certain to bear the signatures, cultural and other, of the particular time and place of its application.

Because all wars and warfare have had essential defining features in common, a single unified general theory of strategy must merit conceptually hegemonic status over their entire historical domain. Some readers may find this an unduly bold claim. Further, it is not wholly unreasonable to assume that any framing and wording of a strategic theory plausibly applicable to all times, places, and circumstances is likely to be so general in its terms that it loses all useful explanatory power. This author believes that there is an eternal and universal theory of strategy that does not pay in surrendered depth for its historical width, although each theorist has expressed it distinctively according to time, place, culture, circumstance, and personal preference.

Presented here is the author's best current effort to present such a general theory. While others may choose to draft the theory differently in some detail of language, as well as in some conflation of, or yet greater distinction between, dicta, most scholars of strategy should be able to agree that the content of these '21 Dicta' is broadly acceptable.

Nature and Character of Strategy

1. Grand strategy is the direction and use made of any or all of the assets of a security community, including its military instrument, for the purposes of policy as decided by politics.

2. Military strategy is the direction and use made of force and the threat of force for the purposes of policy as decided by politics.

3. Strategy is the only bridge built and held to connect policy purposefully with the military and other instruments of power and influence.

4. Strategy serves politics instrumentally by generating net strategic effect.

5. Strategy is adversarial; it functions in both peace and war, and it always seeks a measure of control over enemies (and often over allies and neutrals, also).

6. Strategy usually requires deception, and the results are frequently ironic.

7. Strategy is human.

8. The meaning and character of strategies are driven, though not dictated and wholly determined, by their contexts, all of which are constantly in play and can realistically be understood to constitute just one compounded super context—namely, strategy.

9. Strategy has a permanent nature, while strategies (usually plans, formal or informal, expressing contingent operational intentions) have a variable character driven, but not mandated, by their unique and changing contexts, the needs of which are expressed in the decisions of unique individuals.

Developing Strategy

10. Strategy typically is developed by a process of dialogue and negotiation.

11. Strategy is a value-charged zone of ideas and behaviour.

12. Historically, specific strategies often are driven, and always are shaped, by culture and personality, while strategy in general theory is not.

13. The strategy bridge must be held by competent strategists.

Executing Strategy

14. Strategy is more difficult to devise and execute than are policy, operations, and tactics: friction of all kinds comprise phenomena inseparable from the making and conduct of strategies.

15. Strategy can be expressed in strategies that are direct or indirect, sequential or cumulative, attritional or manoeuverist-annihilating, persisting or raiding (more or less expeditionary), coercive or brute force, offensive or defensive, symmetrical or asymmetrical, or a complex combination of these nominal but often false alternatives.

16. All strategies are shaped by their particular geographical contexts, but strategy itself is not.

17. Strategy is an unchanging, indeed unchangeable, human activity in thought and behaviour, set in a variably dynamic technological context.

18. Unlike strategy, all strategies are temporal.

19. Strategy is logistical.

20. Strategic theory is the most fundamental source of military doctrine, while doctrine is a notable enabler of, and guide for, strategies.

Consequences of Strategy

21. All military behaviour is tactical in execution, but must have operational and strategic effect, intended and otherwise.

The theory presented above should not be rote-learnt and repeated as a credo. Instead, it should be considered only as the most recent iteration of a work always in progress. The practicing grand and military strategist, civilian and military, ought to be so familiar with these guidelines, and their generically practical implications should be so well understood, that these dicta approach the status of an instinctive knowledge. The practicing strategist may consider the general theory as comprehensive rules of engagement with his or her subject. It provides a checklist of matters vital to strategy, albeit one that constitutes a true *Gestalt*, not a menu from which to select after the style of 'pick and mix'.

STRATEGIC THEORY AND POLITICAL PURPOSE

No matter how scornful self-professedly pragmatic soldiers have been of strategic and military theory, they could not help but be informed by ideas—sound and otherwise, and no matter how acquired—that purported to connect force with its consequences when threatened or applied. Military behaviour has strategic consequences understood as strategic effect, whether or not its political masters have ever licensed and agreed on a coherent, explicit strategy that sought to match political purpose to action by available means guided by congruent operational direction. When belligerents and potential belligerents have competed with organized force as an important currency of struggle, they have been performing with and for strategic effect, in pursuit of political rewards.

Since war and warfare cannot be thoroughly self-referential, save to true militarists, its purpose has to be political. Clausewitz insisted that military effort should be matched with the political goals of the state. In addition, he insisted that politicians should understand both the war that is undertaken and the capability of the military instrument that is to be employed.[14]

There is an important place for operational and tactical opportunism, with military commanders seizing unanticipated, fleeting chances to confound their enemies. However, opportunism is a strategic virtue only when it is informed by a strategic sense. In warfare, as in other human behaviours, one should not do things for no better reason other than that they can be done. Successful warfare is success that ultimately has political meaning. If generals are not educated in war, as contrasted with warfare, their expertise is likely to serve only operational objectives. Similarly, if politicians are educated only in politics and in policy desiderata, their higher level guidance of the warfare that they have licensed is apt to be episodic, hugely inadequate, and potentially catastrophic.

Strategy-making is a combined civil–military function, albeit one with the military emphatically in the subordinate role. The soldier has acute need of strategic direction by civilians who at least comprehend the basics of strategy. The eternal challenge to strategy-making and execution is the understandable default tendency for people to retreat into their respective comfort zones of established skill-sets. In other words, the policymakers do politics, which certainly is essential; the generals do warfare, which also is necessary; but no one may be doing war and strategy consistently and competently.

It is not the function of strategic theory to educate politicians so that they can play general or challenge contemporary military practice, though that can be a danger when civilians persuade themselves that their political genius has concealed a thus far latent military genius. Rather, general strategic theory is needed to help people who must think strategically understand the nature of the subject, its structure, the identity of its parts, and broadly the relations between them. This should greatly facilitate the essential if 'unequal dialogue' between policymakers and soldiers.[15] The theory should equip policymakers to ask soldiers questions to which the soldiers should be able to give convincing answers.

Wars Evolve; So Must Strategy

The historical record of strategic incompetence shows unmistakeably that understanding of the function of strategy, and hence appreciation of its importance, has been rare. Important among the reasons why this has occurred, and continues to do so, is intellectual failure to grasp the nature of strategy. Clausewitz asserts that

> Once it has been determined, from the political conditions, what a war is meant to achieve and what it can achieve, it is easy to chart the course. But great strength of character, as well as great lucidity and firmness of mind, are required in order to follow through steadily, to carry out the plan, and not to be thrown off course by thousands of diversions.[16]

What is wrong with Clausewitz's argument is its implicit assumption that war is a static challenge that logically can be answered by a matching (grand) strategic effort. To call this misleading would risk understatement. In historical practice, near universally and eternally, wars have not had a fixed character—though all wars share a common nature.[17] Rather, it is most sensible to consider wars as organically evolving episodes, not as events with all major features fixed and certain from their outset to their conclusion. This is not merely a minor scholastic quibble, because if wars commonly evolve, it follows that the contextually responsive strategies with which belligerents conduct them must also adapt and adjust. Practicing strategists and those who write about them should be educated to respect the semi-sovereignty, the near autonomy, of warfare with its distinctive 'grammar', notwithstanding the formal authority of politics as policy.[18] In his recent powerful critique of the 'cultural turn' in Western strategic analysis, Patrick Porter has argued perceptively and significantly that:

> There may not be one universal soldier, uniform across time and space. But war has a culture of its own. Even as enemies stress their differences rhetorically, conflict with its reciprocity and strategic interaction creates new syntheses.[19]

Porter also writes of war with suitably favourable acknowledgement of Clausewitz's conceptualization, as having a 'competitive reciprocal nature'.[20] Rephrased and slightly expanded, every war is a unique episode created by the belligerent duellists through their combined effect upon each other. The war that policy-makers and strategists envisage prior to the initial clash of arms is, by definition, wholly virtual. The actual conflict will be a unique creation that is more than, and different from, merely the sum of its competing parts. Thus, strategy's general theory must be authoritative and stable in nature, but the strategies with which it is conducted competitively and bloodily must be adaptable. Contrary to the apparent implication in Clausewitz's insistence upon maintenance of the aim in the face of tempting distractions, the practicing strategist has to be ready to adapt as the unique and unpredictable, though not necessarily unanticipateable, course of a war unfolds.

Effective Strategy, Politically Misguided: World War I

When Clausewitz as quoted and cited above is married to deep respect for the integrity of the authority of the generic strategic function of ends, ways, and means, the historical result can be appalling. To illustrate: properly obedient to the logic of strategy, the Great War of 1914–18 persisted for four-and-a-quarter years because political 'ends' demanded a particular type of victory. If the political 'end' of the defeat of what was interpreted as a German bid for hegemony was to be thwarted conclusively (victory), the main strength of Germany's army had to be overcome in battle. This logic translated quite properly into repeated, increasingly massive, and, inevitably, with experience, ever more tactically competent effort on the Western Front. Year after year from 1914 through 1918, the Western Allies declined to be diverted by the apparent potential of alternative possible strategic roads to a sufficient victory. Given the political ends, and viewed in long historical retrospect with the incalculable benefit of hindsight, the Allies were right in persisting on the Western Front year after year. In retrospect, experience demonstrated clearly that such a victory could be achieved only by an attritional strategy, not by a manoeuverist one. The Allies faithfully provided the military and other 'means', and were obliged reluctantly and by default eventually to settle for an attritional approach.

In a strictly functional sense, then, from the Allied perspective World War I was a strategic triumph. The reason why the term 'victory,' as applied to the Allied achievement in 1918, has long been regarded as ironic (though this was not the case at the time) was because that victory came to be viewed as Pyrrhic. The problem lay not in strategy—which, as noted, ultimately worked well enough for the Allies—but in the political goal that the military strategists were required to reach. The popular enough policy objective of defeating Germany necessarily was reflected in a strategy of exhaustion, because there were no strategic alternatives capable of delivering the necessary measure of success. As learning institutions, the armies of all major participants performed admirably in their invention of modern combined-arms warfare.[21] But years hence, the victors' societies came to regret bitterly the cost of the attritional military victory of 1918.

Historically, ill-informed commentators, including many historians, foolishly laid most of the blame at the door of alleged hugely incompetent generals. More sensibly regarded, a generational cohort of military commanders on average not significantly worse than any other exercised strategy(ies) that were obligatory if they were to meet their objectives. Given the tactical context of the period, and above all given the political mission that sponsored their command performance, there simply were no obviously notably cheaper paths to the victory that was their assigned goal. Clearly, what failed was not the triadic logic of strategy, nor even the practical application of that strategy. Instead, error reposed to a catastrophic degree in the politics and policy that insisted upon the enemy's military defeat in a major war between mighty coalitions.

THE THEORY TO PRACTICE STRATEGY

The discussion above demonstrates that the theory and practice of strategy comprise a single subject. As the practice of strategy over millennia has benefited, more and less, from the individual strategists' highly variable understanding of its nature, as explained in theory, so the theory reflects an episodic endeavour to interpret historical practice and malpractice.

Clausewitz was emphatic in distinguishing between the theory and the practice of strategy. He commanded that '[a]ll theories, however, must stick to categories of phenomena and can never take account of a truly unique case; this must be left to judgment and talent'.[22] Also he explains famously that:

> Theory cannot equip the mind with formulas for solving problems, nor can it mark the narrow path on which the sole solution is supposed to lie by planting a hedge of principles on either side. But it can give the mind insight into the great mass of phenomena and of their relationships, then leave it free to rise into the higher realms of action.[23]

The case studies in this book are all examples of the practice of theory, as well as— simultaneously—of the historical practice from which theory was written and rewritten (or passed on in an oral tradition as strategic and military tradition and lore). What should the practice of strategy through millennia be permitted to say to us as theorists? Three points can serve to cover the field and stand as conclusions to this essay on the nexus between the theory and practice of strategy.

First, appreciation of the full context for the practice of the strategy function is vital. It is not enough for a polity's ends, ways, and means to be impressively in balance each with the others. It is no less important that they be mutually supportive and enabling for political purposes that are prudently chosen for their relevance to challenges exogenous to the strategy-making process itself. The adversarial dimension to strategy frequently fails to attract the respect in strategic practice that it merits. Erroneous assumptions about current, and especially anticipated future, dangers are entirely commonplace.

A crucial test of the adequacy of a national strategy is its resilience when confronted with greater than anticipated menace, as well as a true 'black-swan' peril.[24] The domestic management of a defence establishment in peacetime can be so challenging that targeted worry about possible or probable future adversaries tends to recede yet further over the horizon of practical concern. Michael Howard identifies the senior officer's 'real business' unequivocally as 'the conduct of war', but he has also written memorably that 'the complex problem of running an army at all is liable to occupy his [senior officer's] mind and skill so completely that it is very easy to forget what it is being run *for*'.[25]

Second, in order for strategy to be executed, all levels of enabling effort must be held together by the strategic sense that defines the overall mission. This point should be obvious, but its implications have frequently been missed in practice.[26] In principle, there is no doubt as to the hierarchy that rank-orders ascending authority, but in practice the rank-orders of real importance often are determined by everything other than official hierarchical relationships. There is a powerful 'localist' pull at every level—political/policy, strategic, operational, tactical, and technological. This means that even though the entire enterprise of war prevention or war conduct requires some tolerably effective reciprocal enablement among the levels of effort, concerns at each level are all but magnetically attracted to solutions that appear to make tunnel-vision sense at that level, but possibly only at that level.

The challenge for the military strategist, let alone the grand strategist, is to try to ensure that the appropriate strategic sense guides every level of enabling endeavour in a manner consistent with sufficient effectiveness at each level. When a strategist discovers that there is no available solution to a chronic problem at one level of military effort, he or she will need to emphasize effectiveness at another level by way of compensation. For example, the operational level of land warfare died on the wire, shot to pieces on the Western Front (and at Gallipoli) in World War I. Protracted grisly experience proved that there was no operational-level solution to the problem of overcoming modern defences. Thus, the only road to victory was that of a new tactical competence, which by expensive attritional effect eventually succeeded in breaking, though not quite breaking through, the German Army. The year 1918 saw a strategic and operational victory of a sort, achieved by cumulative tactical effort.[27]

Hard fighting against the main body of an enemy's military power certainly is a path to success, provided one is prepared to pay a heavy price and one's human and material assets are decidedly superior to those of the enemy. The challenge to strategy is to identify ways of encouraging operational and tactical subordinates to find and apply solutions to their problems that work well enough at their respective levels, while maintaining strategic cohesion in the whole endeavour. It is all too easy for tactical and operational solutions to be found and applied at those levels and for those levels, with scant if any practical recognition of the overall commander's strategic intent. Unless the strategist achieves and sustains a strategic grip on the nominally enabling operational, tactical, and technical efforts, the result is near certain to be a seriously disharmonious effort in war-making.

Prominent among the steps the strategist should take to advance the prospects for harmony is the selection of subordinates for operational level command who both have a strategic sense and are 'on message' for the strategy of the day. Ulysses S. Grant's confident and well-rewarded choices of William Tecumseh Sherman and Philip H. Sheridan provide an excellent illustration.

Third and finally, history is eloquent in insisting that strategic genius is rare. This very fact means that the merely competent as well as the notably lucky tend to succeed more often than one might expect. It is easy to be so impressed by the number and intensity of both enervating and potentially disabling factors confronting the practicing strategist that one wonders why and how it is that purposeful strategy can succeed. Neither practicing strategists nor historians can completely resist a condition that can be called strategic autism. Self-absorption by the strategist, or for the historian an undue focus on only one side of a struggle, can hardly help but have the consequence of demoting the role and potential significance of the enemy and his effort.

Practicing strategists are, of course, obliged to concentrate on how to win. But, as people who should be well educated by strategy's general theory, they should always be aware that the enemy always contributes, sometimes critically, to his own defeat. This happy enduring fact does not mean that strategists need not strive to undo the foe at all levels of war-making. However, it does mean that the adversary, too, is certain to suffer from many harassing sources of 'friction', not least those that fall in the category of gratuitously self-inflicted wounds.[28] Not only do belligerents win wars, belligerents also necessarily lose them. Anyone who has taught strategic history should be aware of the difference in answers to a basic question that can be phrased in (at least) two seemingly contrasting ways: 'Why did Nazi Germany lose World War II?'; or, 'Why did the Allies win World War II in Europe?'

The point in need of clearest registration is that strategy is not conducted by perfectly omni-competent, wholly rational and reasonable, culturally non-specific Strategic Persons. Successful strategic performance often is the one better described as the least flawed rather than the more brilliant. Serious immersion in strategic theory should immunize the practicing strategist against many avoidable errors, not excluding the need to anticipate contingencies occasioned by the enemy exercising his independent, if also interdependent, will. In the true classics on strategy, only Sun Tzu and the Baron Henri Antoine de Jomini advance strategic ideas together with a guarantee of success for those who follow them faithfully.[29]

NOTES

1. Anachronism is discussed at some length in Colin S. Gray, *The Strategy Bridge: Theory for Practice* (Oxford, 2010), 267–77.
2. Three recent books add considerably to the historical 'width' in our appreciation of strategic thought. See Victor Davis Hanson (ed.), *Makers of Ancient Strategy: From the*

Persian Wars to the Fall of Rome (Princeton, 2010); Beatrice Heuser, *The Evolution of Strategy: Thinking War from Antiquity to the Present* (Cambridge, 2010); and Beatrice Heuser, *The Strategy Makers: Thoughts on War and Society from Machiavelli to Clausewitz* (Santa Barbara, 2010).

3. Alexander P. Kazhdan (ed), *The Oxford Dictionary of Byzantium*, 3 (Oxford, 1991), 2174; and Warren Treadgold, *A History of the Byzantine State and Society* (Stanford, 1997), 349.

4. George T. Dennis (ed. and trans.), *Three Byzantine Military Treatises* (Washington, DC, 1985), 21.

5. Sun Tzu, *The Art of War*, ed. and trans. Samuel Griffith (Oxford, 1963), 63.

6. Carl von Clausewitz, *On War*, ed. and trans. Michael Howard and Peter Paret (Princeton, 1976), 128 (emphasis in the original).

7. Ibid., 177.

8. See Athanasios G. Platias and Constantinos Koliopoulos, *Thucydides on Strategy: Athenian and Spartan Grand Strategies in the Peloponnesian War and their Relevance Today* (London, 2010).

9. Michael Howard, *The Causes of Wars and Other Essays* (London, 1983), 214 (emphasis added).

10. Harold R. Winton, 'An Imperfect Jewel: Military Theory and the Military Profession', *Journal of Strategic Studies*, forthcoming.

11. See Colin S. Gray, *Schools for Strategy: Teaching Strategy for 21st Century Conflict* (Carlisle, PA, November 2009).

12. This terse summary of the general theory of strategy is borrowed from Colin S. Gray, *The Strategy Bridge: Theory for Practice* (Oxford, 2010), 262–3.

13. A full explanation of the nature and function of strategic theory is offered in Gray, *The Strategy Bridge*.

14. Clausewitz, *On War*, 88–9, 608.

15. See Eliot A. Cohen, *Supreme Command: Soldiers, Statesmen, and Leadership in Wartime* (New York, 2002).

16. Ibid., 178.

17. Compare ibid., 90 with 606.

18. Ibid., 605.

19. Patrick Porter, *Military Orientalism: Eastern War Through Western Eyes* (London, 2009), 191.

20. Ibid.

21. See Jonathan B.A. Bailey, 'The First World War and the Birth of Modern Warfare', in Macgregor Knox and Williamson Murray (eds.), *The Dynamics of Military Revolutions, 1300–2050* (Cambridge, 2001), ch. 8.

22. Ibid., 139.

23. Ibid., 578.

24. See Nassim Nicholas Taleb, *The Black Swan: The Impact of the Highly Improbable* (New York, 2010).

25. Howard, *The Causes of Wars and Other Essays*, 214 (emphasis in the original).

26. Historical examples are so legion that one is spoilt for choice for the purpose of illustration. To cite just one exceptionally clear example of the 'best practice' of strategy challenged by a clear case of 'bad practice', readers are invited to examine the victory of RAF Fighter Command under Air Chief Marshal Sir Hugh Dowding in the summer of 1940. Everything that was strategically important, the Command did well enough or better; its mistakes were either near-term correctible or were at least tolerable in their consequences for net strategic effect. See Steven Bungay, *The Most Dangerous Enemy:*

A History of the Battle of Britain (London, 2000); and Colin S. Gray, '"Stuffy" Dowding and the Strategy of Air Defence', forthcoming.

27. See David T. Zabecki, *The German 1918 Offensives: A Case Study in the Operational Level of War* (Abingdon, 2006).

28. Clausewitz, *On War*, 119–212; and Barry D. Watts, *Clausewitzian Friction and Future War*, McNair Paper 68, rev. ed. (Washington, DC, 2004).

29. Sun Tzu, *The Art of War*, 66; and Baron Henri Antoine de Jomini, *The Art of War* (Novato, CA, 1992), 323, 325.

Notes on Contributors

Gábor Ágoston is Associate Professor at the Department of History, Georgetown University. He was born in Hungary and earned his MA and university doctorate from the University of Budapest, and his Ph.D. from the Hungarian Academy of Sciences. Between 1985 and 1998, he taught Hungarian, Ottoman, and Balkan history at the universities of Budapest and Pécs (JPTE). Since joining Georgetown's History Department in 1998, he has taught courses on Ottoman and Middle Eastern history, the Balkans, and the Black Sea. In 2003, he was Visiting Scholar at the Institute of History, University of Vienna. His field of research includes Ottoman military, economic, and social history from the fifteenth to the late eighteenth centuries, early modern Hungarian history, and the comparative military history of the Ottoman, Habsburg, and Romanov empires. He is the author of *Guns for the Sultan: Military Power and the Weapons Industry in the Ottoman Empire* (2005), which challenges the broad generalizations of Eurocentric and orientalist scholarship regarding Ottoman and Islamic societies. He co-edited and co-authored, with Bruce Masters, the first English-language encyclopaedia of the Ottoman empire (2009). In addition, he has published four Hungarian-language books, and more than fifty scholarly articles and book chapters in English, Hungarian, Turkish, German, French, and Italian on Ottoman, European, and Hungarian history.

Jeremy Black is Professor of History at the University of Exeter and a Senior Fellow at the Center for the Study of America and the West at the Foreign Policy Research Institute, Philadelphia. He graduated from Queens' College, Cambridge; did postgraduate work at St John's and Merton colleges, Oxford; and taught at Durham University from 1980 as a lecturer, then professor, before moving to Exeter in 1996. He was awarded an MBE for services to stamp design. Black is also an advisory fellow of the Barsanti Military History Center at the University of North Texas. He has lectured extensively in Australasia, Canada, Denmark, France, Germany, Italy, and the United States. Professor Black is the author of over ninety books, especially on eighteenth-century British politics and international relations, of which the most recent are *Crisis of Empire: Britain and America in the Eighteenth Century* (2008), *War: A Short History* (2009), *The War of 1812: A Napoleonic Perspective* (2009), *War in the Nineteenth Century 1800–1914* (2009), and *Naval Power* (2009).

Anne Curry is Professor of Medieval History and Dean of the Faculty of Humanities at the University of Southampton. She was previously at the University of Reading. Her MA (Manchester, 1977) was a study of Cheshire under Henry IV and Henry V. Her doctoral dissertation (CNAA, Teesside, 1985) focused on the English occupation of Normandy between 1422 and 1450 from the military perspective. She was President of the Historical Association, 2008–11. Professor Curry is co-editor of volume ii of the *Cambridge History of Warfare*. She has published many articles in both English and French on the fifteenth-century phase of the Hundred Years War. Her books include *The Hundred Years War* (1993), *The Battle of Agincourt: Sources and Interpretations* (2000), *Essential Histories: The Hundred Years War* (2002), *Agincourt: A New History* (2005), and *The Parliament Rolls of Medieval England*, volumes x, xi, and xii (2005). She has also co-directed a project funded by the Arts and Humanities Research Council on English soldiers in the later Middle Ages (<http://www.medievalsoldier.org>).

Charles Esdaile is Professor in History at the University of Liverpool. He is a specialist on Spain in the revolutionary and Napoleonic era, and, more specifically, the Peninsular War of 1808–14. A historian working at the interface of military, political, and social history, his areas of study also range over the history of Spain in the whole period from 1788 to 1939, as well as the general history of Napoleon and his empire. His publications include *The Wars of Napoleon* (1995), *Spain in the Liberal Age: From Constitution to Civil War, 1808–1939* (2000), *The French Wars, 1792–1815* (2001), *The Peninsular War: A New History* (2002), *Fighting Napoleon: Guerrillas, Bandits and Adventurers in Spain, 1808–1814* (2004), *Napoleon's Wars: An International History, 1803–1815* (2007), and *Peninsular Eye-Witnesses: The Experience of War in Spain and Portugal* (2008).

Colin S. Gray is a Strategic Theorist and Defence Analyst at the University of Reading who has worked in Britain, Canada, and the United States. He is currently at the Department of International Politics and Strategic Studies at the University of Reading. He has written pioneering and controversial studies on nuclear strategy, arms control, maritime strategy, and geopolitics. He is the author of twenty books, more than 300 articles, and several dozen reports for governments. His most recent publications include *Explorations in Strategy* (1996), *Modern Strategy* (1999), *Strategy for Chaos: Revolutions in Military Affairs and the Evidence of History* (2002), *The Sheriff: America's Defense and the New World Order* (2004), *Strategy and History: Essays on Theory and Practice* (2005), *Another Bloody Century: Future Warfare* (2007), *Fighting Talk: Forty Maxims on War, Peace, and Strategy* (2007), and *The Strategy Bridge: Theory for Practice* (2011).

James D. Kiras is an Associate Professor at the School of Advanced Air and Space Studies (SAASS) at Maxwell Air Force Base, Alabama. He holds a bachelor's degree in history from the University of Massachusetts at Boston, a master's degree in history/international relations from the University of Toronto, and a Ph.D. from the University of Reading. At SAASS, Dr Kiras directs the school's course on irregular warfare, and lectures, publishes, and consults extensively on counter-insurgency, counter-terrorism, special operations, and suicide bombing. He is also an Associate Fellow of the Joint Special Operations University, Hurlburt Field, Florida. Before teaching at SAASS, Dr Kiras was a defence consultant with Booz Allen Hamilton and an analyst at the National Institute for Public Policy. In these jobs, he provided analytic and strategic planning support to the Office of the Secretary of Defense, combatant commands, unified commands, and the Joint Staff. In 2002, he joined the Strategy, Concepts, and Initiatives Team within the Office of the Assistant Secretary of Defense for Special Operations and Low Intensity Conflict. Dr Kiras's first book was titled *Special Operations and Strategy: From World War II to the War on Terrorism* (2006), and most recently he co-authored *Understanding Modern Warfare* (2008).

David J. Lonsdale has been a Lecturer at the University of Hull since September 2006. He was awarded an MA from the University of Aberdeen in 1995, and went on to gain an MA and Ph.D. from the University of Hull in 1996 and 2001, respectively. Prior to his current appointment at Hull, he held the posts of Lecturer in Strategic Studies at the University of Reading (2003–6) and Lecturer in Defence Studies at King's College, London (2000–3), while he was based at the Joint Services Command and Staff College at Shrivenham. His main areas of research are strategic studies and military history. In particular, he specializes in strategic theory and its application to historical and contemporary strategic settings. His recent publications include *The Nature of War in the Information Age: Clausewitzian Future* (2003); 'Strategy: The Challenge of Complexity', *Defence Studies*, 7/1 (Winter 2006–7); 'Clausewitz and War in the Information Age', in Hew Strachan and Andreas Herberg-Rothe (eds), *Clausewitz in the Twenty-First Century* (2007); *Alexander the Great: Lessons in Strategy* (2007); 'Blair's Record on Defence: A Strategic Analysis', in Matt Beech and Simon Lee (eds), *Ten Years of New Labour* (2008); and 'Strategy', in David Jordan et al. (eds), *Understanding Modern Warfare* (2008).

Edward N. Luttwak is a Senior Associate at the Center for Strategic and International Studies in Washington, DC. Dr. Luttwak received his Ph.D. from the Johns Hopkins University, in 2004 he was awarded an honorary degree by the University of Bath. He has served as a consultant to the Office of the Secretary of Defense, the National Security Council, the US Department of State, the US Army, Navy, and Air Force, and a number of allied governments, as well as international corporations and financial institutions. He speaks French, Italian, and Spanish, among other languages, is a frequent lecturer at universities and military colleges in the United States and abroad, and has testified before several congressional committees and presidential commissions. He serves on the editorial board of the *Washington Quarterly* and *Géopolitique* (Paris), and is the author of numerous articles and several books, including *The Grand Strategy of the Roman Empire* (1976), *Coup d'État: A Practical Handbook* (1985), *The Endangered American Dream* (1993), *Turbo-Capitalism: Winners and Losers in the Global Economy* (1999), and *The Grand Strategy of the Byzantine Empire* (2009). His new edition of *Strategy: The Logic of War and Peace* (2001) has been published in Chinese, French, German, Hebrew, Italian, Estonian, and Turkish, as well as English.

Williamson Murray is a Consultant at the Institute for Defense Analyses in Alexandria, Virginia, where he has been working on the Iraqi Perspectives Project. He is also a Visiting Professor at the US Naval Academy at Annapolis. He graduated from Yale University in 1963, then served five years as an officer in the US Air Force, including a tour in South-East Asia with the 314th Tactical Airlift Wing. He then returned to Yale, where he received his Ph.D. in military–diplomatic history, working under Hans Gatzke and Donald Kagan. After teaching for two years he moved to the Ohio State University in 1977 and retired in 1995 as Professor Emeritus of History. Dr. Murray has taught at a number of academic and military institutions, including the Air War College, the US Military Academy at West Point, and the Naval War College. He is the author of *The Change in the European Balance of Power, 1938–1939: The Path to Ruin* (1984), *Luftwaffe* (1985), *German Military Effectiveness* (1992), *The Air War in the*

Persian Gulf (1995), and *Air War, 1914–1945* (1999). He also co-authored *The Iraq War: A Military History* (2003), and has edited a number of books and articles on military matters, held numerous fellowships and chairs, and lectured throughout the world.

John Andreas Olsen is the Deputy Commander and Chief of the NATO Advisory Team at NATO Headquarters, Sarajevo, and Visiting Professor of operational art and tactics at the Swedish National Defence College. Previously, he was the Dean of the Norwegian Defence University College and head of its division for strategic studies. He is an active-duty colonel in the Norwegian Air Force and a graduate of the German Command and Staff College (2005). Recent assignments include tours as the Norwegian liaison officer to the German Operational Command in Potsdam and as the military assistant to the attaché in Berlin. Olsen has a doctorate in history and international relations from De Montfort University, a master's degree in contemporary British literature and politics from the University of Warwick, and a master's degree in English and a bachelor's degree in engineering from the University of Trondheim. He is the author of *Strategic Air Power in Desert Storm* (2003) and *John Warden and the Renaissance of American Air Power* (2007), and the editor of several books, including *On New Wars* (2006), *A History of Air Warfare* (2010), *The Evolution of Operational Art: From Napoleon to the Present* (2011), and *Global Air Power* (2011).

David Parrott is a Fellow and Tutor at New College and Lecturer in History at the University of Oxford. He read for his BA degree in modern history at Christ Church, Oxford, and studied for his doctorate at Wolfson College, Oxford. In 1985, he was appointed to a lectureship at the University of York, and in 1992 took up his present post. In 1998, he was appointed to the visiting post of Directeur d'Études at the École pratique des hautes études, Paris, and in 2004, he gave the Lees Knowles Lectures in Military History at the University of Cambridge. His research interests are in sixteenth- and seventeenth-century European political, military, and administrative history, specifically France and Italy during the Thirty Years War. His publications include *Richelieu's Army: War, Government and Society in France, 1624–42* (2001); 'War and International Relations in Seventeenth-Century Europe', in J. Bergin (ed.), *The Oxford History of Seventeenth-Century Europe* (2001); 'Strategy and Tactics in the Thirty Years' War: The 'Military Revolution'', reprinted in C. J. Rogers (ed.), *The Military Revolution Debate* (1995); and 'The Utility of Fortifications in Early Modern Europe: Italian Princes and their Citadels, 1540–1640', *War in History*, 7/2 (2000). His forthcoming book concerns the military, political, and social aspects of the privatization of war in the sixteenth and seventeenth centuries.

Israel Shatzman has been a Professor at the Hebrew University of Jerusalem since 1985 and held various teaching positions there since 1963. He received his bachelor's degree in history and Hebrew literature in 1959, an MA in history and classics in 1961, and a Ph.D. in ancient history in 1967, all at the Hebrew University of Jerusalem. He has been Visiting Scholar at Gonville and Caius College, Cambridge (1968–9), Harvard University (1981–2), and Columbia University (1998); Visiting Fellow at Wolfson College, Oxford (1986–7); and Visiting Professor at the Department of Ancient History, University of California, Berkeley

(1993–4). More recently, he has been Director of the Jewish National and University Library (1990–97), Chairman of the Committee of Directors of University Libraries (1994–7), and President of the Israel Society for the Promotion of Classical Studies (1999–2003). In addition to numerous articles, he has published (in English) *Senatorial Wealth and Roman Politics* (1975) and *The Armies of the Hasmonaeans and Herod* (1991), and the following books in Hebrew: *History of the Roman Republic* (1989), *Society and Economy in the Hellenistic World* (1991), *The Roman Empire and its Legacy* (2002), *Rome: Imperialism and Empire* (co-authored with R. Zelnick-Abramovitz) (2003), and *The Polis: Regimes, Change of Regimes and Revolutions. Anthology with Introduction and Short Commentary* (2005).

Martin van Creveld was born in the Netherlands but was raised and educated in Israel. After receiving his master's degree at the Hebrew University of Jerusalem, he obtained a Ph.D. in history at the London School of Economics and Political Science. Since 1971, he has been on the faculty of the History Department at the Hebrew University, where he is currently a professor. He is one of the world's leading experts on military history and strategy, with a special interest in the future of war. Professor van Creveld has been a consultant to the defence establishments of several countries, and has taught or lectured at defence colleges, both military and civilian, from Canada to New Zealand and from Norway to South Africa. He has also appeared on countless television and radio programmes as well as written for, and been interviewed by, hundreds of papers and magazines around the world. He has authored twenty books, including *Supplying War* (1978), *Command in War* (1985), *The Transformation of War* (1991), *The Rise and Decline of the State* (1999), *The Changing Face of War: Lessons of Combat from the Marne to Iraq* (2006), *The Culture of War* (2008), and *The Age of Airpower* (2011).

Selected Bibliography

Adcock, F. E., *The Greek and Macedonian Art of War* (Berkeley, 1957).
—— *The Roman Art of War under the Republic* (Cambridge, MA, 1940).
Ágoston, G., *Guns for the Sultan: Military Power and the Weapons Industry in the Ottoman Empire* (Cambridge, 2005).
Ahrweiler, H., *Byzance et la mer: La marine de guerre, la politique et les institutions maritimes de Byzance aux VIIe–XVe siècles* (Paris, 1966).
Aksan, V. H., and D. Goffman (eds), *The Early Modern Ottomans: Remapping the Empire* (New York, 2007).
Albrecht, D., *Maximilian von Bayern, 1573–1651* (Munich, 1998).
Allmand, C. T., *The Hundred Years War* (Cambridge, 1988).
—— *Lancastrian Normandy: The History of a Medieval Occupation 1415–1450* (Oxford, 1983).
Anderson, A. D., *On the Verge of War: International Relations and the Jülich-Kleve Succession Crisis, 1609–1614* (Boston, 1999).
Anderson, J. K., *Military Theory and Practice in the Age of Xenophon* (Berkeley, 1970).
Appian, *Civil Wars* (London, 1996).
Armitage, D., and M. J. Braddick (eds), *The British Atlantic World* (London, 2002).
Arnold, J. R., *Grant Wins the War: Decision at Vicksburg* (New York, 1997).
Arrian, *The Campaigns of Alexander* (London, 1971).
Ashdown, P., *Fate, Chance and Desperate Men: Six Studies of the Role of Chance in Twentieth Century History* (Brighton, 2009).
Austin, N. J. E., and N. B. Rankov, *Exploratio* (London, 1995).
Ayton, A. J., and P. Preston, *The Battle of Crécy* (Woodbridge, 2005).
Bagnall, N., *The Punic Wars: Rome, Carthage and the Struggle for the Mediterranean* (London, 1999).
Balaghi, S., *Saddam Hussein: A Biography* (Westport, CT, 2008).
Ball, D., and J. Richelson (eds), *Strategic Nuclear Targeting* (Ithaca, NY, 1986).
Barkan, Ö. Lûtfi, *The Middle East and the Balkans under the Ottoman Empire: Essays on Economy and Society* (Bloomington, IN, 1993).
—— *Osmanlı Devleti'nin Sosyal ve Ekonomik Tarihi: Osmanlı Devlet Arşivleri Üzerinde Tetkikler-Makaleler*, ed. H. Özdeğer (Istanbul, 2000).
Barker, J., *Conquest: The English Kingdom of France* (London, 2009).
Barker, K., and R. J. P. Kain (eds), *Maps and History in South-West England* (Exeter, 1991).
Barkey, K., *Empire of Difference: The Ottomans in Comparative Perspective* (Cambridge, 2008).
Barrass, G. S., *The Great Cold War: A Journey Through the Hall of Mirrors* (Stanford, CA, 2009).
Barth, F., *Political Leadership among Swat Pathans*, LSE Monographs on Social Anthropology, 19 (London, 1959).
Bartholomees, B. Jr, J. (ed.), *U.S. Army War College Guide to National Security Policy and Strategy*, 2nd rev. edn (Carlisle Barracks, PA, June 2006).
Bérenger, J., *Turenne* (Paris, 1987).
Bergin, J., *The Rise of Richelieu* (New Haven, 1991).
Berntsen, G., and R. Pezzullo, *Jawbreaker: The Attack on Bin Laden and Al-Qaeda* (New York, 2005).
Best, G., *War and Society in Revolutionary Europe* (London, 1982).

Bishop, B. C., and J. C. N. Coulston, *Roman Military Equipment*, 2nd edn (Oxford, 2006).

Black, J., *Geopolitics* (London, 2009).

Bloch, M., *Strange Defeat* (Oxford, 1949).

Blockley, R. C., *East Roman Foreign Policy: Formation and Conduct from Diocletian to Anastasius* (Leeds, 1992).

—— *The Fragmentary Classicising Historians of the Later Roman Empire* (Liverpool, 1983).

Bond, B., *France and Belgium 1939–1940* (London, 1979).

Bond, G., *The Grand Expedition: The British Invasion of Holland, 1809* (Athens, GA, 1979).

Bosworth, A. B., *Alexander and the East: The Tragedy of Triumph* (Oxford, 1998).

—— *Conquest and Empire: The Reign of Alexander the Great* (Cambridge, 1988).

Bremer, L. P., and M. Mcconnell, *My Year in Iraq: The Struggle to Build a Future of Hope* (New York, 2006).

Brisand, J.-C., *Zarqawi: The New Face of Al-Qaeda* (New York, 2005).

Briscoe, C., R. L. Kiper, J. A. Schroder, and K. I. Sepp, *Weapon of Choice: U.S. Army Special Operations Forces in Afghanistan* (Fort Leavenworth, KS, 2003).

—— et al., *All Roads Lead to Baghdad: Army Special Operations Forces in Iraq* (Fort Bragg, NC, 2006).

Brodie, B., *War and Politics* (New York, 1973).

Broers, M., *Europe, 1799–1815* (London, 1996).

Broucek, P., *Der Schwedenfeldzug nach Niederösterreich, 1645–46* (Vienna, 1967).

Brummett, P. J., *Ottoman Seapower and Levantine Diplomacy in the Age of Discovery* (Albany, NY, 1994).

Brunt, P. A., *Roman Imperial Themes* (Oxford, 1990).

Bueil, Jean de, *Le Jouvencel par Jean de Bueil suivi du commentaire de Guillaume Trignant*, 2 vols (Paris, 1887–9).

Bungay, S., *The Most Dangerous Enemy: A History of the Battle of Britain* (London, 2000).

Burkhardt, J., *Der Dreißigjährige Krieg* (Frankfurt am Main, 1992).

Bury, J. B., *History of the Later Roman Empire: From the Death of Theodosius I to the Death of Justinian* (New York, 1958).

Cahen, C., *The Formation of Turkey: The Seljukid Sultanate of Rum: Eleventh to Fourteenth Century*, ed. and trans. P. M. Holt (London, 2001).

Cameron, A. (ed.), *The Byzantine and Early Islamic Near East*, iii (Princeton, 1995).

—— B. Ward-Perkins, and M. Whitby (eds), *The Cambridge Ancient History*, xiv (Cambridge, 2000).

Capponi, N., *Victory of the West: The Story of the Battle of Lepanto* (London, 2006).

Caroe, Sir Olaf, *The Pathans*, rev. edn (Karachi, 1985).

Cartledge, P., P. Garnsey, and E. Gruen (eds), *Hellenistic Constructs* (Berkeley and Los Angeles, 1997).

Cassin-Scott, J., *The Greek and Persian Wars 500–323 BC* (Oxford, 1977).

Catton, B., *Grant Takes Command* (Boston, 1969).

Central Intelligence Agency, *CIA World Factbook 2009* <https://www.cia.gov/library/publications/the-world-factbook>.

Chandler, D. G. *The Campaigns of Napoleon* (London, 1966).

—— (ed.), *On the Napoleonic Wars: Collected Essays* (London, 1994).

Chevalier, R., *Roman Roads* (London, 1976).

Chickering, R., and S. Foerster (eds), *Great War, Total War* (Cambridge, 2000).

Churchill, W. S., *The Second World War*, i (London, 1948).

Clancy, T., with T. Zinni and T. Koltz, *Battle Ready* (New York, 2005).

Clausewitz, Carl Von, *On War*, ed. and trans. M. Howard and P. Paret (London and Princeton, 1993).

—— *On War*, ed. A. Rapoport (London, 1968).

Claydon, T., *Europe and the Making of England, 1660–1760* (Cambridge, 2007).

Cochran, T. B., W. M. Arkin, R. S. Norris, and M. M. Hoenig, *Nuclear Weapons Databook*, iv: *Soviet Nuclear Weapons* (New York, 1989).

Cohen, E. A. *Supreme Command: Soldiers, Statesmen, and Leadership in Wartime* (New York, 2002).

Coll, S., *Ghost Wars: The Secret History of the CIA, Afghanistan, and Bin Laden from the Soviet Invasion to September 10, 2001* (New York, 2004).

Conklin, J., *Dialogue Mapping: Building Shared Understanding of Wicked Problems* (New York, 2005).

Contamine, P., *War in the Middle Ages*, trans. M. C. E. Jones (Oxford, 1984).

Coox, A. D., *The Anatomy of a Small War: The Soviet-Japanese Struggle for Changkufeng/ Khasan, 1938* (Westport, CT, 1977).

Cordesman, A., *The Iraq War: Strategy, Tactics, and Military Lessons* (Westport, CT, 2003).

Cornell, T. J., *The Beginnings of Rome* (London, 1995).

Cornish, P., *British Military Planning for the Defence of Germany, 1945–50* (Basingstoke, 1996).

Cosneau, E., *Les Grands Traités de la guerre de Cent Ans* (Paris, 1889).

Crowhurst, P., *The French War on Trade: Privateering, 1793–1815* (London, 1989).

Curry, A., *Agincourt: A New History* (Stroud, 2005).

—— *The Battle Of Agincourt: Sources And Interpretations* (Woodbridge, 2000).

—— *The Hundred Years War* (Basingstoke, 1993; 2nd edn, 2003).

—— M. Hughes (eds), *Arms, Armies and Fortifications in the Hundred Years War* (Woodbridge, 1994).

Dallek, R., *Harry S. Truman* (New York, 2008).

Dann, U., *Hanover and Great Britain, 1740–1760* (Leicester, 1991).

Delbrük, H., *History of the Art of War within the Framework of Political History*, 2 vols, trans. of the 3rd, German edn (1920; Westport, CT, 1975).

—— *Warfare in Antiquity* (Lincoln, NE, 1975).

Dennis G. T. (ed. and trans.), *Three Byzantine Military Treatises* (Washington, DC, 1985).

Dickinson, H. T. (ed.), *Britain and the French Revolution, 1789–1815* (Basingstoke, 1989).

Documents on German Foreign Policy, ser. D, vol. ix (London, 1956).

Dower, J. W., *War without Mercy: Race and Power in the Pacific War* (New York, 1986).

Duffy, C., *Borodino and the War of 1812* (London, 1973).

Eckstein, A. M., *Mediterranean Anarchy, Interstate War, and the Rise of Rome* (Berkeley and Los Angeles, 2006).

—— *Senate and General* (Berkeley and Los Angeles, 1987).

Egler, A., *Die Spanier in der linksrheinischen Pfalz, 1620–32: Invasion, Verwaltung, Rekatholisierung* (Mainz, 1971).

Ehrenpreis, S., *Kaiserliche Gerichtsbarkeit und Konfessionskonflikt: Der Reichshofrat unter Rudolf II (1576–1612)* (Göttingen, 2006).

Elliott, J. H., *The Count-Duke of Olivares: The Statesman in an Age of Decline* (New Haven, 1986).

—— *Empires of the Atlantic World: Britain and Spain in America, 1492–1830* (New Haven, 2006).

—— *Richelieu and Olivares* (Cambridge, 1984).

Elliott-Bateman, M., *The Fourth Dimension of Warfare*, i: *Intelligence, Subversion, and Resistance* (New York, 1970).

Emsley, C., *British Society and the French Wars, 1793–1815* (London, 1979).

Engels, D. W., *Alexander the Great and the Logistics of the Macedonian Army* (Berkeley, 1980).

Englund, P., *Die Verwüstung Deutschlands: Eine Geschichte des Dreißigjährigen Krieges* (Stuttgart, 2001).

Erdkamp, P., *Hunger and the Sword: Warfare and Food Supply in Roman Republican Wars (264–30 B.C.)* (Amsterdam, 1998).
—— (ed.), *A Companion to the Roman Army* (Oxford, 2006).
—— (ed.), *The Roman Army and the Economy* (Amsterdam, 2002).
Ernst, H., *Madrid und Wien, 1632–1637* (Münster, 1991).
Etheridge, J., *Replacement Operations: The Use of CONUS Replacement Centers to Support the Warfighting CINC*, US Army War College Military Studies Program Paper (Carlisle Barracks, PA, January 1992).
Etzold, T. H., and J. L. Gaddis (eds), *Containment: Documents on American Policy and Strategy, 1945–50* (New York, 1978).
Evagrius Scholasticus, *The Ecclesiastical History of Evagrius Scholasticus*, trans. M. Whitby (Liverpool, 2000).
Evans, R. J. W., *The Making of the Habsburg Monarchy, 1500–1700* (Oxford, 1979).
Ewans, M., *Afghanistan: A Short History of its Peoples and Politics* (New York, 2002).
Externbrink, S., *Le Cœur du monde: Frankreich und die norditalienische Staaten (Mantua, Parma, Savoyen) im Zeitalter Richelieus, 1624–35* (Munich, 1997).
Farrar, L. L. (ed.), *War: A Historical, Political and Social Study* (Santa Barbara, CA, 1978).
Ferguson, N., *Der falsche Krieg: Der Erste Weltkrieg und das 20. Jahrhundert* (Stuttgart, 1998).
Ferrill, A., *The Origins of War: From the Stone Age to Alexander the Great* (London, 1985).
Finkel, C., *Osman's Dream: The Story of the Ottoman Empire, 1300–1923* (New York, 2005).
Fishman, B. (ed.), *Bombers, Bank Accounts and Bleedout: Al-Qa'ida's Road In and Out of Iraq* (West Point, NY, 2008).
Flayhart, W. H., *Counterpoint to Trafalgar: The Anglo-Russian Invasion of Naples, 1805–1806* (Columbia, SC, 1992).
Fleet, K. (ed.), *Byzantium to Turkey, 1071–1453* (Cambridge, 2009).
Fodor, A and G. Dávid (eds), *Ottomans, Hungarians, and Habsburgs in Central Europe: The Military Confines in the Era of Ottoman Conquest* (Leiden, 2000).
Fontenot, G., E. J. Degen, and D. Tohn, *On Point: The United States Army in Operation Iraqi Freedom* (Fort Leavenworth, KS, 2004).
Foote, S., *The Civil War, a Narrative*, ii: *Fredericksburg to Meridian* (New York, 1963).
Fouracre, P. (ed.), *The New Cambridge Medieval History*, i (Cambridge, 2005).
Freedman, L., *The Evolution of Nuclear Strategy*, 3rd edn (Basingstoke, 2003).
Frost, R., *The Northern Wars 1558–1721* (London, 2000).
Fuchs, M., T. Oborni, and G. Újvári (eds), *Kaiser Ferdinand I: Ein mitteleuropäischer Herrscher* (Münster, 2005).
Fuller, J. F. C., *The Generalship of Alexander the Great* (Ware, 1998).
—— *Grant and Lee: A Study in Personality and Generalship* (Bloomington, IN, 1982).
Fuller, W. C., *Strategy and Power in Russia, 1600–1914* (New York, 1992).
Gaddis, J. L., P. Gordon, E. May, and J. Rosenberg (eds), *Cold War Statesmen Confront the Bomb: Nuclear Diplomacy since 1945* (Oxford, 1999).
Genç, M., and E. Özvar (eds), *Osmanlı Maliyesi Kurumları ve Bütçeler*, 2 vols (Istanbul, 2006).
Gillingham, J., *The Angevin Empire*, 2nd edn (London, 2001).
Giustozzi, A., *Koran, Kalashnikov, and Laptop: The Neo-Taliban Insurgency in Afghanistan* (New York, 2008).
Glubb, J., *War in the Desert: An R.A.F. Frontier Campaign* (London, 1960).
Golden, P. B., *Introduction to the History of the Turkic Peoples* (Wiesbaden, 1992).
Goldsworthy, A., *The Punic Wars* (London, 2000).
Goodwin, D. K., *Team of Rivals: The Political Genius of Abraham Lincoln* (New York, 2006).
Gordon, M. R., and B. E. Trainor, *Cobra II: The Inside Story of the Invasion and Occupation of Iraq* (New York, 2006).

Graham, D., and S. Bidwell, *Tug of War: The Battle for Italy, 1943–1945* (New York, 1986).

Grant, U. S., *The Personal Memoirs of U. S. Grant*, 2 vols (New York, 1885).

Grau, L., and M. Gress (ed. and trans.), *The Soviet-Afghan War: How a Superpower Fought and Lost* (Lawrence, Ks, 2002).

Gray, C. S., *Modern Strategy* (Oxford, 1999).

—— *Schools for Strategy: Teaching Strategy for the 21st Century* (Carlisle Barracks, PA, November 2009).

—— *The Strategy Bridge: Theory for Practice* (Oxford, 2010).

Grehan, J., *The Lines of Torres Vedras: The Cornerstone of Wellington's Strategy in the Peninsular War* (London, 2000).

Grimsley, M., *The Hard Hand of War: Union Military Policy towards Southern Civilians, 1861–1865* (Cambridge, 2008).

—— *The Virginia Campaign, May–June 1864* (Lincoln, NE, 2005).

—— C. J. Rogers (eds), *Civilians in the Path of War* (Lincoln, NE, 2002).

Grygiel, J. J., *Great Powers and Geopolitical Change* (Baltimore, 2006).

Guibert, J. de, *Essai général de tactique (1772)*, ed. J.-P. Bois (Paris, 2004).

Guilmartin, J. F., *Gunpowder and Galleys: Changing Technology and Mediterranean Warfare at Sea in the Sixteenth Century* (London, 1974).

Guthrie, W., *The Later Thirty Years War: From the Battle of Wittstock to the Treaty of Westphalia* (Westport, CT, 2003).

Haan, H., *Der Regensburger Kurfürstentag von 1636/37* (Münster, 1967).

Habeck, M. R., *Storm of Steel: The Development of Armor Doctrine in Germany and the Soviet Union, 1919–1939* (Ithaca, NY, 2003).

Halaçoğlu, Y., *Osmanlılarda Ulaşım ve Haberleşme (Menziller)* (Ankara, 2002).

Haldon, J., *The Byzantine Wars: Battles and Campaigns of the Byzantine Era* (Stroud, 2001).

—— (ed.), *Byzantine Warfare* (Princeton, 2007).

Hall, C. D., *Wellington's Navy: Seapower and the Peninsular War, 1807–1814* (London, 2004).

Halpern, P. G., *A Naval History of World War I* (London, 1994).

Halsall, G., *Barbarian Migrations and the Roman West, 376–568* (Cambridge, 2007).

Hammond, N. G. L., *The Genius of Alexander the Great* (London, 1998).

Hanson, V. D., *The Wars of the Ancient Greeks: And their Invention of Western Military Culture* (London, 1999).

—— (ed.), *Hoplites: The Classical Greek Battle Experience* (London, 1993).

—— *The Western Way of War: Infantry Battle in Classical Greece* (Berkeley, 1989).

—— (ed.), *Makers of Ancient Strategy: From the Persian Wars to the Fall of Rome* (Princeton, 2010).

Harding, R., *Amphibious Warfare in the Eighteenth Century: The British Expedition to the West Indies, 1740–1742* (Woodbridge, 1991).

Harris, W. V., *War and Imperialism in Republican Rome 327–70 BC* (Oxford, 1979).

—— (ed.), *The Imperialism of Mid-Republican Rome* (Rome, 1984).

Hattendorf, J. B., *England in the War of the Spanish Succession: A Study of the English View and Conduct of Grand Strategy, 1701–1712* (New York, 1987).

—— (ed.), *Naval Strategy and Policy in the Mediterranean: Past, Present, and Future* (London, 2000).

Heilmann, J., *Die Feldzüge der Bayern in den Jahren 1643, 1644, 1645 unter den Befehlen des Feldmarschalls Franz Freiherrn von Mercy* (Leipzig, 1851).

Hess, A. C., *The Forgotten Frontier: A History of the Sixteenth-Century Ibero-African Frontier* (Chicago, 1978).

Heuser, B., *The Evolution of Strategy: Thinking War from Antiquity to the Present* (Cambridge, 2010).

—— *The Strategy Makers: Thoughts on War and Society from Machiavelli to Clausewitz* (Santa Barbara, 2010).

Heywood, C., *Writing Ottoman History: Documents and Interpretations* (Aldershot, 2002).

Hildebrandt, R. (ed.), *Quellen und Regesten zu den Augsburger Handelshäusern Paler und Rehlinger, 1539-1642*, 2 vols (Stuttgart, 2004).

Hines, C., E. M. Mishulovich, and J. F. Shull, *Soviet Intentions, 1965-1985*, 2 vols (McLean, VA, 1995).

Hitler, A., *The Speeches of Adolf Hitler, April 1922–August 1939*, ed. N. Baynes, 2 vols (London, 1942).

Höbelt, L., *Ferdinand III* (Graz, 2008).

Hochedlinger, M., *Austria's Wars of Emergence: War, State and Society in the Habsburg Monarchy, 1683-1797* (Harlow, 2003).

Höfer, E., *Der Ende des Dreißigjährigen Krieges: Strategie und Kriegsbild* (Cologne, 1997).

Hoffman, F., *Conflict in the 21st Century: The Rise of Hybrid Wars* (Arlington, VA, 2007).

Holloway, D., *Stalin and the Bomb: The Soviet Union and Atomic Energy, 1939-1956* (New Haven, 1994).

Hornblower, S., and A. Spawforth (eds), *The Oxford Classical Dictionary*, 3rd edn (Oxford, 1996).

Hough, R., *The Longest Battle: The War at Sea, 1939-1945* (London, 2003).

Howard, M., *The Causes of Wars and other essays* (London, 1983).

Huber, T. (ed.), *Compound Warfare: That Fatal Knot* (Fort Leavenworth, KS, 2002).

Hughes, J. M., *To the Maginot Line* (Cambridge, MA, 2006).

Hull, I. V., *Absolute Destruction: Military Culture and the Practices of War in Imperial Germany* (Ithaca, NY, 2005).

Hussey, J. M. (ed.), *The Cambridge Medieval History*, iv/1 (Cambridge, 1966).

Icos, *Poppy for Medicine: Licensing Poppy for the Production of Essential Medicines: An Integrated Counter-Narcotics, Development, and Counter-Insurgency Model for Afghanistan* (London, June 2007).

Imber, C., *The Crusade of Varna, 1443–45* (Aldershot, 2006).

—— *The Ottoman Empire, 1300-1650: The Structure of Power* (London and New York, 2002).

—— *Studies in Ottoman History and Law* (Istanbul, 1996).

Immler, G., *Kurfürst Maximilian I. und der Westfälische Friedenkongreß: Die bayerische auswärtige Politik von 1644 bis zum Ulmer Waffenstillstand* (Münster, 1992).

İnalcık, H., *Fatih Devri Üzerinde Tetkikler ve Vesikalar* (Istanbul, 1954).

—— *Osmanlı İmparatorluğu: Toplum ve Ekonomi Üzerinde Arşiv Çalışmaları, İncemelemeler* (Istanbul, 1993).

—— C. Kafadar, *Süleymân the Second [i.e. the First] and his Time* (Istanbul, 1993).

—— D. Quataert, *An Economic and Social History of the Ottoman Empire, 1300-1914*, i (Cambridge, 1994).

International Crisis Group, *In Their Own Words: Reading the Iraqi Insurgency*, Middle East Report, 50 (Brussels, 16 Feb. 2006).

—— *Taliban Propaganda: Winning the War of Words?* Asia Report, 158 (Brussels, July 2008).

Jacobsen, H., and J. Rohwehr, *Decisive Battles of World War II* (New York, 1965).

Jensen, K. M. (ed.), *Origins of the Cold War: The Novikov, Kennan, and Roberts 'Long Telegram' of 1946* (Washington, DC, 1991).

Jomini, A. H. de, *The Art of War* (West Point, NY, 1862).

Jones, A. H. M., *The Later Roman Empire* (Oxford, 1964).

Jones, M. C. E., *Ducal Brittany 1364-1399* (Oxford, 1970).

Jordan, D., et al., *Understanding Modern Warfare* (Cambridge, 2008).

Judt, T., *Postwar: A History of Europe since 1945* (London, 2005).

Kaegi, W. E., *Byzantium and the Early Islamic Conquests* (Cambridge, 1992).

Kafadar, C., *Between Two Worlds: The Construction of the Ottoman State* (Berkeley, 1995).

Kagan, K., *The Surge: A Military History* (New York, 2009).

Kagay, D. J., and I. J. A. Villalon (eds), *The Hundred Years War: A Wider Focus* (Leiden, 2005).

Kallet-Marx, R. M., *Hegemony to Empire* (Berkeley and Los Angeles, 1995).

Kara, G. (ed.), *Between the Danube and the Caucasus* (Budapest, 1987).

Kautilya, *The Arthashastra*, ed. and trans. L. N. Rangarajan (New Delhi, 1992).

Kazhdan, A. P., (ed.), *The Oxford Dictionary of Byzantium*, 3 (Oxford, 1991).

Keegan, J., *The Mask of Command* (London, 1988).

Kennedy, P. M., *The Rise and Fall of British Naval Mastery* (London, 1976).

Kennedy, P., *The Rise and Fall of the Great Powers* (New York, 1987).

Kennett, L., *The First Air War* (New York, 1991).

Keppie, L., *The Making of the Roman Army* (Oxford, 1984).

Khazanov, A. M., *Nomads and the Outside World*, 2nd edn (Madison, WI, 1994).

Kilcullen, D., *The Accidental Guerrilla: Fighting Small Wars in the Midst of a Big One* (Oxford, 2009).

Kirkaldy, A. W., *Industry and Finance: War Expedients and Reconstruction* (London, 1921).

Kleinschmidt, H. K., *The Nemesis of Power* (London, 2000).

Knox, M., and W. Murray, *The Dynamics of Military Revolution, 1300–2050* (Cambridge, 2000).

Kravan, V., J. M. Lefort, and C. Morrisson (eds), *Hommes et richesses dans l'Empire byzantin*, i (Paris, 1989).

Kunisch, J., *Der kleine Krieg: Studien zum Heerwesen des Absolutismus* (Wiesbaden, 1973).

Kunt, M., and C. Woodhead (eds), *Süleyman the Magnificent and his Age: The Ottoman Empire in the Early Modern World* (London, 1995).

Lane Fox, R., *Alexander the Great* (Harmondsworth, 1986).

Laurence, R., *The Roads of Roman Italy* (London, 1999).

LeDonne, J. P., *The Grand Strategy of the Russian Empire, 1650–1831* (Oxford, 2004).

Leffler, M. P., *A Preponderence of Power: National Security, the Truman Administration and the Cold War* (Stanford, Ca, 1992).

—— O. A. Westad (eds), *The Cambridge History of the Cold War*, i: *Origins, 1945–1962* (Cambridge, 2009).

Leggiere, M., *Napoleon and Berlin: The Napoleonic Wars in Prussia, 1813* (Stroud, 2002).

Lendon, J. E., *Soldiers and Ghosts* (New Haven, 2005).

Letters and Papers Illustrative of the Wars of the English in France, ed. J. Stevenson, Rolls Series, 22, 2 vols (London, 1861–4).

Liddell Hart, B. H., *The Decisive Wars of History* (London, 1929).

—— *The Ghost of Napoleon: A History of Military Thought from the Eighteenth to the Twentieth Century* (London, 1933).

—— *Strategy*, 2nd edn (London, 1967).

Lindner, R. P., *Explorations in Ottoman Prehistory* (Ann Arbor, 2007).

Lintott, A., *The Constitution of the Roman Republic* (Oxford, 1999).

Lippmann, W., *The Cold War: A Study in U.S. Foreign Policy* (New York, 1947).

Little, L. K. (ed.), *Plague and the End of Antiquity: The Pandemic of 541–750* (Cambridge, 2006).

Lloyd, A. B. (ed.), *Battle in Antiquity* (London, 1996).

Lockhart, P., *Denmark in the Thirty Years' War, 1618–48: King Christian IV and the Decline of the Oldenburg State* (Selinsgrove, 1996).

Lorentzen, T., *Die Schwedische Armee im Dreißigjährigen Kriege und ihre Abdankung* (Leipzig, 1894).

Low, P., *Interstate Relations in Classical Greece* (Cambridge, 2007).

Lowry, H. W., *The Nature of the Early Ottoman State* (Albany, NY, 2003).

Lucas, H. S., *The Low Countries and the Hundred Years War 1326–1347* (Ann Arbor, 1929; repr. Philadelphia, 1976).

Luttwak, E. N., *Strategy: The Logic of War and Peace* (Cambridge, MA, 2001).

—— *The Grand Strategy of the Byzantine Empire* (London, 2009).

—— *The Grand Strategy of the Roman Empire from the First Century AD to the Third* (Baltimore, 1976).

Mcdonnell, M., *Roman Manliness: Virtus and the Roman Republic* (Cambridge, 2006).

Mackesy, P., *War without Victory: The Downfall of Pitt, 1799–1802* (Oxford, 1984).

Mackinder, H. J., *Democratic Ideals and Reality* (1919; New York, 1962).

McMichael, S., *Stumbling Bear: Soviet Military Performance in Afghanistan* (London, 1991).

Mcpherson, J. M., *Battle Cry of Freedom: The Civil War Era* (Oxford, 1988).

Macrory, P., *The Fierce Pawns* (Philadelphia, PA, 1966).

Maenchen-Helfen, O. J., *The World of the Huns* (Berkeley, 1973).

Mahan, A. T., *The Influence of Sea-Power upon the French Revolution and Empire*, 2 vols (London, 1892).

Mango, C., and G. Dragon (eds), *Constantinople and its Hinterland* (Aldershot, 1995).

Mann, G., *Wallenstein: His Life*, trans. C. Kessler (London, 1976).

Marsden, E. W., *Greek and Roman Artillery: Historical Development* (Oxford, 1969).

Mastny, V., *The Cold War and Soviet Insecurity: The Stalin Years* (New York, 1996).

—— S. G. Holtsmark, and A. Wenger (eds), *War Plans and Alliances in the Cold War: Threat Perceptions in the East and West* (Abingdon, 2006).

Messenger, C., *The Blitzkrieg Story* (New York, 1976).

Milward, A., *The German Economy at War, 1939–1945* (London, 1965).

—— *War, Economy and Society, 1939–1945* (Berkeley, 1979).

Modelski, G., and W. R. Thompson, *Seapower in Global Politics, 1494–1993* (Seattle, 1988).

Molnar, A., et al., *Undergrounds in Insurgent, Revolutionary, and Resistance Warfare* (Washington, Dc, 1963).

Montefiore, S. S., *Stalin: The Court of the Red Tsar* (New York, 2003).

Monticone, A., *La battaglia di Caporetto* (Udine, 1999).

Morrow, J., *The Great War in the Air* (Washington, DC, 1993).

Mosier, J., *The Blitzkrieg Myth* (New York, 2003).

Mueller, J., *The Remnants of War* (Ithaca, NY, 2004).

Mueller-Hillebrand, B., *Das Heer*, 3 vols (Darmstadt, 1954–69).

Muir, R., *Britain and the Defeat of Napoleon, 1807–1815* (London, 1996).

Murphey, R., *Ottoman Warfare, 1500–1700* (New Brunswick, NJ, 1999).

Murray, W., and J. Lacey (eds), *Grand Strategy* (Cambridge, forthcoming).

———— (eds), *The Making of Peace: Rulers, States, and the Aftermath of War* (Cambridge, 2009).

—— R. Scales Jr, *The Iraq War: A Military History* (Cambridge, MA, 2003).

Nagai, Takashi, *The Bells of Nagasaki* (Tokyo, 1984).

Napier, W., *History of the War in the Peninsula and the South of France from the Year 1807 to the Year 1814* (London, 1828–40).

National Security Council, *National Strategy for Victory in Iraq* (Washington, DC, November 2005).

Newhall, R. A., *The English Conquest of Normandy 1416–24* (New Haven, 1924).

Olsen, John Andreas (ed.), *On New Wars* (Oslo, 2007).

—— Martin Van Creveld (eds), *The Evolution of Operational Art: From Napoleon to the Present* (Oxford, 2011).

Oman, C., *A History of the Peninsular War*, 7 vols (Oxford, 1902–30).

Omissi, D., *Air Power and Colonial Control: The Royal Air Force, 1919–1939* (Manchester, 1990).

Osiander, A., *The States System of Europe, 1640–1990: Peacemaking and the Conditions of International Stability* (Oxford, 1994).

Ostrogorsky, G., *History of the Byzantine State*, trans. Joan Hussey (Oxford, 1968).

Overy, R. J., *The Air War, 1939–1945* (London, 1980).

Özbaran, S., *The Ottoman Response to European Expansion: Studies on Ottoman–Portuguese Relations in the Indian Ocean and Ottoman Administration in the Arab Lands during the Sixteenth Century* (Istanbul, 1994).

Palmer, J. J. N., *England, France and Christendom 1377–99* (London, 1972).

Parker, G., *The Grand Strategy of Philip II* (New Haven, 1998).

—— *The Military Revolution: Military Innovation and the Rise of the West, 1500–1800*, 2nd edn (Cambridge, 1996).

—— *The Thirty Years War* (London, 1984).

Parrott, D., *The Business of War: Military Enterprise and Military Revolution in Early Modern Europe* (Cambridge, forthcoming).

—— *Richelieu's Army: War, Government and Society in France, 1624–42* (Cambridge, 2001).

Payne, K. B., *The Great American Gamble: Deterrence Theory and Practice from the Cold War to the Twenty-First Century* (Fairfax, VA, 2008).

Peacock, A. C. S. (ed.), *The Frontiers of the Ottoman World* (Oxford, 2009).

Peirce, L. P., *The Imperial Harem: Women and Sovereignty in the Ottoman Empire* (New York, 1993).

Perjés, G., *The Fall of the Medieval Kingdom of Hungary: Mohács 1526–Buda 1541* (Boulder, CO, 1989).

Perroy, É., *The Hundred Years War*, trans. W. B. Wells (New York, 1965).

Pestana, C. G., *Protestant Empire: Religion and the Making of the British Atlantic World* (Philadelphia, 2009).

Peters, G., *Seeds of Terror: How Heroin Is Bankrolling the Taliban and Al Qaeda* (New York, 2009).

Phang, S. A., *Roman Military Service* (Cambridge, 2008).

Platias, A. G. and Constantinos Koliopoulos, *Thucydides on Strategy: Athenian and Spartan Grand Strategies in the Peloponnesian War and their Relevance Today* (London, 2010).

Plokhy, S. M., *Yalta: The Price of Peace* (New York, 2010).

Pohl, W., *Die Awaren: Ein Steppenvolk in Mitteleuropa 567–822 n. Chr.* (Munich, 2002).

Polisensky, J., *Tragic Triangle: The Netherlands, Spain and Bohemia, 1617–21* (Prague, 1991).

Porter, P., *Military Orientalism: Eastern War Through Western Eyes* (London, 2009).

Prestwich, M., *Armies and Warfare in the Middle Ages: The English Experience* (New Haven, 1996).

—— *Edward I* (London, 1988).

Pritchett, W. K., *The Greek State at War*, 4 vols (Berkeley, 1971–85).

Procopius, trans. H. B. Dewing, 7 vols. (London, 1961–78).

Pryor, J. H., and E. M. Jeffreys, *The Age of the Dromon: The Byzantine Navy ca 500–1204* (Leiden, 2006).

Pseudo-Dionysius Of Tel-Mahre, *Chronicle: known also as The Chronicle of Zuqnin, Part III*, trans. W. Witakowski (Liverpool, 1996).

Pursell, B., *The Winter King: Frederick V of the Palatinate and the Coming of the Thirty Years' War* (Aldershot, 2003).

Ragsdale, H., *Détente in the Napoleonic Era: Bonaparte and the Russians* (Lawrence, KS, 1980).

Répaci, A., *Da Sarajevo al 'maggio radioso': L'Italia verso la prima guerra mondiale* (Milan, 1985).

Repgen, K. (ed.), *Krieg und Politik, 1618–1648* (Münster, 1988).

Rich, J., and G. Shipley (eds), *War and Society in the Roman World* (London, 1993).

Ricks, T., *The Gamble: General David Petraeus and the American Military Adventure in Iraq, 2006–2008* (New York, 2009).

Riley, J., *Napoleon and the World War of 1813: Lessons in Coalition Warfighting* (London, 2000).

—— *Napoleon as a General: Command from the Battlefield to Grand Strategy* (London, 2007).

Roberts, M., *Essays in Swedish History* (London, 1967).

—— *From Oxenstierna to Charles XII* (Cambridge, 1991).

—— *Gustavus Adolphus: A History of Sweden, 1611–1632*, 2 vols (London, 1958).

Robinson, L., *Tell Me How This Ends: General David Petraeus and the Search for a Way Out of Iraq* (New York, 2008).

Rodger, N. A. M., *The Command of the Ocean: A Naval History of Great Britain, 1649–1815* (London, 2004).

Rodríguez-Salgado, M., *The Changing Face of Empire: Charles V, Philip II and Habsburg Authority, 1551–59* (Cambridge, 1988).

Rogers, C. J., *War Cruel and Sharp: English Strategy under Edward III 1327–1360* (Woodbridge, 2000).

—— (ed.), *The Wars of Edward III* (Woodbridge, 1999).

Rosenstein, N., *Imperatores Victi* (Berkeley and Los Angeles, 1990).

Ross, S. T., *American War Plans, 1945–1950* (London, 1996).

Roth, J. P., *The Logistics of the Roman Army at War (264 B.C.–A.D. 235)* (Leiden, 1999).

Rubin, B., *The Fragmentation of Afghanistan: State Formation and Collapse in the International System* (New Haven, 1995).

Ruppert, K., *Die kaiserliche Politik auf dem Westfälischen Friedenkongreß (1643–48)* (Münster, 1979).

Russell, P. E., *English Intervention in Spain and Portugal in the Time of Edward III and Richard II* (Oxford, 1955).

Sabine, P., H. van Wees, and M. Whitby (eds), *The Cambridge History of Greek and Roman Warfare*, i (Cambridge, 2007).

Salm, H., *Armeefinanzierung im Dreißigjährigen Krieg: Der Niederrheinisch-Westfälische Reichskreis, 1635–1650* (Münster, 1990).

Salmon, E. T., *The Making of Roman Italy* (London, 1982).

—— *Roman Colonization under the Republic* (London, 1969).

Sartre, J.-P., *Nausée* (Paris, 1938).

Schama, S., *Revolution in the Netherlands, 1780–1813* (London, 1977).

Scheidel, W. (ed.), *Debating Roman Demography* (Leiden, 2001).

Schelling, T. C., *Arms and Influence* (New Haven, 1966).

—— *The Strategy of Conflict* (Cambridge, Ma, 1960).

Schlenke, M., *England und das friderizianische Preussen, 1740–1763* (Munich, 1963).

Schofield, V., *Afghan Frontier: Feuding and Fighting in Central Asia* (London, 2003).

Schroeder, P. W., *The Transformation of European Politics 1763–1848* (Oxford, 1994).

Sears, S. W., *Chancellorsville* (Boston, 1996).

—— *Gettysburg* (New York, 2004).

—— *The Landscape Turned Red: The Battle of Antietam* (New York, 1983).

Seaton, A., *The Soviet Army, 1918 to the Present* (New York, 1986).

Sekunda, N., *The Army of Alexander the Great* (Oxford, 1984).

—— *The Persian Army* (Oxford, 1992).

Seymour, W. (ed.), *A History of the Ordnance Survey* (Folkestone, 1980).

Shepard, J., and S. Franklin (eds), *Byzantine Diplomacy* (Aldershot, 1992).

Sherk, R. K., *Rome and the Greek East* (Cambridge, 1984).

Sherman, W. T., *Memoirs* (New York, 1875).

Siegel, M. L., *The Moral Disarmament of France: Education, Pacifism, and Patriotism, 1914–1940* (Cambridge, 2004).

Simms, B., *Three Victories and a Defeat: The Rise and Fall of the First British Empire, 1714–1783* (London, 2007).

—— T. Riotte (eds), *The Hanoverian Dimension in British History, 1714–1837* (Cambridge, 2007).

Sinno, A., *Organizations at War in Afghanistan and Beyond* (Ithaca, NY, 2008).

Smith, R., *The Utility of Force: The Art of War in the Modern World* (New York, 2008).

Spykman, N. J., *America's Strategy in World Politics: The United States and the Balance of Power* (New York, 1942).

—— *The Geography of the Peace* (New York, 1944).

Earl of Stanhope, Philip Henry Stanhope, *Notes of Conversations with the Duke of Wellington* (London, 1889).

Steinberg, S. H., *The Thirty Years War and the Conflict for European Hegemony, 1600–1660* (London, 1966).

Stephens, Alan and Nicola Baker, *Making Sense of War: Strategy of the 21st Century* (New York, 2006).

Stone, N., *The Eastern Front, 1914–1917* (London, 1975).

Stratford, J. (ed.), *The Lancastrian Court* (Stamford, 2003).

Strickland, M. (ed.), *Armies, Chivalry and Warfare in Medieval Britain and France* (Stamford, 1998).

Sumption, J., *The Hundred Years War*, i: *Trial by Battle* (London, 1990); ii: *Trial by Fire* (London, 1999); iii: *Divided Houses* (London, 2009).

Suvorov, V., *Den-M* (Moscow, 1994).

—— *Icebreaker: Who Started the Second World War?* (New York, 1990).

Taleb, N. N., *The Black Swan: The Impact of the Highly Improbable* (New York, 2010).

Tardy, L., *Beyond the Ottoman Empire: 14th-16th Century Hungarian Diplomacy in the East* (Szeged, 1978).

Tarn, W. W., *Hellenistic Military and Naval Developments* (Chicago, 1930).

Tezcan, B., *The Second Ottoman Empire: Political and Social Transformation in the Early Modern World* (Cambridge, 2010).

Thompson, A. C., *Britain, Hanover and the Protestant Interest, 1688–1756* (Woodbridge, 2006).

Thucydides, *History of the Peloponnesian War*, trans. C. F. Smith (Cambridge, MA, 1951).

—— *The Landmark Thucydides: A Comprehensive Guide to 'The Peloponnesian War'*, ed. R. B. Strassler (New York, 1996).

Till, G. (ed.), *The Development of British Naval Thinking* (Abingdon, 2006).

Tracy, J. D., *Emperor Charles V, Impresario of War: Campaign Strategy, International Finance, and Domestic Politics* (Cambridge, 2002).

Treadgold, W. *A History of the Byzantine State and Society* (Stanford, 1997).

Trim, D., and F. Tallett (eds), *European Warfare, 1350–1750* (Cambridge, 2010).

Trinquier, R., *Modern Warfare: A French View of Counterinsurgency*, trans. D. Lee (1964; Westport, CT, 2006).

Tzu, Sun *The Art of War*, ed. and trans. S. B. Griffith (Oxford, 1963; repr. London, 1971).

Vale, M. G. A., *The Origins of the Hundred Years War: The Angevin Legacy 1250–1340* (Oxford, 1996).

Valensi, L., *The Birth of the Despot: Venice and the Sublime Porte* (Ithaca, NY, 1993).

van Creveld, M., *The Culture of War* (New York, 2008).

—— *Fighting Power: German and US Army Performance, 1939–1945* (Westport, CT, 1982).

—— *Men, Women and War* (London, 2001).

—— *Supplying War: Logistics from Wallenstein to Patton* (Cambridge, 1978; repr. Cambridge, 1997).

—— *The Transformation of War* (New York, 1991).

van Wees, H., *Greek Warfare: Myths and Realities* (London, 2004).

Veinstein, G. (ed.), *Soliman le Magnifique et son temps* (Paris, 1992).

Villermont, A. de, *Ernest de Mansfeldt*, 2 vols (Brussels, 1866).

von Aretin, K. O., *Das Alte Reich, 1648–1806*, 4 vols (Stuttgart, 1993).

Vryonis Jr, S., *The Decline of Medieval Hellenism in Asia Minor and the Process of Islamization from the Eleventh through the Fifteenth Century* (Berkeley and Los Angeles, 1971).

Walker, S. J., *Prompt and Utter Destruction: President Truman and the Use of Atomic Bombs against Japan* (Chapel Hill, NC, 1997).

Waller, J., *Beyond the Khyber Pass: The Road to British Disaster in the First Afghan War* (Austin, TX, 1990).

Waltz, K. N., *Theory of International Politics* (New York, 1979).

Warry, J., *Warfare in the Classical World: War and the Ancient Civilisations of Greece and Rome* (London, 1998).

Wedgwood, C. V., *The Thirty Years War* (London, 1938).

Westad, O. A., *The Global Cold War: Third World Interventions and the Making of our Times* (Cambridge, 2007).

—— *The Long Peace: Inquiries into the History of the Cold War* (Oxford, 1987).

—— (ed.), *Reviewing the Cold War: Approaches, Interpretations, Theory* (London, 2001).

Whitby, M. and M., *The History of Theophylact Simocatta* (Oxford, 1986).

Wiesehofer, J., *Ancient Persia* (London, 2001).

Wilmott, H. P., *Empires in the Balance: Japanese and Allied Pacific Strategies to April 1942* (Annapolis, MD, 1983).

Wilson, K., *The Sense of the People: Politics, Culture and Imperialism in England, 1715–1785* (Cambridge, 1998).

Wilson, P. H., *Europe's Tragedy: A History of the Thirty Years War* (London, 2009).

—— *The Holy Roman Empire 1495–1806* (London, 1999).

Wittek, P., *The Rise of the Ottoman Empire* (London, 1938).

Wolf, P., et al. (eds), *Der Winterkönig: Friedrich von der Pfalz: Bayern und Europa im Zeitalter des Dreißigjährigen Krieges* (Augsburg, 2003).

Woods, J. E., *The Aqquyunlu: Clan, Confederation, Empire* (Salt Lake City, 1999).

Woods, K., et al., *The Iraqi Perspectives Project: A View of Operation Iraqi Freedom from Saddam's Senior Leadership* (Norfolk, VA, 2006).

Woodward, B., *Bush at War* (New York, 2002).

Woolgar, C. M. (ed.), *Wellington Studies*, 3 vols (Southampton, 1996).

Worthington, I., *Alexander the Great: A Reader* (London, 2002).

Wright, D., et al., *On Point II: Transition to the New Campaign: The United States Army in Operation Iraqi Freedom, May 2003–January 2005* (Fort Leavenworth, KS, 2008).

Young, B. (ed.), *Decisive Battles of the Second World War* (London, 1967).

Zabecki, D. T., *The German 1918 Offensives: A Case Study in the Operational Level of War* (Abingdon, 2006).

Zachariadou, E. A. (ed.), *Natural Disasters in the Ottoman Empire* (Rethymnon, 1999).

Index

The index entries appear in word-by-word alphabetical order.

CPSIA information can be obtained at www.ICGtesting.com
Printed in the USA
BVOW11*0200160414

350754BV00006B/178/P